D0938602

# THE HORN HANDBOOK

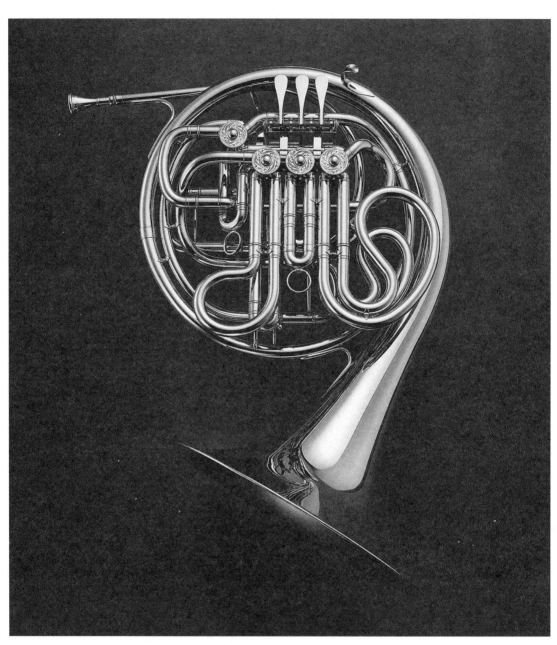

# VERNE REYNOLDS

# THE
# HORN
# HANDBOOK

**AMADEUS PRESS**
Reinhard G. Pauly, General Editor
*Portland, Oregon*

ISBN 1-57467-016-6

Printed in Hong Kong

Amadeus Press
The Haseltine Building
133 S.W. Second Avenue, Suite 450
Portland, Oregon 97204, U.S.A.


Library of Congress Cataloging-in-Publication Data
Reynolds, Verne.
The horn handbook / Verne Reynolds.
        p.       cm.
Includes index.
ISBN 1-57467-016-6
1. Horn (Musical instrument)—Instruction and study—Handbooks, manuals, etc. I. Title.
MT420.R49    1996      96-13672
     788.9′4193—dc20       CIP
            MN

To Shirley

# CONTENTS

# PREFACE

Anyone privileged to have served more than forty years as a teacher of horn in three of America's finest schools of music has accumulated fond memories of past students and events, profited from having to develop answers to why and how, and felt a deep responsibility to be of service to those who have chosen to make horn playing the dominant part of their musical lives. Central to this service is the venerable private lesson, for it is during these hours that traditions are handed down, enthusiasms nurtured, curiosities stirred, standards imposed, and decisions reached. Private lessons are the wellspring from which a lifelong source of inspiration and musical energy can flow.

Playing the horn well enough to be commercially acceptable is usually accomplished after years of excellent training and experience. To be employed as a performer of serious music signifies high attainment, especially when one considers the large number of young people enrolled in our music schools. It often means that the last formal lesson has been taken and that henceforward the player's future depends to a large extent upon the fund of practical wisdom acquired from private instruction and ensemble participation. No longer, happily, are physical and musical gifts alone sufficient to assure success. Musical talent—that combination of intelligence, ears, industry, and other more elusive elements of aptitude—is essential; without it we can never develop beyond technique. To evolve from talent to fulfillment, from technique to artistry, from personal accomplishment to contribution, we must establish working patterns and principles derived from the lessons and examples of teachers, expanded by maturing convictions.

I hope that this book will provide a framework upon which horn players can construct their own methods of practicing. It is meant to be of value to anyone who is serious about playing the horn and to those who wish to organize their work habits. It seeks to make methodical those elements of playing which are calisthenic in nature, and to encourage study and analysis where historical, theoretical, or aesthetic considerations are important. Although not directed exclusively to any age group or level of accomplishment, this book deals with matters usually confronted between the beginning of serious study of the horn and the end of formal training. These are the years in which practice patterns are established. After the last lesson has been taken we all face the necessity of becoming our own teachers. The training years should provide a wide range of musical and intellectual experiences upon which to draw for guidance in the solution of future problems.

In addition to outlining procedures for developing the essential physical techniques of breathing, attack, release, slur, tonguing, etc., emphasis is on expanding the musical mind through ear training, score study, and investigation of historical styles and performance practices. Horn players are urged to search beyond the narrow path of their orchestral parts to discover the broad fields of great music that do not include our instrument. While studying the madrigals of Thomas Weelkes or the piano music of George Crumb does not strengthen the embouchure, it does serve to bridge some of the gaps between composers and performers and thereby strengthens our understanding of the musical universe. It also reminds us that very little great music is written for the horn. Those with intelligence, imagination, skill, and zeal might be moved to become creators as well as consumers of music.

A *handbook* is defined as a manual, a set of directions, or a concise reference book. It is hoped that this handbook will be used as a reference for specific elements of horn technique, for efficient and effective practice, and for the theoretical and stylistic analysis of some of the standard horn repertory. The works chosen for discussion are those that are usually encountered for the first time during the high school and college years and continue to be studied and performed during the playing years.

For the discussion of etudes, solos, chamber music, and orchestral parts, this book will be most useful if the music itself is at hand for constant inspection. All of the music examined is readily available in modern editions and should become part of every horn player's personal music library. References are made to page numbers, rehearsal numbers and letters, and measure numbers, so that the reader can connect the text to a larger view of the music than could be provided by short examples. Much emphasis is placed upon hearing music by looking at its printed pages. Hearing music in this way is an important part of learning about the music we play. For most players this approach requires an extended period of ear training; this training should be considered a normal part of becoming a musician. One cannot imagine any area of musical activity—performance, teaching, composing, arranging, historical research, theoretical analysis, criticism, conducting—not made more excellent by its practitioner's ability to hear the music. Everyone is made richer by listening to recordings made by fine artists. Much is lost, however, when recordings are used to escape from the work of learning the pitches, rhythms, forms, composition techniques, and historical and theoretical precedents of any piece of music. From a study of these items can grow sturdy musical convictions and authoritative performances. From a dependence upon recordings can grow pale imitations of someone else's convictions.

There are many reasons for the extraordinary growth in all areas of horn playing during the latter half of the twentieth century. Instruction is better and starts early; instructional materials are abundant; recordings by the world's great artists are available; brass chamber music is firmly established both commercially and academically; workshops are well-attended; the quality of some new instruments is high; historical and pedagogical information is obtainable in brass journals and other publications; electronic and other teaching and playing aids are plentiful.

Any discussion of modern horn playing must begin with Dennis Brain. His superb recordings remain a source of inspiration and joy, and dispelled, at once and forever, the acceptance of inadequate technique or questionable musicianship. Before Dennis Brain, technical shortcomings were condoned because "the horn is a difficult instrument." Of course the horn is difficult. Before Dennis Brain, musicianship for horn players consisted of having a traditional tone quality, agreeable intonation, and reliable rhythm. Of course tone quality, intonation, and rhythm are indispensable. Before Dennis Brain, a new composition for horn was considered to be well-written if it did not venture beyond the technical status quo. Of course composers should be rational. Before Dennis Brain, orchestral horn players rarely played concertos, even with their own orchestras, rarely played chamber music, rarely advanced technically and musically beyond the requirements of their orchestral parts. Today our leading horn players are active in chamber music, solo playing, teaching, jazz, recording, and commissioning and performing new works. Some actually are composers.

Volume I, no. 1 of *The Horn Call*, which is the journal of the International Horn Society, is dated February, 1971. Since then it has continued to print articles of interest to horn players of all levels of accomplishment. The International Horn Society sponsors annual workshops that bring together players from many countries, and from these activities have grown many regional workshops, which include recitals, lectures, and master classes. There are now several small music publishing companies devoted to brass music whose catalogs contain a listing of music for horn. Some record companies reproduce and distribute solo and chamber music albums produced by horn players and other brass artists. Most of our larger cities have youth orchestras whose horn sections are coached by local professionals, with the result that young players can enter college with some orchestral experience. Since the advent of the DMA degree in performance, many communities through their colleges have well-trained and experienced teachers. These are all indications of a healthy and expanding art.

With so many people being trained and professional and academic opportunities so limited, excellence becomes, as it always should have been, the criterion for success. No one has ever produced a successful formula for performing excellence that did not include practicing. Students spend incalculable hours practicing. Professionals spend more hours playing, but with each new musical or technical challenge it is practice time again, or should be. Practice is the engine that drives improvement; without practice we stagnate. Teachers of young children devise ways to make practice fun, but for the serious player, practice begins to be profitable at the moment it becomes work, defined as the exertion of strength or faculties to reach a goal. Since our goal is to attain excellence, it follows that our work (practice) will be enhanced by the application of excellent methods.

Horn players suffer, whether they realize it or not, from the stigma attached to not being singers, pianists, or string players. The amount and, regrettably, the quality of much of the horn literature does not equal that written for the voice or for most of the other instruments. During the nineteenth and early twentieth centuries, when nearly every composer played the piano, the literature for the piano prospered naturally. Opera, songs with piano, and string music all flourished during this period, while the horn was struggling with the perfection of the valve system and the development of a more or less standard model of instrument. Mechanically, the instrument has now completed most of its evolution with the happy result that we now have several models from which to choose for specific purposes.

The first half of the twenty-first century could be the beginning of a true golden age of horn playing. There are, however, two obstacles on the path to this age. One is the reluctance of horn players to reach out beyond their own playing to become active in the creation of superb new music for our instrument. The necessity for taking responsibility for the state of the literature should be a natural part of the musical development of all players and can be instilled by teachers to students during the training years. Chamber music with the horn and solo literature for the horn are the areas showing the greatest need for exciting new works. Can any musician forget hearing the Britten Serenade for Tenor, Horn and Strings for the first time? We live in an age of fine players and fine composers. Surely these two forces can be brought together to produce other such musical landmarks.

The other obstacle is the reluctance of horn players to continue growth toward becoming more complete musicians once the training years are passed and employment is obtained. There, again, teachers can create, by example and insistence, a curiosity and enthusiasm in young players that can lead to interesting and productive lives. Too often nearly all of the theoretical skills and historical background obtained at great cost in parent dollars and student effort are never put to use after formal training stops. This is a great waste for the individuals and for the art of music, since both are deprived of benefits that could flow from this training.

Together with fond memories, teachers accumulate debts of gratitude to pupils and colleagues. This book can only acknowledge that these debts are outstanding; it does not presume to repay them. Special thanks are owed to Ilene Chanon, Kristen Hanson, J. D. Shaw, and Rebecca Stake for their generous help in typing the drafts. Catherine Zeh Fitch prepared the final text with devotion, sagacity, and skill. These musicians represent the finest of young horn player-scholars, and give us good reason for optimism.

# CHAPTER 1

# PRACTICE

The most critical session of practice each day is the first. It should be viewed as a time of awakening, both physically and mentally. It might also provide the one time during the day when we can confront with total honesty and calm deliberation the fundamental elements of horn playing. *Confront* is the correct word since it is the opposite of *evade*.

There are several prerequisites to this benign confrontation. First, seek practicing space in which it is possible to feel isolated. A sense of isolation is conducive to concentration. The practice space should allow the player to hear realistically. Most music school practice rooms and teaching studios seek to deaden, confine, and absorb sound rather than to provide a space in which sound can develop. Realizing this, and if given choices, we should find a home base for practice that is neither decidedly dead nor deafeningly alive. Most of our practice should be done in our home base room, since we must be able to evaluate progress from a fixed point. We should also, perhaps once a week, practice in another room such as a large classroom or recital hall in order to broaden our listening experience. It is quite flattering and entertaining to play in a large room with a high ceiling, wood paneling, lots of window glass, and a cement floor. This is just as unrealistic as playing in a small room with a carpet, acoustically treated walls, and heavy drapes. Most professional players of any instrument insist that their practice space give their ears a clear and undistorted portrayal of their sound.

The first hour of practice should serve as a daily confirmation of the joy that flows from a beautiful tone quality, an elegant phrase, and a flawless execution. After some searching, one could gather several short melodies, preferably not from the horn literature, and play at least one of these every day, not ritualistically, but always concentrating, listening, enjoying.

Just as it is necessary to recognize deficiency, it is essential to acknowledge accomplishment. The acknowledgment of accomplishment is most helpful when it is followed immediately by analysis. If we know what we did to achieve the desired result we should be able to develop consistency. If something works well once it might have been a happy accident. If, after some analysis, we can discover and describe what made it work, then we can apply thoughtful repetition to ensure that it works every time. This process of thoughtful repetition after analysis is a most efficient and productive way to practice.

The first hour of practice is a good time to discover the benefits of applying the principle of work and rest. There are many examples of this principle in nature, such as the need of plants for daily alternation of light and dark, a yearly alternation of growth and dormancy. Hearts beat and rest, lungs rest between breaths. We are awake, we sleep. Athletes learn the benefits of following hard workouts with rest and restoration.

Brass players, through mouthpiece pressure, deprive the lips of some of their normal blood supply. This deprivation eventually results in fatigue. The more severe the fatigue, the more necessary it is to prolong the rest. A strong, well-developed embouchure can withstand most of the debilitating effects of pressure caused by an all-Strauss orchestral program or a two hour brass quintet concert. Within these concerts are many rests supplied by well-advised composers. A momentary relaxation of the embouchure at phrase endings, rests within and between movements, between works, and at intermission serve to postpone the ultimate fatigue.

It is crucial to rest the embouchure at the first and every sign of fatigue during the first hour of practice. If the warm-up produces fatigue, it has defeated its purpose. For the conscientious student it must at first seem wasteful to allow seconds and even minutes to go by without playing, but it is necessary and beneficial. This builds strength because we are not constantly punishing a tired muscle. Forget "no pain, no gain," since we are working with a part of our body that does not accumulate mass through exercise. In general, a good night's sleep followed by a sensible warm-up should restore the embouchure to good playing condition.

A well-managed symphony orchestra is very orderly in its scheduling of rehearsals and concerts. This makes it possible for players to adjust practicing and other activities to maintain a plateau of strength and energy. College music students who are faced with daily individual practice, orchestra or band rehearsals, chamber music, recital preparation, auditions, and lessons, in addition to a full academic load of courses, often find that they are always playing on tired lips. This can be the result of too little, too much, or too irregular playing. The college years can provide a framework of experience for developing and maintaining a balance between work and rest.

Various strategies should be tried and evaluated during the college years if those years are to be preparatory to professional life. Some players believe firmly in "warming down" after a concert or late practice session. This usually consists of some very relaxed playing in the middle and low registers, which tends to relieve the embouchure of some of the effects of pressure. Some players believe in having one twenty-four hour period during the week with either no playing or, at most, only a light warm-up. Other players are flexible and decide from day to day when no playing, or a light or heavy day is appropriate. These strategies should be tested and evaluated during the college years so that the player has confidence in their immediate and long-term effects. It is a great comfort to know how our embouchure will feel on the evening of the big concert. Hoping for a good concert is not enough, but a well-tested routine will certainly help.

It is generally agreed that physical exercise in sensible amounts is a good thing. Music is a sedentary profession and requires the balancing effects of physical exercise. Performing has its own kinds of stress, some of which can be relieved through a regular program of exercise.

Another benefit of regular physical exertion is the improvement it brings to the quality and quantity of sleep. Anxiety over a recital or concert, an exam, an audition, a term paper, or other pressures can result in loss of sleep. A well-regulated and diligently pursued program of exercise helps us sleep longer and better, and there is an obvious relation between working and resting the embouchure and working and resting the body.

A vital ingredient of practicing is the recognition of practice as a link between the past and the future. We are all products of our past experiences, good and bad. If, for example, during a solo recital one has barely enough endurance to make it through the last piece, an evaluation of past practice habits might reveal the type of changes necessary to gain that type of endurance. Similarly, one learns from experience the differences in preparation for playing J. S. Bach's first Brandenburg Concerto and the Mahler Fifth Symphony, or between a wind quintet concert and a brass quintet concert. Perhaps this realization of difference can be compared with experiences in vegetable gardening. A soil amendment of limestone produces wonderful lettuces but terrible potatoes.

Practice also links to the future. For the student, the most obvious link is between the practice room and the teacher's studio. Seven days in the practice room should produce one good hour in the studio. This first link in our chain of experiences between the practice room and the teacher's studio is important because patterns are set in preparation for future links.

The object of practice is eventual public performance. Part of every practice session should be devoted to actually practicing performing. Each day of the week, one through seven, might see an increase in the time allotted to the practice of performing so that the final session before the lesson approximates the actual playing conditions of the lesson. This in no way repeals any of the laws of practice such as slow before fast, thoughtful repetition, taping and listening, concentration, discipline in the use of time through planning, realistic evaluation of accomplishment, and insistence upon perfection. *Perfection* is defined here as that which meets the supreme standard of excellence.

Perfection begins but does not end with accuracy. Accomplishment in the areas of tone quality, intonation, endurance, technique, and musicianship is admirable but meaningless if canceled by lack of accuracy. For some horn players accuracy is confined to "hitting" notes. For day one and two of the practice cycle, this might suffice. But soon the elements of dynamics, rhythm, phrasing, intonation, and style become components of accuracy. Just as perfection must be complete, accuracy must be complete.

Teacher and student might agree that a certain portion of each lesson is reserved during which an assigned passage of appropriate length and difficulty is played to perfection. The teacher (in future, the audition committee, conductor, audience, music critic, record producer, but never the student) decides immediately whether the standard of excellence has been met. We are constantly evaluated by listeners whether we like it or not, whether it is fair or not, whether it is informed or not. Let us hope that the teacher is fair and informed, and that the student welcomes the teacher's uncompromising evaluation. The student can self-impose the same standard in increasing severity during the practice cycle. If day seven produces the same result as day two, adjustments in practice habits are necessary. Playing up to this standard will not happen suddenly and miraculously in the teacher's studio and certainly will not happen suddenly and miraculously on more public occasions. It is more likely to happen as a result of having practiced playing perfectly. Realistic evaluation by the teacher and realistic comparisons with players of greater accomplishment can be helpful in establishing mileposts on our road to excellence. One is reminded of the twelve-year-old tennis player who boasted to his coach that he had won every match that he had ever played. "Congratulations," replied the coach, "but with whom did you play?"

For these performing experiences in the teacher's studio, teacher and student must understand their own role as well as the other's role in the process. For the teacher to function as arbiter, both parties should understand that the teacher will shift quickly from stern judge to benevolent mentor. If the decision is negative, the teacher must point the way to a better performance the following week. If the decision is positive, congratulations are in order and the next event in the ongoing series of performing experiences is agreed upon. The student must fit the process into the weekly practice cycle and understand its relation to the world of auditions, rehearsals, concerts, and recording sessions. An experienced and wise teacher can use these performing experiences to prepare the student for the time when only perfection is good enough.

The link between the practice room and the teacher's studio is strengthened further by the student's knowledge that a strict reckoning and appraisal is due every seven days if the lessons are weekly. Professional orchestral life has a somewhat similar cycle of preparation and performance. Chamber music and solo recitals have less structured timing between preparation and performance, but the principle is identical. The links are joined most precisely between the last practice session and the lesson, and between the last rehearsal and the concert. Forget "bad rehearsal, good concert," and any other cliché that might be temporarily soothing but is nonsensical folklore. Popular psychology should not become a substitute for logic. A quick self-diagnosis of the ever popular "mental block," for example, only delays the moment when the technical, physical, or musical problem must be faced honestly and dealt with thoroughly.

## Breathing

Practicing the horn can be divided into three general categories: (1) calisthenic, (2) technical, (3) musical. There is some overlapping among the three, since there can be a calisthenic benefit from technical and musical practice and, if done thoughtfully, technical and musical benefit from calisthenic practice.

Calisthenic practice can be described as focusing attention on those matters which make it physically possible to achieve a musical expression. Calisthenic practice should include mental preparation, breathing, warm-up, attacks, long tones, releases, tonguing, slurring, dynamics, air capacity, endurance, and all of the registers. Some players might wish to add to the list, but none of those mentioned should be omitted.

Mental preparation is the prelude to concentration. To bring all of one's powers, faculties, and activities to bear upon an action, it is necessary to find ways to eliminate distractions. Since musicians deal with rhythm and sound, a good preliminary exercise is to listen to the metronome at 40 beats per minute. A beginning level of concentration is achieved when one can predict with utmost precision when the next beat will occur. This exercise is not effective at 60 beats per minute and higher because at those speeds the rhythmic ear readily solves the problem and boredom takes over. Boredom leads to distraction, which destroys concentration. Now extend the exercise by dividing mentally every two beats into three, five, and seven. This procedure also must be done with utmost precision. A further benefit is the increased ability to apply a mental background of subdivisions to the more uncommon rhythmic groupings. Exercises of this type provide an opportunity to confront some of the mental components of performance in a calm and orderly way, and thus take the first step in developing an analytical approach to practice.

Practice demands analysis. Rhythm, pitch, dynamics, style, and tone quality must be evaluated constantly during practice. Even the best sense of rhythm (defined here as measured motion) needs an occasional metronome-check; even the finest ears can benefit from a glance at the electronic tuner. Dynamics, style, and tone quality are more subjective and personal, but to ignore them during practice leads to an acceptance of status quo.

We have now listened to the metronome at 40 and have added a mental subdivision of three, five, and seven. The next step is to practice the physical action of taking in the air. With the metronome off, start by opening the mouth as far as is comfortable by bringing down the lower jaw. Try to achieve the largest and most relaxed opening of the throat, which should feel very natural as the result of dropping the jaw. Take six breaths with the jaw completely open while making sure that the air travels in a horizontal line. This allows an intake of air very close to that of a yawn. Listen closely during these six breaths to make sure that the sound of the intake is low, dark, and hollow. By comparison, a more vertical breath makes a bright, whistling sound. Vertical breathing causes the air during intake to strike the roof of the mouth just behind the upper teeth. Vertical breathing seems to be satisfactory for most of the breathing we do away from the instrument. Runners, actors, singers, and wind players cannot operate efficiently and naturally with a vertical air intake.

After taking the six breaths with the lower jaw completely open, take another series of six breaths. In this series, breath number one should be with the jaw open as before. On each succeeding breath, two through six, raise the lower jaw slightly so that on breath six the lower jaw is in playing position for a middle register note. Check constantly during these breaths to make sure that only the jaw is rising. The throat should have the same open feeling whether the jaw is up or down. Think of the air intake as being quite low in the mouth. The sound of the intake should remain the same whether the jaw is up or down. Listen and observe constantly.

The expansion of the upper body as the result of the air intake should also be horizontal. For comparison, take, occasionally, the worst possible breath. With the jaw in playing position, breathe vertically just behind the upper teeth, pull up the abdominal muscles, chest, and shoulders. At the top of this awful breath, hold the air in this position and ask yourself whether you want to play the horn while feeling this way.

After establishing a good breathing pattern without the metronome, turn on the metronome still set at 40. After listening to the beats, start by taking breaths that consume five beats. The intake of air should start slowly and increase in speed and intensity so that on the fifth beat the intake is the most active. At the fifth beat, hold the air and check how your body feels. If you have taken a horizontal breath you will find that your abdominal muscles have expanded outward and feel firm, your chest has expanded outward and only a little upward, and the top of your chest feels full of air. Shoulders and arms should feel relaxed. Slowly exhale the air and try to maintain the firmness of the abdominal muscles until all of the air is gone. This firmness of the abdominal muscles during the exhale is called support, and can be achieved only by allowing the muscles to expand outward during the intake of air. Occasionally, again, it is helpful to take another worst possible breath by pushing out and down on the abdominal muscles before the intake and breathing vertically by pulling the chest and shoulders upward. You find that you can take in very little air when the abdominal support is set before intake. As the air is exhaled, the abdominal muscles return to their original inward position but do not lose their firmness until after all of the air is gone. The body support is set as the result of the air intake and achieves its firmness at the end of the breath, not at the beginning. After several of these slow, five-beat breaths, one can do several in four beats, then three, then two, and finally in one beat. One should feel exactly the same at the top of the intake, whether the intake lasts five beats or one beat. The tendency is to begin to breathe more vertically as the breathing time is decreased. Gradually working from five beats to one beat will allow a control of the process.

Now we should try to control the exhale. Start with a five-beat intake and a one-beat exhale. Control the intake exactly as before, and on the exhale try to maintain the abdominal firmness until all of the air is gone. The air is exhaled quite rapidly at a metronome setting of 40. Try to take a lot of air. Try to get speed on the exhale. Maintain a grip on the air during the exhale by keeping the abdominal muscles firm even as they pull in while the air leaves. Do at least six of these breaths at the ratio of five beats intake, one beat exhale. The pattern then develops: four-beat intake, two-beat exhale; three-beat intake, three-beat exhale; two-beat intake, four-beat exhale; one-beat intake, five-beat exhale. We should make a relaxed embouchure during the exhale but should not try to buzz a pitch. The steps described above are outlined as follows:

1. Listen to the metronome at 40 beats per minute.
2. Mentally divide each beat into three, five, and seven parts.
3. Take six breaths with the lower jaw completely open;
4. six breaths gradually closing the jaw;
5. six breaths that last five beats each;
6. six breaths that last four beats each;
7. six breaths that last three beats each;
8. six breaths that last two beats each;
9. six breaths that last one beat each;
10. five-beat breath, one-beat exhale;
11. four-beat breath, two-beat exhale;
12. three-beat breath, three-beat exhale;
13. two-beat breath, four-beat exhale;
14. one-beat breath, five-beat exhale.

## Warm-up and related embouchure concerns

There are as many warm-up routines as there are players and teachers. This is as it should be. The beginner will obviously have a warm-up that differs greatly from that of the middle-aged professional. The warm-up should change and develop as the player changes and develops. I hope that students will use the following patterns as suggestions for beginning their own collection of warm-up routines. A spiral bound or loose leaf notebook with staff paper, pencil, ruler, and eraser comprise all the equipment that is needed.

We should begin by consulting a music dictionary for information about the harmonic series. This information is usually found in the section on acoustics. After reading all about the harmonic series, copy it with the appropriate numbers under each note. These numbers will be referred to as *partials* in these patterns. Be sure to copy the harmonic series that has C as its first note. Reading about the harmonic series will create a desire to discover more about acoustics and the other wind instruments. Investigative projects such as this should become an important part of every player's musical life. Information gained by one's own efforts always leads to other topics, which in turn multiply. Since acoustics and the harmonic series are basic to any sound production, they should be of interest to every musician.

The term *warm-up* is used here as a convenient way to encompass the mental and physical activities that precede the playing of the instrument in a musical sense. For horn players, the warm-up should gently and gradually awaken all of the elements of playing and particularly those related to response and flexibility.

It is interesting to observe the warm-up of professional tennis players. No match begins until the players have warmed up their forehands, backhands, overheads, and serves. The physical actions in these warm-up shots are calm, slow, with perfect form and control, and without extremes of exertion. Golfers warm up each shot immediately before its execution, thereby establishing a slow motion pattern for the actual stroke. Athletic warm-up serves to refresh, remind, and rehearse the physical fundamentals of the game. It can also inform the player, and possibly the opponent, how the various shots feel on a particular day. The warm-up is the last event before the actual playing begins. It has been preceded by countless hours on the tennis court or golf course, during which every stroke and stratagem is practiced to perfection before the "performance." One should not belabor unduly the parallels between athletes and performing musicians, but we can apply some of their principles of conditioning and response. No athlete would continue with a warm-up that produces fatigue, but brass players often use a punishing ritual forced on them by a well-meaning but rigid teacher. Athletes warm up easily and with minimum effort but practice with a controlled intensity; brass players too often warm up strenuously and practice with less than total intensity. Athletes have a clear separation between warm-up and workout. Runners do a lot of stretching before they run so that leg and other muscles are ready for the dash or marathon; yet brass players tend to play before everything is flexible and responsive.

Listening to the metronome, subdividing its beats, and performing the breathing exercises described above are all mental and physical preparation for producing the first tone of the day. There are several good reasons that this first tone should be written middle C for horn in F. It is a pitch readily produced by all but the beginner. It is a true middle register note, and one that can be sounded without the embouchure effort of a high pitch or the response concern of a low pitch. If this is the first tone played each day we can use it as ear training if we try to imagine and then sing its pitch before we play it. By this device a tonal memory is established. Thinking, singing, and playing are thus linked from the beginning of each day.

A volume level of *mezzo piano* is good for the beginning of the warm-up, since it provides enough air flow to secure and maintain the vibration of the lips. The force of the tongue stroke should be sufficient to activate the lips but not so aggressive as to cause an accent. Tongue strokes are discussed in the section on attacks.

Part I of the warm-up uses middle C as an embouchure anchor point. During the rests, remove the mouthpiece from the lips so that the embouchure can be re-formed for each note. Each note thus becomes a first note, felt and heard before it is played.

Example 1-1

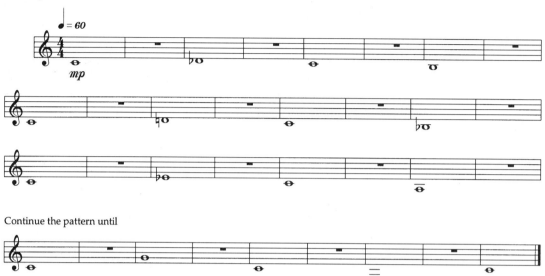

Continue the pattern until

This exercise goes well beyond just activating the vibrations of the lips, although this is its principal warm-up function. It establishes a middle register anchor point for the embouchure; strengthens middle C in our pitch memory; allows us to hear each succeeding interval in relation to C; requires a re-forming of the embouchure for each pitch; challenges us to think before, during, and after each note; exemplifies the work and rest principle; and illustrates that horn players can, indeed, think while they play.

Part II also starts on middle C and spans the two octaves between the second and eighth partials of the harmonic series. "Middle" C is an interesting term. For horn players it is descriptive because our normal range is two octaves above and nearly two octaves below this note. There is a precise system of identifying notes according to their registers. For horn players, our octaves are classified by the following scheme:

$$C \qquad c \qquad c^1 \text{("middle" C)} \qquad c^2 \qquad c^3 \text{("high" C).}$$

These numbers are not related to partial numbers.

Example 1-2

All notes are played open on the F horn. This exercise can be extended by the addition of valves until all three are used. The seventh partial, identified here as B-flat, will sound quite flat but should not be "tuned," but rather enjoyed for its natural and archaic quality. This is the sound that Benjamin Britten used so effectively in the Prologue and Epilogue of his Serenade for Tenor, Horn and Strings. The fifth partial is low in pitch and should be tuned, since it is a part of the normal fingering pattern. Notice how the notes begin to feel slippery with valves 2 + 3 and even more so with 1 + 3, and 1 + 2 + 3. This is because we are adding only the cylindrical tubing of the valve slides and the horn becomes more and more unbalanced between its conical and cylindrical tubing. This notifies us that 1 + 3 and 1 + 2 + 3 are best avoided whenever there is a suitable alternate.

Part III extends the upward range by adding four notes to the harmonic series. At least thirty seconds of rest should precede this exercise.

Example 1-3

As in Part II, we may add all of the fingers until 1 + 2 + 3 are used. Choose a tempo that will accommodate all of the notes of the pattern in one breath. Notice how an expanding air flow helps the upward slurs. We can experiment to find the amount of air flow expansion that is helpful in securing the higher notes but does not create a crescendo. If any of the upper notes do not speak easily, do not force them with embouchure pressure but simply reverse the direction of the pattern at that point and proceed back down to the starting note. If at any time there is any feeling of embouchure fatigue, we must stop and rest for at least one full minute before continuing. When there is fatigue we are no longer warming up.

Part IV is a tongue response and lip trill exercise.

Example 1-4

All of the slurred notes should be played on the F horn; the tongued notes should be played with conventional fingerings. This exercise can be extended downward, as in Part II. It is more important to play this exercise with precision, evenness, and control than with speed. Our goal should be quarter note equals 132–138 for both the tongued and slurred notes. Another approach might be to practice only the slurred measures and to gain speed as the intervals become smaller. This is a good exercise to practice while observing the embouchure in a mirror. Notice how the muscular activity is greater on the larger intervals. We should experiment until we find the smallest motions that will produce the desired control and reliability. Try to minimize any inward and outward motion of the mouth's corners in the slurred measures by keeping the corners firm on the lower pitches. Similarly, any excess up and down motion of the jaw in both the slurred and tongued measures can be controlled by maintaining a solid and consistent grip on the lower half of the mouthpiece. This is especially helpful for players with a noticeable overbite. For warming up, this exercise should be played with the lightest practical pressure on the upper half of the mouthpiece, solid mouthpiece contact on the lower lip, firm corners, and small motions. Ideally, there should be little difference in mouthpiece pressure between *piano* and *mezzo forte*. At *forte* and *fortissimo*, some additional pressure may be necessary to maintain the air seal around the mouthpiece.

Part V. Players whose embouchures have developed sufficiently to play the sixteenth partial (the magic high C) can now approach the top notes of the horn by slurring through all of the partials between four and sixteen.

Example 1-5

All of these notes should be played on the open F horn. Notice and enjoy the pitches that do not conform to their equivalents on the piano. As in previous exercises, this pattern may be extended downward. Experiment with tempo and volume. *Mezzo forte* and 120 are good starting points. As before, if the vibration stops or a note does not respond easily during the ascent, reverse the direction. Stop and rest at any sign of fatigue.

This exercise knits together the middle and upper registers. When starting from the middle register, notice the temptation to set the embouchure more closed, knowing that we are going for a high note. It might seem contradictory to say that the high register should be played as openly as possible. We should remind ourselves that mouthpiece pressure on the upper lip and the gradual tightening of the embouchure continue to make the aperture more and more closed as we ascend. A steady and substantial air flow helps to keep the aperture open, as does an understanding that pressure on the upper lip will flatten and eventually close the aperture. This can be shown by a simple experiment. While looking at a mirror, form an embouchure without the mouthpiece, blow through it and begin to apply pressure to the middle of the upper lip with the tip of the little finger. Notice how this pressure chokes off the air in the middle of the mouth (inside the mouthpiece when it is in place) and diverts it to the sides of the mouth when it could not go through the mouthpiece. This explains why it is easier to play the high register at *forte* than at *piano*, since the rapid flow of air necessary to produce *forte* will tend to "blow" open the aperture. An aperture that is blown open will result in a hard and bright sound (scream trumpet comes to mind) compared with an aperture whose size and shape are controlled by limiting the pressure and holding the corners firmly. Covering a two-octave range is a complex undertaking, but perhaps the following points can serve as a checklist for this exercise:

1. normal embouchure setting on first notes
2. gradual firming of the corners on the ascent
3. least possible pressure on upper lip
4. solid grip on lower half of the mouthpiece
5. gradual increase in air flow during ascent
6. increased body support during descent.

It might also seem contradictory to say that the low register should be played as closed as possible. As we descend, our embouchure becomes less firm and especially so on notes lower than $c^1$. For most embouchures, a curious thing begins to happen between $c^1$ and g. In this range we reach a point where any more loosening of the corners will result in an aperture too open and too relaxed to maintain a vibration consistent with the pitch we expect to produce. It is especially difficult to attack low notes with this too-relaxed embouchure because the slight explosion of the air caused by the tongue stroke opens the aperture even more, if only momentarily. Upon reaching this point in the range we, fortunately, have another resource to call upon. This resource is the lower jaw. Using a mirror and with just the mouthpiece in hand, blow an imaginary $c^1$ and begin to pull down the lower jaw very slightly and very gradually. When you reach what feels like c (not $c^1$), notice that the lips outside the mouthpiece begin to pull apart. At this point the corners must be retightened while the jaw continues to drop. This retightening will assure that the lips can maintain the vibration as the jaw drops even further. This area between $c^1$ and g is often called the "break." Since no two embouchures are exactly alike, the references to specific pitches may not be accurate in every case. The break could begin as much as a perfect fourth lower than $c^1$ but rarely much higher. A few players are blessed with no discernible break. For others, the maneuvers described above will provide a smooth and reliable way to connect the registers, since the setting of the mouthpiece on the lips never changes. This takes practice. We do train the lower jaw and the corner muscles to control aperture size and tension. We do not have a separate embouchure setting for each register.

None of the above is connected with the dreaded and agonizing procedure known as an embouchure change. Changing the embouchure usually consists of (1) moving the mouthpiece from one side to a more central location, (2) moving the mouthpiece to conform to the traditional setting of two-thirds upper lip, one-third lower lip, (3) fixing the corners to correct an excessive pucker or smile, (4) adjusting the angle of the mouthpiece to distribute the pressure, and (5) adjusting the lower jaw. Fortunate, indeed, is the young player whose beginning teacher insisted on attending to these matters as early as possible. Apparently some teachers believe that a "natural" embouchure is the best embouchure and leave the thirteen-year-old to experiment until a setting is discovered that will produce a sound. While admitting that the parallel is somewhat labored, would a violin teacher delegate the discovery of proper finger, hand, wrist, elbow, and shoulder position to the four-year-old beginner? One hopes not. Arriving at an embouchure setting that gives the young player a physical base needing only small amendments as it strengthens should be the primary goal of both the teacher and student during the first few weeks and months of study. During the high school years, our young player presumably has acquired playing responsibilities in school or community groups that make it difficult to play effectively while undergoing a major embouchure change. Much valuable and expensive college experience is diluted or delayed by having to work on physical fundamentals when a maturing musicianship is needed.

There are teachers well known for their success in changing embouchures during the college years. These teachers, and they are to be admired greatly, admit that we hear more about their successes than their failures. In this age of advanced orthodontia, there is less reason to accept an aberrant embouchure because of irregular teeth, and even less reason to continue with it in the hope that somehow, some day, all will be well. This failure to change an incorrect embouchure passes along the problem from the beginning teacher, who could have handled it quickly and effectively, to succeeding teachers, who must then confront well-established habits.

In early development of the embouchure patience is paramount for both teacher and pupil. For young players, the glamour attached to being able to play high notes far outshines the virtues of a solid middle register, rich tone quality, rhythmic accuracy, and good intonation. Thin and squeaky high notes can be obtained on an undeveloped embouchure by pressure, a stretched and smiling embouchure, and a small mouthpiece, none of which will lead to a fine career. As these warm-up exercises suggest, we should establish the middle register first, then extend this base into the high register, and finally develop the low register.

It is never too soon to apply pencil to staff paper. These exercises and their extensions have purposely not been written out in their entirety in the hope that young players will grasp the opportunity to do so and begin, thereby, a life-long habit of creating study material for themselves and for others. Write observations about these exercises in your notebook, but when making marks on any page of music please follow these suggestions:

1. Use a pencil in anticipation of corrections.
2. Never obscure anything printed.
3. Write as small as will be legible.
4. Write lightly enough to be easily erased.
5. Write the fewest and most precise words.
6. Think before writing.

By writing out the notes of these exercises, some of the mysteries of music notation will be solved. While there are several excellent books on music notation now available, most questions can be answered by a detailed examination of printed music. Few of us can remember our first attempts at penmanship, but it evolved to a point where we can read our writing, even if no one else can. Not so with music notation. It must be written so that anyone who can read music can read it. Music notation has its own widely accepted rules and traditions that must be followed when writing by hand or by computer.

Part VI. The warm-up should contain several loud long tones in the lower register, beginning almost anywhere below the staff and continuing downward chromatically. These long tones should be played with the least possible pressure but with firm corners. Playing these loud, relaxed low-register long tones is excellent for removing any stiffness caused by the higher notes in Part V. Some brass players play these tones immediately before coming on stage for a solo recital or chamber music concert so that the first notes of the performance feel alive and healthy. Trombonists, or course, love to play these loud notes whether there is a concert or not.

Many horn players experience uneasy moments at the beginning of concerts because too much time has elapsed between the last warm-up notes and the first note on stage. For orchestral players this happens when the conductor is late entering the stage, or insists upon lecturing the audience before the music can begin. For chamber music concerts, the stage manager will occasionally summon the players to the wings only to announce that the concert will begin five or ten minutes late to accommodate late-comers. These and similar experiences add to the hazards of playing.

Parts I through VI form the main warm-up of the day and should be done rather early in the morning. Before other practice sessions and afternoon rehearsals, a shortened version can be developed following the same general pattern. Before evening concerts we should devise a warm-up that takes into account how much playing we have done that day, how strenuous are the works to be played, and specific passages needing review. If an orchestral concert begins with the Overture to *Oberon*, by Carl Maria von Weber, we should play its first notes enough times to be ready for this type of playing. If a concert begins with the Fourth Symphony of Tchaikovsky, we should prepare accordingly.

During the training years, students with the help of their teachers should periodically examine and evaluate their warm-up. We have to find a balance between staying with a routine long enough to produce the desired results, and being willing to change when the warm-up is not satisfactory. A sixteen-year-old might have to adjust the warm-up every few months if the embouchure is gaining strength rapidly. The twenty-six-year-old professional might have to alter some of the patterns to conform to the demands of the job. The forty-six-year-old veteran will seek to preserve reliability and predictability and will probably be reluctant to change a routine that continues to work.

In general a warm-up is working if

1. The embouchure feels alive and strong after the warm-up and for the rest of the day. This condition depends largely upon achieving a good balance between work and rest, gradually working from middle to extreme registers, and having the patience not to hurry.

2. There are few, if any, bad days. Since in professional life there can be no bad days, we should use the training years to build and maintain a plateau of strength and flexibility. Every embouchure reacts to what we did or did not do yesterday, last week, last month. One of the principal reasons for a warm-up is to repair damage caused by over-work. Ideally, we should play as well on the morning after a big concert as on the morning before, and a sensible warm-up after a good night's sleep will do much to revive a depleted embouchure. On these occasions we should spend more time in the middle register playing softly, more time with the mouthpiece off the lips, and should never play any high register notes before they can be played easily. To do otherwise only adds to the fatigue and causes us to play on last night's tired lips.

3. Range and endurance are maintained or continue to improve. This improvement is one of the most reliable indications that our daily habits are working.

Keeping a detailed record of the amount and type of playing we do gives us a basis for establishing cause and effect. Although the warm-up is but one factor connected with range and endurance, it is a good starting place for diagnosing problems of strength. For students to play, every few months, completely through their warm-up in the presence of the teacher can be very helpful. This is not wasted lesson time, because an experienced teacher can identify hazards and suggest corrections.

4. One plays as well at 9:30 A.M. as at 9:30 P.M. Some brass players have convinced themselves that they cannot play well in the morning. In the professional world, we must play our best at all times and this includes many morning rehearsals, morning recording sessions, and even morning concerts. During the training years we can develop a procedure that makes us ready to play our best at 9:30 A.M., or before if necessary. Our first warm-up note should begin at least one and one-half hours before we expect to play. This interval allows a thirty to forty minute warm-up, some time to rest, travel time to the hall, and another short warm-up at the hall. These times are approximate and do not allow for a long commute, or for other conditions.

There may still be a few players who advocate no warm-up at all. Apparently this wisdom is grounded on the certainty that at some future time one will have to perform without a warm-up. We are left with the confused logic of foregoing all of the benefits of warming up in preparation for the few times that we might not be able to warm up.

After the last low notes of the warm-up have been played, we can rest a few moments to think about the remainder of this first practice hour and how it relates to the rest of the day's activities. We have completed our mental preparation, breathing exercises, and warm-up. Remaining on our daily list are attacks, long tones, releases, tonguing, and slurring. Exercises pertaining to dynamics, air capacity, strength, and the various registers are quite strenuous and need not be done every day. Each can be scheduled for work on separate days during a normal week. High-register work probably should not be done on consecutive days, since the embouchure will profit from at least one day's interval before the next high-register work-out.

The warm-up, as outlined here, has worked well for many fine players. Each part is flexible enough to permit adjustments of duration, speed, or register without violating the tenets of work and rest.

## Attacks

The following discussions of attacks, long tones, releases, tonguing, and slurring are grouped together and can be categorized as calisthenic, since they are repeated physical exertions for the sake of training and improvement. The same can be said for jogging, weight-lifting, and using a treadmill or stationary bicycle. A visit to a health center reveals that most of its patrons are reading, wearing headphones, or are looking at television screens. This suggests that once the physical motions have begun little mental effort is necessary beyond that required to produce repetition. One could, presumably, study the Chinese language while pedaling a stationary bicycle and receive the same aerobic and muscular benefit. Exactly the opposite is true when horn players are repeating exercises designed for the improvement of a specific action. Mental preparation before the action, listening during the action, and analysis after the action produce improvement.

Mental preparation consists of a preconception of the physical action (how does it work?); listening is an accounting of the success or failure of the actions as they are performed (did it work?); analysis seeks answers (why did it work or fail?). Think; hear; evaluate. Mental preparation should be most thorough before starting each category, such as attack, long tones, etc. Between repetitions, it should be done very quickly so that it becomes a spontaneous part of the physical action. Mental preparation must include predictions: if we do X correctly, then Y and Z should result. Listening must be done with every repetition so that we can determine whether the results are satisfactory. Practicing without listening is pointless. Analysis can be lengthy and detailed whether there is success or failure. Why we succeeded is just as important to know as why we failed. Detailed analysis need not be undertaken after every repetition, but a series of failures must be interrupted so that we do not continue to practice failure. A series of successes should be allowed to continue, since it produces a justifiable expectation of more success. Twelve consecutive successful attacks on a difficult note deserve self-congratulations as well as an understanding of the process by which they became possible. This controlled practicing fits nicely into the principle of work and rest. The mind works while the embouchure rests.

It is unfortunate that the third item on our list of daily calisthenic exercises is commonly referred to as *attack*. This seems a needlessly belligerent term, but rather than inventing a more decorous synonym we will continue with *attack*, since brass players understand that even the most gentle of note beginnings is called an attack. Horn players also understand that we must develop a large assortment of attacking styles. Since the method of beginning notes is closely associated with volume, practicing attacks by using each of the following dynamic indications: *ff, f, mf, mp, p, pp*, is useful. As a basic goal, each dynamic level should be practiced to achieve a balance between tongue stroke and air flow. If the force of the tongue stroke exceeds the intensity of the air flow, an accent results. An accent can be an effective and colorful expression and should be practiced separately as such. The tongue stroke and air flow must be timed precisely. A hesitant tongue stroke produces late and uncertain responses. A late air flow produces inaccuracies. The metronome is very helpful in timing the air intake with the tongue stroke and air flow. There should be no pause at the top of the intake, but rather the air should change directions immediately with the tongue stroke. The tongue should not rest against the back of the upper teeth before the stroke but should have an uninterrupted motion.

Upon examination you will find that the tongue is slightly tapered at its front and can be rather thick and broad. From behind the upper teeth a quick withdrawal of this breadth (there is no tip of the tongue), when timed precisely with the beginning of the air flow, can cause the lips to vibrate. Once the intake has begun, there must be no pause in the sequence of air intake–tongue stroke–air flow. A rhythmically controlled, slightly audible air intake and precise tongue strokes are indispensable in wind chamber music.

This process must become natural and automatic. Therefore, it is best achieved by thoughtful repetition. Set the metronome at 40 and listen for a few beats. Select any comfortable middle register note and play at least four attacks at *fortissimo*. Listen carefully to make sure that they are balanced between tongue stroke and air flow intensity and all are identical in volume. Each note should be held three beats with one beat silent for breathing between notes. On the same note, play each of the other dynamic levels from *forte* to *pianissimo* at least four times. Listen and evaluate constantly. It is helpful to associate each level with a well-known work: the opening of the Tchaikovsky Fourth Symphony for *fortissimo*, the solo in the introduction to the fourth movement of the Brahms First Symphony for *forte*, etc. Occasionally, play each of the six dynamic levels consecutively from *fortissimo* to *pianissimo*, and from *pianissimo* to *fortissimo*. On alternate days, practice these attacks in either the high register or in the low register. Practice itself does not make perfect, but thoughtful repetition enhances reliability. These attack exercises should follow a thorough warm-up and should never be attempted on fatigued lips.

No attack may be considered successful if it is not accurate. A large factor in accuracy, tongued or slurred, is the player's ability to form links among how a pitch looks, how it feels, and how it sounds. These links become more important as the notes become higher, although it is possible for any player, at any time, to miss any note on the horn regardless of height. First notes are most often missed if they are not linked by feel and pitch to another note. Everything else set aside, it is easier to play an F-sharp if we have just played an F-sharp.

Accuracy in transposition becomes difficult as the transposition increases the distance from the safe haven of horn in F. The first note in the first horn part of the second movement of the Brahms Second Symphony is a perfect example. It does not look, feel, or sound at all like the same note written for horn in F, since the transposition of B-natural places the pitch a tritone away from our home base of horn in F. In this case, our first note of the second movement is a concert F-sharp. F-sharp is the third of the D major triad. A D major triad is the last chord in the first movement. If we have trained ourselves to remember pitches, we can link these two movements together by mentally retaining an F-sharp during the pause between movements.

It is possible to construct exercises that require the player to sing a pitch, play the same pitch, and link the played pitch to the next written pitch. The following exercise is not difficult, since each three-measure group forms either a major or a minor triad. All twelve notes of the chromatic scale are used. It is no accident that this exercise begins on $c^1$.

Example 1-6

1. Always play with the metronome set at 40 beats per minute.
2. Hear the next pitch on the second beat.
3. Sing or hum the next pitch on the third beat.
4. Breathe on the fourth beat.
5. Remove the mouthpiece from the lips between notes.
6. Play the exercise in all the usual transpositions.

Example 1-7

This series of twelve notes is a typical tone row or set. As such, it can be modified and extended by the usual twelve-tone techniques of inversion, retrograde, and retrograde inversion. These terms and the mechanics of the twelve-tone technique are taught in college music theory courses and should not puzzle the advanced music student. For players who have not yet begun their theory training, here is an opportunity to investigate a composition technique that began early in the twentieth century and is still used by some composers. It is also an opportunity to gather information about Arnold Schoenberg (1874–1951), who developed the technique. An independent study of the system and of Arnold Schoenberg could begin, but not end, with reading about Schoenberg in a good music dictionary such as *The New Grove Dictionary of Music and Musicians*, a conversation with a private teacher, or a visit to a library. Libraries exist to collect, store, and provide information and we should consider them to be an essential part of our musical literacy. Much of the music written in the twentieth century, or any century, can be intimidating to those not familiar with its origins, techniques, and aesthetics. What musician would not profit from an intelligent application of a knowledge of the techniques that composers have used, for better or worse, for most of the twentieth century? What horn player's attacks could not be improved by devising and practicing an exercise based upon the twelve-tone technique?

Achieving a reliable embouchure response to a physical sequence of air intake–tongue stroke–air flow should lead to a consideration of the application of these skills in a musically pleasing and stylistically appropriate manner. Because the horn is included in every historical period from the Baroque to the present, we must learn about the styles associated with each era. There is currently much interest in recreating authentic performance practices. Modern replicas of early instruments, including the natural horn, are available. Many of our finest players and teachers are convinced that a horn player's technique is not complete without the skill and understanding necessary to play the natural horn successfully, or to play the modern instrument in a historically valid style. History and literature courses for college students include the study of performance styles. A growing number of recordings are made by conscientious and informed artists playing on historically acceptable instruments. Results of research by musicologists and performers are published in books and periodicals such as the International Horn Society's *The Horn Call*. To isolate ourselves from this information will delay or deny the development of attitudes and techniques necessary for stylistic growth.

In connection with styles of attack, compiling a list of all of the performing groups that include horns would prove interesting. This list would create other lists, since under symphony orchestra we must consider the various historical periods, national characteristics, tra-

ditions, sections within the orchestra with which we play, dynamics, and conductors' suggestions. Such lists have meaning only to the extent that they nourish further thought. The
extremes of attack are easy to define. The differences in attacking a *fortissimo* note in a big band
compared with the same note *pianissimo* in a wind quintet illustrate these extremes. Extremes
are also found within a single work. A study of the horn parts in *La Mer* by Claude Debussy
reveals the necessity for developing a large fund of attacking techniques. Between these
extremes lie many subtleties.

As suggested above, attacks are closely related to volume; thus, attacks must be practiced
at all levels of volume. Within each volume level are still other considerations. Does the music
require an attack that is pointed and aggressive, or one that is perfectly balanced between
tongue stroke and air flow? Should the attack imitate a clarinet, snare drum, or violin? Could
one theorize a gentle *fortissimo* attack or an aggressive *pianissimo* attack?

Young players are urged to write out, complete with transpositions, the exercises suggested in Examples 1-6 and 1-7 or to create their own exercises based on these models. Doing
so combines ear training with the physical precision of attacks, adds more exercises to the fund
of study material, and creates a gauge against which progress can be measured. These exercises direct our mental and physical efforts toward the accuracy of first notes after a breath or
after a longer silence. No horn player believes that the battle for accuracy has been won when
only the first notes have been conquered. The same orderliness and reasoned discipline can
be applied to all the notes of a phrase, slurred or tongued, if in the practice room we continue
to prepare (think), listen (hear), and analyze (evaluate).

A forehand that is reliable, strong, and varied is one of the pillars of every tennis player's
game. It begins with an elusive gift called talent, is developed through fine coaching and
orderly practice, and becomes natural through thoughtful repetition. In the heat of the match
there is no time for the equivalents in tennis of think, hear, evaluate. Thoughtful repetition
has transformed these steps into a natural, instinctive, and continual flow. Attacks are one of
the pillars of horn playing. From teaching and orderly practice develop reliable and varied
attacks. Thoughtful repetition transforms *think, hear*, and *evaluate* into a natural, instinctive,
and continual flow of musical expression. Natural gifts are expanded into eloquence.

## Long tones

We never outgrow our need for long tones. They allow us to concentrate on

1. breathing techniques
2. body support
3. attack and response
4. intonation
5. release
6. mouthpiece pressure.

Long tones should be practiced with the aid of the metronome and the tuner. The
metronome helps in the rhythmic control of starting and ending the tone. The tuner allows
us to check whether it is sharp, flat, or just right and to evaluate the steadiness of pitch in the

attack, duration, and release. It can also show us how volume affects pitch, how the pitch of the various registers reacts to volume, and how pitch is influenced by where we are in air supply. It reveals how temperature affects pitch. A cold horn in a warm room will sound flat. A warm horn in a cold room will sound sharp if we push in the slides and play constantly. A horn that feels cold to the touch will produce a flat pitch no matter what the room temperature might be.

During the warm-up it is advisable to confine long tones to notes between $g^1$ and $c^2$. *Piano*, *mezzo piano*, and *mezzo forte* may be used, but dynamic extremes must be avoided. The warm-up long tones provide an opportunity to investigate how mouthpiece pressure relates to intonation, range, tone quality, and volume. Too little pressure as a way of life results in a small, dull, unfocused tone quality, a middle register only, and minimum embouchure strength and endurance. Too much pressure produces a hard, bright sound, a choked-off high register, and little endurance on notes above the staff. Other symptoms of excessive pressure include a persistent, red half-circle on the skin above the upper lip, and a noticeable, but temporary, improvement in strength, high register, and flexibility after three or four days of not playing. Obviously one cannot build a horn playing career on not playing for several consecutive days even if one argued the principle of work and rest.

Excessive pressure often is the result of the young player's attempts to play the high register before the embouchure is strong enough to do so. For a player at age thirteen, it might take three or four years to develop this strength properly. Perhaps a ten-year-old is better served by singing or learning the piano until the body is matured sufficiently, at least, to hold the instrument correctly. All of these "facts of life" demand patience from young players, their teachers, and their band directors, whose career advancement depends on their young horn players' ability to play high and loud.

The relaxed long tones, played in the middle register for the daily warm-up, must not be done without specific purposes in mind. One day each week might be devoted to experimenting with pressure. The extremes of too much or too little pressure are easily identified, as described above. We should remind ourselves occasionally of how these extremes feel and what they produce. We should then work away from these extremes to find the amount of pressure that produces a centered, ringing tone quality, since it is beauty of sound that suffers most from errant pressure. By applying small amounts of more or less pressure during long tones, we can accumulate a fund of information concerning the effects of pressure, for good or evil, on each note, each volume level, each register. This approach takes time and thought, as all practice should. Teachers can be very helpful through their observations on the effects of pressure, but only the player can find the right amount. Each player can evolve a very personal understanding of this important matter, rather than having a stern method imposed from without.

Every teacher of college-age horn players has experienced the trauma of attempting to relieve the effects of excessive pressure. Months or years of college opportunities and experiences are lost while teacher and student struggle with this physically and emotionally debilitating problem. As with other aspects of embouchure, pressure should be a normal part of early training, thereby obviating a difficult and uncertain remedy at an inopportune time.

As a part of the warm-up, long tones need not consume more than five minutes. On the days chosen to concentrate on the effects of mouthpiece pressure, we could double the amount of time.

Long tones are important in our daily practice quite apart from their function in the warm-up. They allow us to compare how our bodies feel during the first fifteen percent of the air supply with how we feel during the last fifteen percent. The last fifteen percent is decisive in the development of a large air capacity. We have all experienced that moment of nearly running out of air. We are faced with some unfortunate choices: we can play faster, we can reduce the volume, we can insert a breath at an inappropriate place, we can shorten the last note, or we can stop playing. If we can find ways to delay arriving at the last part of the air supply, we can strengthen our volume and increase our comfortable phrase length. Through our breathing exercises we have practiced taking in a lot of air by inhaling horizontally and raising the speed of the intake. Throughout the exhale, we try to maintain a grip on the air by keeping the abdominal muscles firm as they pull inward. During the early part of the exhale, the air inside us continues to act as part of the support until we have used fifty to sixty percent of it. At that point, we must begin to rely more and more on abdominal muscle support. This is impossible if we have allowed these muscles to draw inward at a rate faster then we are expelling the air. There should be a direct ratio between where we are in the air supply and where we are in the abdominal muscles' return to their inward starting position. Do not allow the muscle return to get ahead of the air flow or these muscles will not be able to help us during the last part of the air supply.

We can construct exercises that require us to use the last part of the air supply in a most vigorous manner. This is done by playing a crescendo at the very moment that we are running out of air. Running out of air is often mistaken for lack of body support.

Example 1-8

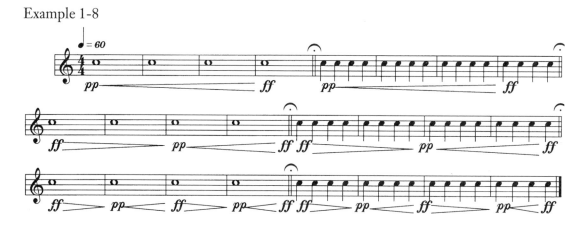

1. Set the metronome at 60 beats per minute and turn on the tuner.

2. Try to apply all of the knowledge and experience gained from the breathing exercises.

3. If, for the first few days or weeks, the last measures of the crescendo are not fulfilled, keep trying.

4. Do not save air on the crescendo. Use the air even if you cannot complete the four measures.

5. The tuner will show you the effect of volume on pitch.

6. Try to apply what you have discovered about pressure during the warm-up long tones.

7. Keep a record of your improvement. You will hardly notice the difference between 60 and 58. The difference between 60 and 50 is considerable. Our goal is a true *fortissimo* at 40. Move from 60 to 40 in easy stages.

8. This is an excellent low register exercise for both volume and capacity.

9. Use the resting time at the double bars to analyze and evaluate. This habit sets a pattern of concentration during rests in rehearsals and concerts.

10. The exercises are strenuous for the embouchure and for the breathing mechanism. They should never be done before the warm-up is completed and belong more in the second hour of practice.

11. Though neither easy nor fun, these exercises reward the serious player by producing a strong, abundant, and efficient air supply. The horn, after all, is played with air.

## Releases

Releases can be practiced in connection with long tones. The most common release is that used by clarinetists, who take great pride in their ability to fade away in a most enchanting manner.

With the metronome at 60, we can practice diminuendo in a series of notes that decrease in length from four beats to one beat. You will notice that at one beat the diminuendo would more properly be called a tapered release. To bring the note from *mezzo forte* to *pianissimo* in one beat takes practice but will add an elegance not always heard in horn playing. The quick tapered release is most useful on the last notes of lyrical phrases. Then it becomes a natural part of the music rather than a part of the physical action. Sometimes, however, we must do exactly the opposite. To disguise our breathing when there is very little time to breathe, we must release with no decrease in volume, breathe very quickly, and reenter at the same volume with no accent. This type of release and reentry can be practiced as a series of long tones connected by quick breaths.

A most satisfying and rewarding release exercise is to practice the first three notes of the Overture to *Oberon*, by Carl Maria von Weber. This three-note pattern can start on most any pitch. Try to bring the third note down to silence. Ask a fine clarinetist to play this pattern and listen to the release.

At release and reentry points, some horn players are concerned only with breathing and reentry and do not consider the release to be an expressive device. In lyrical playing we might think of a breathing place as a seam, which is defined as a line formed by sewing together two pieces of cloth. Sometimes the seam is used as a decorative element; at other times it is appropriate to disguise the seam. Just as the designer and the tailor decide which type of seam is suitable, the musician decides which type of musical seam is suitable. The musician decides which type of musical seam is desirable before choosing a physical action that produces the desired result. The physical action must be practiced until it becomes a natural part of technique.

Having a bountiful air supply provides more options for musical decisions. Within reasonable limits, breathing places must be determined from musical conviction rather than out of physical necessity.

## Tonguing

A fast single tongue is the horn player's good friend. A reasonable, but necessary, single tonguing speed allows us to play four notes on each beat when the metronome is set at 138–144. Some players seem to have been born with a fast tongue; others need to develop speed. The tongue can tire quickly, causing us to lose speed after several groups of notes.

We should test our single tonguing speed every week or so. Try to find a metronome setting that will allow the tongue to produce four notes on each beat at a comfortable speed. For increasing the single tongue speed, set the metronome one or two notches faster than the comfortable speed. At this faster speed, you will notice that after several groups the tongue will tire. The tongue has a remarkable ability to refresh itself with just a few beats of rest. Trying to force the tongue to move faster when it is fatigued does absolutely no good. Speed is developed by using the work and rest principle. If, when practicing for speed with the metronome, fatigue becomes apparent, simply rest for six or eight beats and continue. When working to eliminate fatigue, we should do the opposite. Find your comfortable speed and reduce the metronome setting one or two notches. Practicing at this slightly reduced speed will allow the tongue to strengthen by playing more groups before fatigue takes its toll. Do not be discouraged if your comfortable speed begins at 96 or lower. By keeping weekly records you will notice that you are progressing toward the goal of 138–144.

It is best to practice these groups of four notes as four repeated pitches on each note of a chromatic scale, one octave up and down. Middle register is best, since the low register responds more slowly and the high register has its own fatigue problems. When, after several months, the ideal tonguing speed and strength are attained, we can extend our practice to extreme registers.

A fast, reliable single tongue is more necessary on the horn than on the trumpet. Consider that the C trumpet is less than one-half the length of just the B-flat side of our instrument. The trumpet tubing is more cylindrical than horn tubing. The trumpet bell normally faces forward; ours faces back. Even a large trumpet mouthpiece seems amusingly small and shallow compared with an average horn mouthpiece. For all of these reasons, horn players need to develop a reliable, steady, strong, fast, single tongue in all registers and dynamics.

Practicing multiple tonguing by slowly articulating "tu ku," or "tu tu ku" probably does no great harm. Like all slow practice, it assures us that we can do the procedure slowly. We are still faced with the necessity of rapidly articulating "tu ku," or "tu tu ku." For double tonguing we should practice the basic unit of "tu ku tu":

Example 1-9

A metronome setting of 120 would seem to be a reasonable speed for beginning this exercise. When this is producing a good result, we can practice two units:

Example 1-10

By adding units we strengthen the process in speed and endurance. We can follow the same general procedure for practicing triple tonguing by isolating its basic unit:

Example 1-11

One hundred is a good metronome setting for beginning this triple tongue exercise.

Occasionally we should hear these tonguing exercises on tape. Since we are working for clarity as well as speed, it is necessary for us to hear how this really sounds. Sometimes we mistake the effort for the result.

Following, yet again, the principle of work and rest, some horn players feel that we should practice single and multiple tonguing every other day, allowing a day of rest after a strenuous workout. Each of us should experiment to determine what works best.

So far the discussion of tonguing has dealt with speed, endurance, and clarity of fast tonguing. One cannot imagine a fine performance of the Mozart Quintet for Horn and Strings, K. 407, if the horn player's single tonguing lacks speed, lightness, and clarity. Nor is it possible to play the horn parts in the Rimsky-Korsakov *Scheherezade* without a multiple tongue technique that has speed and endurance. Composers, in their wisdom, have written these tonguing techniques far more often for trumpet than for horn, but when we are faced with the necessity we must be able to produce.

Another type of tonguing is legato tonguing. This tongue stroke is used to connect notes rather than to separate them, as in staccato playing. Most horn players feel that the legato tongue is closer to "du" than to "tu." Saying "du tu du tu du tu" rather slowly demonstrates the more explosive quality of "tu." Speeding up the tempo reveals that at faster speeds the "du" becomes more like "tu."

A true legato tongue requires that the air flow be constant and unaffected by the tongue's motion. Since the legato tongue is often used in phrases with slow-moving note values, the temptation is great to move the tongue forward too soon and too slowly. If the tongue starts too soon and remains against the teeth for even a short time, the vibration stops, a space is created, and the legato is destroyed. Even the most gentle of tongue strokes must consist of a continuous action, as fast as possible, and at the exact moment the note is to arrive. A slow tongue stroke causes a space between notes; a fast tongue stroke allows the air to remain constant so that the vibration may continue.

A simple experiment will show the effects of a slow-moving tongue stroke. Without the horn or the mouthpiece, make an embouchure and blow through it without buzzing. Take notice of where the tongue is in a normal blowing position. Slowly move the tongue forward. Notice how the sound of the air is disturbed as soon as the tongue starts forward. Notice, also, that the air sound stops when the tongue reaches the teeth. This shows us the following: the tongue can disturb the air flow with only a slight motion; the tongue moves only a short distance before it strikes the back of the teeth; the tongue need stay against the back of the teeth only an instant before it stops the air and consequently the vibration.

Beginning players with undeveloped embouchures must use the "tu" stroke almost exclusively until their lips will respond to the more gentle "du." A more advanced player will want to start using "du" on notes after silence and not confine its use to connecting notes within a phrase. Since we do not always play with other brass players we must develop tongue strokes that fit well in a wind quintet, a soft string passage, or practically any *pianissimo* entrance. In the concerto literature, the first note we play in the second movement of the Strauss First Horn Concerto is an appropriate place to use a gentle attack. In the horn parts of the Brahms Violin Concerto are many entrances that demand an attack without accent or harshness. Measure 35 in the second movement is an example of an entrance in which we must imitate the violin on a figure that the soloist has just played.

Example 1-12

This is no place to enforce the amateur's rule of tonguing a little harder to make sure we get a good attack. A good attack is one that serves the music.

Of course it is the extremes of volume that present problems of balance between tongue stroke and air flow. We should work outward from the middle of the dynamic range:

Example 1-13

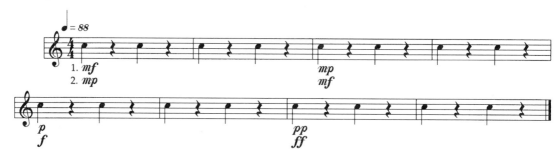

*Pianissimo* attacks are difficult because we must start the vibration with very little air. *Pianissimo* attacks often speak late because the air flow begins late. If this happens during the exercise, go back to a higher dynamic level and approach *pianissimo* again. Never add explosiveness to the tongue stroke but rather concentrate on achieving a good balance between air flow and tongue stroke. A gentle tongue stroke combined with a late air flow produces inaccuracies. Notice when moving from *mezzo piano* to *fortissimo* that the tongue stroke becomes more and more like "tu" as the volume increases. Alternating attacks between the two dynamic extremes is interesting and helpful. Doing this confirms that the air flow must start precisely with the tongue stroke no matter what volume level we use. Those who gather statistics on missed notes report that soft attacks are most often missed from below and loud attacks are most often missed from above. This will hardly be astonishing news to horn players.

The legato tongue is very effective in fast-moving notes. Its use is mainly a matter of stylistic choice; a legato tongue is not appropriate for the third movement of the Mozart Fourth Horn Concerto, but seems just right for the last page of the Hindemith Alto Horn Sonata. Practicing the legato tongue works well in etudes such as Kopprasch that have four sixteenth-notes on each beat. Notice that this stroke becomes less effective when we exceed a metronome setting of 126–132. Notice also that repeated pitches require a slightly more energetic stroke.

The point of practicing these tongue strokes is to build up a variety of attacking styles. We are then in a position to make music and not just use the tongue to start a note. We also expand our confidence that we can, indeed, call upon these resources in performance and not be tempted to revert to a style of articulation that serves only to explode air past our lips in the hope that they will vibrate the correct pitch.

There are, however, occasions when we might use the image of explosion to help with marcato, accent, sforzando, and *forte piano*. For brass players, these articulations are more effective when they are preceded by silence, even a very short silence. This can be confirmed by trying to play a series of sforzando attacks with a legato tongue stroke. The silence needed to produce the sforzando attack is obtained by allowing the air pressure to build up while the tongue is momentarily held against the teeth. This is precisely what we strive so mightily to avoid in legato tonguing. In a series of fast marcato notes we must hasten to return the tongue to the teeth in order to seal off the air flow sufficiently to produce the next explosion. At a slower speed there is enough time to allow the note its normal decay before the next tongue stroke. In an accent, the same procedure applies but must be modified according to the prevailing dynamic level. Accents in *fortissimo* require the tongue to rest against the teeth longer and be withdrawn more forcefully than an accent in *piano*. Accents and sforzando are similar in physical action. *Sforzando* means forced and is an extension of the accent. It is also modified by the prevailing dynamic level. It is more often used as an orchestral marking than in solo or chamber music literature, and it is very effective when played by four or more horns. In its literal application, *forte piano* requires us to perform an accent sufficient to produce a *forte* level of volume and to subtract immediately enough air to sustain a *piano* level. It is the most flexible of these markings because we can adjust it according to the prevailing dynamic level, we can stay with the *forte* a longer or shorter time, and we can use a greater or lesser amount of *forte* in any dynamic level according to style or historical period. A *forte piano* written by Mahler would seem to have a greater force than one written by Mozart. All of these articulations should be practiced separately after having arrived at an understanding of their musical applications. They should be taped and played back, since they have a surprising way of feeling forceful but sounding bland.

As with every specific technique, tongue strokes should be practiced until they become natural and reliable. The practicing of physical actions must of necessity be prolonged, repetitious, and thoughtful and must have a musical destination in mind. Having fun while practicing is just fine so long as practice does not end when it is no longer fun. Practicing, like thinking, becomes the most profitable at the moment it becomes the most difficult.

To digress for a moment, I do not quarrel with the fun component so necessary to the public school music establishment. This enterprise must be kept entertaining enough to attract and retain sufficient numbers to field a distinguished marching band. Attraction and retention defines success. The same can be said of many college music programs. The bright side is that public school music programs provide jobs for college music graduates, revenues for band uniform and twirling baton manufacturers, profit for publishers of band and choral music designed and produced for this market, and earnings for companies whose instruments play easily if not always well. The lamentable side is that a young player can spend up to twelve years in a public school music program and not play, sing, or hear a Morley madrigal, a Mozart aria, a Beethoven string quartet, a Chopin prelude, a Brahms Liebeslieder Waltz, Vaughan-Williams's *The Lark Ascending*, or anything by Webern. No one would pretend that playing in a band—grade school, high school, college, or community, even if it is fun—yields the same musical dividend as studying with a dedicated, experienced, and wise private teacher. Few would not agree that a superbly conceived, structured, staffed, and supported band program can be fun when it is led by a dedicated, experienced, and wise director. Music in schools is an enormous, entrenched enterprise which is here, we hope, to stay. One has to admire its ability to survive in spite of being a favorite target of budget cutting. Its success should be measured by how well it creates a passion to learn about our incomparable art, not by precision at the half-time of an athletic event, and by how well it creates a life-long enthusiasm for the pursuit of excellence, not by how well it provides temporary pleasure. Practicing tongue strokes provides the pleasure (fun, if you will) that accompanies genuine accomplishment.

## Slurring

Musicians agree that a slur is a curved line placed under or over a group of notes to indicate that those notes should be played smoothly. The tongue is used to begin the first note and may be used within the slur somewhat in the same way a violinist changes the direction of the bow, providing its use does not violate the spirit of smoothness. In other slurred phrases the tongue is not used again after the first note. Within the curved line may be dots, dashes, accents, and even sforzando and *forte piano*, all of which require the use of the tongue. The same curved line can indicate phrase length and possible breathing places. A slur could be called a phrase boundary when it encloses many notes. Within the boundary there can be several tongued notes added to adorn the phrase and to give it shape and definition. Seldom are these articulations used to separate the smaller units within the phrase. A composer occasionally, and intentionally one hopes, includes silence within the phrase boundary, thus offering the player an opportunity to employ the elegance of tapered release and non-accented reentry. A brass player cannot succeed without being able to connect notes without using the tongue, or without a complete assortment of tongue strokes to articulate notes within a legato phrase. These techniques are linked to the elemental instrument of expression. The human voice was heard before the sea shell or the animal horn was blown. It is comforting to reflect that in the latter part of the twentieth century, musicians must still be able to make their instruments sing.

Slurs, since they connect notes of different pitches, are either upward or downward; repeated pitches must be retongued. The most simple and nearly automatic of upward slurs are half-step slurs fingered 2 to open:

Example 1-14

Theoretically it should be quite impossible to miss the second note, since we approach an open note from a note having the least possible added valve slide tubing. Nonetheless, some of us have managed to do so. Keeping the air flow steady, raising the second finger, and letting the spring do its work should produce a smooth slur. This exercise illustrates the merits of subtracting tubing on upward slurs.

Playing this series of slurs is revealing:

Example 1-15

As the interval becomes larger, notice the increasing necessity to maintain the air flow while the embouchure moves us from one pitch to the next. Strangely, the best way to discover how the embouchure acts during the slur is to separate the notes and examine how the second note feels compared with the first. In this way the embouchure learns how to adjust during the slurring process. After separating and evaluating the feel of both notes we can then begin to rejoin them by making the notes longer until the separation no longer exists. Slurring is a subtle and complex blending of air flow, embouchure adjustment, and memory of how each note sounds and feels. It defies description in all but its rudimentary terms. Fortunately, if our embouchure can produce the two or more pitches separately, we can use our accumulated physical memory to join them while the air continues its flow. Physical memory evolves into feel, and feel evolves into instinct and eventually becomes natural.

Composers seem to enjoy writing fast slurred lines made up of small intervals. The Second Horn Concerto of Richard Strauss is an example. Composers also enjoy writing slurs of an octave or more. The method of practicing slurs by separating and rejoining them becomes even more necessary as the interval becomes larger. In a two-octave slur the embouchure must know how the second note sounds and feels while it is producing the first note. Fast wide slurs are difficult because the embouchure has little time to predict the feel of the second note. We must practice wide slurs slowly enough to be able to calculate the pitch and feel of the second note while we are playing the first note. Yes, we can think while we play. Not to think is to shoot at an unheard and unfelt target. Here is another case in which thoughtful repetition produces results.

Downward slurs require the same continuity of lip vibrations as upward slurs. Downward slurs more often involve making the tube length longer either by adding fingers or by moving from the B-flat horn down to the F horn and adding fingers. As the horn is lengthened, a proportionate amount of air must be added to allow the increased length immediately to become a part of the vibrating column of air.

We can practice downward slurs by reversing the direction of Example 1-15. Notice how subtly and gradually the need for added air between the notes begins to be felt as the intervals widen. For those of us not born with perfect slurs, it seems logical to separate the elements of slurring and then rejoin them in the following sequence:

1. Hear the pitches.
2. Play each pitch separately.
3. Compare how the pitches feel.
4. Sing the first pitch while hearing the next pitch.
5. Play the first pitch while hearing the next pitch.
6. Tongue both notes with a separation.
7. Tongue both notes with a slight separation.
8. Connect the notes with a solid but legato tongue.
9. Connect the two notes with a light legato tongue.
10. Connect the two notes with air.

## Large ensemble rehearsals

The next link in our chain of practice experiences is between the practice room and the rehearsal. One should never entertain the attitude that "it's only a rehearsal." Practice should be private, but rehearsals are public because they are heard and witnessed by colleagues. The music, our colleagues, and our employers deserve our very best at all times.

Our performance at the first rehearsal for a concert reflects the thoroughness of preparation. The first rehearsal also sets the psychological framework for the remaining rehearsals and concerts. If we do not have a good first rehearsal of the Beethoven Seventh Symphony, for example, we are left with a wound that probably will not heal completely before the concert. This wound becomes a scar that can affect future performances. For the Beethoven Seventh Symphony, horn players, before the first rehearsal, must have worked out the dotted rhythm, soft high attacks, loud high attacks, A-horn transposition and intonation, breathing places in the loud passages, and the endurance necessary to do all of this. To arrive at a rehearsal with doubts about any of these components is the first step toward a long battle with performance nerves. Conversely, confidence is the manifestation of the expectation of playing well. A bad first rehearsal cannot lead to a justifiable expectation of playing well at the second rehearsal. Better to be thoroughly prepared at the first rehearsal. This thoroughness is the link to the practice room.

In our leading orchestras, not much rehearsal time is given to an often-played work such as the Beethoven Seventh Symphony. Other orchestras devote more time to such works. In either case, preparation for the first (perhaps only) and subsequent rehearsals is good insurance for success. Unfortunately, many student-training orchestras allow the rehearsals to consume weeks and even months. This gives the student players the impression that rehearsals are the proper place to learn the part. Many schools of music place a high priority on playing the best possible concerts even if it takes months of rehearsing, thereby limiting the literature that can be learned and destroying the linkage of practice-rehearsal-concert. This kind of training does little to prepare students for professional life. An understanding, experienced, dedicated, and fearless training orchestra conductor achieves a good balance between rehearsal time and concert. The experience must be for the players' growth and development and not for the conductor's.

Thorough preparation extends well beyond the practice room and should not be confined to the literature that is currently being rehearsed. The serious horn student desiring membership in a professional orchestra should, during the training years, compile a personal dictionary of Italian, French, and German musical terms. This is best done in German, for example, by examining the scores of all of the works, not just orchestral works, of Mahler, Schoenberg, Richard Strauss, Webern, Berg, and others.

It is not enough to find a definition in a dictionary, "memorize" it, and forget it; to look at the score to *Don Juan* and ignore *Don Quixote*; or to deface a horn part with hand-written definitions. As each new term is discovered, it should be defined and entered into our own personal dictionary of terms. Work on this project should be a regularly scheduled item on our weekly agenda.

Italian terms have been used most frequently by composers. Would it not be helpful to know why a composer used *ritenuto* and not *ritardando*? The Italian section of our dictionary will be shorter than the German section, but since musicians communicate so often through spoken Italian, would it not be helpful if our pronunciation were precise? Would it not be helpful to know that there is no such thing as "double *forte*"?

The French section of our dictionary can be compiled in the same way, and during this project how wonderful it would be to discover *Escales* by Jacques Ibert. The listing of instruments should not be overlooked in any work, orchestral or otherwise. Understanding and correct pronunciation and usage will flow from our investigations. Such investigations are not, of course, a substitute for formal study of languages. Every college campus has language teachers and every music faculty has teachers and performers well-trained in languages. Singers can help with pronunciation so that we never again will say "mezzo forty."

The serious and intellectually gifted horn student who desires to enter the world of academic music as performer, teacher, and scholar must, during the training years and beyond, gather as much information about music as possible and develop interests more far-reaching than the narrow confines of orchestral horn parts. Every technique and insight gained in theory and history courses should add to our intellectual capital.

Just as our training years should produce a dictionary of musical terms, these same years should produce a personal library of orchestral, chamber music, and solo literature. Books of orchestral excerpts bring together what the editor believes to be the most important solo and tutti passages from favorite works and are convenient for preparing for auditions. Nearly every orchestral work contains at least one passage whose difficulty is unforeseen because of its innocent appearance. If we have complete parts, we can practice the first note in the second horn part in the Beethoven Fourth Symphony, and the coda of the last movement of the Beethoven Fifth Symphony. These are but two examples of orchestral passages not to be left for reading at the first rehearsal.

Rehearsing is another form of practicing. When we are in our own practice room, we work to control every part of our playing. Who, what, when, where, why, how, how often, and how long are all chosen by the player. In orchestral or band rehearsals, who, when, where, how often, and how long are determined by a master schedule agreed upon by the management and the conductor. How, what, and why are the conductor's choices. Except for conductorless ensembles, players have little or no voice in these matters. College-age players preparing for a career in a professional orchestra or military band should keep this system in mind and should look upon every large ensemble rehearsal as an opportunity to practice performing to the highest standard.

Unfortunately, we are not always conducted by the finest musicians or by the finest human beings during our training and young professional years. The podium does not invariably attract people with both of these exemplary qualities. We have all heard conductors say unfortunate things, have witnessed their inadequate preparation and skill, and have been the target of their ill-conceived comments. From these and other negative experiences, attitudes are formed. Though inevitable, these experiences should not dilute our desire to learn during the training years, or lower our standards of conduct and performance during the professional years.

Not uncommonly, young players complain that their conductor tried to tell them how to play, or told them that they were sharp, flat, ahead, behind, too soft, too loud, too short, too long. If one of these comments were offered shortly after the conductor had beaten incorrectly, we can understand that the young player will question the conductor's qualifications and right to evaluate. The conductor's right to evaluate and comment is inalienable; the conductor's competence to do so is another matter. The student will be confused and angry. The professional will remember the times that the orchestra rescued the performance from the clutches of the conductor's inadequacy.

Being bored in a large ensemble rehearsal says more about the player than about the rehearsal. Orchestral brass players do not play as often as woodwind or string players, and percussionists, happily, play hardly at all. During these non-playing times, we can choose to be mentally active or to drift off into dormancy. Why should a horn player choose not to look and listen while the strings are being rehearsed? Is it because the possibility of musical growth ceases when the orchestral contract is signed? Why would a horn player choose not to observe how the composer, woodwinds, percussion, and conductor all combine to produce a magical sound? Is boredom really more attractive than curiosity? Why would an orchestral player not want to know more and still more about music? Why do orchestral players take pride in not remembering what was on last night's program? Apparently there is a point where "professionalism" can block artistic development. Not to participate fully in all rehearsals during the training years is the first step in forming an apathetic attitude toward the very thing we have chosen to do. Full participation includes observing how the conductor tries to shape a phrase in the first violins. Does it matter if the phrase starts up-bow or down-bow? Why?

How do the horn parts contribute to the seamless sequences of the first twenty-three measures of the second movement of the Brahms Third Symphony? Why does the music of Debussy and Mahler sound so dissimilar when their life spans were nearly identical? Questions never end if they begin with a desire to discover.

Our relations with conductors will be more positive if our preparation, attention, receptivity to suggestions, and general conduct convey a message of cooperation and reliability. Our preparation must not be confined to works we have not played. How embarrassing to misread one of the transpositions in the last movement of the Dvořák "New World" Symphony because we neglected to review such a standard work. Impressions made at first rehearsals of a new program are important because they ratify or repudiate that we are experienced and always prepared. From these impressions, reputations are built for better or worse.

No special rules, other than those of civil conduct and common sense, govern behavior during conducted rehearsals. Civility demands promptness, attention, an agreeable tone of voice, a willing demeanor. Common sense tells us that the conductor is boss in all musical matters. Players' preferences are not open for discussion during the rehearsal. We should speak pleasantly when it becomes necessary to speak; a nod usually suffices to confirm that a message is received and understood. We should not feel offended if the conductor rarely acknowledges our presence. It could mean that the part is being played according to the conductor's wishes.

Our relations with members of our own section are governed by the rules of civility and good will. The bond between the first and second horns can be a very special one if it is built and nurtured on trust, respect, and appreciation. We have to trust that our partner will enter accurately, on time, in tune, and at the proper dynamic level. We must be able to respect our colleague's judgment, honesty, and reliability in all matters, and the appreciation for work well done should flow in both directions. There have been cases in which the first and second players have not spoken to each other in years and have managed to convey their contempt for each other in various ways, but still have made fine music together. This is tragic and is more worthy of the playground than the concert stage. One is always saddened to hear of arrogant, boastful, pompous, insensitive, rude, tasteless people playing the horn.

A wise and gifted training orchestra conductor can insist on high standards of behavior in musical matters. A wise, experienced, and caring teacher will find a place to include instruction in all of these concerns. Horn quartet coaching sessions are an ideal time to talk about orchestral etiquette. The teacher's personal example can be a powerful force.

## The class lesson

American higher musical education has never looked very favorably upon the class lesson. Used as an extension of the private lesson it can be made to serve as a temporary link between the teacher's studio and public performance. If the teacher is fortunate enough to have a sizable class, an acoustically appropriate room, and the opportunity to assemble the class on a fairly regular basis, the class sessions can be an excellent learning occasion for the teacher, for students chosen to play, and for other class members.

The teacher learns how the student reacts to a setting more public than the teaching studio. The teacher learns which new approaches have been absorbed and in which areas the student reverts to older habits. The students learn how much nerves can weaken control. The student learns how important it is to play well during the first section of the work and how first impressions can affect both the player and the listeners. Through the gentle guidance of the teacher, the student learns how to view a particular performance in relation to a further goal. The listening class members can hear new literature, can learn to listen analytically, and can see and hear how colleagues deal with problems similar to their own.

Ideally, class lessons are held weekly and occupy a fixed place in the schedule. Class lessons should always be viewed as an addition to, not a substitute for, solo recitals, or for the work normally done in private lessons. If the teacher decides that these classes are primarily performance opportunities, the semester's work should be scheduled to allow everyone to play as often as possible. Each week's class should be planned well in advance so that everyone can prepare according to schedule. Just as solo recitals must be planned to allow adequate preparation time, these class performances should be scheduled after considering the students' other responsibilities. Once set in the schedule, all class performances must take place. In the professional world, the show really does go on. No last minute blues, no trading of times, no postponements, no cancellations. A commitment is a contract to be fulfilled honorably by students and professionals. For students, it is good experience in personal discipline and for professionals there is no choice.

Realistic decisions on literature must be made by the teacher in consultation with the student. The Schumann Adagio and Allegro is not a sensible choice for someone concerned about high register and endurance. Unrealistic decisions provide the soil in which the seeds of nervousness are planted. It is so much better for the student and teacher to agree on a natural and inevitable succession of increasingly difficult literature that must be prepared thoroughly before performance. Otherwise the student will suffer the long-term consequences of playing the wrong music at the wrong time. Horn players thrive on success; they also remember failure. A series of successful performances leads to a realistic expectation of the continuation of successful performances, but only if the literature is chosen wisely and prepared completely. College horn students are often reluctant to study again those works they had played in junior high or high school. The teacher must weigh the benefits of learning a new work against those of repeating a work and playing it better. Class standing also plays a part in selecting repertory. Asking three freshmen to play the same work in the same class session is not a good idea. Asking three seniors or graduate students to play the same work as a preparation for professional auditions is not a bad idea. Whenever possible, these class performances should have the appropriate accompaniment.

There is always the possibility of assigning etudes for class performance. Etudes suggest the possibility of discussing technical matters. Class lessons, however, are not the place for detailed criticism and analysis of an individual's performance. The teacher's comments should be more for the guidance of the listeners than for the punctilious correction of the player. Orchestral parts could be included in these classes, but most of this literature should be studied in the private lesson and the orchestral repertory class.

Inviting guest speakers and players is always good. The speakers need not speak about the horn, nor must the players always play the horn. Would it not be interesting to invite a theorist, a musicologist, a conductor, and an opera stage director to converse about Richard Strauss?

Occasionally the teacher can use the class lessons to work through a student's nerve problems. If a student has suffered an unsuccessful performance because of nerves, the teacher and student can agree that for the next several class sessions three or four minutes will be devoted to playing long tones in the middle register. The purpose of this is to give the student an opportunity to play well before an audience. The student must practice these long tones before each class and thereby strengthen the link between practice and performance. When, after several short sessions of long tones, the student is able to achieve good responses, a straight and steady tone with no dry-mouth, then some middle-register scales could be the next step. After success with scales the student should be ready for simple middle-register melodies, then longer and less simple music can be played, followed by more advanced material. This process uses the class as a laboratory for the practice of performing publicly. It works best when there is complete honesty and disclosure. The teacher explains to the class that small portions of every session for several weeks will be devoted to helping one of their friends work on performance anxiety. The whole expanding process of moving from long tones to more difficult literature must be outlined to the class members. This procedure is good for their own growth, and it points out that their presence is necessary for the success of the operation and that their collegial support is vital.

Teachers should think about their own role in the class lesson. It goes far beyond planning and supervision. Each teacher should decide how to present comments after each performance. One way is to make notes while the student is playing and speak to the class from these notes. The teacher should remind the class of the fine moments in the performance and explain how these moments were achieved. This is not the time to list each technical and musical flaw. These can be discussed at the next private lesson. Flattery is transparent, gracious honesty is appreciated, and brevity is essential. Both the teacher and the class should listen actively and analytically. A mental checklist of accuracy, tone quality, intonation, dynamics, style, preparation, presentation, and stage presence provides a framework for analytical listening. From analysis we can extract those parts that could be beneficial to our own playing and teaching. At least we will have more to say and think about after a performance than, "I liked it," or, "It was neat."

## Practice summary

Horn players who practice three hours a day, seven days a week will invest 1092 hours per year in this activity. Before we congratulate ourselves too heartily we should remember that pianists, string players, and other non-brass players practice much more. There is no magic in practicing exactly three hours every day, but during the college years it is a reasonable average to maintain. Six hours every other day maintains the average but does not produce the same results as regular, daily practice.

The most effective practice is that which prevents us from repeating mistakes. The most productive word in the practice room is *why*. It takes time to put the horn down, ask why, and ponder the question. We have seen how the work and rest principle is basic to horn playing; here is an opportunity to use the resting time to analyze our own mistakes. Very often the answer to why is connected to hearing. We cannot correct a mistake we did not hear. We cannot play a rhythm that we cannot hear. We will be lucky to play a pitch that we cannot hear. The same applies to intonation, dynamics, style, and accuracy.

Our trained ears confirm that a mistake has, indeed, been made. Our analysis leads us to the general area of concern, that is, air, embouchure, fingers, reading, concentration, lack of physical effort. Far too many mistakes occur simply because we did not try hard enough. We must not "try it again" without knowing what caused the mistake and what we will do to try to correct it. Relating the mistake to its general area is a large step toward improvement.

Solutions often will work one day and not other days. This predicament falls into the general areas of concentration and effort. A physical action becomes natural, instinctive, and reliable only after we have found the right amount of mental and physical effort required to complete the action. If the action is new to us we cannot expect that it will be easy, natural, and reliable until it has undergone many thoughtful repetitions. Slow practice allows us time to concentrate on each physical part of the action. Gradually faster practice allows us to blend each physical action into the musical effect. Fast practice allows us to proceed according to established habit.

We have seen how practice can be divided into (1) calisthenic, (2) technical, (3) musical. The calisthenic category, most of which is included in the warm-up, can easily deteriorate into a monotonous performance of an implacable procedure unless we understand why we must do breathing exercises, attacks, long tones and all the rest of it. We should remind ourselves that when we practice long tones, our attacks, body support, intonation, volume, tone quality, releases, air capacity, and embouchure strength are also being practiced. The tape recorder, the electronic tuner, the metronome, and the teacher's eyes and ears, as well as the player's own, can provide information on improvement. Teachers and students should keep notes on improvement. These notes could evolve into a record of what works and what does not, thereby becoming a resource for future decisions.

It seems reasonable that technical practice is in the center of our calisthenic-technical-musical triad. The technical is dependent upon the calisthenic, since we cannot practice anything technical until calisthenic practice has given us the rudimentary skills to do so. To attempt a high-register etude, for example, before our embouchure can produce notes above the staff is damaging and futile. Calisthenic practice separates the various physical actions in order that each may become healthy and reliable. Technical practice brings together physical actions as they are required to produce a musical expression. For pianists the calisthenic practice of scales and arpeggios, followed by technical practice of Czerny etudes, make possible the musical practice of anything written by Chopin. It strains the analogy to suggest that our tonguing exercises, followed by Kopprasch etudes, lead to the Weber *Concertino*. The framework, nevertheless, is the same.

We all have been convinced that slow precedes fast in practicing technically intricate passages, but few ask why this is so. Slow practice allows us to hear mistakes and gives us time to train our embouchure, breathing, and fingers, through deliberate steps, to place each note securely. Slow practice also lets us check intonation, dynamics, and rhythm. Faultless slow practice does not guarantee faultless fast playing. If we have been practicing with the metronome at 60 we must be prepared to return to 60 many times if 72 is not perfect. If our goal is 100 and we have played the passage perfectly one time at 100, a different kind of practicing begins. Now we have to practice playing it perfectly $X$ number of consecutive times at the proper speed. This could include several temporary returns to a slower tempo, but not without asking why. Quite often success depends upon one or two notes. We must identify the offending notes, ascertain the nature and cause of the mistake, practice these notes many times, and only then begin to add notes in front of the now-corrected notes until we arrive at the beginning of the passage. What is learned today may be gone tomorrow. We should be prepared to repeat the process on as many days as necessary to achieve control. What teacher has not heard, "I don't understand it. This was perfect yesterday"?

Musical practice is the most demanding because of its complexity and subjectivity. We have known players with mastery over the calisthenic and technical who have mistaken those skills for musicianship. We have known players who have not developed the physical and temperamental control necessary to convey their splendid musical thoughts. Some players are content when all of the notes are played in strict conformity with tradition. This predilection is not all bad if the tradition arose from the composer's intention and not from the technical and musical inadequacies of the past.

A young player does well to follow the teacher's example. It is assumed that the teacher has broad experience, historical and stylistic understanding, and the ability to describe or demonstrate the desired musical effect. In this way a cornerstone of musicianship is laid at the same time that calisthenic and technical progress is being made. Not having, as yet, a strong high register or a thunderous *fortissimo* does not absolve the teacher or the player from the consequences of a delayed or impoverished musicianship. From the beginning of serious study, a young player must hear the finest horn playing by listening to the teacher or to recordings. This is especially important if otherwise the only horn playing a student would hear is that of colleagues in school ensembles.

As early as possible, the student should be asked to listen, describe, and imitate a phrase that the teacher has just played or sung. These three actions are in the proper order, since we cannot reproduce what we cannot hear; being asked to describe what has been played focuses attention on essential points; imitating the teacher completes the possibility of analysis and imitation of the student's own singing or playing. Young players, once they rise above their embarrassment, sing more musically than they play because vocal expression is likely to be instinctive and natural and not constrained by the machinery of the instrument. Taken in small steps, the young student can be led along the path by listening, describing, imitating.

A more mature student can be asked to make and defend musical choices. One can imagine the teacher asking the student to work out three distinctly different approaches to a lyrical etude. At the next lesson the student will play and defend each of the three versions and choose the best one. This choice must also be explained and defended. It is no longer enough to say, "I like it." *Why*, again, is the key word. We should trust our instincts and experiences up to a point. An experienced player very often gets it right the first time because instinct and experience have combined. There is always the exciting possibility of doing exactly the opposite of the instinctive. Contrariness gives us another choice. The mature player of superb technique and musicianship might be tempted to solve all musical problems with only solutions that have worked well before. This decision could be called style, or it could be evidence of contented stagnation.

Teachers of horn players of any age have a responsibility to balance the calisthenic, technical, and musical in the student's playing, thinking, and sense of proportion. They are obviously connected, and the first two are indispensable to the third. Teachers also have the opportunity of initiating in the student an enthusiasm for discovering music other than that written for horn. Some of this discovered music can be related to horn playing and can rightfully be labeled musical practice, but much of it should be heard, enjoyed, and discussed for its own sake and for the purpose of musical growth. Horn literature is but one beautiful planet in the musical cosmos.

Teachers must create and preserve a studio atmosphere in which students are comfortable in the discussion of musical or other concerns. Teachers must urge students to define problems in precise terms and not to rely upon jargon or flippant cliché. Often the teacher must listen for a long time before offering a solution. It is possible that with every sentence the student has taken a step toward a solution or has increased the teacher's understanding of the student and the problem. In musical matters, students must have reason to trust the teacher's judgment. This trust is earned through honesty and by having solutions that work.

# CHAPTER 2
# ETUDES

## Kopprasch

We have seen how practice can be apportioned into three flexible categories of calisthenic, technical, and musical. Etudes, by definition and by their nature, belong mainly in the technical area. The traditional horn etudes of the 19th century, such as those by Gallay, Mueller, and Kopprasch, concentrate on scales, arpeggios, or articulation patterns, and an entire etude may be devoted to just one of these technical matters. They are highly repetitious, tonally predictable, and often have the same note values throughout. They probably represent the level of horn technique expected of fine horn players of the era in which they were written. Except for an occasional lyrical piece, this genre of etude does not require very much musical perception, but rather an understanding of purpose and potential benefits. Each etude as it is assigned should be examined by both teacher and student to determine its general character, intent, and structure. These etudes are especially valuable, since they can be modified in many ways to become even more effective. For example, nearly every etude can be practiced an octave lower for low-register development. They can be transposed into any other reasonable location; their rhythmic patterns, dynamics, and speed can be adjusted. To many young ears these etudes may seem boring, and if played only in their original configurations, may be so. If used as sketches deserving of expansion they can serve as a treasured resource for building a solid, traditional technique. We should never feel that we have finished with these etudes, never to play them again. By using some imagination they can be used throughout one's playing career for diagnosis and rehabilitation of the fundamental techniques.

The first historically significant etudes encountered by serious young horn players are those written by C. Kopprasch. Their use signifies that the student has graduated from method books and is ready to work on essential technical matters. The 1992 Robert King *Brass Player's Guide* lists seven editions of the *Kopprasch Sixty Studies*, most of which are divided into two volumes. A quick glance through Volume I confirms that the etudes are exercises in scales, arpeggios, and articulation patterns, with some attention given to the lip trill and wide leaps. Only two of the thirty-four etudes in Volume I are lyrical in nature and content. For this discussion, the Carl Fischer edition of 1939 as revised by Fr. Gumbert and Albin Frehse was consulted. We are all indebted to Norman Schweikert, the distinguished horn player and tireless scholar, for letting us know in the May 1971 edition of *The Horn Call* that Fr. Gumbert is actually Friedrich Gumpert (1841–1906). We assume, not having evidence to the contrary, that dynamics, articulation, and other editing marks are those written by Kopprasch and those added by Gumpert and Frehse. Another fine edition, published by International Music Company in 1960, edited by Oscar Franz, revised by Albin Frehse, and newly edited by James Chambers, is quite similar to the Gumpert-Frehse edition.

Etude No. 1 in Book I is a rather slow, tongued scale study. Its general appearance suggests that a legato tongue stroke is appropriate. A metronome setting of quarter-note equals 60 requires that good breathing techniques are used, since many phrases begin *piano* and crescendo to *forte*. Its range is nearly three octaves, which creates an opportunity to observe how the embouchure reacts to the legato tongue stroke in the various registers. Assuming that these etudes are played on a standard model double horn in F and B-flat, we should listen carefully to make sure that the first note played after changing from one side of the horn to the other is perfectly in tune and matches its predecessor in volume and tone quality. In this etude the crucial notes are $g^1$ on the F horn and $a^1$ on the B-flat horn. Without any adjustment by the player the $a^1$ will often be sharp and somewhat bright-sounding if fingered 1 + 2. Similarly, $g^1$ on the F horn often sounds flat when preceded by $a^1$ on the B-flat horn. A glance at the electronic tuner will certainly help. Tone quality is a matter of judgment, but it is generally true that the qualities of the two sides of the double horn differ more in loud playing than in soft. Loud playing tends to drive the pitch of the $a^1$ even higher. Fortunately, our efforts to keep the $a^1$ down in pitch will take away some of the brightness and help the smoothness of passing from the B-flat to the F horn. The ear can be taught to accept questionable intonation or to demand perfect intonation. The more times that we hear ourselves playing this $a^1$ to $g^1$ interval perfectly, the greater the demand becomes. Since this etude has no intervals other than half steps and whole steps, it presents an opportunity to listen for the difference in size and flavor of these intervals. They must sound as different as possible, with the half step tightly together and the whole step properly spaced. A good prelude to this exercise is to play, while watching the tuner, a slow chromatic scale from the lowest note to the highest note of the etude and then back down, and then do the same with a whole tone scale. Playing the scales will reveal that we do not always play pitches at the same place ascending and descending. This is a wonderful etude because its simplicity is both a virtue and a challenge. It could be an etude that we play every day.

Etude No. 2 is another study in legato articulation, this time in major and minor thirds. The editors suggest that every ascending four-measure phrase should begin *piano* and end *forte*, and that every descending phrase start *forte* and end *piano*. This is very natural, but we should reverse the dynamics occasionally. Every phrase ends with a fermata. Some thought should be given to the length of each fermata. Translating the Italian *fermata* into the English *hold* or *pause* does not alter its function of causing a break in the rhythmic motion. We should never arrive at the length of a fermata by adding a specific number of beats. The length should be governed by several factors, including the nature of the music that precedes it. In this etude each fermata is preceded by fourteen quarter-notes. The regularity of this rhythmic motion suggests a fermata long enough for the mind's ear to erase the pulse created by the quarter-notes. Players tend to be more impatient than listeners with the length of the fermata, but we cannot forget its function or its dramatic potential. In this etude we can experiment with varying the length of each fermata. Perhaps those in *forte* could be longer or shorter than those in *piano*. Since the etude ends with a low note, this last fermata could be astonishingly long. We should recall that in the Rondo of the Mozart Third Horn Concerto there are two fermatas. The fermata near the beginning of the movement need not be as long as the one near the end. The second fermata must erase the feeling of pulse that has accumulated for almost the whole movement. Unfortunately, the length of each fermata is in the hands of the conductor. As in Etude No. 1 we must listen for the exact size of the minor third and the major third. Nearly every measure has the potential for faulty interval size. The first measure is a good example, since it contains one note that is probably all right ($c^1$), two notes that could be flat ($e^1$ and $d^1$), and one sharp note ($f^1$). It is not enough that notes register on the tuner as sharp, flat, or just right. They must sound right to the player's ear in their intervallic context. This is the beginning of both linear and horizontal intonation. We must be able to hear pitches in relation to previous pitches but also in relation to pitches sounding simultaneously with our own.

Etude No. 3 and Etude No. 4 should be played at *fortissimo* and at *pianissimo* in addition to the printed dynamics. Playing at *fortissimo* can show us where extra effort must be applied to maintain an even level of volume, regardless of register. The tape recorder can illustrate whether the notes on the F horn are projecting with the same intensity as those on the B-flat horn. At *pianissimo* we must guard against the natural urge to increase the volume on the ascending lines. Both etudes are marked sempre staccato but there is no reason not to practice them with a legato tongue occasionally. These two etudes seem ideal for beginning the serious study of transposition. Most young players have had some experience with transposition and perhaps have resorted to using pencil marks to identify pitches in the more familiar horn in F. Some players have contrived elaborate formulations for each transposition. These schemes usually involve changing the clef and adding or subtracting sharps or flats. If these stratagems work, so be it. It does seem that these cumbersome machinations seek to avoid the hard work of learning each transposition so thoroughly that it becomes automatically and perpetually reliable. How simple, direct, if old-fashioned, it is to practice these two etudes a half step lower and call it horn in E. At first we must go slowly enough that our eyes can grip each note as we play it and our ears connect the pitch we play with the note we see. The first seriously studied transposition might as well be horn in E so that the intervallic difference is as small as possible. In this "method" of transposition eyes, ears, and fingers all learn the new pitches. It is best to stay with horn in E until most of the etudes in the first volume can be read at a slow but steady pace. E-flat horn logically comes next, followed by D, C, B-natural, low B-flat, high B-flat, A, and G in that order. Learning transposition is somewhat similar to learning languages; learning one helps in learning others. Transpositions should be mastered to the point that there are no transpositions. Every key must be as automatic as horn in F, with only an occasional urge to polish up B-natural in honor of the Brahms Second Symphony. Learning transpositions this way can consume a lot of music for reading. Venturing beyond the safe confines of horn etude literature might even be necessary.

Etude No. 5 introduces the lip trill as a series of slurs between notes that are a whole step apart. At first this etude should be played open on the F horn. Doing so will produce a strange interval between $e^2$ and $f^2$, but just for this exercise we can relax our strict standard on intonation, knowing that this is not the normal fingering for this trill. This is a true calisthenic exercise in that we are concerned only with the physical action that results in a steady, smooth, reliable slur between the two notes. The mirror is helpful when it shows excess motion in the corners or the lower jaw. In our slow practice we should try to find the smallest motions that will move us from one note to the next. Large motions do not produce fast reliable lip trills. Firm corners and a firm grip on the lower half of the mouthpiece is our best approach. As the editors suggest, we can expand this exercise downward one half step at a time by adding the second valve for E, first valve for E-flat, first and second for D, second and third for D-flat, first and third for C, and all three valves for B-natural. Notice how the pitch, tone quality, and physical control deteriorate as the horn becomes longer and longer. Whenever we have a choice of fingering for any note we should try to make the horn as short as possible. This is an etude that demands patience. Nothing is gained by playing faster than we can control the slurs. This etude alone is not a magic carpet to lip trills. Combined with the warm-up exercise illustrated in Fig. 1-4 and the willingness to spend months rather than weeks or days in calm orderly practice, this etude will provide the control and flexibility needed for elegant lip trills.

Etude No. 6 or No. 2 is suitable for beginning the study of memorization because each has short phrases and relies on sequences. Everything here is predictable and logical. After marking off each phrase, defined by the fermatas in No. 2 and by the eighth-notes in No. 6, look at the first phrase to see what it contains. After studying this phrase we should try to reproduce it in our mind's ear while looking at the notes. Do this at least three times. Then try to reproduce it mentally without looking at the notes. When this is successful, play the phrase three times while looking at the notes, then three more times without the notes. This procedure relies on complete concentration at each step. Some phrases will be quite easy but do not omit any of the steps, which can be outlined as follows:

1. Mark off each phrase.
2. Find the pattern within the phrase.
3. Look at the notes.
4. Look at the notes and produce them mentally three times.
5. Produce the notes mentally without looking at the notes.
6. Play the phrase three times with the notes.
7. Play the phrase three times without the notes.

Each step should be perfected in the above order. It is always possible to go back one or more steps to solidify the process. After memorizing the first phrase, repeat the same steps for the second phrase. When the second phrase is memorized, play phrase one again and if all is well play phrase two. Then play the phrases joined together. Continue this procedure until the complete etude is memorized. Do not be distracted or discouraged by a temporary lack of success, or by the simplicity of the process. We are establishing a pattern for memorizing that can be applied in future to more complex works. It follows an orderly sequence of study, analysis, practice, performance.

In Etude No. 7 we have an opportunity to listen to intervals in a harmonic framework. We should begin to trust our ears. If it sounds right, check with the tuner to make sure but do not let the tuner do all of the work. Just as with the metronome, we could become so dependent on the tuner that we only see rather than hear discrepancies in intonation. The metronome is very useful in practicing attacks, releases, and breathing, establishing a beginning tempo, and checking for unsuspected lapses in tempo. It might have some use in pieces, such as marches, in which the maintenance of a rigid tempo is considered virtuous. Etude No. 7 should also be played in all reasonable transpositions and with varied dynamics.

Etude No. 8 is excellent for the practice of memorization. Would it not be interesting to memorize it in F and then, without looking at the notes, try to play it in E or E-flat? This exercise tests our ability to transfer what we hear into what we play. Though sometimes discouraging at first, it is another way to expand the usefulness of our ears. Most ears will improve through hard work; some become excellent.

The ninth etude introduces articulation patterns of tongued and slurred notes within a group. The editors' indication of *tempo giusto* is well chosen. *Giusto* is translated as *strict* or *correct* and, as applied here, means that the sixteenth-notes must be placed evenly whether tongued or slurred. The metronome tells us whether the first notes of the group are on time; only our ears can tell us whether the remaining three notes are correct. Listening to the tape playback is very revealing, since articulated patterns often feel one way and sound quite another. Absolute rhythmic precision is needed at all rates of speed.

No. 10 presents the common articulation pattern of two notes slurred followed by two notes tongued. The critical note is the second note of the slur. Since no tongue is used on the second note, it may have less volume than any of the tongued notes. This is especially true if the volume level is high and the slur is downward. There is also a tendency to shorten the second note as the tongue prepares to articulate the third note in the group. As in Etude No. 9, we must listen to make sure that all four notes in the group are placed evenly. Some players hurry to the second note, pause for a moment before the third note, and, as far as the metronome is concerned, everything is fine. Record it and listen for evenness in volume and rhythm. Playing this exercise in E or D gives the 2 + 3 combination of fingers a good workout.

The editors suggest that a better place for Etude No. 11 would have been preceding No. 44. If the physical action of the lip trill is not fully developed, no harm is done by delaying the study of this etude.

Etude No. 12 is another exercise in two notes slurred, two notes tongued. This articulation pattern is especially appropriate for the horn concertos and the chamber music of the classical period when composers were content to leave such matters to the judgment of the performers. One suspects that horn players of that era were not always as conscientious as modern players in developing a fast, light, reliable single tongue. Not having to tongue every note in a four-note group does help the player who has not, as yet, attained a speedy single tongue. Our ears have been conditioned to accept and expect this articulation pattern, and it certainly has been a favorite of those who have edited music from the classical period. This pattern also works very well when the speed is fast enough to warrant double tonguing. When we have attained a single tonguing speed of four notes to a beat at a metronome setting of 138–144, we are able to make decisions about articulations from musical conviction rather than from technical inadequacy. This etude should be practiced with several different articulation patterns, including all notes single tongued. This is a good place to begin practicing transposition of etudes with key signatures.

Etude No. 13, when transposed down to D or C, becomes an exercise in achieving solid responses in the lower register and offers another opportunity to practice passing through those notes known as the "break." We should always be willing to try some B-flat horn fin-gerings on some notes usually considered to be sacred F horn territory. Decisions on finger-ing should be made after considering tone quality, intonation, volume, and response. Ideally, fingered notes should have the same quality as open notes. Careful listening reveals that the addition of any one valve does not change the quality of the tone very much, although the third (the longest) valve does sound "darker" than the second (the shortest). The addition of the first and second valves makes the horn sound "brighter" and especially so on the B-flat horn because of the sharp bends in the tubing. The third valve produces approximately the same pitch as the combination of one and two but the quality is darker because of the more gentle curves of the tubing. The combination of the second and third valves sounds rich and gives a good response in all but extreme dynamics. Generally, the shorter the horn the better the tone quality. Tone quality remains a matter of opinion, but intonation is not. No one would insist on a fingering that resulted in bad intonation but had a beautiful tone quality. For this reason we do not play $a^1$ open on the B-flat horn. In correcting the intonation of notes that conventional wisdom would finger 1 + 3, or 1 + 2 + 3, our embouchure and our right hand must bring the notes down in pitch so far from their natural centers that the tone quality is seriously distorted. Generally, the shorter the horn the better the intonation. It is our good fortune that the double horn makes alternate fingerings available for every note played 1 + 3, or 1 + 2 + 3 except for the lowest G and F-sharp on the instrument. Response follows the same pattern as quality and intonation. The B-flat horn, being shorter, responds a little more quickly than the F horn. Open notes respond more quickly than fingered notes. This is not always a blessing. In soft entrances the B-flat horn in the low register might sound slightly more explosive than the F horn; in loud entrances the B-flat horn will respond immediately and with a large volume of sound. Fingering comfort should never be a consideration. If we must choose a fingering only because it is easy we have allowed weak finger technique to pre-vail. Bassoonists would be overjoyed if they could play their instrument with three fingers and a thumb on the same hand.

Etude No. 14. Here again is an exercise in slurring and tonguing within a rhythmic group. It is especially rewarding because all of the slurs are downward and many of them require a change from the B-flat horn to the F horn. The first slur in the first measure offers a good example of what is often described as "blowing through" a slur. Since they are not tongued, the second and subsequent notes of slurs are completely dependent on air to make them sound evenly in volume and on time. In downward slurs when we move from the shorter B-flat horn to the longer F horn, we must add a little air to keep the notes even in volume. Of course this can be overdone; let your good ears guide you. The length of the second note must also be considered. We could start from the premise that all notes are full value until proven otherwise. Since the editors did not add anything to shorten the second notes, we may assume that the second notes are as long as the tempo will allow. By not shortening the second note and by blowing through the slur we can arrive at an even volume on the two notes. When listening to the tape, check to see whether the ornamental notes are projected clearly. Ornaments can also feel one way and sound quite another.

Etude No. 15 is a delightful recital piece for horn alone. If we divide up the phrases it becomes an effective piece for two antiphonal horns with one or both players off-stage. Notice how every phrase ends with a quarter-note, and how long these final notes are at a metronome setting of eighth-note equals 66. This etude gives us a fine opportunity to practice tapered releases with some variation in the speed and amount of taper. The *forte* phrases should be played very dramatically and the *piano* phrases rather gently. Do not hurry the 32nd-notes or the ornaments. Perhaps we might think of this as two horns signaling and echoing. On solo recitals this etude must be played from memory. Take some time to consider the proper length for the only fermata. Nearly every etude in this volume has at least one repeat. Notice that when the only repeat is at the end of the etude, we repeat from the beginning, even though there is not a repeat indication in the first measure. For recital performances we should decide whether to observe one or both of the repeats only after playing the etude several times each way. Repeats are not always long and boring.

Etude No. 16. Whereas Etude No. 15 should be played without a musically stifling rigidity of tempo, No. 16 is an exercise in rhythmic discipline. The metronome should be used occasionally to point out our tempo indiscretions, but not so often that the inflexibility it causes begins to be mistaken for musicianship. Perhaps its use can be compared with that of the electronic tuner. No one suggests that the tuner can do more than show us where we go astray and by how much. When we play we have to listen. The metronome becomes most useful after we have turned it off because then we must listen to ourselves rather than the metronome. The rhythmic motion in this etude is hardly perpetual but it must be steady and even and should not vary with the changes of articulation pattern. We should give some thought to the length of the fermata toward the end.

Etude No. 17. Intonation and evenness of volume throughout the two-octave range are the main concerns in this etude. We must not assume that the notes in the lower octave will project exactly as those in the upper octave. As we transpose the etude downward toward low B-flat, the tongue must work more forcefully to maintain volume. It also requires firm corners and good contact with the lower half of the mouthpiece rim. This is a wonderful exercise for those aspiring to become great second horn players. It is a noble calling.

Etude No. 18 should be learned in both E and D before reading it in F. In E the fingering patterns for the upper octave are rather complex, but quite simple in the lower octave. Memorizing this etude is a good idea so that we can watch our fingers. The tips of the fingers should always be in contact with the end of the valve keys. Some players, without realizing it, raise the fingers before depressing the keys, or allow the fingers to rest so far down on the keys that the first joint is flattened. If the stretch from the B-flat key to the little finger hook is too long, the fingers are forced to become flattened rather than arched. A competent instrument repair person can move the little finger hook to shorten the stretch for a more comfortable grip. There are some wonderful devices on the market that are helpful for players with small hands. One goes by the intriguing name of "Duck Foot," and seems to work well for those who play with the bell off the leg. It is best to work out this etude *sempre forte* to make sure that an even volume is maintained.

Etude No. 19. Most of this etude is grouped in a pattern of two slurred notes followed by four tongued notes. The editors have used *piano*, *mezzo forte*, and *forte* as the three volume levels. It is always helpful to establish these levels separately by playing several groups at each level before practicing the complete etude. Every phrase ends with a quarter-note, which should not be shortened or accented. This is an excellent exercise to practice total concentration from beginning to end. Concentration demands that our eyes and our memory supply the necessary information from the page, that we have decided upon the appropriate physical actions to convert the information into music, and that we listen and evaluate the result. In practice we can profit from giving attention to each component separately (information, action, listening) but our success in actual performance depends upon all three of these working simultaneously. Therefore, every day we must practice performing so that these three become one. Writing the word *concentrate* at the top of the page is but a small part of the process.

Etude No. 20. Sometimes it is better not to breathe at every opportunity. Breathing at each eighth-note rest in this exercise is tempting, but doing so deprives us of the opportunity of working on air capacity. In performance we like to arrange the breathing so that we play on the first seventy percent of the air supply whenever the music will allow. In practicing etudes we should look for occasions to work on expanding the latter thirty percent of our air supply. The first two phrases, which crescendo from *piano* to *forte*, and all phrases marked *forte* are excellent for building air capacity. There is no reason to practice this etude at a tempo so fast that the phrase length becomes easy. This should be an exercise in good breathing technique, dynamics, endurance, and fermata length.

Etude No. 21 is marked sempre staccato but we can use this exercise to practice our legato tonguing also. Since it is divided into orderly phrase lengths, we should practice our memorization routine on this etude. After it is learned and memorized in F, try to play it in any reasonable transposition without looking at the notes.

Etude No. 22. Since this is the first time in these etudes that we have seen the word *espressivo*, we should rejoice. In its broadest sense, espressivo refers to those elements of performance that cannot be indicated by symbols. Before the seventeenth century, commonly understood symbols and inherited conventions made further indications of tempo and volume unnecessary. As vocal music grew, and with the rise of instrumental music, composers began to add more guidance in matters other than speed and volume. By the end of the nineteenth century composers were using words and symbols to ask for nuances, both rhythmic and dynamic, and gradations of speed and volume. Gustav Mahler filled his pages with words of advice, warnings, descriptions, and numerous other directions. Some twentieth-century composers place combinations of symbols on almost every note, and with the emergence of new notation, composers often supply several pages of performance notes. All of this points to the need for performers to study the history of notation, the history of performance practice, and the stylistic elements of the various historical periods and individual composers, and to become familiar with the most recent developments in notation. Only then will we have a historical and aesthetic framework upon which to build a valid expressive storehouse.

Orchestral horn players are not given much liberty, being confined in tempo by the conductor, in volume by the orchestration, and in personal stylistic choices by custom and habit. In chamber music and solo playing the restrictions on expressive freedom are presumably those of historical accuracy and good taste born of intelligence nurtured by study and experience. There is also that mysterious thing called talent, without which music becomes recitation.

Except to establish a basic tempo, the metronome must not be used in Etude No. 22 since rhythmic nuances are completely suffocated by its beating. In a most general way phrases should move ahead in tempo and then relax toward their natural conclusions. This is not to be identified as accelerando and ritardando. Accelerando and ritardando are most effective when they are noticed as such. Shaping a phrase with motion is most effective when it cannot be recognized as a departure from the basic tempo. In much the same way phrases which move upward should gain in volume and those which arch in contour may also arch in volume. Each phrase should be examined to test the appropriateness of this approach. Not every descending line need lose volume. Many phrases have a point of destination often made obvious by the contour of the line; at other times made less obvious by a harmonic subtlety. On rare occasions non-espressivo can be very expressive.

Singing in the privacy of the practice room is a good way to discover the natural shape and flow of lines. It is also a form of ear-training if we try to produce precise pitches. Listen to what your voice does naturally as the lines rise and fall, and do not give up because your singing voice does not please you. If we convince ourselves that we cannot sing, we forfeit a most valuable asset. Musicians have always learned by imitation, intentionally or otherwise. A good teacher loves to be imitated in the hope that it will lead to a more personal expression by the student. It is very sad that most young wind players hear very little music other than that played by themselves. Attending recitals by singers, pianists, and string players could be called practicing if we concentrate on how the performers achieve expressive results. Recordings are fine if the technical dazzle does not deafen us to the more musical qualities. The worst thing that we can do to a phrase is to do nothing. We might as well leave the notes on the page if we cannot bring them to life. The elevation of lyrical playing to at least the status of technical display should start very early in the pursuit of a personal style that is founded in excellence. Can anyone doubt that Dennis Brain imitated his father as a first step towards his own musical greatness?

In Etude No. 22 we can make a start on finding ways to use our calisthenic and technical accomplishments for musical purposes. The editors suggest that we should breathe after the first measure. Generally it is preferable to breathe after a longer note value to accommodate an elegant release and an unhurried reentry. If we decide on a metronome setting of eighth-note equals 60, and if we have developed sufficient air capacity, we can delay the breath until after the third beat in the second measure, thereby achieving a longer line and a nice arch in the phrase. Physical comfort insists that we breathe after the first measure; the music insists that we do not stop the line so soon after its beginning. The ornament must be played as slowly as the tempo will allow so that it does not disturb the relaxed feeling of the music at this point. Each note of the ornament must sound clearly. After the breath in the second measure the trill is followed by two ornamental notes often called *nachschlag*. This ornament also must be played at a speed in keeping with the character of the music. We do this by starting the ornament soon enough that it has time to sound unhurried. Our next breath should be after the dotted quarter-note in the fifth measure. Since we are in an ascending line with a crescendo, we should use our technique of nontapered release and a quick reentry to keep this line moving to the F-sharp. This F-sharp is the highest note in the etude thus far. We may dwell on the F-sharp slightly before moving ahead with the remaining sixteenth-notes. Take plenty of time with the release and the reentry in the sixth measure, since this breath should last until after the third beat in the eighth measure. The editors have suggested other breathing places but we should be willing to take the difficult approach if the musical result is honorable. In the eighth measure we can practice the art of making this breathing place sound very natural by using a long release and not hurrying the reentry. We can breathe after the first dotted eighth-note in the tenth measure, but be on time with the sixteenth note. The editors suggest a diminuendo in the tenth measure, but we might consider keeping all of the energy until the last quarter-note, which should be long and tapered. The double bar marks a natural halfway point in the music so we should not be exactly on time with the first note in measure eleven. The crescendo on the rising line in measure twelve could be enhanced by forward motion after lengthening, slightly, the G-sharp. We should try to avoid the breath suggested at the end of the eleventh measure, but should breathe after the third beat in measure twelve and not again until the quarter-rest in measure fourteen. We must not hurry the entrance in the next measure, or hurry the ornament with which it begins. Since the music in measure fifteen is a reminiscence of the beginning, play it more softly and gently, at least until the third beat of measure sixteen. Measure eighteen is the top of the piece for both height and volume. We can make the most of this by breathing after the first eighth-note, stretching the tempo slightly on the slur up to the G, and then breathing after the third beat. This breath should last until after the first dotted eighth-note in the last measure.

All of this slightly painful, measure-by-measure investigation is pointless if it results in the music's sounding labored and pedantic. In practicing lyrical playing we should do exactly what we do in technical practice, which is to go well beyond our goal and then bring it back to reality. Exaggerate every crescendo, diminuendo, forward movement, relaxation of tempo, and variation of volume, before settling on the proper amount. If we always work on the deficit side of expressive devices we will never reach the optimum. If we work on the surplus side we are more likely to achieve a natural but controlled feeling by relaxing from the extravagant. Occasionally we can create a stunningly dramatic moment through this process, but only if the music calls for it. We will never know if we do not try.

We have seen how closely breathing and phrasing are connected. We have also seen that breathing places do not always coincide with the ends of phrases but can be disguised to minimize breaks in the line. Practicing lyrical etudes includes looking at the music measure by measure in search of ideas that the human mind and spirit can add to transform symbols into singing. Practice also includes trial, error, and substitution. Practicing technical etudes often means gaining control of speed and every kind of accuracy. Practicing lyrical etudes always means finding what the music has to say before finding a way to say it. We must have the patience to practice slow music with the same discipline, concentration, thoughtful repetition, thoroughness, and joy that we lavish upon technical display. To err technically might be human; musical transgressions can never be forgiven.

Etude No. 23 and Etude No. 24 follow the pattern announced in their first measures. The large slurs in No. 23 should be practiced with an expanding air flow. No. 24 has quicktongued leaps, many of which cross over between the two sides of the double horn. We should not search for easier fingerings but should use this etude to give the thumb a good workout. Horn in G would be most appropriate for this etude.

Etude No. 25, in spite of its key signature and accidentals, is an excellent etude for horn in E as well as other transpositions. Try seeing how much of this etude can be played from memory in F after having worked it out in several other transpositions not including F.

Etude No. 26 concentrates on quick narrow slurs upward and downward. There is no reason not to tongue this etude occasionally. After achieving some speed on this exercise we might imagine that it is the horn part in a wind quintet from the classical period, and try to emulate the lightness with which this figure can be played by our colleagues on their more highly mechanized instruments. Everything becomes more difficult in transpositions, including one octave lower in F.

Etude No. 27 is another study in slurred and tongued notes within a rhythmic group. Be sure to play a full quarter-note when it is the last note of a phrase.

Etude No. 28 should be practiced slowly enough that we can feel the four sixteenth-notes contained in the dotted eighth and sixteenth figure. It should also be practiced quite rapidly. Notice how we must use what seems to be an extra amount of tongue on the sixteenth-note when we play this familiar rhythm quickly. This etude should be taped and played back to check rhythmic accuracy and evenness of volume between the dotted eighth- and sixteenth-notes.

Etude No. 29. Rapidly changing dynamics and registers are less a concern when played andante than allegro. A legato tongue stroke seems appropriate.

Etude No. 30 could be practiced all tongued, all slurred, or as printed. Playing it all slurred and one octave lower in F will improve our fluency in low-register slurring.

Etude No. 31 is still another two-slurred, two-tongued exercise that can be practiced at various speeds, including a speed fast enough to justify using the double tongue.

Etude No. 32 is a wonderful exercise for getting the low notes to speak on time after a large leap downward. Check the mirror occasionally to see whether there is excessive motion on the leap downward. There is good reason to practice this etude in all dynamic levels, including the extremes. The Gumpert-Frehse edition has no suggested volume level; the Chambers edition suggests *mezzo forte*. Both suggest *sempre staccato*, but that does not preclude using a longer tongue stroke also.

Etude No. 33 uses the same notes again and again, with only a little relief in the middle section. We could pencil in changes of transposition every two measures in preparation for playing the Prelude to the third act of *Lohengrin* by Richard Wagner.

Etude No. 34 is an example of Kopprasch at his most predictable and repetitious. We can surely find other ways of practicing this etude by changing the articulation patterns, slurring, transposition, dynamics, and rhythm.

The etudes in Book II are longer and somewhat more chromatic than most of those in Book I, and they follow the same patterns of tonal sequences and articulations. Because they are so similar to the studies in Book I it is hoped that the observations above can be applied to Book II. Since only six of the sixty etudes in both volumes are lyrical, balancing the etude diet with transcriptions of vocalises or similar material is necessary.

Kopprasch etudes will reward careful patience with a disciplined basic technique consisting of accuracy, two and one-half octave range, well-defined dynamic levels, sensitivity to aberrations in intonation, understanding of traditional notation and common Italian musical terms, and endurance sufficient to play a one-page etude. They can also form a link between the entertainment approach of most elementary method books and the serious, thoughtful work of establishing a solid technical foundation.

It may seem that I have taken much liberty with the Gumpert-Frehse edition of these fine etudes. If so, it was not done out of an absence of admiration and gratitude for the work of the editors or of the composer. While we have no reliable dates for Kopprasch, nor do we know his first name (Carl?), there is reason to believe that these etudes were written in the early years of the nineteenth century. That they continue to be a mainstay in the horn literature speaks for their excellence.

Etudes written for the sole purpose of technical development and not meant for public performance should, in the privacy of the practice room and teaching studio, be allowed to serve their purpose to the fullest extent. Those, such as No. 15, that might be played in recital, should be presented in a manner consistent with the composer's musical intentions as nearly as can be determined.

# Gallay

Jacques François Gallay (1795–1874) was a French virtuoso who became Professor of Horn at the Paris Conservatory in 1842 and taught there until his death. He wrote a remarkable number of etudes, which have been edited and collected in opus numbers 13, 27, 32, 37, 43, 53, 57, and 58. Of particular interest are the *Grand Caprices* in Opus 32 because they do not always follow the predictable course of sequences and repetitious rhythmic and articulation patterns. Several etudes in Op. 32 have unmeasured, cadenza-like passages that are in great contrast to the severe style of Kopprasch. Opus 27, containing forty etudes in the Chambers edition, is the most interesting of all. The first nineteen etudes follow the Kopprasch model and, from their general appearance, could have been written by Kopprasch. Etudes No. 20 through No. 40 are unmeasured and offer good training in imaginative, free playing. Brass players, having no training literature comparable in musical quality to that of pianists, for example, should welcome every occasion to develop a solo style tempered only by good taste and judgment. This does not weaken our ability to conform to the restraints imposed in orchestral or band playing.

All of the unmeasured preludes in Op. 27 are short. When transposed down a perfect fifth or more, they make excellent low-register exercises. Etudes 21, 23, 25, and 34, when played in any transposition and in almost any order, are unusual recital pieces. We should not try to "bar" these etudes or force them into the more conventional groupings, thereby destroying the very quality that gives them purpose and charm.

# Maxime-Alphonse

## Book 4

Horn players are indebted to Maxime-Alphonse for giving us six volumes of etudes ranging from the short and rather easy to the long and very difficult. Book 4 represents a reasonable advance in difficulty from the etudes of Kopprasch, Mueller, and Gallay. Most of the etudes in Book 4 are strictly technical and concentrate on a specific activity. They are not as chromatic as those in Books 5 and 6, nor do they contain as many rhythmic complexities. Many of them can be altered in ways that make them even more effective.

Etude No. 1 has leaps to the top of the staff and above. The last thirty measures are especially good as an assignment to perfect accuracy. It is well edited with a variety of dynamic marks and the breath marks are well placed. It does become more difficult as it proceeds, making it necessary not to let down the concentration when playing through the etude, thus also testing the short-term endurance because there are no breaks in the music. Exaggerating the accents is advisable (particularly those on $c^1$) for several practice sessions, and then relaxing them to a musically agreeable severity after volume and accuracy are assured.

Etude No. 2 is a study in short repeated pitches. Usually it is the second of the repeated pitches that does not project well unless we give it a little extra tongue. Repeated pitches below the staff and in soft volume levels must be very short in this etude.

Etude No. 3. The first four lines of this etude should be played with a legato tongue stroke. Since it is a scale exercise, we must be very precise with the size of the half steps and whole steps. No volume should be lost on the two-octave descending passages. This should be checked on a tape playback because, again, it might feel as though we are maintaining a steady volume when in fact we are mistaking effort for result. In the latter part of the etude there are several suggestions for fingering that do not apply to the standard F and B-flat double horn. "3e (c. asc.)" refers to the third valve on a French instrument which raises the pitch a major second. The third valve on our instruments lowers the pitch by approximately a minor third. All of the measures marked 1 + 2 can be played with this combination on the F side of the horn, but for etude practice, using the normal F and B-flat double horn fingerings is more beneficial.

Etude No. 4 is a repetitious study of the dotted eighth-, sixteenth-note rhythm in compound meter. There is always the possibility that the sixteenth-note will appear too soon, causing the figure to sound as though it were subdivided in three rather than in four. At moderate to fast tempi, this figure becomes more a matter of feeling than arithmetic. When subdivided in three, this rhythm sounds easy-going and relaxed; when subdivided in four it can sound vigorous and lively.

Etude No. 5 should be perfected exactly as written and then practiced in the following ways:

1. one octave lower in F, *fortissimo*, quarter-note equals 60
2. horn in G, *pianissimo*
3. any transposition, any speed
4. as written, every note on the F horn
5. any transposition, every note on the B-flat horn.

One octave lower at quarter-note equals 60 is excellent for working on air capacity. Try to take as few breaths as possible and maintain a firm body support on the last fifteen percent of the air supply. Since there are accents on nearly every slur we must observe them and play exactly as written. At other times we can strive for smooth slurs.

Etude No. 6 may also be extended by playing one octave lower and all tongued.

Etude No. 7 is a Kopprasch-style arpeggio exercise. It also can be altered by transposition, speed, and tonguing length. Listen carefully to ensure that all octaves match in pitch.

Etude No. 8 begins and ends with a lovely *mélancholique*. These measures should be copied by hand in order to make three or more editions of the dynamics, phrasing, and articulations. No horn player has ever suffered permanent damage from the application of pencil to staff paper. These editions should be made after the etude has been worked out completely as printed. Composers often have given but one word, such as *espressivo* or *mélancholique*, and have seemed content to leave everything else to the player's good judgment. We can use this etude to expand our expressiveness. The more choices we have at our command, the less likely we are to rely on the obvious. The middle section of this etude should be played with a legato tongue stroke. The last thirteen measures of the middle section could be selected by the teacher as a test of accuracy.

Etude No. 9 is a theme with eight variations in which the notes are always the same, but articulations and rhythms are changed. The turns in variation seven should be played as slowly as the tempo will allow. In variation eight, the composer has included a suggestion for playing the trills and turns in a rhythmically controlled manner. We might also practice playing the trills freely. The whole step trills on $f^1$ and $e^1$-flat are better when fingered on the F horn; all half-step trills are fingered normally. The lip trills on $f^2$ and $e^2$-flat are excellent on the B-flat horn.

Etude No. 10 gives the 2 + 3 combination a good workout. Brass players have been led to believe that music written in sharp keys is difficult, awkward and possibly ill-conceived. If true, this might apply to this etude, which has only one note, repeated several times, that is normally fingered open. Problems in intonation and accuracy increase with each addition of valve tubing. One would rather believe that this is the reason for our antipathy towards sharp keys. The whole first section or the last section might be assigned for accuracy.

Etude No. 11 requires a bold, aggressive manner in the outer sections and a smooth, lyrical style for the middle section. Calculate very carefully to discover where the note after the doubly dotted note should be placed. The middle section has only a few directions for expression. We could be quite free with both volume and movement, or we might play it very simply. This is another opportunity to experiment with several approaches and to choose the most pleasing and appropriate. When played one octave lower in F, the outer sections of this etude are excellent for developing volume on troublesome notes just below the bottom of the staff.

Etude No. 12 begs to be altered to become an exercise in volume and air capacity. When played one octave lower in D, very slowly, and *fortissimo*, this etude provides challenging physical and mental exercise.

Etude No. 13. There is a lot of detail in the first half of this etude that must be observed. The dots outside the ties call for a space before the next note but not a rearticulation. The dashes are a reminder that the notes to which they are attached are full length; this does not allow any space for the tongue to prepare for the following accent. Maxime-Alphonse was a very clever composer!

Etude No. 14 is another exercise in dotted rhythm. At the tempo indicated, this rhythm could easily lapse into a triplet feeling, which dilutes its natural vigor.

Etude No. 15 could also be played much slower and in the lower transpositions.

Etude No. 16 has, again, a lot of detail that must be understood and practiced. Notice the difference between the wedge-shaped mark and the dash. In this case the wedge is placed outside the slur so that it shortens the note but does not imply a rearticulation. This mark is used more often on tongued notes at higher volume levels, and in that context is understood to be a combination of accent and dot.

Etude No. 17 should be practiced exactly as printed. It could also serve as another exercise in low-register development by playing it in the lower transpositions and somewhat slower. At the speed indicated this is an excellent study in slurred flexibility.

Etude No. 18 has, again, much detail that must sound very clear and precise. The dot under the slur in measure 21 is surely a misprint. The general feeling is one of neatness and sparkle.

Etude No. 19 should be practiced as written and in E-flat, with careful attention to placing the sixth eighth-note in the measures and the second of the two sixteenth-notes. A mental background of subdivided eighth-notes is needed to ensure proper length on the longer note values.

Etude No. 20 could be studied as a preparation for the *Concertino* by Carl Maria von Weber or the Rossini Prelude, Theme, and Variations. Nothing is lost by delaying work on this etude until such time that it might be considered for recital.

## Book 5

The etudes in Book 5 take horn technique another step forward. Teacher and student might consider working on these etudes in an order other than consecutive. One might begin with 16, followed by 20, 12, and 9, before starting with the first etude and going in order through the book. In this way, we start with the most elaborate etudes in the volume, work them out thoroughly and put them aside, and then work at them again with, one hopes, added capability. This is a good plan for working on the large concertos by Reinhold Glière, Gordon Jacob, and the Second Concerto by Strauss. Work at them, go to other solo works, and return several times. Since it is especially difficult to play these and similar works the first time, we should devise slightly unusual but effective practicing patterns to meet these occasions. Many violinists delay playing the Brahms Concerto publicly until they feel ready for it; some conductors wisely postpone the Beethoven Ninth Symphony indefinitely.

Etudes No. 1 and 2 could be studied as companions since they each concentrate on long and short tongue strokes. No. 1 is brief and not difficult, and is a good choice for perfecting accuracy. Accuracy includes every detail of dynamics and note lengths. In Etude No. 2 the first line of the second page has two crescendo markings that take us through those annoying notes near the bottom of the staff. An enterprising horn student will want to create a sequential exercise pattern revolving around these notes. This etude also emphasizes short repeated pitches, which can be troublesome when played *piano* near the bottom of the staff. Firm corners, a good grip on the lower half of the mouthpiece rim, and quick, hard strokes should make these notes speak on time and project well. Etude No. 2 should be played with more animation than speed.

In Etude No. 3 the diminuendo mark should be attached to the dotted quarter-note in the second measure of the phrase. This applies throughout the etude. Since lyrical phrases often end on a long note value, we must be sure that, as far as volume is concerned, we have not played the end of the phrase before arriving at the last note. Last notes must also be interesting. There are not many dynamic marks in this etude—a signal for us to create our own. The 6/8 should be practiced in several transpositions, including one octave lower in F and horn in G.

Etude No. 4 has so many sharps that not to practice it in E-flat and B-flat would be wasteful. There is nothing very challenging here in F.

Etude No. 5 is most useful when practiced as follows:

1. exactly as written
2. down one octave, slurred or tongued
3. down one octave, *fortissimo* at eighth-note equals 46, tongued or slurred
4. as written, all on the F horn
5. as written, double tongued.

The greatest benefit is earned when this etude is used to improve volume, intonation, articulation, and smoothness of the low register.

Etudes No. 6 and No. 7 could be practiced as companions. Etude No. 7 is excellent for transposition including G and A. They both are very lightly edited and do not offer much beyond practice of accuracy.

Etude No. 8 is more varied and interesting. The second measure appears to have no special hazard, but it does illustrate the need to look, occasionally, at our fingers. We are so accustomed to changing fingers on nearly every note that we become reluctant to do otherwise. In measure 2 beginning with $f^2$, each descending fourth is played with the same finger, thus causing some momentary perplexity. This can be remedied by observing when the repeated fingers occur and by playing this pattern many times while looking at our fingers. Common and often unnoticed undesirable habits are raising the fingers before depressing the valve key, holding one or more fingers off the valve key, allowing the first joint to flatten, or fingering too far down on the valve key. The opening of this etude should be played very boisterously. At each double bar we could find a different feeling to portray. This could involve editing some of the dynamics, or an occasional change of tempo, but it will allow us to search the music for expressive ideas and possibly rescue the etude from a mere mechanical reproduction of its notes.

Etude No. 9 has an opening section that should be played with all the dynamic and rhythmic nuances implied by the term *expressif*. Notice how the first two phrases end with a long note value after a succession of more active notes. This suggests moving ahead in both motion and volume to the final note. Long final notes of phrases are boring only when they are stationary. At the speed indicated, this is a note long enough to require control over where we begin to taper the release. We should stay with our accumulated volume long enough to establish it as a final note, but not so long that the release sounds abrupt. We could start the taper during the second beat. The second phrase appears to be an echo, but we might feel that it should be more bold than the first phrase. Experiment with both approaches until both phrases are pleasing and natural. The ascent to the *forte* should be as dramatic as possible. On the ascent there should be no diminuendo on the quarter-notes after the accents. We should try to find the amount of forward motion that will enhance the crescendo on the rising line, but not so much as to suggest an accelerando, which is contrary to the composer's intention. If we agree that the music thus far has a stately quality, our choices of expressive gestures must not be in conflict with this feeling. Leave no doubt that the high A is the top if the piece in intensity. What a disappointment it would be to finger this note open on the B-flat horn only to sacrifice intonation to safety. The remainder of the etude is a repetitious drill in technical precision.

Etude No. 10 is written so that the rhythmic figures do not fit into their expected place in the measures. The accents on beats 1 and 4 seem out of place but apparently that is the point.

Etude No. 11 has a refreshing amount of variety and detail. We must play the 32nd-notes as late as possible and with a strong tongue stroke so that the accents do not make them sound weak in comparison. Be very precise with the triplet figure containing the sixteenth-note. Remember that the third note must appear in its rightful place without regard for the alteration of the second note. This can be practiced by leaving out the second note for one or two beats and then replacing it. The Allegretto must be played, as the composer suggests, quite gently. Be sure to differentiate between the speed of the ornaments and the speed of the following sixteenth-notes. The section before the da capo is excellent for perfecting accuracy, particularly when played in D horn. C-flat, F-flat, and B-double-flat are all legal.

Etude No. 12 is a jovial piece. It is well edited with many suggestions for breathing. All the directions should be translated and entered into the French section of our dictionary of terms. Of course, this has been done in each etude thus far.

In Etude No. 13 we can become accustomed to using 2 + 3 on $c^2$-sharp and $d^2$-sharp when they occur consecutively, ascending or descending. This complete etude is a good test of accuracy because of the stopped notes and because of the added tubing on the 2 + 3 notes.

Etudes No. 14 and No. 15 are highly repetitious and predictable. In these two etudes we could relax our rule about making the fingering "easier" and search for alternate fingerings that reduce the great physical effort of moving from 2 + 3 to 1, and we might even play some notes on the B-flat side of the horn that are normally considered to be F horn territory. Put all fingerings to the test: how does it sound, and is it in tune?

In Etude No. 16 the first two phrases when played *forte* and at the tempo indicated are good gauges of our air capacity. We must not play at a lesser volume or at a quicker pace to ensure that we can complete the phrases, but rather should keep trying, while making sure that our breathing and body support are correct. Since both phrases are ten beats in length, it is interesting to hold the highest notes and the lowest notes at *forte* for ten beats and compare how each feels. The group of six notes at the beginning must be "blown through," which means that the air flow must expand during the figure; not to do so results in a diminuendo. The real test here is whether the last notes of the group are as well projected as the first notes. The dotted rhythms must never sound as though they had been subdivided into three parts. Check the practice tape to hear whether the notes just before the accents are heard clearly. This, again, could be a case of feeling one way and sounding another. Look for at least three ways to play the turn in the third phrase. One way is to consume the entire beat with five even notes. Listen to the tape and choose the one that fits the music, but not necessarily the one most easily produced. Experiment with different lengths for the tongued sixteenth-notes in the phrases marked *piano*. This might be a good time to invoke the rule that notes are full value until proven otherwise. Having no guidance from the composer, we are left with our taste and judgment to decide the matter and with our technique to bring it to musical life. The first four lines are rich in technical and musical details; one must not give way to the other. We must be willing to practice the music as diligently as we practice the techniques needed to produce the notes, and not be content with work half done. In the Allegretto we must not invent a crescendo. This is not to say that dynamic shaping is forbidden, but to arrive at the measure before the *forte* with a volume greater than *piano* is to cancel the subito effect and deny the composer's intention. If we are ready to work on Book 5, surely we are past taking the easy path. The final Allegretto is excellent for the insistence upon complete technical accuracy. After Etude No. 16 has been worked out with great diligence, it should be taped and saved for future comparison. This etude is one of the treasures of the horn study literature.

Etude No. 17 is a study in agility in its outer sections. The middle section should be played very dramatically by taking full advantage of every accent and crescendo. The tempo indicated is slow enough that all of the slurred 32nd-notes can sound distinctly. The notes are not very difficult; the style is crucial. The middle section could be played quite freely. The outer sections are played with a light tongue stroke, no accents, and just enough separation of notes to accommodate all of the repeated pitches.

Etude No. 18 is long and quite repetitious but does demand rhythmic precision. The dotted eighth-, sixteenth-note figures must always sound subdivided into four parts. The metronome marking seems very fast but is probably worth striving to achieve.

Etude No. 19 is a wonderful flexibility exercise as written and at the speed indicated. It is also very good as still another slow, loud, low-register etude, tongued or slurred. All of these low-register exercises are perfect for the latter part of the final practice hour of the day. Every horn player needs a solid low register, and these etudes, along with their other considerable virtues, will certainly aid our efforts to become complete horn players. A few players enter this life with a gift for low notes; most of us have to confront the low register with tenacity, zeal, and firm corners of the embouchure. It is good to play, occasionally, all of our low-register etudes very softly, tongued or slurred.

Etude No. 20 is a long virtuoso piece with a lot of variety. It could be called a Grand Concert Etude if we would write our own stunning cadenza. Take advantage of the fermatas on the double bars both for the musical effect and regeneration of the embouchure they provide. There are several different dotted and doubly dotted figures in this etude. Each must be precisely correct. After studying Etude No. 20 we might look again at Kopprasch, Gallay, and Books 4, 5, and 6 by Maxime-Alphonse for a suite of etudes for recitals. At least one etude should be in the low register.

## Book 6

This volume continues to extend the technical boundaries of horn playing. Glancing through the book, one is astonished by the amount of ink on the pages. Nearly everything is notated in sixteenth-notes or 32nd-notes. There are so many notes that some lines contain only two measures.

Horn myths, timeworn and delusory, persist. One of the more unfortunate warns us that practicing technique will result in an inferior tone quality. One has only to hear the magnificent tones produced by today's virtuoso horn players; they all spent much time on technique. Another myth advises us not to practice any etude after Kopprasch, Book II, because etudes do not win orchestral auditions, excerpts do. We should look at the path cleared for us by Dennis Brain, Barry Tuckwell, Hermann Baumann, and more, who were not content to be confined to orchestral parts, but created a renaissance of solo playing and recording. Granted, one could play the orchestral parts of Brahms without struggling with Book 6 of Maxime-Alphonse. With the greatest reverence to Johannes Brahms, there is now much more to horn playing.

Etude No. 1. Most of the first page is an exercise in moving quickly through the registers. The second page is beneficial for training our eyes to gather information very quickly. At a slow practice speed the eyes can grasp each note as it is played. As we gain speed the eyes must recall information obtained from previous practice sessions. At the speed indicated there is no time for the eyes to look at each note but instead they must capture and summarize whole patterns instantly. These patterns contain as many as eight notes in one beat at quarter-note equals 80. Since harmonic implications in this etude are quite predictable, and the melodic shapes are often sequential, our mind's ear can help in transferring these configurations into sound. This assumes that we have been diligent in ear-training, and that we continue to develop our ears by singing everything that we play. Dull, sluggish, pitch-illiterate ears deprive us of this most helpful component of transforming notation into music. Our embouchure, air, and fingers are completely dependent upon eyes, ears, and mind.

The first measure of Etude No. 1 sets a trap for us. It is tempting to breathe on the eighth-rest, making it necessary to recover very quickly for the high G-sharp. Try not breathing here but after the quarter-note A. Breathing can be so automatic that we are not aware of it. Breathing can also be risky. The ornaments should be ornamental and not played at a speed that could be mistaken for sixteenth-notes. At letter A we should choose our articulation length after considering that the composer has written no dots until E. At the speed indicated, a completely legato tongue stroke will sound sluggish and a bristling staccato will not contrast well with what follows at E. There is an agreeable middle length consisting of slight separations but no accents. The stroke at this tempo is the same one that is appropriate for repeated pitches. Pick any middle-register note and practice this tongue stroke until it sounds right and feels reliable. The more gentle tongue strokes can cause inaccuracies until we become completely accustomed to them. At H we must use the permission granted by *très expressif* to explore beyond the composer's markings. When we see motion at the end of a measure, as in the first and third measures of H, it is often an invitation to move ahead or shape the six-note groups by starting them slowly and regaining speed. Since the second phrase imitates the first it suggests an echo, but we could also consider a more aggressive approach. The second half of the etude should be practiced one section at a time. Much of the second half is sequential to and repeats earlier material, thus easing the burden if past work has been thorough. One could be forgiven a slower tempo at T. Make sure that X is more dramatic than the beginning.

Etude No. 2 is a study in lengths and styles. There are many accents in this etude and they occur in all volume levels. As observed earlier, when practicing accents it is advisable to exaggerate the force of the tongue for several sessions and then make them less severe, if need be, when confidence and accuracy are secure. Accents require confidence. Unfortunately, every horn player can recall occasions when a loud, exposed, important, high-register accent went embarrassingly astray. Reluctant to reopen the wound, we tend to approach accents with caution. We need to assure ourselves that we can, indeed, play accents in every register and intensity. We gain this assurance by hearing ourselves play accents successfully many, many times. Here again is an opportunity to create our own personal accent exercise.

Etude No. 3 is full of variety. From the beginning to E we should play with our own subtle nuances of volume and motion. The dashes over the final notes before breaths imply taking extra time with the last note and the reentry. The metronome marking is misleading because 50 usually foretells little motion. Upon checking with the metronome, we are pleased to discover an agreeable flow to the lines. After setting the general tempo with the metronome we must turn it off immediately because our purpose here is to play freely. At B we can take a little extra time with the ornaments so that they fit into the leisurely flow of the music. At C we can create an interesting line by combining forward motion with crescendo and rising pitches. Between E and J we can resort to practicing with the metronome if we are incapable of maintaining a steady pace without it. Sooner, rather than later, we have to control speed mentally. Yes, we have to think and listen while we play. The foot is even more damaging than the metronome; its addiction is very hard to overcome, but we shall. At each letter L through Q we should work to project a different character. The composer asks us to keep the same tempo so we have volume, note length, and accents with which to work.

In Etude No. 4 the middle section is played very smoothly. We could also practice this *pianissimo*. At O the bottoms and the tops of the line should be at the same volume. The outer sections need not detain us very long.

Etude No. 6 covers a variety of styles, since each section has its own flavor. A pompous *pesante* works well for the beginning to G. At G we shift quickly to a more elegant style by abandoning the heavy tongue for a smooth connected feeling. *Expressif* invites shaping the motion and the volume. At letter G, every ornament must be clear and quick, but not harsh. At letter I, every G must be on time. The composer advises that the scales be played very rapidly. Would he consider a fingered glissando? Letter L begs us to search through our collection of expressive gems. As we have done before, we should copy L through M and prepare at least three editions with lots of detail. This project can be worked on away from the horn, in complete privacy, and with much singing, shouting, and waving of arms. We start by singing each phrase to discover what our instincts and experience tells us to do naturally. After working out each phrase separately we can survey our pencil marks, looking for consistencies to maintain and duplications to avoid.

Decisions must be made and tested against taste, imagination, and reason. It comes as no surprise that there are twenty-four measures between L and M. One expects to find the phrases packaged neatly into four- or eight-measure boxes. Not so. The first sixteen measures have phrases in three- and five-measure lengths; only the last eight measures are in neat two-measure parcels. A surprise comes in the last two measures, where suddenly we have the highest notes in pitch and volume. All of this suggests that the first sixteen measures be played in an amiable manner with many small nuances of dynamics and motion. The first six of our final eight measures must not hint at the outburst coming in the last two measures. With this outline in mind, fantasy and understanding must join to breathe life into the composer's creation. Find those points that need a little extra time to relax. They often coincide with breathing places and phrase endings. Remember that breathing is an indispensable ingredient of life and all of music, whether it is played on a wind instrument or not. Find the rhythmic groups that could be enhanced by motion, forward or reverse; repeated figures come to mind. Not every reentry must be exactly on time. Predictability breeds boredom. In the catalog of musical sins, boring is on the same page as lazy. These musical subtleties must be taped and played back so that our nuances are not lost in understatement. Similarly, we must be on guard against extravagance, although yesterday's extravagance could develop into tomorrow's good judgment. In an etude book overflowing with technical snarls, it is comforting to find serenity and warmth.

Etude No. 7 is long, difficult, and exhausting to practice. We could consider working on only those measures that the composer has marked to be played five or ten times. Each will require calm perseverance. The most difficult of these occur at H and at L; the second and third notes of the descending triplets are the most troublesome. We must recognize that grinding away at these measures on tired lips is bad for accuracy, embouchure, and confidence. After making sure that we can sing the required pitches, we should try practicing these measures at *mezzo piano* and gradually work toward *forte* and *fortissimo*. Doing so fixes the notes in the embouchure, reduces the probability of practicing mistakes, and improves confidence without ravaging the embouchure. In *pianissimo* passages we could start at *mezzo piano* and gradually decrease the volume. This works as long as we are not content to settle for something more than *pianissimo* or less than *fortissimo*. P is also difficult. Maxime-Alphonse asks us to play it ten times but does not provide a dynamic level. We can take advantage of this omission and practice it at *pianissimo* one day and at *fortissimo* the next.

In Etude No. 8 we use the same approach of practicing only the most difficult sections as selected by the composer before starting at the beginning and working through. Here we have two places marked *20 fois*. We may wish to add G and V to the list. From M to T there are eight sections marked for special practice, but they are all quite similar. Many of these difficult measures contain notes just below the bottom of the staff. Now is the time to remind ourselves of firm embouchure corners, good grip on the lower half of the mouthpiece rim, jaw placement consistent with the desired pitch, and slow before fast.

The opening of Etude No. 9 until E is very attractive with its large lines and small surprises. There are several high G-sharps and high As. If we choose the safer fingerings of 2 for the G-sharp and open for the A, we must be certain that those notes are not low in pitch. The normal fingering of 2 + 3, and 1 + 2 lengthen the tubing considerably and, therefore, feel not as secure as 2 and open. We would not dream of playing these notes one octave lower with 2 and open because they are so obviously flat. Trading intonation for security is not a good transaction. Beginning at E the inevitable repetitions begin and the etude becomes an exercise in flexibility.

Etude No. 10 looks more difficult and more interesting than it proves to be. No horn player's career will suffer from not having worked on this etude.

The practice and perfection of difficult etudes during the training years establish work habits that remain productive throughout the professional years. These habits form a link between the intense concentration in the practice room and the physical and mental control in the public arena. Given the enormous number of horn players now being trained, the ever expanding technique required for contemporary works, and the noble desire of intelligent players to raise the standards of accomplishment, the days are past when technical training was complete with Maxime-Alphonse, whose etudes nonetheless remain a magnificent achievement. Fortunately, several French and American horn player-teacher-composers have contributed etude literature for the late twentieth century and beyond.

## Alain Weber and Charles Chaynes

The French etude tradition continues through the studies of Alain Weber and Charles Chaynes. The *Thirteen Studies* by Alain Weber, published in 1959, become more difficult and interesting as the book progresses. The player has to remain constantly alert for unexpected note choices in sequential patterns. We rejoice to see the occasional "odd" meters of 5/8, 7/8, and even 6/8 + 2/8. On recital programs, Etude No. 12 is a good choice as a last piece in a group for unaccompanied horn. These etudes are excellent as preparation for solo works by Bitsch, Bozza, Desportes, Dukas, Echevarria, Françaix, Poulenc, Saint-Saëns, Tomasi, and for other works calling for agility and freedom of expression.

The *Fifteen Studies for Horn* by Charles Chaynes have been expertly edited by Lucien Thévet, who supplied articulations and metronome marks. There are many changes of meter and complex rhythms in conventional meters throughout the book. The second study shifts from 5/8 to 6/8 with accents in unforeseen places. It also has the virtue of requiring the player to maintain the pulse during the rests. It seems almost like a page from the horn part of the Bozza Sonatine for Brass Quintet. Etude No. 8 is quite similar with the addition of a few glissandi. The Chaynes studies are generally more difficult than the Weber studies but have the same insistence on mental quickness, physical agility, and stylistic perception. This is not developed easily by American players trained only to play the orchestral horn parts of German and Austrian composers. Nothing is lost by seeking out study literature that adds agility and freedom to our playing.

## Georges Barboteu

The most advanced, by far, of the twentieth-century French etudes are the *Vingt Études Concertantes* by Georges Barboteu (1924–). He continues a long line of professors at the Paris

Conservatoire who have written study and solo literature for the horn. His etudes progress gradually from tonal, early in the book, to the jazz of No. 19 and the thorny maze of No. 20. For each study he has written a few sentences of advice on style and possible transpositions. These comments have been translated into English, Italian, and German. The collection is published by Editions Choudens in a large, easily-read format. There are a few well-placed breath marks, but most of the breathing coincides with phrase lengths, thus giving the music a natural feeling.

The book begins with a strictly tonal study followed immediately by two glorious lyrical pieces. Since etudes No. 2 and No. 3 contain every dynamic level between *pianissimo* and *forte*, we should establish each level as realistically as possible before each day's work on these etudes. This helps us to avoid the dreaded mezzo nothing in which all dynamic levels are pulled mysteriously to the middle and lose their special identities. In Etude No. 2 only seven of the eighty measures are *forte*, thus giving us the added task of providing dynamic contrasts in only the middle and lower levels. If one ever doubted the wisdom of developing a wide range of volume, this etude proves the necessity of having the largest possible spectrum in which to work. The greater the distance stretches from *pianissimo* to *fortissimo*, the greater the possibility for interesting nuances within and between levels. The nearest we have to a dramatic top to the piece is the one measure marked *forte* in the third line on page 5. We are, therefore, well-advised by the composer to play this etude simply and easily. Phrase endings and reentrances can be leisurely but not unvarying, since there are so many quarter-rest stopping points. Variety is the spice of pacing.

Etude No. 3 is more nimble and just on the brink of sounding fast. In the middle section it is tempting to play the *pianissimo* and the *piano* levels a little more loudly to facilitate the slurs, generally, and the leaps to the top of the staff, specifically. Don't. The outer sections consist of small shapes and large arches. They are of differing lengths. Each note should move dynamically forward or back. Nothing is static here. One majestic slur at *forte* up to the high B-flat is the crowning moment. The slur to the high A six measures later should not compete with the B-flat because we are already in descent toward the final slur up to the *pianissimo* high G. Evidently this etude has special significance for the composer, since he recommends its study before all others. It is rich in detail, thoughtful in design, and strangely melancholy in feeling.

If we reflect back to the Kopprasch and Maxime-Alphonse etudes we recall that most of the emphasis was on playing the notes. With the Barboteu etudes, the emphasis expands to playing the notes as interestingly as we can and as close to the composer's intention as we can discover from studying the notation. Making music is a noble goal but defies definition. We can only hope to describe some of the process. In these etudes all of the detail, the insistence on perfection as we hear it, the subtlety and variety of tongue strokes, air capacity, rhythmic integrity, and enduring strength of embouchure and purpose will be summoned for the sake of the music.

In Etude No. 4 we are back to tonal scales. The Modéré has treacherously soft leaps and terrifying high entrances. It is hoped that previous work has smoothed the path.

In Etude No. 5, entitled *Médiévale*, the Aeolian mode is pursued, abandoned, and recaptured several times. There is an occasional *forte* but most of the etude and most of the high playing is soft.

It may seem paradoxical that the work we do in robust long tones and approaching the high register with expanding volume is what strengthens the embouchure so that it can produce a soft high register. After having achieved a solid full-volume high register, we must begin to use this strength to scale back the air gradually. Granted, this type of strength varies from day to day and reflects how we have treated our embouchure in the recent past. Soft high notes are not comfortable on lips that were punished the day before. Once high-register strength is achieved, high soft playing is a good gauge of its actual strength. Lacking strength, we can always revert to adding air to help the high register, but, of course, this is not possible in an honest *pianissimo*.

In the chapter on practice, a reference was made to the differences in preparation leading to a performance of the Bach Brandenburg Concerto No. 1 and the Mahler Fifth Symphony. For the Bach we must have practiced countless hours of vigorous, high long tones (push-ups if you will) to gather strength. Several days before the performance we must begin to reduce the volume while maintaining the necessary strength through work and rest. For the Mahler we must also have practiced countless hours of vigorous, high long tones to gather strength. Several days before the performance we must continue the vigorous high playing but never so much as to exhaust the embouchure. Hard work and good rest maintains strength for either type of playing. The Mahler is strenuous but not unreasonably high. The Bach has high moments but is not unreasonably strenuous.

Etude No. 5 is completely edited. The composer has used the dash symbol as (1) a reminder of length, (2) stress, and (3) an admonition against accent. All three of these usages could be applied to the first note in measure six. The dash under the slur in measure ten is used for stress, and in the same measure it is used on the tongued G to rule out accent. Each other dash should be studied to determine its appropriate interpretation.

Traditional notation provides fairly accurate information on pitch (where is the note in the staff?), and duration (what is the metric value of the note?). Less strict is the information that we get from symbols pertaining to how we play the pitches and durations. The interpretation of these "how" symbols determines to a large extent the way we interpret a piece of music. Just the word *dash* can have at least these general meanings: to break; to frustrate; to finish rapidly; a small quantity; a stroke of a pen; a line longer than a hyphen; a short note; a member of the Morse Code alphabet; a musical symbol. Those who translate and interpret language must know the word, the idiom, the style within the idiom, and the context to be able to choose the appropriate meaning of *dash*. Exactly the same can be said of the performing musician confronting the dash or any other interpretative symbol. With sufficient knowledge, experience, skill, judgment, and taste, interpretation becomes a matter of opinion rather than a slavish adherence to definition.

Etude No. 6 is a surprisingly fast waltz with difficult downward slurs, soft high playing, speedy single tonguing, quick accents, and copiously edited details of articulation, dynamics, and nuances. In music so fast and so laden with traps, dividing the etude into workable segments according to patterns would be wise. The first four measures form a familiar pattern of two slurred and two tongued notes. We recall from Kopprasch that the crucial notes are the second of the slurred notes. These four measures could be practiced until they can be played reliably, and then taped and played back to confirm that all notes sound as clearly projected as they feel. The next pattern begins in measure 5 and consists of downward slurs, mainly perfect fourths. From Maxime-Alphonse Book 5, Etude No. 8, we remember the fingering hazards of perfect fourths. This pattern is scattered throughout the etude. The same procedure of work, tape, and playback should be followed. The displaced accents beginning in m. 25 are next, followed by the lavish arch that spans mm. 25 to 43. The quick tonguing in mm. 94–96 deserves our special attention and we will probably, but regretfully, have to resort to triple tonguing because of the speed. After these larger and recurring patterns are divided and conquered, we can search for other pitfalls such as the glissando, the quick afterbeats, and the ornaments. We can then begin to join a few lines together to see which patterns remain solid in continuity. You will discover that at this speed nearly every breath must be taken very quickly. Locate places where the breathing works well in isolation but less well in context. One of these places is the long arch beginning in m. 30 because there is no opportunity to take a satisfactory breath before starting the ascent. Take the best breath that you can at the eighth-rest in m. 30, and the best of luck. There is no musical preparation for the abrupt ending so we must follow the composer's directions to play the penultimate measure slowly (the second quarter-note must be noticeably late) and the last note exuberantly long. Etude No. 6 is a brilliant piece for recitals, but only for the strong and the brave.

Etude No. 7 is a study in the variety of phrase shapes. Most of the phrases are two measures in length and have convenient breathing places in plain sight. Most of the phrases move upward, at least at their beginning. The rising line suggests forward movement and some increase in volume. These two expressive devices—motion and volume—give life and warmth to the succession of pitches. Some phrases rise and then fall, but not necessarily to their starting point. In these phrases we could follow the line upward with motion and volume, but recede only slightly as the line recedes. The first two measure in Etude No. 7 illustrate this shape. The second phrase, beginning in m. 3, rises and returns to very near its starting point. Here we can enrich the arch shape by joining motion and volume to the rise and fall of pitches. The third phrase, beginning at the fifth measure, continues to rise with very little fall and ends almost two octaves higher than it began. The forward thrust is clear. There are other phrases that begin high, proceed downward, and then come back up either to a half-way point or continue on toward their starting note. This inverted-arch shape is interesting because of the possibility that the motion and volume could be contrary to the direction of the pitches. Beginning in the fifth measure of the Più mosso section, the composer outlines an arch three times in a rising sequence, leading to a *forte*, accented figure. There again the forward energy is obvious. The player will want to go through the rest of the etude looking for the shapes of phrases and thinking about how to use motion and volume to give further meaning to shape. This etude contains a rich variety of phrase contours that deserve our attention and understanding.

Practice on this etude begins not with playing the notes but with looking at the notes in the hope of discovering connections among phrase shape, motion, and volume. Practice continues with the singing of each phrase, complete with motion and inflections. Listen carefully to how you sing; you might even tape it. When you arrive at something that pleases you and you understand what you did and why it is pleasing, only then try to achieve the same result on the horn. By this process our instincts, experience, imagination, and judgment allow us to sing without the hindrance of metal and machinery. *We* make the musical decisions, not the horn.

Not every line that rises should move forward or gain volume, although those are very natural things to do. Not every arch requires that motion and volume follow the pitches up and down, although that also is natural. A phrase can be completely stationary; its attractiveness lies in its infrequency.

The third section, marked poco più mosso, presents an interesting challenge with its quick and ever changing note values and volume levels. Freedom of the lines has been provided by the composer with the variety of rhythmic figures and the avoidance of stress on main beats. Here is an unusual example of playing note values very strictly to achieve freedom. Have we, at long last, discovered a musical use for the metronome? The music sounds just as fast as it looks. There can be no notes or figures ghosted or skimmed.

In the first and last lines we are asked to use no vibrato. For American horn players this is curious because we assume the opposite: vibrato is not used unless we are directed to do so. Due to the pervading German tradition in most American orchestras, vibrato is verboten for horn players even in the French repertoire. In chamber music and solo playing, vibrato is one more expressive device to be used with judgment and taste. If vibrato is the first impression and the only attribute remembered about our playing, we have reason to suspect excess.

Etude No. 8 is written in changing meters and, as the composer indicates, exercises the eye. It also exercises our ability to keep a steady mental background of subdivision. Counting through the rests is often more difficult than playing through the notes because we are so accustomed to relying on a regular pulse to guide our entrance after a rest. In this etude the rests are not resting places for the mind but are silences through which we must count. The section marked scherzo is full of surprises that test our retention of information gained in previous practice sessions. There seems to be at least one fleeting reference to the Ravel Piano Concerto in G minor. We should use this etude exactly as the composer suggests. Horn players are all too infrequently required to think as they play and come to believe that it cannot be done.

Etude No. 9. After the first eight etudes, No. 9 begins to look like the more typical Barboteu with its wild looping figures, its downward slurs, and its sudden flights to the high register. A quick check with the metronome reveals that it is not as fast as it looks. This etude also includes every volume level from *fortissimo* to *pianissimo* and each must have its own distinctive character. Setting each level before practicing this and similar etudes is always a good plan. There are no great technical entanglements here, but it is quite taxing for the embouchure because of the tessitura and volume.

Etude No. 10 qualifies as a grand etude. It is boisterous, full of accents, echoes, and variety, and has a wonderful *fortissimo* top just before the main material returns. It is not an etude that is practiced by playing through. Tongue strokes ranging from the most gentle *pianissimo* to *fortissimo* accents must be observed, produced, and checked on the tape playback. Horn players tend to lose interest in accents when asked to play a lot of them, with the result that the accents can become bland. Loud accents can be harsh, irritating, noisy, and with a dramatic amount of brass in the attack. This characteristic brassy sound (the horn can produce it the best of all brass instruments) is a legitimate part of horn playing, and like every other expressive device it must be practiced for control and applied with discretion. In our zeal to cultivate a tone quality described as rich, dark, and mellow, we become reluctant to approach the other side of the color chart described as thin, bright, and shrill. It might be helpful to think of loud accents as the ignition of a Roman candle with its huge burst of luminous energy followed immediately by a glowing radiance. In this etude there are accents at every volume level except *pianissimo*. Each should be practiced separately as well as in context. The last note should not lose its stopped "sizzle" until well into the fermata. This note could be the most interesting in the piece.

With Etude No. 11 we begin the latter half of the book, with its increasing demands on lips, tongue, ears, eyes, and fingers. It also abounds in *bouché, cuivré, déchirant*, flutter tongue, glissandi, trills, meter changes, no vibrato, poco vibrato, and jazz.

*Bouché* is stopped. *Cuivré* is brassy. *Bouché cuivré* is stopped and brassy. With stopped playing as with open playing, there are always questions of pitch and tone quality. These questions are more difficult for players whose hands are small. For the small of hand we can find a way to seal off enough of the bell to produce a typical stopped sound while not going into the bell so far as to cause severe pitch problems. We will never seal off the bell completely with our hand. If we could, there would be no sound. We should try to find a hand position that stops the air sufficiently for our purpose. Leakage of air occurs when the backs of the fingers are not held against the inside of the bell. This part of the seal is accomplished by relaxing the fingers just enough to allow them to conform to the contour of the bell. Take a moment to inspect the area inside the bell that our fingers will touch. Notice how confined this area is. Try inserting the hand into the bell while looking at the bell. The fingers should be straight, not curled, and their backs should touch the metal only up to the second joint. Draw the hand out of the bell while still in this position. From the first finger to the little finger should be a shape that corresponds to the curve of the inside of the bell. With the hand still in this position move the thumb down toward the nail of the first finger. Notice that the fingers flatten and a triangular space for air leakage is created between the thumb and first finger. When stopping the horn, the thumb must be held against the first finger but not back far enough to raise its knuckle, thereby causing another air leak. For the same reason the thumb must not fall below the first finger. The heel of the hand completes the seal. It is fleshy enough to conform to the bell's shape but must be held firmly enough against the metal to seal effectively. This hand position can be described as an attempt to feel as much of the metal as possible. Ideally, we should go from our open hand position straight across the bell with the heel of the hand to the stopped position. With an average to large hand, and if the seal is not leaking excessively, this hand shape will produce a good pitch and a typical stopped quality in all volume levels. Players with smaller hands can take comfort in knowing that, with practice, the middle and lower stopped notes can be bent down with the embouchure. This bending seems to improve the tone quality and the pitch in loud playing, but does not improve the quality in soft playing.

Conventional fingerings of one half-step lower on the F horn work well until we reach the bottom and the top of the staff. The lower notes on the F horn become foggy, unstable, and sharp. The higher notes become difficult to locate, especially in soft playing, and the pitch becomes uncertain. We should all invest enough time with the tuner to find alternate fingerings for the extreme register notes. The B-flat horn does provide some extra fingering possibilities. After locating fingerings that work well for any troublesome notes, we should make our own personal fingering chart for stopped notes. These fingerings might be quite different from your teacher's or colleague's fingerings because every embouchure, every hand, every model of bell is different. By going through the process of searching for alternate fingerings and writing out our own chart, we come to know our instrument better. We know that by trying to close the bell we distort the natural workings of the horn. Acousticians, through their own charts, can tell you how.

For many years there has existed a stopping mute. Horn players are curiously reluctant to make full use of this simple, reliable, relatively inexpensive tool. With this mute the pitch is stable if the instrument is tuned properly; it extends the stopped range downward considerably; in soft playing it retains the typically sibilant sound and does not become dull; in loud playing it has a rattled edge; and it will do a decent "wah-wah" when, with our right hand, we open and close its open end. The notes feel more secure in the embouchure because the leakage is confined to a concentrated, not a diffuse, area. Horn players usually buy a stopping mute rather late in their training and perhaps because of this, look upon it as a frill. Not so. To remove any averse feelings we might devote five minutes a day to this mute until we are comfortable with it and enjoy its unique advantages. We can use our regular stopped fingerings. It is sometimes called a transposing mute for the same reason that our straight mute is called non-transposing. Horn players often smile contentedly at the array of mutes displayed by brass quintet trumpet players. We have human flesh, a straight mute, and a stopping mute. Who could ask for anything more?

In Etude No. 11 the Barboteu style is evident throughout. Wide-ranging lines, sudden shifts of pace, and a three-octave downward slope illustrate the composer's spirit of adventure. By his inclusion of a good deal of fourths, fifths, and octaves (all traditional signaling intervals) he reminds us that, in spite of the chromaticisms, this is indeed horn music. Look carefully at the Meno mosso section on page 23. Each stopped G has a sforzando and a diminuendo. Each G is in a higher dynamic level than its predecessor. Each G leads to the stopped A-flat, which has its sforzando in *forte* but no diminuendo. The measures preceding each stopped note become increasingly agitated as the sequences advance. Here is a perfect example of motion and volume working together to produce drama. If we understand the phrase construction we are ready to move beyond merely reciting the notes. This is a beautifully conceived pattern of events deserving of our best technical and intellectual efforts.

At first glance it seems strange that, with all of its virtuosity, this etude is described by the composer as a lyrical study. If we recall the word *coloratura*, meaning colored or decorated by runs, trills, and cadenzas, we have a better understanding of this music. Coloratura horn playing has a nice resonance, but how can we transform all of these notes into a lyrical study? Part of the answer rests with our having a technique so complete that we no longer struggle with notes, but can channel our technical energy into musical expression. By glancing through the etude we could make a list of technical items the composer has included. Extreme registers, fast single tonguing, varied tongue strokes, lip trills, and stopped notes can be practiced apart from this etude and most are part of the warm-up. We must all be able and willing, through honest appraisal, to face our shortcomings. Technical weakness is like tooth decay. It does not go away and will plague us until it is remedied. No one etude or etude book will shoot the magic arrow. Our disciplined approach to calisthenic and technical practice will tell us where we stand.

After working out each technical problem we can look at the musical architecture. It is clearly divided into five sections with a da capo coda. We could begin by finding a word or two to describe each section. The first section seems bold, and when it returns it could be very bold. Aggressive tongue strokes and a forward motion on the scale lines are appropriate for the style. We should make the most of the one gentle measure marked *piano subito* but return quickly to the dash and energy of the scale lines. The second section is unsettled, with its constant changes of pace, and the meno mosso indicates a more tentative attitude. There are several shifts from triple to duple or quadruple and we can emphasize these by keeping the speed of the note values as far apart as the tempo and arithmetic will allow. The music is always changing and is never relaxed. All note values must be exact because this is the way the composer has chosen to signify a fidgety feeling. The third section, marked più mosso, could be titled "Calls and Echoes," reminding us of some of the horn's outdoor history. The calls are played with an assertive, trumpet-like style. The echoes come back changed in color, volume, and speed. In nature they return lower in pitch. The calls are strictly in tempo; the echoes are leisurely in their arrival, statement, and departure. The fourth section is drama. As discussed above, it features the repeated Es and the plunge to the very low note. Allow all of the entrances and exits a little extra time at the beginning but move ahead with them as the music presses on to the *fortissimo espress*. Take a lot of time before starting the next section. Silence can also be dramatic. In recitals, do not move before starting the fifth section, which has a frivolous character and should seem never to stop in spite of the rests. It leads very smoothly back to the beginning, which is even more confident and outspoken than the first time it is played. If we were to include this etude on a recital, it could be listed on the program thus:

---

Etude No. 11, from *Vingt Études Concertantes*
by George Barboteu (1924–)
Bold
Unsettled
Calls and Echoes
Drama
Frivolity
Very Bold

---

These observations must not be construed as a prescription for performance, but are offered as a method for arriving at strong and intelligent musical convictions. We work from the general to the specific: find what the music is, and then find ways to play it. This is the correct order of events, since technique, or the lack of it, should not make musical decisions for us. Most composers are happy to hear a performer say, "I feel it this way." They are overjoyed if the tempo is correct.

At times we are faced with having to practice and perform music that we dislike. This etude, frankly, is not likable until we have some understanding of it. Too often players will make a quick judgment based on a lack of information, lack of familiarity with the idiom, or lack of technique. Music history teems with accounts of critics' missing the point. With our present wisdom and sophistication it seems impossible that anyone could ever have evaluated the Brahms Violin Concerto as too long, dull, and not suited to the instrument. It would have seemed so to violinists lacking the insight to understand it and the technique to play it. It is not a matter of giving the music a chance but rather our acquiring enough knowledge and experience to make informed decisions and having enough technique and musicianship to act upon them.

Etude No. 12 is completely different from No. 11, but the composer's distinctive style is evident throughout. *Rollicking* is the obvious word here. To rollick is to play in an easy, boisterous, jovial manner. Easy? Nearly every measure has potential pitfalls of unruly rhythms, sudden changes of volume, and unexpected note choices, all at a very fast tempo. After working out each technical detail of this etude, it must be practiced in longer sections, and then practiced with many playings-through. Events are upon us so rapidly and so constantly. Playing through tests our concentration, our memory, and our short-term endurance. There is always the hazard of accumulating slowness in fast pieces. We can guard against slowness here by not playing more slowly in the triple measures than in the duple measures. The metronome can assist us. Then turn off the metronome. At the tempo indicated this etude lasts one minute and nineteen seconds. In spite of several stops, it is a piece in perpetual motion. Boisterous? It certainly is turbulent, but not always loud. There is some resemblance to the rather carefree nature of most 6/8 movements of classical horn concertos. If a work can be rowdy but civilized, this is it. Jovial? There is not one moment of gloom from beginning to end.

Etude No. 13. When horn players sing in the practice room they often do so to identify pitches. This certainly applies to Etude No. 13 because nearly every measure has at least one interval that falls into the awkward category. In the first three measures we are asked to alternate between perfect fourths and tritones. One assumes that the singing of perfect fourths upward or downward presents no problems for a horn player advanced enough to be working on Barboteu. Tritones remain a mystery to some ears. Musical folklore tells us that tritones are difficult to sing and are, therefore, best avoided, at least in tonal music. As a starting point we can use its proximity to the perfect fourth—one half-step larger—and the perfect fifth—one half-step smaller. Tritones have a notational hazard because they sound the same when written as an augmented fourth or as a diminished fifth. Nevertheless, we must work at this interval until it is as automatic and direct as any other interval. Many players find that the tritone, once learned, is easily lost. Even after it has been learned thoroughly it should be tested regularly, since it can vanish mysteriously overnight.

One might say that it is more important to be able to sing this etude than to play it. Few American horn players have very much experience with solfège, few have perfect pitch, and most are convinced that they cannot sing. All of this begs for early and continued ear training. It is rather late in the game to begin ear training at the age of eighteen. For this etude a good plan is to divide it according to its double bars and work on each measure until every interval can be sung. Keep a list of troublesome intervals and give them special attention apart from the etude. The tritone is surely at the top of the list. After the second double bar the rhythms become more complex. After working out the pitches try to sing the pitches and the rhythms. At times we must make octave adjustments to accommodate the voice's range. When pitches and rhythms are satisfactory, we are ready to begin practicing the etude on the horn. Precision of pitch and integrity of rhythm are more important than vocal tone quality. No horn player's career will be damaged by singing in a choir, by participating in a voice class, or by having private vocal lessons. These are more stones in our wall of skills and experiences.

This etude is a gold mine of dynamic detail. We should try to incorporate these details into our singing whenever possible. Sforzando, accents, trills, *cuivré*, crescendo, diminuendo, *bouché*, and flutter-tongue can all be done with the voice.

The Epilogue calls for a straight mute. Every horn player needs mutes that are in tune, will produce the complete range with no bad notes in the low register, and have a wide volume range. Good mutes seem expensive but with careful handling they should last many years. Twisting and grinding the mute into the bell is not necessary. With a little practice we can get a feel for the depth of insertion that provides a sufficiently snug fit. Most horn players are comfortable holding the mute while it is in the bell. Others feel that the mute is dampened in loud playing if it is held. A good mute has a tuning device on the inside.

Late twentieth-century composers make extensive use of the mute in orchestral and chamber music, but only occasionally in solo works with orchestra. Practicing with mutes regularly, especially in the extreme registers and dynamics, is beneficial. Playing with a good mute in the bell should not feel very different from open playing at *mezzo forte* in the middle register.

Horn players often have a box full of mouthpieces and a drawer full of mutes. Some horn players have experimented with the corks on their extra mutes in search of a very loud mute, or a very soft mute. Generally, the higher the corks, the louder the sound. Corks do compress with years of use. Every good mute deserves the replacing of its corks when the time comes.

We should not hurry through Etude No. 13. At this stage of development we can profit from working on more than one etude at a time, since the dividends of impeccable pitch and honest rhythm will help everything we play.

The first half of Etude No. 14 is a study in tongue strokes, wide slurs, changes of meter and dynamic nuances. Notice that in the first half nearly every note has some indication of length or style of articulation. This is not unusual in late twentieth-century music. Most of the etude is gentle in dynamics and relaxed in nature despite its sinister metronome marking. There is another Barboteu grand descent from the high C down to the low register. This is inverted three measures from the end. Neat, sleek, and elegant are the words for this etude.

At the beginning of Etude No. 15 there is a note from the composer that the Prelude should be played very freely. We could take the next step and remove the bar lines, giving us even more freedom to follow our musical instincts. It is a prelude composed of short fragments, most of which end on a long note value. We must keep the dynamic shape of these final notes interesting, and we can vary the timing of the reentries. Three- and four-note groupings within phrases can be moved forward or held back as the phrase demands, and the phrases themselves must not be stagnant in volume and motion. This again is a well-edited etude, and in addition to responding to the composer's markings we should create nuances of our own. The second half of the etude is a Scherzo, which looks faster than it sounds because it is in 3/8 and not 3/4. Except for the coda, the Scherzo is light in volume and spirit.

Etude No. 16 continues the pattern of training eyes and ears with constantly changing rhythms and unexpected intervals. There are sudden leaps to high notes, arpeggios covering a wide range, and another long and twisting dive into the low register. This is a good etude for the continuation of memory training as begun in the Kopprasch etudes. We should use the same techniques of hearing before playing, after dividing the etude into manageable segments. The phrase lengths rarely exceed four measures, and this could be convenient for separating and rejoining.

Memorizing this etude will not be possible without using all of the energies of eyes and ears, concentration and perseverance. The more elusive of these are concentration and perseverance. Barboteu is not Kopprasch, with whom we can coast along on predictable sequences and repetitions. This is not Maxime-Alphonse, some of whose challenges are eased by familiar tonal language. In Barboteu we must know, hear, feel, remember, predict, and be able to play every unexpected detail. Pianists describe the technical difficulties of contemporary music as being more acute because the fingers have never been there before. The same pianist might say, when asked to transpose the accompaniment of a Schubert song, "If I can hear it I can play it." Horn players should be able to say, "I can play it from memory if I can hear it." Perseverance does not come easily to horn players because so much of the music we play is easy, both physically and mentally. The instrument is not easy but most orchestral horn parts contain only a few demanding moments. Beginning method books, because they are aimed at the very young, go to extraordinary means to make all things easy. Training materials, generally, do not challenge the mind, the ear, or musicianship until we arrive at

Maxime-Alphonse Book 4. Orchestral parts, once learned, change only slightly from one performance to the next, and from one conductor to the next. It is tempting for some horn players to stay in a steady state of accomplishment and not venture into the future. Perseverance is not fun, since its rewards are always in the future. Perseverance is built one accomplishment at a time. By acknowledging each accomplishment as being partly the result of perseverance we gain confidence to rise to the next level. Concentration, as a technique, and perseverance as driving energy can be applied to any task.

Etude No. 17 presents the same hurdles of seeing, hearing, and attention to detail as the previous etude. The practice procedure is the same: hear everything before playing anything. There is an abundance of tritones in this etude, but the good work done in Etude No. 13 should be of help. It is comforting to see an etude with rising and falling lines in almost equal proportion. At any volume level we must guard against the automatic and often unrecognized loss of volume on descending lines.

Etude No. 18 is the most thorny and elaborate encountered thus far. Nearly every measure makes extraordinary demands on our skills of physical technique, our ears, and our ability to transform notation into music. There is so much editing detail on the first page that after hearing all of the pitches we should sing through this page with both the pitches and the nuances. Jazz musicians invent the most delightful vocalizations of articulations, rhythmic figures, and dynamic nuances and seem able to make a valid connection between these vocalizations and their performances on their instruments. This etude, while not jazz, offers another way to make details of nuance and articulation a vital part of the music rather than something added to the surface. The trumpet playing of Louis Armstrong and Dizzy Gillespie sounded very much like their singing. Should we not profit from the example of these two masters?

Etude No. 19 is a jazz piece and a good one for recital programs. No one would pretend that the study of this one etude will do very much toward understanding the style. It is complex and subtle and must be absorbed and practiced over a long period. Jazz musicians work and play in their own stylistic world, and it is up to us to go to the best of them for counsel and criticism. Most any fine jazz musician would be happy to sing through this etude for us with vocalizations appropriate for each musical gesture. For jazz musicians, traditional rhythmic figures are not a matter of arithmetic, but of "feel," as manifested by vocalization, not conversation. One cannot write the rhythms, articulations, and nuances, but we can begin by listening and imitating. This is how the jazz feeling is perpetuated. The truly great jazz musicians absorb the tradition through listening, imitating, and then adding something uniquely their own. No one could ever confuse the trumpet playing of Louis Armstrong with that of Dizzy Gillespie because their styles, well-grounded in tradition, are so personal. In every community and every school of music there are jazz musicians. All too often classically trained musicians fence themselves off from the riches of the jazz heritage, which endures in the face of the latest commercial degradation.

The miracle of jazz lies in its capacity to feel very loose while confined to a strict beat. Therefore, we should play this etude with a drummer, as the composer suggests, and practice it with a metronome. This does not stifle expressive freedom as it does in other styles, but gives us a framework around which our melodic lines can move according to style and idiom.

Etude No. 20 brings this remarkable collection to a fitting close. It is written in short fragments, every one of which contains a technical, rhythmic, or musical point. This etude must seem shocking to the eyes of horn players not wishing to be disturbed by the possibility of expanding their technique. As menacing as it appears, there is nothing on these pages that is incomprehensible, unplayable, or not found in chamber music or solo works written for the horn in the latter part of the twentieth century. The etudes of Maxime-Alphonse, Alain Weber, Charles Chaynes, and Georges Barboteu continue the wonderful French tradition of technical and musical etudes. We are all indebted to them for their efforts and skills, and we are richer for their extraordinary accomplishments.

Most of America's finest horn players are also teachers. A few of them have written etude books or have in other ways made valuable contributions to the teaching literature. These efforts include editing solo works and chamber music, writing articles and books on horn playing, composing and arranging, compiling orchestral excerpts, and writing method books for beginners. These activities are often the result of a teacher's dissatisfaction with a specific area of the teaching literature or an honest desire to research a topic or person. Although method books lie outside the reach of this book, they are an important part of the early development of horn players when used by a wise teacher and a keen student. Method books usually have photographs of the playing position, embouchure, and right-hand position, as well as fingering charts and advice on breathing, tonguing, and slurring. They also contain simple exercises and melodies. Teachers who specialize in the noble and difficult art of beginning instruction often compile their own methods, and some of these make their way into print. There is also some material available for class instruction of beginners. Photographs and fingering charts are helpful; fine players who can teach beginners are invaluable.

We are fortunate, indeed, to have in our universities and conservatories so many fine players who teach the instrument and perhaps other courses, play in resident chamber music groups and the local symphony orchestra, coach chamber music, conduct the school's horn choir, play solo recitals, make recordings, commission new works, and pursue their own scholarly and creative projects. The steady improvement in performance standards and pedagogical materials is due mainly to these player-teacher-scholars.

## Douglas Hill

Among the most distinguished is Douglas Hill of the University of Wisconsin at Madison. His book, *Extended Techniques for the Horn*, through its text and cassette, discusses and illustrates techniques, other than the familiar, that composers have been using for at least thirty years. Included are air sounds, quarter-tones, vocalizations, mouthpiece sounds, various tongue effects, half valve, and much for horn players interested in preparing for the present and the future. This book is orderly and thorough, and although it is not an etude book, it covers a neglected part of horn technique. The examples are played by Douglas Hill on the cassette that accompanies the text. His playing on the cassette and on a solo album entitled *A Solo Voice* confirm that he is a musician of extraordinary skill, intelligence, and sensitivity.

## James Decker

James Decker has long been one of the predominant horn players in the Los Angeles recording studios. Through his work with students at the University of Southern California, where he is Professor of Horn, he has produced a book, an audio cassette, and a video, entitled *Horn*. He presents basic drills with exercises for long tones, tonguing, rhythmic precision, scales, arpeggios, natural horn, flexibility, legato, stopped and echo horn, endurance, lip trill, and orchestral excerpts. The audio cassette is narrated by Mr. Decker and his commentary is direct and practical. The video features the playing of young professionals, who demonstrate the examples in the book. The drills and examples are printed in the text and the student is invited to listen and to play along with the video. The last part of the book is meant to be used in a class setting. The intonation and group rhythmic studies are especially helpful for training an orchestral horn section.

Douglas Hill and James Decker have produced training materials strengthened by sound. Their efforts are the result of long experience and diligent research. The real work of the horn world is being done by players who can teach and write, and through zeal and intelligence are able to pass along their wisdom to those who want to learn.

## Gunther Schuller

In his *Studies for Unaccompanied Horn*, Gunther Schuller, whose musical activities are so varied and vast as to defy hyphenation, has combined the pattern repetitions of Kopprasch with his own imagination and skill in etudes that are meant to prepare the player for the latter part of the twentieth century and beyond. They are especially good for interval study. To be able to sing Nos. 1, 4, 9, and 11 should be the goal of every horn player. Others of these etudes concentrate on slurring over a wide range, meter changes, wide leaps, stopped playing, flutter tonguing, and trills. Study No. 12 will begin to prepare the player for the horn part that Gunther Schuller wrote in his Music for Brass Quintet.

No discussion of educational materials for horn should be without an expression of respect and gratitude for the work of Philip Farkas. His book *The Art of French Horn Playing*, published in 1956, will remain a monument to his devotion to the instrument, his ability to write with unaffected precision, and his complete knowledge of his craft. His other two books, *The Art of Brass Playing* (1962) and *The Art of Musicianship* (1976), are further evidence that he was, indeed, the model player-teacher who played beautifully, taught with dedication, and wrote superbly.

## *48 Etudes*, by Verne Reynolds

These etudes were written during 1954–1959 while I was on the faculty of the Indiana University School of Music. At that time there was nothing beyond Book 6 of Maxime-Alphonse for the technical and musical training of gifted horn players. Instead of leading the advance of technique and musicianship, the writers of etudes and method books seemed content to reseed the ground harvested by Kopprasch, Mueller, Gallay, and Kling. Several of my students at Indiana practiced the 48 Etudes as they were being written and helped confirm that they were playable after a lot of practice and were rewarding. Many students, then as now, feel that the metronome indications are too fast. For the tongued etudes the speeds as printed lie well within our bench mark of four single-tongued notes at 138–144. The difficulty and the subsequent benefit is not speed of tongue, but in tonguing leaps more wide than the interval of a third. This is true, also, of slurring. Most horn players can slur a chromatic or diatonic scale faster than they can tongue it. When we leave the old familiar patterns, the difficulties arise.

Therefore, the first twenty-four etudes are interval studies. Beginning with the half-step each interval up to the octave is studied in order. Each has its own tongued and its own slurred etude. The etudes are almost equally divided between slow and fast; three have sections of various speeds. We have seen in earlier studies that there was little attempt to balance the technical with the lyrical. Within reason, any of these etudes can be transposed. It does not make sense to transpose a bass clef etude into horn in A but it might be amusing. Some of them can be practiced by treating horn in F as a transposition (which it is for most of the non-horn playing world) and mastering several other transpositions before practicing them in F. Etude No. 1 is excellent for this.

These etudes do not allow the player to coast along on instinct or experience. They seek to exercise and develop the ability to transform notation into sound quickly and accurately. How do pianists, flutists, and clarinetists manage to play so many notes so rapidly? The machinery certainly helps if it is operated properly. How is it that a violinist, lacking such machinery, is able to play so rapidly? Pre-Suzuki violinists and pianists were trained on a regimen of etudes that prepared them for the concertos of Beethoven, Paganini, Brahms, Rachmaninov, and Prokofiev and not for the orchestral parts of the accompaniments. Until recently, horn players were trained to win an orchestral audition and live happily every after. These etudes were designed to meet the needs of the complete horn player who can reap the personal joy of solo playing, the musical wealth of chamber music, and for whom Richard Strauss is a lot more than tone poems.

Etude No. 1 is a rather conservative study of tongued half-steps within a narrow range, with only an occasional large leap. It is no accident that it starts on middle C. This etude does not tax the speed of the single tongue. Surely, after playing Maxime-Alphonse and Barboteu we expect the tongue to operate at 120. The fingers are constantly in motion. There are hints of patterns but they are dissolved quickly. I am pleased that the publisher chose to spread this etude over two pages. This places most of the notes about one quarter-inch apart. For comparison, turn to the last etude and notice the spacing of the note heads. In Etude No. 1 the wide spacing of notes requires the eyes to move quite rapidly. With the music stand at its normal position look at the first note of the first etude and see how many more notes your eyes can identify without leaving the first note. Do the same with the first note in the last line of Etude No. 48. It seems obvious that the wider spacing should require our eyes to move more rapidly from note to note or from group to group. The notes themselves are spaced more widely but the information between the note heads slows down the eye speed. If the first two groups of Etude No. 1 were written as an ascending C major scale, the eyes would transmit that information very rapidly and be ready for the next groups. Here, with vital information on nearly every note, our eyes must stay long enough on each note to decode and signal information. This is one of the reasons that we read and practice slowly so that our eyes can do their work. The eyes do not need to see a C major scale very many times before the appropriate signal is sent or before memory takes over. As we have seen in the Kopprasch etudes, memory depends more on hearing, repetition, and concentration and less on seeing as the memory strengthens. It is hoped that Etude No. 1 will be practiced for reasons beyond speed of tongue.

Etude No. 2 continues with the half-step and introduces the element of fitting two slurred notes into a three-note metric grouping. Notice that we complete six measures before there is an articulation on the first beat. The second phrase does the opposite by placing the articulations on every first beat but divides the measures into three groups of two notes rather than two groups of three notes. This pattern must continue to sound 6/8 and not 3/4. There is always a tendency to drop the volume and shorten the second note of a two-note slur. This does help the clarity of articulation on the note after the slurred note but can also create a duple feeling in conflict with the triple nature of 6/8. This is often exactly what the composer had in mind and is especially effective when the duple grouping works contrarily to an established triple pulse. In Etude No. 2 we decide which phrases should emphasize the duple feeling, and give the first of the slurred notes a little extra tongue and allow the second note to decrease slightly in volume. When we wish to maintain a feeling of 6/8 in spite of the two-note groupings, the second notes of the slurs must not be weakened in volume or be shortened. In both events the second note must never be hurried. Since the notes and the speed of this etude are not difficult, we can concentrate on these rhythmic nuances.

Etude No. 3 might be appropriate for a recital program. The interval has now become a whole step. Except for a few soft moments it is a robust piece and is played with short, solid tongue strokes. Too often it is played faster than marked and thus becomes more difficult because there is less time for breathing. Notice that the stopped notes remain at a *forte* volume. They are not echoes but are changes of color. We have to tongue vigorously to match the volume of the open notes. In the last line, space slightly before the accents. The last three measures, including the release of the final note, must be exactly in tempo.

Etude No. 4 is an exercise for fingers, eyes, and memory. We all should check our fingers occasionally to see whether they are slightly arched, and not more than one quarter-inch past the end of the key. Since our fingers are likely to be on their best behavior while we are checking on them, we might take a moment to form our hand into playing position away from the instrument. Start with the first three fingers straight out and then bend down their tips to form an arch while maintaining a natural separation between the fingers. Now move the thumb and little finger to simulate grasping the B-flat key and the little finger hook. Stop just short of the point where the thumb and the little finger begin to feel stretched. With the horn in playing position check to see whether your hand position is approximately the same on the horn as off the horn. Horns and hands come in all sizes and many configurations, but horn makers try to make this part of their instruments fit the hands of most of their buyers. Players with small hands and short fingers often add dimes or pennies to the finger keys to lengthen them for a more comfortable fit. Players with large hands often have the little finger hook moved. Tension and discomfort in the left wrist and arm is not uncommon among horn players. Flat fingers, a long stretch between the thumb and little fingers, and high shoulders are often the cause.

The first finger frequently rises from the finger key when either or both of the other fingers move. This tendency can become so habitual that we are not aware of the first finger's misfeasance. The second finger acts on its own or combines with either the first or third fingers, but rarely both. It is the finger that is most likely to creep down on the finger key and become flattened. It does not rise off its key as often as the first finger, but seems willing to do so. The third finger is the least used and the most sluggish. If the placement of the little finger hook causes a stretch, the third finger will be pulled in that direction and will not line up with its key. Ideally, each finger will appear to be a straight extension of its key. In a figure that repeats the combinations of 1 + 2 and 2 + 3 the first finger wants to rise off its key as the third finger moves. We may allow ourselves one exemption to the rule of always maintaining flesh on the keys. During a trill for which the best fingering is 2 + 3 to 3, the trill is faster and more even when the first finger is up off its key. This seems to free the second finger.

This etude has also been printed with extra space between the notes. At the speed indicated the eyes cannot convey every bit of information quickly enough for us to react, so we begin to rely on the memory that has been accumulating during slow practice. We remember patterns and lines so that a quick glance serves as a reminder but does not dwell on every single note. Our slow practice will be of greater benefit when we realize that its purpose is to create stored information. These memories are subsequently called forth by our eyes and we react. Establishing memories takes time and concentration but is the principal reward of slow practice. Physical memories are also accumulated. They allow the fingers and embouchure to act in an established order. Diligently practiced mistakes are often difficult to correct because we have practiced them so conscientiously. Slow practice prunes out mistakes; fast practice solidifies what is correct. The last four lines of Etude No. 4 should be memorized and played in front of a mirror to see what the fingers are doing.

Etude No. 4 seeks to establish 5 as a natural feeling. We play 2/4, 3/8, 3/4, 4/4, 6/8, and 9/8 every day. 5/8 remains exotic because we continue to be obsessed with whether the measure is 2 + 3 or 3 + 2. This burden has been given to us by music publishers who insist that 5/8 must be divided one way or the other and by conductors who believe that by dividing 5/8 they can conquer it. Let us start by agreeing never to divide 5/8 as a matter of course, comfort, or convenience. Let us agree also that we will divide 5/8 only when the music is served by doing so. Fortunately, 5/4 has not suffered the same fate as 5/8. Does anyone ever think of the second movement of the Tchaikovsky Sixth Symphony as 2 + 3 even though every measure of the movement is printed 2 + 3? 5/8 is nearly always faster than 5/4, but does it follow that five fast notes must be divided some way, but of course, never into 1 + 4 or 4 + 1? In 5/8 composers must always beam five notes together when no musical division is intended or justifiable. Five notes can be just as beautiful as 2 + 3 or 3 + 2.

We should practice Etude No. 5 several different ways. First, we speak the rhythms using any convenient sound; "tu" works well. Accent, slightly, each first eighth-note but no others, and do not force an accent elsewhere in the measure if the first beat is vacant. Do not sing any pitches, since changes of pitch can give a false sense of grouping. We can start speaking the etude with the metronome set at 66 to the measure. After two lines are spoken, turn off the metronome and continue without breaking stride. Increase the speed over several practice sessions until 76 is reached. Only then should we start playing the notes on the horn. When the 5 feeling is solid the notes are easy, since there are no high or low notes and only moderate leaps. 5/8 has remained difficult only because we have persisted in dividing it.

Etude No. 6 continues the study of five beats in the measure. The etude is in four sections, each of which is announced by the recurring half-note phrases. Before playing a note of this etude we want to determine the shape and character of each section. Noticing the general direction of lines will suggest rhythmic and dynamic shapes, but the highest and the loudest notes are not always as important as the lowest and the softest. Singing any of these phrases during this first stage of preparation is just fine. By singing first, our musical instincts are more likely to guide us. By playing first, our instincts and our training prompt us to play only the notes and the rhythm.

I hope that the reader will forgive my youthful indiscretion of not having included a printed request to play this etude quite freely. The note values must remain valid but never metronomically rigid. In this etude the lines are generally upward and the energy is often forward, with a relaxation of both at phrase endings. Natural phrase shape is linked to respiration and vocalization. We sing with increasing energy and rising pitch just after we have filled our lungs with air. We sing with less vigor and volume as we near the end of our air supply. The musician has to decide, after examining the notation, whether or not the traditional phrase shape is appropriate. At times we must combine two or more phrases to create a longer line. We accomplish this by not relaxing the speed or reducing the volume at breathing points. At other times the music demands that every phrase has its own distinctive shape. Both the composer and the performer have to be alert to the good and the evil in repetition and expectation. Repetitions of phrase shape creates the expectation of more repetitions. Only our sensitivities can tell us when enough is enough. There are no rules. Are we not fortunate that Maurice Ravel knew when to end the *Bolero*?

In the first section, beginning at measure 5, there is an obvious urge to point the volume and energy to the high B and slightly beyond. We are probably well advised not to resist this urge. This tells us to take quick breaths without losing volume or speed. Beginning at measure 16 we have a series of short gestures and hints of sequences. We must decide whether the two places marked *forte* are of equal intensity or whether one should predominate. We also have to decide whether the motion takes us to the high A or to the low E. Either could be dramatic, but the choice must be made from musical certainty and not from physical vulnerability. In the third section, which begins with the triplets, there is so much activity that adding a lot of dynamic finery would seem excessive. At times it is all right to play exactly what the composer has written. Contemporary music is often thoroughly and precisely marked with symbols of expression. Older composers seemed more willing to rely on such words as *espressivo*. The last fifteen measures act as a coda. Here we could decide to let the beauty of the low register come through unhindered by very much rhythmic or dynamic nuance. The composer has written note values of increasing length to signal the end of the piece. Please do not go near the metronome or try to divide the 5/4. Neither is necessary and either or both will harm the music.

Etude No. 7 contains no musical profundities to ponder. It is a simple exercise in joining all of the registers. *Sempre forte* is a gentle reminder not to lose volume in the outer registers and to project the F horn enough to match the B-flat. With Etude No. 7 we have reached the major third on our journey to the octave. Beginning with the perfect fourth the interval size combined with speed begins to feel more and more difficult. As usual, downward is more cumbersome than upward and the middle register is easier than anything else. Increasing the size of the interval by half-step increments should allow the technique to grow gradually. These etudes were designed to advance the technique and not to conform to a traditionally conservative estimate of its limits. To say that a piece of music is well-written for the instrument is not always the highest praise.

For Etude No. 8 we can follow our procedure of looking at the structure before the actual practice begins. When we see the word *lento* we expect the music to be slow. A quick glance at the etude reveals that in its outer sections the rate of activity is measured in eighth-notes, while the middle section is almost stationary because of all of the half-notes. At quarter-note equals 60, the eighth-notes move along easily while the half-notes seem to last forever. This is the key to the structure and it invites us to keep the outer sections alive with motion and the middle section very still. From the beginning to the double bar we can follow the printed suggestions for nuances but we must decide what to do with the two phrases that rise to *forte*. Should the phrase with the higher pitches be louder, softer, or the same as the *forte* phrase with the lower pitches? The best way to decide is to play both phrases three or more ways on three or more days and then begin to decide. A firm decision made on day one might have to be reversed after the whole piece has been learned. In the third section, this problem has been solved by the use of *fortissimo*, the magic high C, and the gradual descent to the lowest E-flat. The middle section could be described as inverted echoes, since what is echoed has more presence because it is open. It is always tempting to "move" slowly-moving music. In a more typical ABA form, the contrasting B often makes its point by being faster than the A sections. Here the contrary is true although the metronome speed has not changed. Adding volume to the high stopped notes is also tempting just to be safe. This amounts to a choice between playing the notes or playing the music. Surely in an etude for advanced players we can choose the more difficult in the hope that by so doing we add to our technique and confidence. Musical convictions are not sacrificed to inadequate technique. In the middle section it is fun to sing the first notes after the rests before playing them.

In Etude No. 9 the dotted eighth-note, sixteenth pattern is presented in two speeds. The Adagio is slow enough to allow a mental subdivision of sixteenth-notes and thereby help us to place the fourth sixteenth-note. In the Presto there is no time for subdivision. Notice that the Presto sections alternate between repeated pitches and pitches that move. It is curious how much faster this Presto is now than it was thirty years ago. Achieving the necessary speed still depends on tonguing the sixteenth-note soon enough. The tongue must move immediately after the dotted eighth-note or the speed suffers.

We all feel quite virtuous when we practice slowly and methodically, but in Etude No. 9 we can experiment with reducing the amount of slow practice and adding time to practicing the fast, dotted-eighth tongue stroke on repeated pitches. Years of slow practice will not produce a fast tongue. The phrases without repeated pitches will need more time to become solid.

Etude No. 10 presents no new problems but offers another opportunity to play freely and expressively. For the D above the staff we should begin with the normal fingering of 1 + 2 and then test several other fingerings with the tuner. We are now in a register of the horn where it is important that the fingerings we choose feel right in the embouchure as well as being in tune. We certainly do not want to ask the embouchure to tune such a high note. Every horn, mouthpiece, and embouchure produces different results above the staff. Check every combination of fingers until you find one that feels secure and is in tune. Fortunately, the horn literature is not, at this writing, overabundant with high Ds.

Most horn players will agree that Etude No. 11 is difficult because of the speed and the tritone interval. *Sempre forte* reminds us not to allow an automatic diminuendo on downward slopes and to match the volume of the low register with the rest of the horn. It should be practiced very mechanically by perfecting each phrase before moving ahead. There is no urgent need to play all the way through this etude, or to link up the phrases. It is not necessary to complete this etude before starting another. It is an etude that we could return to many times if we can bring ourselves to do so. This etude and the next should solve the mystery of the tritone once and for all.

In Etude No. 12 the player chooses the speed that seems most suitable for the music. It has no bar lines, no time signature, and no metronome marking. It does have dynamics, slurs, and fermatas. One, two, and three beams have been used to group the notes together. The beams indicate only a general and comparative relationship of speed. The notes in the groups with one beam will be played more slowly than notes in groups having two or three beams, but no exact relationship should be sought, nor should notes having one or two beams be thought of as eighth-notes or sixteenth-notes. There should be no metric pulse, but we can organize the etude into phrases or sentences because the music always moves toward a long final note.

Some musicians hear the tritone as a sad and lonely interval. This might be a starting point for both speed and style. Nearly everything is slurred, thus ruling out an aggressive use of the tongue. There are phrases in which as many as thirty-five notes are beamed together. We can shape these notes in several different ways by using motion and dynamics, either separately or together. The most common shape is one that starts slowly and softly and increases the speed and the volume. Dynamic suggestions are abundant in this etude, but shape and motion, being more subtle and personal, are left to the player's good judgment.

The first two lines begin and end with a tritone notated as half-notes. The tritones at the ends of the lines will be much faster than those at the beginnings of the lines if we move forward in the intervening notes. The motion, not the notation as half-notes, determines speed. Consistency is not always a primary musical concern. In the third line the stopped signal should be noticeably slower and softer than the open statement. The next sequence of thirty-five notes beamed together could start very fast, continue fast to the crescendo, and slow down on the last five notes. Since the first two phrases begin slowly and are accelerated, we should consider doing something quite different on the third phrase. The time between the release of the fermatas and the reentries must be varied. When there is a drastic change of register, volume, or speed, a delayed or unexpectedly quick reentry can be effective. A good example of this is the reentry on the *pianissimo* high A after the *fortissimo* low E-flat. Counting the number of notes in the figures marked *veloce* is not necessary, but playing not fewer than printed would be nice. In the last line, each downward tritone should be conspicuously slower than its predecessor. The last three notes can be very long; breathing before and between these notes is necessary and commendable.

The common beam and no bar line notation is used frequently for free, unaccompanied works. Composers like this technique because they and the player are relieved of metric constraints. The composer can exercise control over pitches, volume, speed, articulation, and nuances, but still give the player freedom to make personal choices. In studying a freely notated work, the player uses the same methods that apply to more traditionally notated music. We have to search for the general character of the music and find how it is put together. Those are often the easy questions. As the questions become more specific we must make choices that enhance and make clear our convictions about the music. If we are convinced that the tritone is a mournful interval, our choices of speed, volume, and articulation should not contradict that conviction unless there is strong evidence that the tritone has suddenly become carefree. Every teacher has been asked, "Is this right?" When the question pertains to expressive matters, we should alter the question to, "Is it right for the music?"

We often have to balance a phrase against one or more phrases of the same type. In Etude No. 12 we have to invent a variety of ways to play the phrases that advance toward a long final note. We look for high points in energy, volume, and pitch. We also must find moments of motionless calm. When in doubt we can try to find five ways to play a phrase, and then begin to discard those that are unsuitable until one or two are left to consider. This is good musical and mental exercise. It requires a thorough examination of the music and allows intelligence and taste to govern our decisions.

Etude No. 13 is similar to Etude No. 7. The interval has grown to become a perfect fifth and the speed is commensurably slower. This etude also emphasizes the need to match the volume of all of the registers.

The middle section of Etude No. 14 seems to be more difficult; the patterns cover a large range or change directions suddenly. The outer sections recall the use of the perfect intervals for signals and fanfares. Perfect fourths, fifths, and octaves are readily available and rather easily produced in the lower and middle registers of natural brass instruments. The perfect interval heritage is manifest in the opening of the Brahms Horn Trio, and throughout the work. Other examples can be found in the Beethoven symphonies, Wagner operas, and more recently in the Britten Serenade for Tenor, Horn and Strings, and in the Persichetti *Parable VIII*. One hopes that with an expanded technique for horn players and more elaborate schemes for composers, this ancient treasure is not buried. The outer sections of Etude No. 14 are very quiet and are meant to evoke a reverence for times past.

The beginning and ending of Etude No. 15 are exercises in restraint. The first several measures are so slow that we must rely on the beauty of the tone and the rising line to create an expectation of what is to follow. In the last ten measures the notes should stay in tempo but each entrance should be somewhat slower that its predecessor. This stratagem creates a feeling of premonition of the end of the music.

It is worthwhile to spend some time with the tuner to perfect the interval of a minor sixth. Its distinctive flavor is lost when the interval in either direction is too wide. The minor sixth is, of course, an interval in its own right, but it is also an inversion of the major third. We have always been told that the major third, which defines the major mode, is bright and happy, and the minor third, defining the minor mode, is dark and sad. A strange thing happens when these thirds are inverted. Inverting the bright major third results in a dark minor sixth; inverting the dark minor third produces a bright major sixth. So goes the theory. To some ears these differences in color persist even when the intervals are out of their tonal context.

In our examination of the music we might try to discover whether the music is sad because of the interval, or whether it is sad music that contains a lot of minor sixths. The high point of the piece is the pitch and volume peak on the A-flat. In approaching this peak we have a rhythmic sequence and a crescendo, both of which could indicate moving forward. Going against the familiar is always interesting and, occasionally, rewarding. Here we could push on with the crescendo, but hold back with the tempo and delay the arrival at the summit.

For this etude it is advisable to tune every minor sixth in each direction between $g^2$ and g by looking at the tuner and by playing with a colleague.

Etude No. 16 is an exercise in long and short tongue strokes in the middle register. There is an occasional high note but much of this etude is set near the bottom of the staff. This register is often neglected by players who have developed strong high notes. Second and fourth orchestral horn players must be able to match the volume of first and third players whose parts are usually written in a range more easily projected. The opening of the Tchaikovsky Symphony No. 4 offers a perfect illustration of the higher parts being in a more advantageous range. In an earlier discussion of the troublesome notes on either side of middle C, it was noted that these notes require firm corners of the embouchure, a solid grip on the lower half of the mouthpiece rim, and a slightly lower jaw position. These three points can be checked with a mirror and by mental observation. Problems, if any, with this range become more acute at the volume extremes. A *fortissimo* $d^1$ needs the embouchure position described above to prevent the strong flow of air from causing an enlarged aperture. A *pianissimo* $d^1$ needs the same firmness to produce an immediate response to the tongue stroke.

Each section of this etude can be practiced separately. Within each section the phrases should be practiced separately by proceeding gradually from slow to fast. This method of practice is more efficient than trying to speed up many lines of music during one practice session.

Etude No. 17 is an etude of leaps. Horn players know that the accuracy of downward leaps can suffer if we cannot hear them or feel them, or when we lose energy on the descent. This is also an etude of matching the volume throughout the range. Since the measures alternate between triple and duple, an occasional check with the metronome will reveal any rhythmic misbehavior. Do not practice with the metronome.

Etude No. 18 does not appear to be a lazy waltz, but we should try to make it sound relaxed. Set the metronome at 50 (not at 56 as printed) and listen to it for about sixteen beats. Turn off the metronome and sing silently the first thirty-two measures. In this way we can establish an unhurried pace. Since we probably could not persuade anyone to waltz to this etude, we can use some rhythmic shaping in the sixteenth-note passages. The first two phrases could start slowly, arch forward, and relax toward the end. Two phrases is the limit for this treatment because three consecutive phrases shaped identically could be predictable and tiresome. In the third and fourth phrases we should linger on the highest notes. If we have accumulated some speed during the sixteenth-notes it would be nice to relax going into the return of the first material, and to play the theme slightly slower and softer than the beginning. At the last double bar there is a short eruption of activity which could exceed any previous speed. The last line fades away with only its memories.

In this etude we are asked to revisit the swirl and elegant dignity of the waltz. The real technical difficulty lies with the slurring of wide intervals. Some of the difficulty can be overcome by practicing considerably more loudly than marked. This establishes an aggressive air flow, which is at the heart of fast, wide slurs. The volume can be modified gradually as the embouchure learns how the notes feel. This is no time to starve the embouchure for air. Our goal is to perfect the technique of quick, wide slurs so that the music, like the dance, is animated but at ease.

Etude No. 19 brings us to the minor seventh. Once again we begin to work on the interval in a tongued, not a slurred, setting. As you recall from the discussion of slurring, the embouchure can become more readily accustomed to the size of the interval if the interval is tongued (separated) before being slurred (connected). There is no special musical message hidden in this etude, leaving us free to concentrate on the calisthenic exercise of leaping.

In Etude No. 20 we can add just a touch of jazz rhythmic flavor. When there are only two eighth-notes slurred together we should shorten the second note. Saying "be-bop" a few times gives a good vocal image of this rhythmic nuance. This feeling is impossible to portray in conventional technical language, but, like so much of jazz, its words derive from the art. The more flowing phrases can be completely legato and the three- and four-note groups of eighth-notes are played in a legitimate manner. The occasional two-note figure "swings," another word that evolved from the music.

Etude No. 21 is a legato tongue study in which all of the dynamic levels and most of the range is covered. The major seventh interval should be played as wide as possible to give it an urgent feeling. It is an interval that seems to demand movement and resolution when played upward. When played downward it has a more placid quality. We should all see this interval on the tuner. Our ears can easily become content with a bland major seventh.

Etude No. 22 tests our ears and our ability to predict how the next note feels and sounds. The theme is slow enough that we can think at least one pitch ahead of the pitch we are playing. Each variation has its own character and the player might want to search for the words that most accurately describe that character. We see the word *espressivo* on the first note and we assume that this carries through the complete etude because it is never canceled by *non espressivo*. Because there are so few nuances suggested, the player becomes responsible for studying each variation to find its own shape and for relating each variation to the whole. This study is particularly necessary in variations IV and VI because the notes move so slowly. It is helpful to write observations about each variation on a separate sheet of paper, rather than on the music, and to add to these comments as the work progresses. The notes are not difficult for an advanced player. The music needs conviction born of study.

Etude No. 23 is an old-fashioned tongued octave exercise. It need never be played all the way through, but each part, as defined by the note values, should be practiced separately. The latter half of the etude stays rather low and is a real test of the embouchure's ability to remain firm and to move out of the low register to the other registers. We may breathe whenever necessary but we should not reset the embouchure at the breathing points. I hope that players will return to this etude many times. It can show us which registers need work.

Etude No. 24 is the last of the interval studies. It roams freely around the whole range and requires a good short-term endurance. Octaves give us no place to hide. They are either exactly in tune or not. Every upward and downward octave should be checked with the tuner. As usual, intonation problems are more numerous in the extreme registers and dynamic levels. The upper notes of downward octave slurs can easily bend down in pitch if the slurring mechanism moves too soon or too slowly.

Few things played on the horn are more dramatic than an octave slur up to the high register. There are several of these slurs in this etude; none must be hurried and each should have an expanding flow of air. The last downward octave should be played with a feeling of arriving home after an arduous and hazardous, but successful, journey.

The first twenty-four etudes have proven to be more beneficial when practiced in their printed order. This, presumably, allows the size of the interval, from the half step to the octave, to expand logically and gradually. Since there are two etudes, one tongued and one slurred, based on each interval, the player can become immersed thoroughly in an interval before going on to the next. These etudes were not written to become more difficult as they progress. If the etudes seem to increase in difficulty, most of the difficulty can be attributed to the increase in the size of the intervals.

Etudes 25 through 48 can be studied in any order, since each confronts a specific technical, physical, or rhythmic matter. Two or more etudes can be worked on simultaneously. Etude No. 48 takes a long time to perfect. It combines well with any etude. Some players like to work on a high etude and a low etude on alternate days.

Etudes 25 through 28 are low-register etudes notated in the bass clef with a few higher notes written in the treble clef. These two clefs work very well for horn in F because they eliminate the need for 8^va, 8^va bassa, and for more than two ledger lines. The player should not be confounded by the sight of three ledger lines in some of these etudes. Bass clef is usually encountered rather late in the training years and most younger players manage to decode one note at a time as needed. Even after the clef is learned thoroughly it can fade away through lack of steady use. These four etudes can serve as a refresher course in bass clef; advanced players may want to return to them periodically.

We are nearing the end of a period when horn players have had to use their good judgment to determine whether bass clef notes sound a fourth higher ("old" notation) or a fifth lower ("new" notation) than written. Nearly every late twentieth-century composer uses the new notation, which allows both treble and bass clef to sound a fifth lower than written. The time has come to assume that the new notation has been used unless the composer has informed us to the contrary. There will still be questions in some earlier orchestral works, but in nearly every case the answer can be found either in common sense or by a quick look at the score.

Horn players too often make physical and musical concessions to the low register. We overlook or condone flaws in intonation, articulation, and phrasing in the low register that would be obvious and unacceptable in the middle and high registers. Low notes should not be viewed as a bothersome adjunct to more important areas of the horn, but should rank in importance alongside a brilliant high register, beautiful tone quality, infallible intonation, and complete accuracy.

Etudes 25 and 28 should be as smooth and legato as they would be if they had been written to sound an octave higher. Breaks in the line occur when the air flow is interrupted by a tongue stroke that starts too soon and stays too long against the back of the teeth. Some of this can be corrected by playing a slow phrase one octave higher and observing how the tongue acts when the lower jaw is in its more normal position. We must also remind ourselves to blow through the tongue stroke. These two etudes should be studied and played with the same care and musical integrity as any of the earlier etudes. If Maxime-Alphonse had written Etude No. 28 he might have written 20 *fois* from the end of measure 23 to measure 31.

In Etudes 26 and 27 we should check the embouchure occasionally in the mirror. If the embouchure looks flabby and loose, the notes are probably responding late or not at all. A constant up and down motion in the lower jaw is a symptom of an insufficient grip on the lower part of the mouthpiece rim and a tongue stroke that travels too far and too slowly. You will recall that we can improve our slurring by first separating the notes and then rejoining them. Low-register separated (staccato) notes can improve by first joining them with a legato tongue stroke and then gradually separating them. While moving from legato to staccato the lower jaw should not begin to move synchronously with the tongue. The "tu" articulation for staccato tonguing opens the aperture more than the "du" used for legato. This makes firm corners of the embouchure necessary for low, short playing. Etude No. 27 has several groups with repeated pitches. If the notes do not change, we cannot justify moving the lower jaw as the tongue does its work.

Etudes 29 through 32 are high-register etudes. In Etude No. 29 there are numerous short rests. At these resting places we should relieve all the pressure of the mouthpiece on the lips so that the embouchure can become refreshed. Here, again, is the work and rest principle. If need be, one can take more time than is notated at the rests. We do not strengthen the high register by punishing the embouchure with continuous playing or by using excess pressure. I hope that every student playing these etudes will have experimented with pressure in all registers to find the amount that is sufficient to maintain the air seal and to center pitches, but not so much as to flatten the upper lip, cause a red ring above the upper lip, or induce fatigue great enough to stop the vibration. Before practicing these four high etudes, the player should hold several long tones and should vary the amount of mouthpiece pressure until memory of a suitable pressure is renewed. $c^2$ to $f^2$ is a good range for these preliminary long tones. After reestablishing the feel of the pressure, try to maintain that amount at least as far up as $a^2$. The last few higher notes might accommodate a little more pressure. In Etude No.

31, high-register pressure is released not by rests but by frequent dips into the comfort of the middle register. It is not as relaxing as resting, so we should not hesitate to create some rests as they are needed.

Even though Etude No. 30 is written in 5/8 it is good preparation for playing those baroque and classical works that are continuously high. About ten days before the rehearsals of the Bach Brandenburg Concerto No. 1 or the Mass in B minor, we should begin to practice this etude, or something similar, to accustom our embouchures to high, nimble playing.

Etude No. 32 is just what it appears to be. Every line is downward after starting on a high note. Every note is *forte*. Every second group passes through the bottom of the staff. All of this has to be played with an even volume. We can practice this etude exactly as written, or we can play from the bottom to the top of the lines. Although written in 9/8, try playing it in 12/8 and, in the added beat, sing or think the next starting pitch. We can also practice only the first and last notes of each arpeggio. The height of the first notes after the rests can cause inaccuracies if we cannot hear the notes and approach them timidly. Hearing the note adds to confidence, which promotes accuracy. In the middle of the etude there are arpeggios that have an accidental on nearly every note and do not fall into familiar patterns. They should be sung at each practice session. Playing all the way through Etude No. 32 is not advisable. Rather, work on a few groups, such as the one starting on high D-flat, by singing the notes and gradually increasing the playing speed. This etude is a good preparation for the first solo in Richard Strauss's *Till Eulenspiegels lustige Streiche*.

Etudes 33 through 36 are scale and arpeggio exercises and are more calisthenic than musical. There is no reason that any of these should not be played at a different speed or with a different articulation or volume than is marked. All four of these etudes observe the Kopprasch tradition of pattern repetition. It is hoped that these patterns are broken frequently and unexpectedly enough to ensure a high level of concentration.

In Etudes 37 through 43 uncommon meters and changing meters are given attention. Etude No. 38 is the only slow, lyrical etude in the group. It is a calm piece with only a few agitated measures. Fast music written in 5/8 or 7/8 is often jagged and aggressive, but in a slow tempo these meters can feel loose and unencumbered by a more regularly occurring pulse. Dividing Etude No. 38 into 4 + 3 or 3 + 4 invites the restrictions of such steady grouping and destroys metric freedom. In this etude the 7/8 meter is effective if its rhythmic implications are more elusive than prominent. It is an etude that requires patience with the slow pace of its beginning and ending, and even the more animated middle section should not stray very far from the basic tempo.

*Cantando* is another in a long list of words that refer to singing. It is also a term that frees us to use dynamic nuances. Practice of this etude starts with singing after having listened to the metronome for several beats. When we sing we must not feel inhibited by the possibility that someone might hear us. This is another good reason for locating practice space where the player feels isolated. Singing is practicing, singing is done in the practice room, and singing is a way to explore our natural musical instincts. We can be extravagant with our use of vocal dynamic nuances when we are studying a work. The horn has an unfortunate tendency to mute these extravagances almost to oblivion. It is better to work back from excess than to be always enfeebled by a shortage of expressive devices. We must listen carefully to what we sing with the hope of incorporating its good qualities into our horn playing. We need not confine our singing to the earlier stages of practice. As the work progresses we can continue to experiment by singing phrases in several different ways in the hope that something glorious will evolve. Etude No. 38 is not difficult technically. Its meter and complex phrase structure are the musical challenges.

Etudes 37, 39, 40, 41, 42, and 43 are all more typical odd-meter studies in which the rests are more difficult than the notes. Each of these etudes should be played with a jovial attitude toward the music and a disciplined approach toward finding ways to enhance its boisterous quality. We can start by keeping all dynamic levels as distinct as possible. Few things stifle exuberance more than the confining of all dynamic categories in the safe shelter of "mezzo nothing." Short notes must be very short, but they can be varied. Accents, even in *pianissimo*, must be flashes of color. The occasional slur must be an unwrinkled legato. Measures of 2/4 and 3/4 must be very square to contrast with the more wayward 3/8, 5/8, and 7/8. Our intent should be one of doing enough rather than not doing too much. The world of the horn has been in 4/4 and B-flat for a long time. A major and 5/8 offer relief from the ordinary.

Etude No. 44, like Etude No. 12, leaves the player free to choose the tempi and the spacing of its events. Its three main elements are (1) slow, ancient-sounding calls, (2) quick upward fanfares, and (3) free melisma. The calls are easily identified, since they are all notated as whole notes with an occasional ornament. The fanfares are notated with two or three beams, and the melismatic lines have one common beam. The dynamic levels are clearly defined, which is not to say that all notes marked *forte* are identical in volume. The absence of rests is not to be construed as the prohibition of silence. Music can thrive on silence and listeners are often grateful for its presence. Silence allows reflection on what has occurred and anticipation of what is to follow. Actors and comedians understand silence. Jack Benny could be very funny without saying a word. The length of silence between events must not be predictable. Prolonged silence must have a purpose. The note after the high C in the fifth line should appear either very soon or astonishingly later than expected. At these dramatic moments we must not move, and surely not pause to take care of the water. The half-step trills should be trilled as fast as possible. The trill from $f^2$ to $g^2$-flat is best fingered 2 + 3 to 3 on the B-flat horn. The activity of the trills should not stop between notes. In the last set of calls the dynamics are printed correctly, and every note is stopped with no edge to the sound. This is one of the recital pieces. There is no "right" way to play it; it is wrong to ignore its historical implication, its elegiac brooding, its momentary outrage, or its final resignation.

Etudes 45, 46, and 47 are calisthenic exercises in multiple tonguing and trilling. The tempo of each etude may be adjusted in either direction. The multiple tonguing exercises are meant to be more informative than instructive. We need to know, periodically, whether our double and triple tonguing are in need of repair and improvement, since we use them rather infrequently. Although these etudes are not meant to be played through without stopping, doing so provides an estimate of the endurance of the tongue and of the embouchure. In Etude No. 47 all whole-step trills, except one, are lip trills and all half-step trills are fingered. If we are ever in doubt about the size of the interval in trills, the key signature in tonal music will always provide the answer. Since C major is unlikely to have a C-sharp, any trill on B is trilled to C-natural. In nontonal music the composer must supply an accidental if needed. In this etude all trills start on the written note, although starting all of the trills from the note above the written note makes another nice etude. Trills should continue for the full value of the note to which they apply. Trills usually do not stop before a *nachschlag*. Some of the trills are on notes of such short value that we have no time to enjoy the luxury of starting these trills slowly. Some attempt should be made to match the speed of the lip trill with that of the fingered trill. When there is a good choice of trill fingerings, we choose the fingering that shortens the instrument. Trilling 2 to open is so much better than trilling 2 to 1 + 3. The lip trill from $f^1$ to $g^1$ is troublesome. On most horns this trill works well as a fingered trill 1 to 1 + 3. Here we have broken two rules: (1) whole-step trills are lip trills and (2) fingered trills should shorten the instrument. Rules are least attractive when they are not helpful.

There is no reason that the stopped exercise is the last. It is an exercise that we revisit for the reconditioning of stopped playing. Once the hand position is established, attention should transfer to reading and accuracy. Although the majority of hand-stopped notes can be fingered the same as horn in E, it is curious that our expertise in E-horn transposition does not seem to help very much. We all need to practice stopped horn with enough regularity that it becomes as solid as E-horn or any other transposition. The notes feel somewhat different from their open equivalents, and especially so in soft dynamic levels. Etude No. 48 requires patience and a good memory for what was accomplished at previous practice sessions. The sudden shifts of volume add to the hazards.

# CHAPTER 3

# PLAYING WITH THE PIANO

Playing solos or sonatas with the piano is, for horn players, mainly confined to the training years. Orchestral players do not routinely play solo recitals; academically based performers play recitals occasionally. Performing with the piano is an established component of our musical activities, and one that, for students, should be viewed as another opportunity for growth. Most of our standard horn concertos are published with piano reductions of the orchestral score. By including these works on school recitals we can gain valuable performance experience before playing them with orchestra.

Wind players are naturally more comfortable playing with other wind players than playing with a pianist. The most obvious reason for discomfort is the fixed pitch of the piano. While pitch can vary among pianos, once the key is struck the pitch is constant. The horn player, and other soloists, including singers, have total responsibility for intonation when performing with the piano.

We must, first of all, prepare our instrument to play with the piano. We tend to set the pitch of our instrument to conform to the general pitch of the organizations in which we play. There simply are no flat bands or orchestras, in spite of the best intentions to "keep the pitch down." When we tune we "tune up" but when we move from the band or orchestra to the piano we most often have to "tune down." Also, the myth still persists that somehow it is less disgraceful to be sharp than flat. Because the piano will dictate the pitch to us we should prepare our instrument well in advance of the first rehearsal with piano. One way is to use our personal tuner to check the pitch of the piano with which we will play. This gives us an accurate estimate of pitch level. With this estimate we can use our tuning slides to make the appropriate adjustments.

The most stable partial for tuning the horn is the sixth, which is written in F as $c^2$ on the B-flat horn and $g^1$ on the F horn. Since the main slide controls the pitch of both sides of a double horn, it is best to tune the B-flat horn ($c^2$) before tuning the F horn ($g^1$). A few student horns have a short and separate B-flat tuning slide, which might be slightly helpful in lowering the B-flat part of the instrument. Two pitches never to be used for tuning are concert A ($e^1$) on the F horn or concert B-flat ($f^1$) on the F horn. Unfortunately these are the two pitches most often sounded to tune orchestras and bands. The fifth partial ($e^1$) is the lowest (in pitch) open note that we commonly use on the instrument, so if we push in the F-tuning slide to raise this note the rest of the F horn notes will be high. The $f^1$, played first finger on the F horn, is high in pitch on most horns so that if we pull out the main slide to remedy this note our F horn will be low. The open sixth partials give a good reading of the general pitch of the horn. Tuning these two sixth partial notes with our tuner is a good first step.

The next step is to compare our tuned sixth partial notes with the actual sound of the piano. This can be difficult at first for some players because we must listen and evaluate while playing our note. The tone quality of the piano is like no other sound that we play with and it takes practice to become adjusted to it. Therefore, we should practice doing just that. Ask a friend to play these notes (concert $f^1$ and $c^1$) and practice matching pitches. Usually the horn plays first, followed immediately by a strong piano note, after which the horn player releases in order to compare pitches. We should change the order frequently, however, so there are no surprises in the future. *Mezzo forte* probably is a good volume for tuning but *pianissimo* and *fortissimo* can be interesting. The horn should be close to room temperature, since a cold horn gives a low pitch. A horn tuned at room temperature will rise in pitch slightly as we play because our breath heats the horn. One can foresee the difficulties connected with playing a piece with many long rests in a cold hall. Also, practice tuning some of the more troublesome pitches—1 + 2 notes on the B-flat horn, all of the fifth partials on the F horn ($e^1$, $e^1$-flat, $d^1$) and, on some horns, notes fingered 2 + 3. The $c^1$-sharp, fingered 1 + 2 on the F horn, qualifies as a fifth partial note but is not flat, since the sharpness of the 1 + 2 fingering raises it sufficiently. With the tuner we see where the pitches are; with the piano we must hear where they are.

Volume and register and their effect on pitch need to be considered when playing with the piano and every other instrument. Generally, in the middle register, pitches tend to rise when played loudly. Curiously, for some players, they also rise when played quite softly. Perhaps this is because most of our playing is done at *mezzo forte* in the middle register and this is where our ears and embouchures are most experienced in controlling pitches. The pitch of the outer registers at any volume varies so much among players that there is no general rule that applies. In our daily calisthenic practice it is wise to monitor the effect of volume and register on pitch.

The steps in preparing to rehearse with a pianist may be outlined as follows:

1. If possible, go to the piano that will be played at the rehearsal or recital and get a pitch-level reading on a tuner.
2. In the practice room tune the sixth partial notes to this reading on the tuner.
3. Practice tuning the sixth partial notes and other more troublesome notes to the practice room piano. This piano might be slightly different in pitch from the rehearsal-recital piano.
4. Check outer register notes at various dynamic levels first with the tuner and then with the piano.

Every rehearsal with piano should start with our two sixth partial tuning notes played on a room-temperature horn. To achieve room temperature might require several moments of preluding. A few puffs of air through the horn will not suffice. At this point, with a realistically warm horn, we will probably have to bring the horn down in pitch, since slides have a mysterious way of gravitating to their band-orchestra settings. Do not fight bringing the pitch down, do not be confused by it, and trust your first reaction to the pitch. If we have to study the pitch longer than one second, the opportunity is lost and we are likely to guess. The odds really are not bad—one out of three—but who wants to gamble on pitch? After every slide adjustment test the pitch with the piano again. Take whatever time is necessary and do not feel intimidated by the presence of the pianist, and never ask for help. The tuner is our helper in the practice room but our ears must do the work for us in the rehearsals and in the recital. Therefore we must practice matching pitches with a piano as a regular part of our practice routine.

Wanting to hasten the tuning process and make our tuning notes sound as nice as possible is natural and understandable. A beautiful tone quality is always esteemed, but some players, without doing so intentionally, will raise or lower the pitch of tuning notes with their embouchure. This makes the tuning note sound just fine but does not tune the horn. We must all be completely honest with our tuning notes.

Preparing the pitch of the horn to play with the piano is, at first, a tedious and time-consuming process. It does become less so as our ears become more experienced. After doing our best with tuning the two open sixth partial notes, and using this as a starting point, there remain all of the other notes to tune as we play. Here is where our hours with the tuner will be most helpful, since the tuner shows our eyes, and we confirm with our ears, which notes must be adjusted. These small adjustments must be practiced until they become instinctive and natural, and until they sound right as well as feel right. A strong, well-developed embouchure can make small pitch adjustments without losing tone quality. Our valve slide settings should be calculated to make minimal the number and amount of these adjustments. For example, on the F horn $d^1$-sharp is low and $f^1$-sharp is often high. Since both notes are played with the second finger, we cannot position the second slide to accommodate both notes. Rather, we place the second slide in a position from which we do not have to make a large adjustment for either note, or for notes fingered 1 + 2, or 2 + 3. The third valve on the F horn is interesting because it is rarely used alone, has a more mellow quality than 1 + 2, and is most often used with the second finger for a-flat and A-flat. With some thoughtful experimentation we might be able to find a more useful setting for this slide. Most young horn players accept the general rule of having all valve slides out approximately one-quarter of an inch. Like most general rules, it works pretty well. Every horn player should experiment with valve slide settings with the goal of making intonation adjustments as efficient and reliable as possible. Also, there is no rule that all valve slides must stay at exactly the same place for every piece, for every transposition, or even for every passage.

A few horn players have been given ears of such excellence that only an occasional check with the tuner is necessary. Others of us must use every technique and device to secure and maintain good intonation. Sadly, there remain those whose intonation will never be reliable.

The term *accompanist* should not, in itself, imply that a lesser level of musicianship is required to produce the piano part of a solo work. The roles of soloist and accompanist are different, but one does not exist without the other except in works written specifically without accompaniment.

As with all other matters of performance, information about the history and art of accompanying can enlarge our understanding of this essential part of our musical life. The attitude that assigns a decreased importance to piano parts evolved during the nineteenth century. When Paganini played there was no doubt that the performer was more important than the music being played and the accompanist was best when hardly noticed. The literature for brass soloist and piano, from J. B. Arban to the present day, consists largely of short pieces whose piano accompaniments supply a harmonic backdrop, a few interludes for the soloist's embouchure to recover, and little of musical interest. The brass solo literature played during the earliest training years is so often of this type that it is natural, therefore, that the pianist's contribution is viewed as contributory, but minor. Pianists do not always look upon accompanying as ensemble playing, and perhaps are fearful that a loss of stature occurs when appearing with other instrumentalists or singers.

In solo literature the roles of soloist and accompanist should be clearly understood by both participants. The accompanist's role is one which allows the soloist total expressive freedom. All freedoms demand responsibility. The soloist's responsibility begins with a thorough preparation and knowledge of the music, which, of course, includes the piano part. For a soloist not to know when to enter is, on a basic level, an obvious sign of inadequate preparation. To play without spirit or conviction is to confess to a lack of percipience, and to rehearse with a pianist before solving rhythmic, physical, technical, and musical mysteries is tasteless and indefensible. A good soloist is reliable. When a certain expressive freedom is agreed upon it should not be changed whimsically and without notice. A good brass soloist welcomes counsel and recognizes that a pianist is likely to have a rich and more varied background of musical experiences. During the college years a student pianist's time is more profitably spent on Bach, Mozart, Beethoven, Chopin, Brahms, Rachmaninov, and Prokofiev than on brass solo accompaniments. Fortunate, indeed, is the college freshman horn student who can work with the same gifted student pianist for the four undergraduate years. Let us hope that this gifted pianist also accompanies singers.

To provide a framework for expressive freedom, the accompanist must remember and be able to reproduce an endless chain of accommodations. It is not enough to mark where the horn player breathes; the accompanist must sense whether the breath is a phrase-ending breath, or one that should pass unnoticed. The ideal accompanist allows the soloist the luxury of confidence that the tempo, if set by the pianist, is always as agreed upon and rehearsed. The Mozart Horn Concerto No. 2 provides one example of the necessity of this dependability, since after the piano introduction we enter with two long-valued notes and cannot immediately adjust the tempo. The pianist must somehow find a balance between obsequiousness and aggression, and decide in which direction to incline at any moment. There is hardly an accompaniment in which the pianist, if only for a few measures, does not take on the role of protagonist, whether or not the soloist is playing. An experienced and sensitive pianist recognizes and cherishes those moments. The superb accompanist enriches the music by freeing and exhilarating the soloist. The superb soloist is thoroughly prepared, has strong musical convictions anchored on scholarship, and recognizes the equality of participation.

Volume and balance between the horn and the piano are not simply matters of loud and soft, nor can they be evaluated apart from the music, the size and acoustical properties of the performance hall, and the tone qualities of the two instruments. Composers know about and make use of the blending tendency of the horn tone. When played with other instruments having somewhat similar quality and volume, the horn can become absorbed by these instruments and lose prominence and projection. The direction of the bell adds to the concern.

Normally the horn part is prepared, both technically and musically, in the isolation of the practice room. With no competition from the absent piano part, every note can be heard clearly by the horn player. Dynamics and breathing places are established without an appraisal of the piano's volume and density of sound. This absence can lead to surprises at the first rehearsal with the piano, particularly if the horn player has been working only from the horn part. A thorough preparation means that we are thoroughly acquainted with the piano part.

Horn players are often startled by having to match or exceed the volume of the piano. Suddenly having to produce more sound means that breathing places that seemed to be logical musically, and comfortable physically, now no longer work. The automatic reaction is to ask the pianist to play more softly, but doing so presents the danger that the piano will sacrifice too much of its identity and become colorlessly subservient. The non-projecting, blending quality of the horn may not represent its true solo voice. When musically appropriate, we should cherish the glorious soft magic of the horn, but in solo playing it should be considered contrast, not habit.

The accompanist exists to furnish harmony, rhythm, and color. An analysis and understanding of the importance of each of these elements is necessary in making decisions on balance and volume. Comment on every harmonic, rhythmic, or color contingency is impossible, but perhaps the following examples will apply. Rapidly changing harmonies need clarity and volume to reach the listener's ear. Conversely, repeated chords or harmonically repetitious rhythmic patterns such as Alberti bass can convey both the harmonic and rhythmic messages without much volume. Piano reductions of the accompaniments of classical period concertos contain much of this type of writing, which, when played too loudly, can become disturbing. Imitative rhythmic figures in the lower part of the keyboard do not project and balance with similar figures on the horn. Short and sharply tongued horn gestures must sound correspondingly aggressive on the piano to be effective. The color of the piano changes dramatically from the bottom to the top of the keyboard. The top cannot compete with the horn's projection, but when the writing for the lower half of the keyboard is thick, some adjustment in volume is often necessary.

Unfortunately, some horn players and other brass players generally regard sonatas with piano as solo playing rather than as chamber music. It is interesting to remember that when the Beethoven Sonata Op. 17 was first performed on 18 April 1800, it was advertised as a sonata for the pianoforte with horn accompaniment. By the end of the nineteenth century, the Joseph Rheinberger Sonata Op. 178 was entitled Sonata for Horn and Pianoforte. Sadly, few other nineteenth-century sonatas include horn. A study of these works will show that the piano constantly shifts from accompaniment to leading voice, from imitating the horn to providing contrast, from sharing melodic lines to providing counterpoint. The horn is more often assigned to a melodic role but in both works it at times serves as accompanist or offers commentary on the piano part. The horn player, in preparing sonatas with piano, must work from the piano score to account for all these factors. Composers, traditionally and to the present, treat sonatas for one instrument and piano as complex works in which the piano is given the larger assortment of musical activities to perform. It is our responsibility to understand both parts from the composer's perspective, and not just from our own more narrow view. In rehearsing sonatas much time and attention must be given to balancing the relative importance of all of the musical ingredients. Of course all of the note values, metronome indications, dynamic marks, slurs, accents, articulations, and other directions must be followed with probity and intelligence, but they must always be taken as helpful clues and not mistaken for the music itself. In sonata playing, the ostentation of the solo piece is cheerfully abandoned for the elevation of chamber music.

## Recitals with piano

Horn players are fortunate for having solo and chamber music literature that includes works by Haydn, Mozart, Beethoven, Schubert, Schumann, Brahms, Strauss, Britten, and other masters. We all regret not having a sonata or a concerto by Brahms, a horn quartet by Beethoven, or any solo works by Stravinsky, Prokofiev, or Shostakovich. The horn recital literature, however small when compared with that for strings, piano, or voice, contains works of beauty and excellence, and it is to those that we should turn for our recital material.

Most student recitals with piano accompaniment should be considered exercises in gaining practical experience. There is no way to obtain this experience other than by doing it. If we agree that each recital should strengthen the player's confidence for future appearances, it follows that the music chosen should be challenging, but not beyond a realistic expectation for success. There must be sufficient time for individual practice and, just as important, enough time for rehearsal with the pianist. The scheduling of recitals should be planned on a semester or yearly basis and must be frequent enough to serve as links in a chain of experiences, rather than as isolated events. These links are

1. short piece during a class lesson
2. concerto movement on a class recital
3. half recital with another player
4. full recital.

Nearly every music school requires a senior recital. This could be a terrifying event if our student horn major has not played a full-length recital until late in the senior year. The expansion from a short piece in a class lesson to the full recital offers the possibility of building on the success of previous experiences. The skills, poise, and confidence gained by frequent, well-prepared solo appearances carry over into professional auditions and other musical activities.

The early training of wind players seldom includes much guidance in stage deportment as compared with that of singers, pianists, or string players. Horn players often have not observed the stage behavior of other recitalists since they, sadly, seem not very interested in music other than that written for the horn. Singers learn rather early how to enter the stage, where to look, how to acknowledge applause, what to wear, how and when to bow, how to exit, when to reenter, how to appear relaxed, though formal, and how to respond to compliments and other small talk after the performance.

Stage deportment consists mainly of good manners. This civility begins with starting the recital exactly on time. To delay the beginning of a recital to accommodate the arrival of late-comers penalizes listeners whose good manners prompted them to be on time. Many concert halls have a policy that prohibits the seating of late arrivals until after the first or subsequent natural break in the music. Unfortunately, other halls condone bad manners by automatically starting performances five or even ten minutes later than the announced time. Starting exactly on time is the first evidence of respect for the audience.

No horn player would ever consider starting a recital without a satisfactory physical warm-up. We have to be assured that our first notes will be a true representation of the music and of our ability to play it, and not the product of nerves or lack of preparation. It is also important to have a few minutes of complete calm and repose before starting the recital. During this period of mental warm-up there must be no last-minute well-wishers asking whether we are nervous, no unnecessary conversation with the accompanist, and only a few well-spaced middle-register notes to keep our warmed-up lips alive. We should focus our attention on the first few phrases that we will play, but should not dwell on what might seem to be the most difficult passages. At this moment they are either prepared or they are not. Rather, we must be physically and mentally ready to begin the recital so that we ratify immediately our belief in ourselves. After the recital, write a summary of the event by listing elements that contributed to success and those that might be altered.

In every recital there is that potentially magic moment when the stage door opens and the audience first sees the artist. Magic is reduced to commonplace if the performer does not immediately establish contact with the audience. This can be done very simply by looking at the audience. To look at the floor while walking from the stage door to the performing area is to ignore the listeners and is, if the recital has started late, a second display of bad manners.

The third such display could occur with the first bow. This bow should communicate our thanks to each audience member for taking the time, making the effort, spending the money, leaving the comfort and safety of home, and postponing work or other pleasures just to see us and hear us. We routinely thank others for simple courtesies extended. How rude it would be, then, to respond to the applause accompanying our entrance with a curt nod of the head. How civilized it is to signify with our bow that we genuinely value their efforts made on our behalf.

Some thought should be given to how we carry and present our instrument when entering and leaving the stage, during rests, and while bowing. The worst way is to hold the horn bell up with the mouthpiece pointed toward the audience. Apparently this style of holding the horn comes to us from the marching band. A better way is to hold the instrument in front of us with the left hand, centered about waist high, bell down with the F slides toward the audience. This presents the instrument in all of its complex glory. A few thoughtful moments before a full length mirror will help establish this. It might feel slightly strange at first, but after some experience, walking and bowing with the instrument held in this manner will soon feel natural.

Just as we make use of audio taping and playback to improve our playing we should use video taping as a tool of training. Video taping is invaluable for the study and improvement of stage deportment. Close-up taping could also reveal mannerisms unknown to the player that could either hinder our playing or detract from the music.

Orchestral players sit, chamber music players sit or stand, soloists stand facing the audience, not the accompanist. Horn soloists should allow a good amount of space between the bell and the piano to avoid having the sound reflect directly off the hard surfaces of the piano. Some horn soloists find exact stage center, left to right, and then position the piano so that the horn bell angles the sound behind the piano. On deep stages we must not have too much space between our bell and the backdrop. Fifteen feet is probably maximum, but since every stage and every surface is different we must experiment. We all know that curtains and carpets are deadly and we must make every effort to avoid them. Jacket or other sleeves can also inhibit and dull the tone quality. Try to keep as much of the right sleeve as is sartorially decorous out of the bell. Plan to wear the recital costume at the final rehearsal. Perhaps this is the reason it is called the dress rehearsal. Occasionally we are asked to play in "the round." This offers the opportunity to be more informal and to change our playing position many times during the performance.

Solo works are played from memory. Chamber music, which includes sonatas, and orchestral works are played while looking at the music. Sonatas may be played without the music but only if both participants play from memory. To play solo works while looking at the music serves to reinforce the belief that brass players are intellectually incapable of memorizing music and are, therefore, exempted from doing what singers, pianists, and string players regard as proper, expected, and routine. We should include memorization in our daily exercises so that it becomes a part of our technique. A horn player faced suddenly, in the senior year of college, with playing a recital from memory has our sympathy. That player has also been swindled by the instruction that allowed this to happen. The experience of playing from memory can be built progressively into the chain of the lesson, class lesson, half recital, and full recital so that confidence in one's memory is attained through a series of successes.

A typical student solo recital might start with a concerto, followed by a sonata, and end with one or more short solo works. Another format might start with the Mozart Quintet K. 407, then continue with a contemporary work or works for horn alone, and end with a contrasting concerto. A third possibility is to start with a short piece from the classical era, then to an all-French group, and end with a large contemporary work. These programs use a three-part framework and allow for a variety of styles covering a large historical span. Often overlooked is the possibility of playing a group of etudes chosen more for their musical than for their technical content. This group could contain works by three or more composers or by a single composer. Some etudes make excellent recital pieces when played in a transposition considerably lower than horn in F, and a short group for low horn could be appropriate. There are a few excellent works for horn alone that work very well for the opening piece.

In planning recitals we must not guess at the length of pieces but should use a stopwatch to arrive at exact timings. When timing music we should also time an appropriate pause between movements. For a one-hour recital, add at least ten minutes for a short intermission and time spent offstage between works. A full-length evening recital might consume one and one half hours or slightly more. A twelve to fifteen minute intermission is appropriate for these longer recitals. It is the player's responsibility to time accurately and to control the pacing of the recital.

No one should play a full recital without having played completely through the program three times in the correct order and with the precise pacing. The first time reveals what remains to be improved, the second confirms that the improvements have, indeed, been made. The third, in the hall, affirms that everything is in order, and that the recital is an extension of two solid performances rather than one unrepeatable fortuity. There should be no unanswered questions when the recital begins.

Recitals offer an opportunity for us to enrich the literature through transcriptions, through adding piano accompaniments to certain etudes, by writing original works for ourselves and others, and by commissioning or otherwise encouraging composers to write for us. We should not be content to continue to reap a harvest from the talent and toil of others.

During the high school and college years, student horn players study the concertos of

Mozart, Richard Strauss, and others, and perform them accompanied by the piano reduction of the orchestral score. Only the most straitened purist would be offended by this practice and deny the student horn player the manifest benefits of this experience. This does not mean that every concerto sounds just fine with the traditional piano reduction of the orchestral score. Perhaps eventually new and improved piano accompaniments to some of the established concerto literature will be welcomed. If the composer has furnished the piano reduction, however, it should be our first choice.

The four Mozart concertos could be played, not necessarily in order, as an all-Mozart program. The Quintet K. 407, Quintet K. 452, and the Sextet K. 522 make a varied chamber music concert featuring the horn. With careful timing and a realistic evaluation of the embouchure strength required, one could put together a Strauss father and son program consisting of the *Nocturne*, Op. 7, the Concerto Op. 8 of Franz Strauss, and almost anything by Richard Strauss. Programs of sonatas by American composers, music written since 1970 (or pick another year), or music for two, three, and four horns are possible and valid, if chosen wisely.

There is a small fund of chamber music that prominently features the horn: Brahms Trio Op. 40, Lennox Berkeley Trio Op. 44, Haydn *Divertimento a Tre*, Bernhard Heiden Quintet for Horn and Strings, Mozart Quintet K. 407, Carl Reinecke Trio Op. 188, are a few examples. The Beethoven Septet Op. 20 and the Schubert Octet are works whose length make them more suitable for a chamber music concert that a solo horn recital. Programming a work for wind quintet or brass quintet on a recital might compare with including a string quartet on a violin recital. It has been done, of course, but dilutes the solo status of the recital.

The works mentioned in the preceding paragraphs are but a fragment of the recital literature for horn. Music publishers' lists reveal an expanding stream of transcriptions and original works; there are numerous recordings of solo literature by the world's great artists; symposiums and workshops have recitals of old and new music; *The Horn Call* of the International Horn Society and similar journals have reviews of newly published literature and works in manuscript. The enrichment of the literature must never be an accomplishment left to others. The preparation and performance of all new music must proceed with zeal, intelligence, and skill; and the creation of enduring music, by whatever means available through our attainments, remains an honored clause in our covenant with the art of music.

## Short works for horn and piano

Among the brass instruments, the horn is fortunate in having a small wealth of short pieces for horn and piano. They form a core of literature that should be a part of every horn player's training. The French composers are well represented, and their works are often lyrical, but with a few flashes of technical brilliance. *Villanelle* by Paul Dukas is one of the finest works of this genre, and it epitomizes the balance between lyricism and technical display. Others, such as the Glazunov *Reverie* and the Richard Strauss Andante, remain true to their rather gentle vocal quality throughout.

Listed below are a few of these works. Each represents its composer's style as heard in larger works and each has earned its deserved place on recital programs. Every horn player and teacher with an interest in solo playing will add their personal favorites to this list.

Marcel Bitsch, *Variations sur une Chanson Française*
Paul Dukas, *Villanelle*
Jean Françaix, *Divertimento*
Alexander Glazunov, *Reverie*
Carl Nielsen, *Canto Serioso*
Francis Poulenc, *Elegie*
Camile Saint-Saëns, *Romance*
Franz Strauss, *Nocturne*
Richard Strauss, Andante

## *Nocturne*, Op. 7, by Franz Strauss

Franz Strauss (1822–1905), teacher, composer, conductor of amateur orchestras, and leading horn player of his time, is now remembered as the father of Richard Strauss, and for being Richard Wagner's favorite horn player. For over forty years he played in the Munich Opera orchestra. There, and at Bayreuth, he was principal horn for the first performances of several Wagner operas. His composition style was conservative, harmonically and formally, and his works for the horn break no new technical ground. His lyrical writing for the horn, as heard in this *Nocturne* and in the slow movement of his Concerto Op. 8, is relaxed, flowing, and looks backward toward Schubert and Mendelssohn rather than ahead toward his son. Horn players today should not be alarmed at the sight of the *Nocturne* being for horn or cello and piano. It was common for music publishers to insist that composers allow their works to be made available for other instruments. Range or suitability was a minor concern, apparently. Even the mighty Johannes Brahms, while insistent that his Trio Op. 40 should be played on the waldhorn, evidently agreed to having its horn part arranged for either cello or viola.

The piano accompaniment of this *Nocturne* is similar to those found in the songs of Schubert, with its arpeggio outlines of the harmony and the interludes predicting the character of the coming section. Much of the accompaniment is located rather low on the keyboard. It gives a rich glow, but under the hands of some pianists can become thick and competitive.

For rehearsals and for this discussion we might number every five measures, since the Universal Edition contains no numbers or letters.

Quarter-note equals 52 seems a reasonable beginning tempo, but, as usual, we must not be constrained by the metronome. We should check our tempo occasionally because slow music does have a way of speeding up when we work only on our own part. The first measure in the piano is simple and straightforward. Its function is to establish D-flat major and to hint at the music ahead. The first two measures of *Auf dem Strom*, by Franz Schubert, start this way also. The pianist can add a touch of elegance by delaying slightly the first sixteenth-note, and by gradually easing into the tempo by the third beat. This tactic can easily be overdone, but if the first measure is metronomic and unimaginative we are off to a dull start. The horn player must not be dreaming during the first measure, since we must make our first note coincide precisely with the pianist's D-flat in the second measure. This must be rehearsed with the pianist so that both parties are completely comfortable. It seems very natural to breathe on the fourth beat in measure one and play on one in the second measure. This is easy in the practice room but we know that first notes can be unpredictable because they follow silence. A quick glance from the beginning to m. 24 reveals that in nine of these measures there are groups of four eighth-notes. Most of the groups are in the latter half of the measure, suggesting forward motion over the bar line. A simple way of achieving this motion is to delay the second eighth-note slightly and then make up for the delay through the three remaining notes. As with all rhythmic nuances, this can be deadly if overdone or when it becomes predictable. Generally, this shaping is more pronounced in agitated moments and less when the music is tranquil. Sometimes we can use it to good effect if an exotic and unexpected harmonic shift needs time to settle in the ear. In the second measure we only hint at this motion, since we want the opening to be very calm. This subtlety must be practiced. The second group of four eighth-notes appears in m. 4. Here we can use a bit more motion because the phrase does not end until the pianist has played across the bar line into m. 6. From the horn part it seems that the phrase is completed in m. 5. Not so. In m. 6 we have the four-note group on a rising line with a crescendo. Here we should not delay the second eighth-note but should move ahead with all four notes. Moving ahead is not to be confused with accelerando. With motion we do our best to disguise the fact that the notes are slightly out of their metronomically appointed slots. *Accelerando* means getting faster; motion implies freedom within a tempo. Fine accompanists, and especially those who have worked with singers and instrumentalists other than brass players, make playing freely easy.

Notice the interesting harmony when we go from m. 7 to m. 8. The harmony needs a little time to make its effect. We have now reached the dynamic high point thus far, so we must play with a full *mezzo forte* in m. 8 and carry the volume through the long note in m. 9. This is a strong cadence and our volume should reflect that.

At the end of m. 9 there is another interesting harmonic progression, which must not be hurried. The ornament in m. 12 need not upset the calm feeling at this point if we place the first ornamental note rather soon after the sixteenth-note. For clarity the crucial note is the second ornamental note. If it sounds hurried or lost we might resort to playing the third beat as five even notes. After hearing a tape play-back we can decide how to play the ornament. We are listening for a clarity that does not interfere with the prevailing calm. Beginning with the latter half of m. 13 everything moves forward with the quickening note values and the crescendo. In m. 15 we arrive at *forte* and have another group of four eighth-notes. These four notes and the following sixteenth-notes are best played in a foursquare manner. In m. 16 the diminuendo returns our volume to *forte* so that the resolution in m. 17 is strong. At the end of m. 17 the pianist brings us back to *piano* and, in doing so, should take enough time to restore the tranquillity needed for the return of the first material in m. 18. In the Universal Edition the horn part has no dynamic marking at the beginning but has a *piano* in m. 18. The piano part has *piano* in both places. We might wish to start m. 18 a little more softly than the beginning.

In m. 20 we can take some time on the first sixteenth-note and then move ahead through the next two measures until the A-flat in m. 23. Here we should delay the E-natural and then move through the rest of the triplets. Pianists often are reluctant to continue the crescendo in m. 24, but prefer to get softer at the very moment that the composer urges us to push toward the cadence in m. 25. The piano part in the latter half of m. 25 through m. 29 is unhurried and does not stray very far from *piano*. Our octaves are unobtrusive and perfectly in tune.

The middle section, marked *più animato e marcato*, is animated mostly by the composer's choice of note values and by our style of tongue strokes. Quarter-note equals 84 seems a good tempo for m. 33. The pianist can move forward slightly on the octave triplets but should place the second quarter-notes in mm. 33–36 just a little late for emphasis. Measures 37–40, marked risoluto, must have a feeling of bold steadiness. In m. 39 the sixteenth-notes can have an interesting shape if we use the tactic of dwelling slightly on the first note and making up any lost time on the remaining notes. This allows the third beat to be exactly on time and does not argue with the rather square succession of quarter-notes in the accompaniment. Pianists are urged to arpeggiate the chords in m. 39 slowly enough to point out the wonderful dissonance caused by the A-natural. Surely the flat on the fourth beat belongs to the A and not to the B where it is written. There is not much time for the written accelerando to accomplish very much. If we make a small amount of accelerando we can push the activity and the volume into the first note of the Tempo I. There the pianist should play a resounding F major chord and delay the second sixteenth-note before restoring our speed of quarter-note equals 52. That is the difference between *Tempo I* and *a tempo*.

There is a feeling of remote calm in mm. 42–45 and the pianist's echo can be a true echo—a little late and a little slow. Tempo is resumed after the horn's entrance in m. 46. In m. 48 we should stay long enough on the first eighth-note to establish the deceptive quality of the harmony and then proceed with stern dignity while taking extra time on the octave at the end of the measure. Each second beat in mm. 49–51 should appear a little later than its predecessor and with a slow arpeggiando of the chords.

The piano interlude in mm. 52–57 should remain calm until the outburst of *fortissimo* in m. 56. Notice the almost hidden counterpoint in the left hand in mm. 53–54, and the rising line in mm. 55–56. There should be a feeling of contentment and inevitability upon arriving home in D-flat major.

Some players prefer to treat this return as a reminiscence and play it a little softer and slower than the beginning. The horn line in the piano part has no volume level printed here, nor does the horn part. We should treat this as an omission, and not as a mysterious message from the composer, or an invitation to play *mezzo forte*. There is an awkward ornament in m. 67. It must not sound graceless or hurried. We can easily stretch the tempo sufficiently to accommodate all of the notes, but we must carry the crescendo over the bar line to m. 68. By doing so the *pianissimo* in m. 69 is doubly effective. Notice that in mm. 72–75 there is a strong beat 4 to beat 1 feeling in each measure. Each first beat should be delayed slightly (including the echo in the piano) until the *fortissimo*. This is our final grand moment and it should be played with an unhurried dignity. Notice that the diminuendo from *mezzo forte* is not in m. 78 as we expect, but in the piano part in m. 79. There are several of these strong cadence points in this *Nocturne* and we should observe them.

The coda begins in m. 80. This is a long, uncluttered approach to the end of the piece. We can rely upon the beauty of the horn sound and the richness of the low writing for the piano to sustain us to the end. The piano's sixteenth-notes in mm. 87–90 could lean toward the third beats, and the uppermost notes in each of these measures could be emphasized. In spite of the *pianissimo*, the horn player must find a volume in the last four measures that will project through the piano part. The last note must not be played at an inaudible *pianissimo*. It might be prudent to ask a trusted colleague to check the balance here. Nothing is lost by holding the last note a little longer than written. Much is lost if the ending sounds abrupt.

It may seem that all of this attention to details of motion, shape, and dynamics will result in an artificial or extravagant performance. It could do so if these suggestions are applied extravagantly, artificially, or capriciously. Many young horn players, having undergone the stringency of Kopprasch and suffering the consequences of playing in conducted organizations, are limited to playing the correct notes at the correct time. Accuracy, in all of its manifestations, is indispensable, but it does not follow that accuracy will decrease if we study phrase structure.

We have seen how helpful it is to study a work mentally before physical practice begins. Reading a work should mean that we read with our eyes, ears, and minds before playing it. For an actor to speak lines before understanding the plot, setting, characters, and structure of the play is meaningless. In the Strauss *Nocturne* the structure is very clear with its first section marked *andante quasi adagio*, its middle section marked *più animato e marcato*, its return to the first section at the Tempo I, and a coda, unmarked as such but evident through its slower note values. ABA coda is the theory shorthand for this form.

Our first task is to determine the general character of each section and to search for the elements that maintain the character. In the first section we notice that the use of the groups of four eighth-notes is central to the rhythmic activity within the phrases. We locate the high point of pitch and dynamics. Here they coincide. Looking at the accompaniment we discover the harmony, texture, rhythmic motion, and thematic references that support or oppose the horn part. ABA form relies mainly on B providing noticeable contrast to A. Here the contrast is achieved through speed, volume, tongue strokes, rhythmic energy, and the nature of the accompaniment. After consideration of the interludes before and after the B section, we can find where the music is similar to and different from its first statement. Codas come in all types, shapes, and lengths, and serve a variety of functions. Franz Strauss apparently wanted the coda to extend the peace and calm of the return of A, and to lead us to an even more tranquil ending. By way of contrast we might want to study how Beethoven used the coda in the fourth movement of his Symphony No. 5 for quite a different purpose, or to look at the coda which concludes Dvořák's Symphony No. 9, "From the New World."

In music, convictions should be formed by proceeding from the general to the specific. We now have a general idea of the music in the *Nocturne*. We know its shape and character. We know that the groups of four eighth-notes in the A section are its propelling and unifying rhythmic motive. Four arithmetically and metronomically exact eighth-notes will be punctilious only, and will cause the music to remain stationary. If we agree that phrases often move forward, rather than remain stationary, we have speed and volume to help us move. If we also agree that some phrases after moving forward should move back, we have the withdrawal of speed and volume to help us. Speed without shape only makes the music faster. If we can shape the speed we can control tempo while providing motion within the tempo.

The question then becomes one of amount. A rhythmic shaping so extreme that it destroys the feeling of four eighth-notes is unquestionably excessive, but in the practice room, starting with an excessive amount can be useful. By playing and recognizing what is excessive we can then start to trim the excess until our goals are met. These goals are (1) to retain the integrity of the rhythm, (2) to move forward without accelerando or rushing, and (3) to complete the now shapely group within its allotted time. The amount of shaping will vary according to the occasion. The group in the first measure will have very little shape. The groups in m. 15 might have none or a lot. The same applies to the combining of volume with rhythmic shape. We are all familiar with the word *hairpin* as applied to dynamic rise and fall. It can become almost automatic, and therein lies its hazard. If every rising and falling line has a corresponding rise and fall in volume, the music becomes predictable and monotonous and the phrases become lumpy. Not every musical arch is symmetrical. In Mozart, for example, the top of the phrase often happens very near the end. The first two phrases in the solo part of the first movement of his Horn Concerto No. 2 are examples of carrying motion and volume through the entire phrase.

We must always place the composer in the proper historical era and then look for how the music of a particular composer conforms and conflicts with the general style of the era. Franz Strauss was the musical product of the middle decades of the nineteenth century. *Romantic* is the name given to this period. The expression of beauty and emotion was prized over the elegance of form. New forms, such as the symphonic poem, were invented and older forms were reshaped and elongated. If Franz Strauss had written a symphony, the chances are good that it would have been non-programmatic, formally correct, and considerably shorter than his son's *Symphonia Domestica*. In this *Nocturne*, we have an example of feeling and form working together.

The styles of the romantic and classical periods are the most familiar to late twentieth-century ears because concert programs, music publishing, and recordings all rely heavily on those two periods. Even so, it is never too early or too late for horn players to study music from a stylistic perspective. There are no formulas for musicianship, but there is scholarship, analysis, and the willingness to learn about phrase shape and nuance. By doing nothing beyond the mechanical reproduction of notation we have grammar, but not Emily Dickinson.

Performing musicians are notorious for their impatience with theory, history, and aesthetics. Many orchestral players never pursue theoretical or historical matters beyond the college classroom and seldom glance at program notes. The ensuing intellectual blindness leads to embarrassing stumbling in chamber music, solo playing, and the teaching studio. In these arenas, what we know and can play or otherwise articulate is strictly in our hands and not in the hands of the conductor. Are practitioners of the other artistic professions comparably disinterested in matters beyond their narrow specialty? This lack of curiosity and industry has no simple remedy, but teachers, through intention and example, can begin by endowing the study of music with the same stature as the study of the instrument.

### *Villanelle*, by Paul Dukas

Paul Dukas (1865–1935) is another of a long line of French composers who have written short works for competitions and examinations at the Paris Conservatoire. Written in 1906, *Villanelle* is one of the more prominent of these works and remains a favorite of horn players. We are especially fortunate to have it because Dukas was extremely critical of his own output and allowed few works to survive him. His most familiar orchestral composition is *The Sorcerer's Apprentice*, written in 1897. In addition to serving as professor of composition at the Paris Conservatoire from 1913 to 1935, he was a music critic and wrote many articles for French music journals. His composition style is firmly grounded in traditional tonality and, in *Villanelle*, shows a refreshing lightness of spirit and grace of line.

*Villanelle*, like the Franz Strauss *Nocturne*, is laid out in three well-defined sections, but, unlike the *Nocturne*, the third section has no references to the other sections and serves as a coda. At the beginning Dukas has written a typical horn signal of fourths and fifths. It is preceded by an ornamental figure that can cause problems if we do not breathe on the second half of the first measure. Doing so allows us to take a big, slow breath and set the embouchure for what is to follow. The 1906 Durand edition of *Villanelle* has no metronome marking, but dotted quarter equals 46–50 seems reasonable. Horn players are often reluctant to accent energetically enough in the second measure. This is a reminiscence of the outdoor use of the horn when signals were expected to travel long distances. This signal is echoed a few measures later, and true to the phenomenon of echo, it is softer, less accentuated and a little late in the beginning. The lateness will sound natural if the pianist will relax the latter part of the sixth measure. The pianist should also emphasize slightly the top notes of the descending chords over the pedal F.

The music that follows the echo is one of the glories of the solo literature. Built on the notes of the F harmonic series, it contains the exotic seventh partial (written here as $b^1$-flat), which sounds flat to well-tempered ears. When played without valves, as Dukas suggests, its darkness and depth of pitch create an archaic mystery not heard when this note is played with the machinery of the modern instrument. Most horn players now use valves for this melody, but in the privacy of the practice room or the teacher's studio we could play this passage without valves to experience this unfamiliar quality. If we begin to like what we hear, we might be tempted to capture this sound on the recital stage. Notice that each written $b^1$-flat is in an ascending line. The $b^1$-natural notes serve as a leading tone and should be played quite close in pitch to the following $c^2$. The written B-flats should be as dark and as low as ears and embouchures will allow.

In the Strauss *Nocturne*, a group of four eighth-notes in 4/4 serve to move the music along. In *Villanelle* we have a group of three eighth-notes in 6/8 serving the same purpose. Every one of these groups occurs in the latter half of their measures, and by shaping them forward, as we did in the *Nocturne*, we can create a line that moves ahead without accelerando. After this rhythmic nuance is mastered, it is interesting to set the metronome at eighth-note equals 138 and play through these phrases matching the eighth-notes exactly with the metronome beats. Never again will you be content with a metronomic approach to melodic lines.

At the 4/4 there is another signal with appropriate accents. This signal is more gentle than the one at the beginning of the piece. Following the signal are several directions to play freely. Each of these should be translated and entered into our dictionary of French terms. Here we have seven and eight notes to work with, but the shape always consists of a slight delay followed by moving ahead. The most motion occurs in the phrases marked molto espressivo.

The 2/2 Très vif is the main body of the *Villanelle*. This section has the great virtue of sounding faster to the listener than it feels to the player. A metronome setting of half-note equals 126 seems to capture the lively spirit of the music at a tempo that does not sound tight and on the edge. There are many Ds. Remember that those below the staff are likely to be flat and those on the fourth line are often high. The Risoluto is played exactly in tempo, and the pianist must not rush the chords across the bar line. After the downward arpeggio, hold the low C long enough to secure the note and taper the release.

During the echo phrases we may use our regular stopped horn fingerings, but the tone should not have the usual harsh edge so often associated with stopped playing. The accompaniment is marked *pp* and later *ppp*. If the pianist will follow these directions we can create a magically distant reminiscence of the agitated section just before the Très vif begins. Be sure to find the meaning of *revenez*, and enter it into your dictionary.

There is a wonderful dynamic arch built on the sustained Ds. Think arch shape and not just crescendo and diminuendo to make this effective. Notice exactly where Dukas has placed the *poco rit*. There are only four measures to work with, so the slowing down must start immediately. When composers use the abbreviations for ritardando and ritenuto we are never quite sure which is intended. Here the evidence suggests strongly that the slowing is felt without delay.

More than one soloist has forgotten to bring a mute on stage and not realized it until reaching for it. At that moment there is nothing better to do than to play on as though Dukas had not called for the mute. Be prepared to suffer the jovial scolding of your teacher and the friendly wit of colleagues. There is plenty of time to handle the mute before and after its use. It should not feel to the players, or appear to the audience, that we have to hurry. If we sit during the performance the mute should be on the floor. When we stand the mute can be on a flattened music stand on our right side. In either case we should not play the whole piece with the mute hanging from our right wrist. It is curious how long soft muted notes can sound. This is especially true of lower notes. This whole muted passage must feel very short and should be taped and played back. There is no competition for volume with the piano, so it can be very soft before the crescendo begins. The next entrance is not marked *forte* in the Durand edition, but surely it must be so.

Pianists must be urged to play slowly enough in the four measures before the next 6/8. These measures must be out of the previous tempo and slow enough to create a feeling of expectant calm. In the first of these four measures, the pianist should feel a very late second half of the measure, even though nothing is played on the second beat. In each succeeding measure the second beats should be felt later and later. These measures appear to have little dramatic significance, but when played properly they can lead us into the magic that follows.

The 6/8 is a recollection of the beginning of the *Villanelle* after the opening signal. This time it is played *pianissimo* and moves hardly at all. It is nice to stretch the E-flats slightly. While trilling, listen for the moving notes in the left hand of the pianist and play the *nachschlag* after the sixth eighth-note.

Following the composer's advice to move to the end, the tempo at the 2/2 ought to start at a speed that allows the accelerando to be effective and controlled. Try a tempo of one measure equals 66. This conforms to the stately character of the music for the first twelve measures. When the rapid tonguing begins we can then feel an accelerando to the end. Those who have developed a fast single tongue will be able to produce a fast tempo and an exciting *fortissimo*; those who must triple tongue might be able to play faster but the repeated pitches will not be as clearly defined or the *fortissimo* as brilliant. Those who have a slow single tongue and cannot triple tongue will be at the mercy of their deficiencies. No one will mind if we release the long G a little early to get a good breath and be set for the ascent to the high C.

*Villanelle* is not easy, technically or musically, but it is excellent training for facility and elegance of line. It should not be programmed until it is reasonable to expect that the high C at the end will be solid. The only way to play this note is to smite it, and the *fortissimo* preceding it, with courage and confidence.

### *Divertimento*, by Jean Françaix

French composers have often written music of spontaneity, wit, and elegance. The Françaix *Divertimento*, written in 1959, shows very clearly this part of the Gallic spirit. It is in three short movements and, except for the Aria, everything is quick and mischievous. Horn players must be ready for sharp accents, short, fast, staccato tonguing, clarity in the middle register, an unaffected and cool legato in the Aria, flutter tonguing, and then play a high C-sharp, no less, toward the end of the piece.

The metronome directions seem exactly right for the spirit of the music. Both parts are so skillfully written and carefully edited that by following the composer's wishes there should be few balance problems. The piano part sparkles a lot, but is rich when it needs to be. There is even one gorgeous, but slightly concealed blue note in the Aria.

Our first entrance in the Introduction puts our short middle-register tonguing to the test. This is not so much a matter of projection, since the piano has only *p* against our *mf*, but more a willingness to play a dry, clipped, staccato. American horn players seem uncomfortable with this degree of shortness but it does give us another tongue stroke to master. In legato tonguing we delay the tongue as long as possible between notes so that the air continues to flow and connect the notes. In very short staccato tonguing the tongue returns to the back of the teeth quickly, thereby causing a space between the notes. Keeping the tongue well forward and slightly higher than its normal tonguing position is helpful. Since much of the opening material is rather low in the staff, we might practice this stroke by playing through the rhythms on a single pitch only—the D at the bottom of the staff. This gives us a feeling for how the tongue must work in this register and how it reacts differently to the speed of the eighth-notes and the sixteenth-notes. At this tempo, having to use a slow double tongue on the sixteenth-notes would be tragic. While practicing the tongue stroke on $d^1$ it is wise to exaggerate the accents, and especially those that occur unexpectedly. Here we can relax, but slightly, our rule against practicing with the metronome. Notice that eight measures before rehearsal number 3 the piano has the leading voice, and we should praise the pianist lavishly for a brilliant high D, as well as a stunning *forte* nine measures before rehearsal number 4. Eight measures before number 4 is in great dynamic contrast to the beginning, so we must not neglect to practice short tonguing at the bottom of the staff at a *p* volume. The possibility of dragging the triplets when they are interjected into a duple setting always presents a hazard. There are enough entrances on the second sixteenth-note of a group to invite tardiness. Everyone will enjoy the *con bravura* scale descent at *fortissimo* if we can maintain that volume all the way to the bottom. If this scale gains some speed, we can attribute it to the composer's *con bravura* and the heat of the moment. The pianist's low G should astound.

There is a fermata over the bar line before the Aria begins. It is very effective to have silence and no movement from the players at this moment. If we feel that there is water in the horn then, of course, we must take care of it, but in doing so we lose the moment. If we start with a dry horn and use the lead pipe water key during the short rests in the Introduction we might not have to deal with any water at this point. There is some time at the end of the Cantabile to use the water key again in preparation for the last movement. Blowing out water, twirling the horn, and popping the slides during a work can be annoying for the non-horn playing members of the audience and can detract from the music. Water keys are essential for solo and chamber music performances. Orchestral players have much more time to take care of the water and are not so prominent visually.

The composer's suggested speed for the Aria seems perfect; fast enough to prevent apathy, and slow enough to foster a cool sophistication. Most of the sixteenth-notes have dashes which, in this context, refer to length. If we place the sixteenth-notes late, we are committed to hurrying to the next note. If we place the sixteenth-note early, we have added length but will be on time for the next note. Is it not curious that we achieve length and slowness by being early? Take plenty of time one measure before rehearsal number 7, and have the courage to play a real *pianissimo* at the a tempo. The harmony looks very complex from number 7 to the end but sounds expertly polished. The music is not harmed if we take a quick breath after the tied G-flat four measures before rehearsal number 8. Breathing there will provide a fine, long, low C.

The Canzonetta explodes on the scene with no break from the Aria. There are no shy accents in this movement, including those in *pianissimo*. At rehearsal number 13 the slurred sixteenth-notes are much smoother if the $e^1$ is fingered 1 + 2 on the F horn. The flutter tongue should rattle; *mezzo piano* might be too soft. On the stopped notes after number 16, each player should decide on a fingering for the B-flat. With this fingering, slide up to the B-flat. At this tempo, breathing on the second beat works well. You might want to adjust the volume on the bass clef notes to achieve a thumping good bass line. The *perdendo* after number 17 means, in this case, getting softer but not getting slower.

The Françaix *Divertimento* can be the last piece in an all-French group, it can end the first half of a recital, or it can close the recital. It should not be programmed until the technique is strong, the style is gallant, and the spirit is brave.

### *Variations sur une Chanson Française*, by Marcel Bitsch

To observe the many similarities between the Françaix *Divertimento* and the Bitsch *Variations* gives credit to both compositions. They have the same lightness of heart, clarity of texture, emphasis on technique, and a very attractive lyrical section. Marcel Bitsch chose for his theme a simple, but jaunty, tune. The melody is strictly G major but the short chords underneath it only hint at the tonality. Even though the theme is placed near the bottom of the staff, there should be no balance problems because the piano accompaniment is so transparent. We really must sing the theme several times before deciding on its style and character. Notice that each phrase starts on the latter half of its measure. Emphasizing the second beats, or the third beat in the 9/8, creates an unwanted heaviness. It is wise to check the tuner for the pitch of $d^1$, $e^1$, and $f^1$-sharp on the F horn, and $a^1$ on the B-flat horn. These notes lie at the heart of D major as written for horn in F. Practicing slow scales of the keys of the compositions we are working on is always useful. There are several hazards in this key. They will become evident through working with a tuner.

The fermata separating the theme from the first variation should be long enough to accomplish its purpose of defining the end of the theme. Each variation begins on $a^1$, moves downward similarly to the theme, and then proceeds along its own path. This relieves the players and the listeners from searching for cleverly concealed thematic quotations, and allows us to concentrate on the character of each variation. The composer has chosen to remain with one character throughout each variation. Because style and character are so dependent on tempo, it is essential that we understand and follow the composer's advice for tempo. His words describing the speed of the first variation may not be familiar, but since they also affect the tempo of Variation II we must not guess. Light, short, but not marcato, are the appropriate tongue strokes for the first variation. If we are convinced that the second variation is solid and sturdy, our tongue strokes should reflect that conviction. On several occasions the tied notes evade either the downbeat or the second beat. If we are late in moving after the tie, we invite musical and ensemble problems. Double tonguing the sixteenth-notes will make them sound trivial instead of firm.

When we see a metronome marking of 50 we assume that the music is slow. Not so in Variation III. Here is another example of the necessity of gathering as much information as possible about the music before playing it. The music in Variation III is slower than the music surrounding it, but it does not move slowly. This may be a puzzling statement until we discover that Variation III is really a dance form known as *siciliano*. Dotted rhythms, 6/8 meter, moderate to slow speed and a smooth flowing melodic line over a steady rhythm are all typical of the siciliano. One hopes that horn players, armed with this basic information, would investigate other seventeenth- and eighteenth-century dance forms. Françaix placed dashes on the sixteenth-notes in the Aria from the *Divertimento* to prevent them from being hurried. Evidently Bitsch relies on our knowledge and experience to treat his sixteenth-notes similarly. In the muted phrases the horn must not rise above *piano* in an effort to be heard. The pianist should play the chords very softly and only slightly emphasize the countermelody in the left hand. In the accompanied cadenza each phrase moves forward to a long final note. The energy should build with each succeeding phrase so that the final phrase is quite dramatic. Notice which phrases end in a fermata, and which enter quickly.

Variation IV is the longest and metrically the most complex. The music is written so skillfully that the meter changes become very natural and relaxed. Be happy to take the composer's tempo at the beginning of the variation, because the music gets faster, and faster, and still faster. The accents at the ends of measures beg to be punched. This gives the rhythms an energetic and jagged feeling. In the 7/8 at the più vivo we must count the rests as aggressively as we play the notes. The vertical dotted lines divide the measures into 4 + 3 or 3 + 4 and are not much help beyond that. It is best to develop the feeling of 7 as a unit in the measures that are broken up with rests. Singing the rhythm is always helpful. Perhaps in another hundred years 5 and 7 will become as natural as 4 and 6. Both the horn player and the pianist must master the meter changes before the first rehearsal.

### *Canto Serioso*, by Carl Nielsen

*Canto Serioso* will come as a surprise to those who associate Carl Nielsen with powerful symphonies. Throughout this work is a feeling of melancholy. The many changes of tempo and the low tessitura of the horn part contribute to a restless and dark mood. Dark melancholy is lost if the tempo is too fast. Much of the music looks fast because of all the sixteenth-notes. When reading through without the horn, practicing the horn part, and even rehearsing with the pianist, the search continues for the speed that best serves the music. This is a work of many compartments, each having its own tempo and style, but all bound together by a gloomy resignation. The music, not just the notes, should be our main concern in the practice room and on the recital stage.

At the beginning the music and the phrase lengths seem to fit well into a tempo of quarter-note equals 60. Nielsen has not provided any small dynamic nuances for the first eight measures. This tells us to use our expressive devices rather sparingly. In m. 9 there should be a crescendo in the horn part to correspond to the piano part leading to the *forte* in m. 10. It is tempting to move ahead with the little fanfare figures in m. 11, but by holding back on each group before the rallentando we can bring the music almost to a halt. The Adagio molto is not as fast as it looks. Eighth-note equals 72 will feel slower than the beginning tempo, as the composer wishes, and will not make the triplets sound hurried. In mm. 19 and 20 each group starts slowly and moves ahead, but this motion must not disrupt the quarter-notes in the piano. In mm. 21–23 the piano has the leading voice and there is a serious rallentando in m.

23. Agitato is written in the piano part, but not the horn part. For works with piano it is always a good idea to check one part against the other to discover discrepancies. By observing the agitato we will start our descent into the rallentando from a rather quick tempo. After this outburst of speed and volume the Tempo I is calm again. Notice that the Allegro after the Tempo I does not last very long. It could start quarter-note equals 110 and quickly return to the andante tempo of 60. Everyone will understand if we use the fourth beat four measures from the end for breathing so that the fermata in the final measure can be appropriately long.

The Nielsen *Canto Serioso* does not require a superb high register, great speed of tongue, a giant *fortissimo*, or extraordinary endurance. It does demand that both players understand the intense sadness of the work. We can use our voices in the practice room to experiment with inflections and nuances. We can look at each phrase and ponder its own shape as well as its place in the structure. We can imagine how the piano part must sound to promote the feeling of sorrow. We can insist that both players extract every bit of anguish from this unusual piece of music.

### *Reverie*, by Alexander Glazunov, Op. 24

In this short piece is a Russian richness as well as a restrained melancholy. The pianist displays this opulence with the slow rolling of the D-flat major chords that begin the *Reverie*. Pianists occasionally need some urging to lavish enough care on these sumptuous chords. In the first ten measures are several triplet figures. Those in mm. 2 and 3 are shaped forward. In m. 6 the first triplet should relax enough to complete the phrase. The triplet on the third beat moves ahead again. In m. 8 we invoke the rule that requires duplets after triplets to be "very duple." The same rule could be extended to m. 9 to ensure that the sixteenth-note could never be mistaken for the third member of a triplet. Measure 13 continues the ritardando, leading to a nice bit of enharmonic magic in m. 14. Horn players might want to try a slower tempo than indicated at the beginning of the *Reverie*. Metronome marking 54 seems to impart more of a dream-like quality in keeping with the title than does 66. In m. 15, where the accompaniment is suddenly more active, we could use the metronome marking 66. On the long descent to the low A-flat take enough breaths for a good crescendo and a firm bottom note. Tempo I is marked tranquillo and suggests that the tempo can be a little slower and the volume a little softer than at the beginning. The last twelve measures act as a coda. Glazunov has wisely given the pianist only one measure of ritardando to prepare for a calm coda, which fades away in volume and speed. The stopped echo must be a true *pianissimo* with not a trace of edge to the sound. If the stopped E-flat does not match the open E-flat in pitch we can try first finger on the F horn for the stopped note and then add the thumb to the first finger on the open E-flat. It is wonderful not to breathe before the last two measures. If we do not breathe we will have a short fermata. If we do breathe we can have a long last note. Sometimes musicianship abides in finding the lesser of evils.

## Unaccompanied works

One of the excellent works for unaccompanied horn can be included on recital programs with piano. All of the brass instruments have a growing list of unaccompanied original works and transcriptions. Because of its range, colors, dramatic potential, and ability to portray everything from despair to jubilation, the horn seems particularly suitable for short, unaccompanied works. The Robert King *Brass Player's Guide* has nearly 100 published works for horn without another instrument; there must be many times that number in manuscript. A horn recital that contains a work either written or commissioned by the performer is always encouraging. Some theory courses require that each student write a short work for his or her own instrument. This seems a practical and easy introduction to a lifetime of contribution to the literature.

Unaccompanied works can be played on stage, off stage, from the audience, while walking through the audience on the way to the stage, at various locations on the stage, with no light, dim light, changing light levels, in costume or regular concert attire. All of the techniques that Douglas Hill describes in his book on extended techniques are appropriate and effective when the horn is played alone. All dynamic levels from muted and barely audible *pianissimo* to a ghastly *fortissimo* have been used to good effect.

As with every other area of horn literature, it is impossible to list or discuss every fine work for horn alone. Following are several fine works that are played frequently:

> David Amram, *Blues and Variations for Monk*
> Malcolm Arnold, *Fantasy*
> Sigurd Berge, *Horn Call*
> Don Gillespie, Sonata for Solo Horn
> Douglas Hill, *Jazz Set*
> Otto Ketting, *Intrada*
> Pamela Marshall, *Miniatures*
> Vincent Persichetti, *Parable*, Op. 120

The discussion of etudes included several identified as good candidates for recital programs. There are undoubtedly many others.

In his *Jazz Set*, Douglas Hill has included thirty-one illustrations and explanations of the notation devices he has used. They are very helpful in working out the technical details so vital to the style. The style itself is not natural to many horn players. Fortunately, we have Hill's own fine recording of his *Jazz Set* for guidance. We can also consult players of other instruments whose musical lifeblood is jazz. They seem to be everywhere and always willing to help. The second of the four pieces in the *Jazz Set* is entitled "Cute 'n Sassy." It is wonderfully fresh, constantly alive, and compact, with half valves, flutter valves, kisses, scoops, vibrato, doinks, plops, and play and sing, all under the rubric of bebop.

Vincent Persichetti, as part of his *Parable* series, has given horn players a serious, complex, beautifully crafted and expertly edited work. From its opening perfect fifth to its closing perfect fifth this is, indeed, horn music. It is a slow piece with many fast notes. Though measured, its many changes of meter and tempo create a feeling of a constantly changing rate of speed. There are a few moments of serenity, but most of the *Parable* consists of short, often energetic fragments. We should play each of these fragments for its own rhythmic energy or melodic contour and not try to create longer combinations of events than the composer has indicated. The work is so thoroughly and clearly edited with metronome markings, expressive suggestions, articulation advice, and other directions that if we understand the notation we should be very close to the composer's intent. This piece, in spite of its appearance, is perfectly singable, and we should use our voices as a practice tool for pitches, articulations, rhythms, changes of tempo, and subtle expressive nuances. By realizing that this is music constructed of short incidents, we are charged to play each incident with clarity, spirit, and conviction. By following every direction we can fit each part into an intricate composition. Be prepared to find definitions for several seldom-used Italian musical terms.

# CHAPTER 4

# SONATAS WITH PIANO

## Sonata Op. 17, by Ludwig van Beethoven

The works by Beethoven listed below were written, along with our beloved sonata, between 1795 and 1800.

| OPUS | WORK | YEAR |
|------|------|------|
| 13 | *Sonata Pathétique for Piano* | 1798 |
| 14 | Two Piano Sonatas | 1798–1799 |
| 15 | Piano Concerto No. 1 | 1797 |
| 16 | Quintet for Piano and Winds | 1796 |
| 17 | Sonata for Piano and Horn | 1800 |
| 18 | Six String Quartets | 1798–1800 |
| 19 | Piano Concerto No. 2 | 1795, revised 1798 |
| 20 | Septet | 1800 |
| 21 | Symphony No. 1 | 1799–1800 |

Of these fifteen works, twelve are chamber music, six are for piano, and six include the horn. Each of these works remains in the standard repertory of its medium and ranks with the finest of its type and period. One cannot imagine the string quartet literature without the Op. 18, or the wind literature without either Op. 16 or Op. 20.

The Sonata Op. 17 was performed first on 18 April 1800 by Beethoven and Giovanni Punto. Its dimensions are modest compared with the mighty *Kreutzer Sonata* of 1802, its harmonic content limited compared with the Op. 14, and its dramatic effect nearly absent compared with the ominous *Sonata Pathétique*. These are false comparisons if we consider the limitations of the hand horn technique. That Beethoven wrote a structurally balanced and musically engaging work within those limitations is another manifestation of his extraordinary power of invention.

Beethoven was thirty years old when this sonata was written, with the greatness of Op. 106 and Op. 131 still to come; Punto was fifty-three and near the end of his life. For this discussion, the International Music Company edition was used. No editor's name appears.

The first movement of this sonata could be used in a theory class as a model for late eighteenth-century sonata-allegro form. Everything is in its proper place, in the right harmonic framework, and all held together by the dotted rhythm that opens the piece. This dotted figure is attached to all of the three melodic groupings: first theme at the beginning, second theme at C, closing theme at E. Notice how each thematic group has two parts alternating between the energetic and the more lyrical. This can be seen clearly at the beginning with the horn assigned the dotted figure and the descending triad, followed by the piano with the more gentle, but highly ornamented, material. In the second theme, at C, the order is reversed, since the lyric feeling precedes the more vigorous character of the music at D. The closing themes at E are also divided between these two differing elements. These are very clear examples of how the sonata-allegro form depends upon contrast in its themes. For performers, the real purpose in studying the formal outline of a work is to determine the character of the music. Here the contrasts are clearly defined as either energetic or lyrical. This understanding will enhance the musical integrity of our performance.

The end of the exposition is marked by the traditional double bar and repeat sign. This movement is a superb example of a balanced and clearly defined structure; not to observe the exposition repeat is to amputate the member of sonata-allegro form that distinguishes it from the simple ABA song form. There can be no doubt that composers of this period wanted the exposition played twice, giving the movement an AABA framework. Composers often wrote first and second endings at this point, further indicating that the movement is not fulfilled if the exposition is not repeated. Neither the repeat sign nor the first ending is optional. Just as we would not ever consider playing an F-sharp when Beethoven has written F-natural, how dare we not play the whole movement as he so clearly indicated? Occasionally one hears that the audience might be bored by having to "sit through the exposition twice." This surely is a comment more upon the audience's ability to listen with informed ears than upon Beethoven's musical judgment. A slightly shaky case is sometimes made for not observing the exposition repeat in the longer orchestral works of the late nineteenth century, but even here should we not be allowed to hear a work just as it was conceived by the composer following the practice of the time, rather than conductor *X*'s version? Being bored by the repetition of the exposition of 75 measures in the Op. 17 Sonata indicates an incomprehension of the work, the composer, and the historical period.

After brief references to both the first and second themes the development consists mainly of a modulatory treatment of the downward arpeggio, new material at F, and a vigorous entry to the recapitulation at G. Notice how, except for the first six measures, the development contains no lyrical passages. Beethoven, or a mystery editor, chose to begin the recapitulation at *fortissimo*, rather than at *forte*. This seems appropriate considering the energy of the approach.

The recapitulation is as orderly as the exposition. The final major arpeggios are the only virtuoso moments in the movement. The low Gs two measures before L and six measures before L can be fingered on the modern instrument, but Giovanni Punto had to bend them down with his embouchure.

This is a sonata without a slow movement. Instead, we have seventeen measures of introduction to the Rondo. Again there is the dotted figure, but without the energy of its use in the first movement. The main feature of this introduction is the alternation of the material between the two instruments. Since this section is so short, and the imitation so close, the material should be rhythmically consistent as it passes back and forth. The introduction ends without a cadence but with a direction to begin the Rondo immediately after the fermata. This direction must be observed, thereby joining the two movements.

In the classical era the rondo was a most popular form for final movements, since it provides a stable framework for returns of the main theme while allowing much freedom in transitions and alternating sections. It is a loose form and, like the sonata-allegro, thrives on contrasts. This rondo can be outlined as ABACA with a long and rather free coda consisting mostly of A. The theme is eight measures long, easily recognized with its extraordinary leap of one octave and a tritone. Its harmonic implications are not complex. The most interesting of the alternating themes begins at E and is a rather extended lyrical section. There is one brief virtuoso moment after I, and a flourish at the end, leaving the rest of the movement with a feeling of untroubled cantabile.

This sonata is classic in form, content, and spirit. The study of form is not undertaken to confirm that a movement is, indeed, in rondo or sonata-allegro form but, rather, is another tool to discover important information about the music and how to play it. This discovery leads to the conclusion that the first and last movements are lyrical in nature, thus allowing us to choose an appropriate tempo and style. This discovery will strengthen our own personal musical convictions and will allow us to play Beethoven's glorious music and free us from playing only the instrument.

From the first measure the horn player must confront the matter of tempo and reconcile the tempo with style and character. We have seen how Beethoven, in the first movement, has shifted constantly from the energetic to the lyrical. Within the first two measures the music moves from the aggressive downward arpeggio in the horn to the more cantabile line in the piano. How does one find a tempo that makes peace with such contrasting material? The character of the horn arpeggio depends greatly on volume and style of articulation. The character of the piano line depends on a tempo that does not make the music sound hurried or cluttered. To arrive at an opening tempo, we should consult the horn part from the second measure of A to B. These measures contain the lyrical portion of the first theme. When we find a tempo in which the sixteenth-notes are not cramped and the music sounds relaxed, we can then fit the volume and energy of the arpeggio figure to the tempo of the more lyrical line. One fears that there have been countless performances of this movement in which the tempo was determined by the first few notes of the horn part. We could look at the Allegro moderato and the horn arpeggios and decide quarter-note equals 126 would be just fine. Or we could consider the form, style, and character of the music, and settle on quarter-note equals 100. This is not to say that the music will never relax below 100 or move beyond 120. Just as we need a large arena of volume levels and articulation styles, we need a flexible frame of tempi to accommodate the changing character of the music. Every dotted eighth-sixteenth-note figure in the first movement occurs on the fourth beat. In the second measure we must not confuse the metric issue by playing the low C on the second beat more loudly than the middle C on the first beat. This can happen if, in our zeal to play a solid and quickly responding low C, we use too much tongue on the lower note. A good way to practice this arpeggio is to play the low C as a dotted half-note for several practice sessions and then gradually shorten the note to become a staccato quarter-note. In this way we teach ourselves to blow through the low C and to think about making a well-mannered release. At the second measure of A, the pianist should play the right-hand notes softly enough to provide more harmony than volume or rhythm. The rests in the left hand must be observed strictly. Inevitably, some speed will be gained starting seven measures before C. During the silence one measure before C, the horn player must think four beats in the beginning tempo. By doing so we reestablish the correct tempo for the second theme. The contrast and tranquillity of the second theme are lost if we charge ahead at the speed we attained in the measure before C. It is painless, musically, to bring the tempo back to 100 during the rests.

At C we should use a slightly tapered tongue stroke on the repeated pitches. Calando brings the volume down to *pianissimo*, and we can ease the tempo back slightly. Four measures before D the notes are very short and the crescendo starts immediately. We can take a little time before the leap to the high F. This leap is imitated in the piano, but with a more narrow interval, two measures before D. At D the pianist must release the quarter-notes in the left hand and not sustain them through the rests. This clears out the texture for the horn. The piano's descending chords can start late and return to tempo almost immediately. The cadence at E is quiet, gentle, and slightly relaxed in tempo. The first eight measures of E are dolce and tranquillo. The last four measures before the double bar are crisp and aggressive. The repeat to the beginning starts exactly on time.

After the exposition repeat, the development also starts exactly on time. Following a gentle reference to the second theme the horn and the left hand of the pianist begin a dialogue. The horn arpeggios must be played even more vigorously than at the beginning of the movement because here the piano has become a competing voice. When no pedal is used, the notes in the left hand are heard as an answer to the horn and not as a supporting harmonic line. The texture is open and clear. At F there is a slight pause before the pianist plays the second eighth-note in the left hand. This delay allows the resolution to F major to become settled before the music proceeds. The chord on the second eighth-note should be *piano*, but the sforzando in the right hand is quite pronounced. These sforzando notes should be comparable in volume between the two players. In the approach to the recapitulation at G, we must have the patience necessary to maintain *pianissimo* until the crescendo is marked. The natural forward motion through all of the sixteenth-notes will result in a slightly faster tempo at G than at the beginning of the movement. In the second measure the pianist can ease back to tempo primo.

The recapitulation is very regular, with all of the thematic material returning in the proper order. At I, the second theme is a perfect fourth higher than it was in the exposition. This is no place to starve the horn for air. The low Gs before L are easily hidden by the low thickness of the piano chords. In some editions the sixteenth-notes beginning seven measures before the end of the movement have been slurred. Slurring these notes dilutes their energy and is contrary to the formal plan of alternating a lyrical feeling with a more energetic character. The pianist must not allow any sound to sustain through the quarter-rests.

The second movement has only seventeen measures; thirteen of them contain the dotted rhythm of the first movement. It hovers between F minor and E-flat minor and creates a marked contrast to the outer movements. The dotted figure is played very simply, but exactly, and the volume does not stray very much above *piano*. Eighth-note equals 60 seems an appropriate tempo. The small cadenza in the last measure is quiet and without elaborate rubato.

The word *attacca* means to begin the last movement immediately after the release of the fermata. It does not mean that the fermata is short.

The tempo of the third movement seems to move very naturally at half-note equals 66–72. It is easy to accumulate speed during this movement. If this happens we can control the tempo by playing the more lyrical music at B, C, E, and F not faster than 66. At one of the rehearsals with the pianist, we should play each of the sections separately so that we have these tempi firmly in mind when we play through.

The rondo theme has a sforzando in the second note of its spectacular leap. An answering sforzando occurs one quarter-note later in the piano. These must not be hurried, nor should the pianist slur into the sforzando.

Throughout the movement either the right or left hand of the pianist seems to be busy with arpeggiated accompaniment figures. While most of these passages are soft, they should never become competitive with the horn or pianist's other hand. The first example of this is at B. One measure before B there is a cadence on the third beat. At that point we should relax the tempo to accommodate the cadence. By doing so we can have an elegant release, and an unhurried breath and reentry. B and C give us our first opportunity to sing in this movement. Our next opportunity is at E. Despite the *piano*, it must sound dark and full. Since the pianist's left hand forms an interesting counterpoint to the horn line, the right hand is played very softly. Six measures before F the first note of each triplet should be emphasized slightly, since they also create a nice counterpoint. Beginning at four measures after H, no sounds should sustain through the quarter rests in either hand. The chords in the right hand have to be especially short so that the horn has a clear path. Although some musicians make a rallentando three measures before I, we can consider driving ahead with every note until the fermata. The breath before I has to be sufficient for us to play a sforzando, a long fermata, a controlled diminuendo, and an elegant release.

The arpeggios between I and K are extremely difficult if we arrive there with a tempo in excess of half-note equals 72. The pianist can help by listening carefully enough to meet us on the downbeat of the measures following our arpeggios. The measure before K needs to slow down so that the piano line at K can sound tranquillo. The rallentando should not be so severe that it causes the motion to grind to a complete halt. At the Allegro molto section, the pianist must play everything very short in imitation of the horn. This is especially necessary in the third measure. The movement ends exactly in tempo.

The study and performance of this sonata can be postponed until the player has had sufficient theoretical and historical training to understand its formal structure and its historical context. Or, even better, a teacher who feels that a student is physically ready to play this sonata might wish to use it to illuminate the wonders of Beethoven, the sonata as a classical form, turn of the century Vienna, the natural horn, and the Op. 18 quartets.

## Sonata Op. 178, by Joseph Rheinberger

For the horn player, the nineteenth century is especially notable for the development of the valve and the gradual emergence of the double horn in F and B-flat. From our late twentieth-century perspective, it seems curious that more than seventy years were required to move from the restraints of the valveless horn to the chromatic riches of Strauss and Mahler, and from the Beethoven Op. 17 to the Rheinberger Op. 178.

Joseph Rheinberger (1839–1901), prolific composer of nearly 200 works with opus numbers, teacher, conductor, pianist, and organist, is best known for his compositions for organ. His Sonata Op. 178 is the best of the few larger late nineteenth-century works for horn and piano. In 1967 the Schott Music Corporation published the Rheinberger sonata in an edition by M. S. Kastner. It is printed and covered beautifully, and has the added luxury of measure numbers in both parts. Pianists enjoy having the horn line in the piano part written in C.

From the first four measures of the first movement, we know that this is sturdy horn music well anchored in E-flat major. Strong tongue strokes are appropriate. In mm. 3 and 4 there are downward octave slurs from $d^2$ to $d^1$. The lower note is a fifth partial note extended by the first valve on the F horn, and therefore tends to be low in pitch. We must check this note with the tuner by playing the opening of the movement up to this note and holding it. The sixteenth-notes in the first and third measures must be rhythmically precise. We could consider starting the ritardando at the end of m. 25 instead of m. 26. It does seem abrupt as printed. Beginning in m. 33 we have a duple syncopated figure against the triplets in the piano. We dare not rush to the quarter-notes and must not accent them, even slightly. In mm. 39 and 40, the repeated pitches are separated by the tongue. In m. 44 the opening theme is now accompanied *fortissimo* and must sound even more heroic than at the beginning of the movement. The last note in the horn part in m. 50 should be *piano*, not *fortissimo*. The second theme at m. 54 can start a bit late and continue at a more relaxed pace than the first theme. The sforzando in measure 62 is quite gentle. In m. 71 we begin to recapture the energy and tempo of the beginning of the movement, and by m. 75 we can exceed the opening tempo. The repeat of the exposition begins in the second measure of the first ending. There, of course, we must duplicate our first tempo.

In the development section the piano has the larger share of the action. From m. 114 to m. 138 the horn part is mainly accompaniment. In m. 130 the piano part should be marked *fortissimo* at mm. 132 and 134. The pianist must make a grand ritardando in m. 137.

The recapitulation begins in m. 138 with the first theme accompanied and, again, *fortissimo*. We should plan that this statement of the theme will be the most stentorian of all. The ritardando in m. 143 need not rival the magnificence of that in m. 137. The tempo in m. 144 is very majestic, rather than moving, and the horn player must not rush the two eighth-notes. Here we have a feeling of shouting an ancient call. Surely it is no accident that the composer has chosen C major for this statement of the first theme from which we proclaim our joyous message. After this high point, the music subsides with several references to the gentle second theme. The movement ends with seven measures of straightforward E-flat major.

It is interesting to compare the lengths of the three movements of this sonata. The first movement, with the exposition repeat, is about ten minutes long. Each of the other two movements is six minutes long, making a total of twenty-two minutes. Rheinberger did not scale down his formal dimensions out of deference to the horn or its player. There are longer late romantic sonatas, of course, but the length of this sonata is quite normal for the period. The length of the first movement as it compares with the other two movements is also about right for the period. If we fail to repeat the exposition of the first movement we have destroyed the balance of the sections within the first movement, and have also deranged the length relationship among the movements. If we play the sonata well enough, our listeners will be happy to hear the exposition twice.

Horn players who have worked diligently at developing air capacity will find their reward in the slow movement. It is full of long phrases that beg to remain unbroken. The piano part lies mainly on the lower part of the keyboard and sounds rich, dark, and thick. Both players must consider volume and balance during the first eleven measures. Rheinberger has marked the piano part *pianissimo* and the horn part *piano*. The pianist, therefore, must find a volume level that is high enough to impart warmth and richness, but not so high as to cover the horn line. Similarly, the horn player must search for a sound that is rich but not lavish, soft but not feeble. These are the kind of balances that must be tried and evaluated in the hall and with the piano that will be used for the performances.

Our first real cadence is on the third beat of m. 7. We can hold back the tempo slightly before the piano moves on. In m. 9 we can take a leisurely breath on the downbeat (not on the third eighth-note) and enter with a sforzando that is not orchestrally explosive, but majestically *forte*. Measure 11 has another cadence on the third beat that requires extra time for its own sake and also to allow the chromatic notes in the piano to sound with clarity. From m. 13 to m. 27 the music is relaxed and amiable in preparation for the more dramatic moments which follow at m. 27 and m. 33. If we plan to take a breath at the end of m. 32 we can have a very dramatic ritardando and a luxuriant *forte* for the phrase beginning at m. 33. This breath is taken very late and very quickly. Surely there must be a crescendo in the piano part at m. 40 to match the horn. From m. 46 to the end of the movement there is a feeling of contented calm. Since there is no activity in the last measure, we must take the composer's advice and die away in m. 55. An obvious, but minor, misprint occurs in the piano part in m. 54. This movement is one of the finest treasures of the literature for horn and piano. It fits perfectly between its outer movements; one is tempted, occasionally, to play it as a separate piece.

The piano part of the second movement was thick and dark, but all is transformed to transparency and lightness in the third movement. We should make the most of the ritardando in m. 3 and the fermata in m. 4. This theme returns several times and we want to announce it as dramatically as possible. The fermata in m. 10 need not be very long. In m. 22 the pianist begins a long tarantella-like passage that reappears several times during the movement. In m. 32 the horn begins a statement of the opening thematic material, but this time it cannot slow down to a fermata because the piano is in the midst of its tarantella. The horn player must take a very quick breath after the half-note in m. 36 so as not to hamper the onrushing piano part. From m. 46 to m. 63 the piano is in command and the horn notes must not disturb the pace. In m. 62 it is nice for both players to take extra time before beginning m. 63. No harm is done if we play mm. 63 to 89 at a more relaxed tempo. The editor has neglected to mark the horn part *fortissimo* in m. 89. In m. 108 there is a rather shy restatement of the opening motive. This fermata can be short but the fermata at m. 160 is extra long because here we have a feeling of starting the movement again. Much of the previous thematic material is heard again before we have one last statement of the opening motive in m. 268. This fermata should not be long enough to dull the urgency to drive forward to the end.

## Sonata for Horn and Piano, by Paul Hindemith

Following our plan of studying the music before making major decisions about style and tempo, we discover that throughout the first movement the piano is the main source of rhythmic energy. From the first measure through m. 21 the vigorous dotted rhythm is heard in every measure. Above this rhythm either the horn or the right hand of the pianist sings a lyrical line. To capture the stylistic conflict between the horn and the piano we should set the metronome at quarter-note equals 100 and sing only the rhythm of the piano part. Notice the repeated Cs in the first measure. These repeated notes are a clear signal that the style of the piano part is marcato. The slightly thicker texture on the downbeats indicates that the first beats are well defined and sustained for their full value. There should be a minimum of pedal used in the opening twenty-one measures so that the rhythmic vitality of the piano part is not lessened, and, because of the low position on the keyboard, so that a muddled roar is not created. The pianist's responsibility is to provide a heavy, but open, texture of high volume and a persistent pulse. The horn part remains *forte* but cantabile. From the first measure, Hindemith has defined the roles of the two players. The horn sings while the piano supplies a steady, driving energy. Notice that even in the *pianissimo* beginning in the fourth measure of 2, the roles are the same. Here the rests in the piano part do not permit any sound to linger into the silences and the eighth-notes are separated from the quarter-notes. A steady, unhurried rhythm and open texture will contrast well with the sustained horn line.

Tempo can awaken the music or destroy it. Too often a tempo for the first movement is chosen by the horn player after considering only the length and volume of the first phrase. Of course this phrase is much more comfortable at 120 than 100, but we must never make the music the victim of our inadequacies. If we have worked diligently to increase our capacity, the slower tempo should be possible at *forte*. If we have neglected working on capacity we can play more quickly or play at the correct tempo but at a reduced volume. These are unacceptable choices. We must know how the length and volume of the first phrase relate to our capacity. After setting the metronome at 100 we can play *forte* long tones for sixteen beats, corresponding to the length of the phrase. We can choose various pitches from the phrase but our choices should include the highest and the lowest. For this exercise and for starting the sonata with the piano, we should use a two-beat air intake. If there is air left after the sixteenth beat we can use it to extend our capacity even more. If sound breathing techniques are in place we will not have to conserve air to make it through the phrase, but can feel confident of playing with a vibrant *forte*.

For pianists to accumulate speed between 3 and 4 seems to be easy. A gentle motion through the phrases is just fine, but we must not stray very far from the actual tempo. The music changes abruptly one measure before 4. There, the piano part is even more vigorous than at the beginning while our part maintains its smooth flow. The pianist should make sure that 4 is still quarter-note equals 100.

Our long note at 5 is, in effect, six measures long. We practice this note with the metronome to become accustomed to conserving air for three measures and then adding a small amount of air for the last three measures. When the piano becomes silent in the sixth measure we will have a firm, steady *pianissimo*. Most often we practice long tones at a high volume level, but we should not neglect the other side of the dynamic coin. In holding very soft long tones, it is important that the upper body is very relaxed and the lower body is very firm. By keeping the shoulders down and the throat open during the air intake we can achieve the upper body relaxation. Relaxing the leg muscles, while sitting or standing, by feeling the body weight as flowing downward into the floor is also helpful. These techniques can be practiced apart from this sonata, but they must also be practiced in context, since we have only the normal breathing time to prepare for the long note. We must listen very carefully to the last two A major chords in the piano so that we are not embarrassed by the intonation when the piano is no longer playing.

*Frisch* means lively and fresh. This applies to the style of the articulation as well as to tempo. Quarter-note equals 120–126 seems appropriate. Everything that is not slurred from the *Frisch* to 9 is short and tongued very sharply. The rising perfect fourth is one of the most ancient of horn signals and should be well-spaced rhythmically and the longer second note sustained at full volume.

There is a special moment at 7. Here is the first *fortissimo* of the sonata. It is quite fittingly dramatic to space this perfect fourth more than any of the others. The next *fortissimo* at 8 is a battle between the two instruments for dynamic supremacy. We will need a *fortissimo* that equals the piano's largest volume.

There is another special moment six measures after 9. We could label this as the recapitulation. Like Beethoven, Hindemith chose to bring back the first thematic material at *fortissimo* rather than at *forte*. At the beginning of the measure the pianist can heighten the intensity by holding back the first two beats, after which the tempo is resumed immediately. At 11 all is peace and calm again. Here the players should work for a clear dialogue between the horn part and the pianist's left hand. The left hand is also the leading voice at 13, but at 14 there is three-part counterpoint of equal weight with the right hand's imitation of the horn and the left hand with the rising fourths.

The coda at quarter-note equals 144 seems much faster for the pianist than for the horn player. With the accents in *fortissimo* the piano must sound very percussive in contrast to the horn's broad notes. We can lower the volume at 15 so that we can make the most of the ascending line toward the high A. Between 15 and 16 both parts are battling again, but this time it is a rhythmic battle. Both players must have prepared their parts so thoroughly that each can withstand the dislocated rhythmic jabs of the other. As the composer has indicated, the end of the movement should become more and more broad. Most of this slowing down should be during the F major chords in the last three measures. The last note is held only as long as the horn player can maintain the *fortissimo*. There is no diminuendo and the horn player must not signal the release. Pianists who play chamber music are very good at releasing with singers or wind players. Trust them.

We begin our study of the second movement by singing the first ten measures with the metronome set at quarter-note equals 96. We discover that this sonata does not have a slow movement since all of its movements are approximately the same tempo. 96 is one of the more elusive tempi, so we will continue to check our speed during study and practice. Here is another example of the close relationship between tempo and style. At 96 the music has a feeling of calm movement (*ruhig bewegt*); at 88 it seems to trudge. As usual, we can learn much about the spirit of the music in sonatas by examining the piano part. Except for several measures before and after 26 the piano writing is open and simple. The contrast among the movements is more a matter of texture than speed. Everything in the horn part is smooth and lyrical; even the tongued notes have dashes over them. Simplicity and serenity prevail. At the 9/8 after 21 the piano part is very high and soft, thus allowing the horn to float along in a most unusual setting with only the slightest of dynamic nuances. The composer gives us another long note to hold at *pianissimo* between 22 and 23. Our body support is exactly the same for this note as it is for the long low note in the first movement. While we hold this F-sharp, the piano must adjust the volume between the hands so that the left hand does not compete with the right. The trills are very fast. All of the notes not slurred are staccato, thus adding to the glitter of this remarkable passage.

After the return of the first thematic material we begin to ascend to 26, which is the dramatic and dynamic summit of the movement. In the third measure of 25 the horn and the right hand of the piano have slow-moving, upward lines while the left hand is moving down-ward. Our first reaction is to move ahead in tempo toward the *fortissimo* at 26. This is one of those occasions when we should consider doing exactly the opposite of what our instinct and experience would have us do. By holding back very gradually from the sixth measure of 25 to 26 and by placing great emphasis on the left hand as it moves inexorably to the low E, we can create suspense, drama, and fulfillment. The second quarter-note at 26 should appear late and we should try to extend the glorious E major by playing a very broad and late eighth-note before moving across the bar line. The notes are not difficult to play, but the shape and pac-ing of these measures require understanding and a willingness to do something unusual. In the second measure of 26, the pianist can move ahead slightly to regain tempo primo at the fifth measure of 26. From this point to the end of the movement, the music continues to fade away. The last measure should be quite long and the written A must never be sharp. Neither player should move for several seconds after the music has ended. To blow the water out of the horn while D major still lingers in the listener's ear exhibits lack of sophistication in stage manners and an absence of regard for the music and the audience.

The third movement is boisterous and complex. It seems that the movement has just begun when the music stops and shifts suddenly to a somber *langsam*, which changes tempo several times. The dotted figure in the piano part must be reminiscent of a dirge and the 32nd-notes should be early enough to have a substantial length. Our goal here is to create a complete contrast to the rather rowdy opening of the movement. At the *vorangehen* (a word that should send us to a German dictionary), the mood shifts suddenly again. While we hold our long note, the piano moves the tempo ahead. We must know the piano part well enough to react immediately when the piano stops. In the fifth and seventh measures of 31 we slow the two eighth-notes before the long E begins again so that we can take a relaxed breath. At 32 the low notes in the pianist's left hand are more important than the ostinato in the right hand.

At the 3/2, the scene changes abruptly. All of the tongued notes are short and the piano part must be very crisp. Three measures before 35, the octave imitations work well when the accents in the horn and in the pianist's right hand are very heavy. The left hand must not be so prominent as to obscure the imitation of the octaves. At 35 it becomes quiet for a moment before growing toward the *forte* three measures before 36. At this point Hindemith again has a dialogue between the pianist's left hand and the horn. While the left hand hints at a quota-tion from the second movement, the right hand continues with the ostinato. All of this is so low on the keyboard that it seems wise to sacrifice some of the ostinato volume for the bene-fit of the other lines. Also, since so much of the movement is either *forte* or *fortissimo*, we could consider saving the real volume for the *fortissimo* at 37. Much of the earlier material is repeated between 37 and 41. In the fourth measure of 41 there is a very brittle texture in the piano. Although the left hand is not marked staccato, it should be played very short and *pianissimo*. When the horn enters every note must be short.

In the coda we do exactly as the composer wishes on the interpolated 3/4. In the piano, each 3/4 begins strongly and diminishes. In the horn part we start each 3/4 *forte* and do not diminish against the crescendo in the piano. The coda begins more slowly than the section that precedes it; at 45 we are asked to play again more slowly; three measures from the end the music becomes even slower. It is best to decide how slowly we want to play the last three measures and then adjust the other tempi accordingly. The penultimate measure can be very grand, and the final fermata, as in the first movement, should be held only as long as we can maintain the *fortissimo*.

There are no great technical difficulties in the horn part of this sonata. It is, however, quite strenuous, with much loud and sustained playing. During individual practice and rehearsals together there must be constant attention to volume and balance as they affect the projection of important lines. In solo works, this often means lowering the volume of the piano to allow the horn a clear path. In any well-written sonata, balance is often achieved by raising the volume of the piano to give it musical prominence as the need arises. The pianist can always see the horn part and is able to make accommodations in style, volume, and tempo. Horn players, who do not play from the piano score, must know the piano part. It is impossible to prepare the horn part of this, or any sonata, without having the piano part on the music stand. By preparing our part in this way, we relieve ourselves of any urge to think of the pianist's role as accompaniment in the performance of sonatas.

## Sonata for Alto Horn and Piano, by Paul Hindemith

The full title of this work is Sonata for Alto Horn (Mellophone) in E-flat (also French Horn or Alto Saxophone) and Piano. Only four years separate the Sonata for Horn and Piano (1939) from this sonata (written in 1943 and not published until 1956). After these two sonatas came the horn concerto in 1949.

As a violinist, violist, conductor, theorist, teacher of composition, and author, Paul Hindemith was truly a man of the musical world. As a composer his output was extremely diverse, with such works as a Symphony for Band, madrigals, *Ludus Tonalis*, a five-act opera, easy teaching pieces, and the sublime *Symphonia Serena*. Orchestral horn players enjoy his *Symphonic Metamorphosis on Themes of Carl Maria von Weber* and his Concert Music for Strings and Brass. Between 1935 and 1955 he wrote a sonata for each of the orchestral instruments and piano, as well as sonatas for piano and organ. In any of these sonatas we feel the unique Hindemith touch almost from the first measure. Every work sounds like Hindemith, yet every work is distinctive.

After studying the sonatas of 1939 and 1943, it would be difficult to imagine two more contrasting works written by the same composer for more or less the same instrument. The 1939 sonata is weighty; the Alto Horn Sonata is both vivacious and restrained. The 1939 sonata has no slow movement; the Alto Horn Sonata has two. The 1939 sonata has no extended passages for piano alone; in the Alto Horn Sonata the pianist plays a long virtuoso solo to open the fourth movement. In the 1939 sonata the players speak to us only through the eloquence of their performance; the Alto Horn Sonata has spoken poetry for both the pianist and the horn player. Throughout both sonatas the traditional horn signal intervals of the perfect fourth, perfect fifth, and the octave are abundant.

The first movement of this sonata requires that the players have the patience to play music that moves very slowly. Quarter-note equals 108 does not appear to be a slow speed, but given the 6/4 time signature and a harmonic motion mainly by the half measure, the real pace of the music is dotted half equals 36—slow music indeed. Before starting the first movement at every practice session, at every rehearsal with the pianist, and of course, at the concert, both players must create the tempo in their minds before playing. If the two players are off stage just before the sonata is played, they can sing the opening four measures together very quietly. During the quiet moments on stage just before the music begins, we can, once again, settle into the correct tempo. This is no time for idle or distracted minds.

The magnetism of first beats lends the possibility of moving too quickly through the latter halves of measures toward the downbeats and thereby accumulating an unwanted speed. Patience to play slowly is indeed a virtue. The quarter-notes in the fourth measure of 1 should hold back slightly to end the phrase. Four measures before 2, it is the pianist who must be virtuously slow, and we must not hurry the entrance one measure before 2.

At 2, horn players will surely notice the imitation between the horn part and the right hand of the pianist. The composer has given the horn a clear path to tread here; it is the pianist who must ensure that the imitation is not hidden, and can do so by not allowing any of the sound of the left hand to sustain into the rests. The horn plays this elegant arch four times, each with a different dynamic shape. The pianist, sadly, plays it only three times. In the measure before 3, it is the pianist who has to hold back the quarter-notes before the music begins again. We really must not be faster at 3 than we were at the beginning of the movement. Four measures before 4 the notes are very slow and there is no motion at all in the piano part. We should not attempt to improve these measures by moving them ahead. Our emphasis will be on shaping the arch dynamically as written in the hope that it can be heard as a reminiscence of the arch at 2. Breathing in the fourth measure of 2 and before the fermata is wise. The pianist must not release the sound before we begin our last note. There, again, is a soft, long tone requiring a good breathing technique and body support.

We have just played a very long fermata at the end of a very slow movement. Removing the water before starting the next movement is not appropriate. If the fermata is long enough, we have created a feeling that the movement has ended. We can, therefore, release the fermata, take a breath in the tempo of the second movement, and proceed. If the horn is dry when we begin the sonata and if we have a water key on the leadpipe, we can wait to remove any water until the ten-measure rest after 5.

Occasionally one sees a horn player enter the stage, take a bow, play some tuning notes, and then with much popping and clicking of slides and twirling of horn, go through a lengthy and elaborate water drainage drill. Of course we do not want to have any water in the instrument during the first movement, but the green room and off stage are the proper places to take care of it.

For the second movement, since Hindemith has given only the *2/2* and *lebhaft* to guide us in matters of tempo and style, we should follow our habit of searching through the whole movement, and not just the first several measures, to find clues. A tempo of half-note equals 120 seems to fit the opening thematic material very well. It is fast enough to be lively but not so fast as to feel rushed. At this speed all of the quarter-notes in the piano part sound distinct when they are separated and played marcato. At 16, half-note equals 120 should allow an agile-fingered pianist to make even the left hand sound nimble. Since the music in this movement has dash and spirit, all of the quarter-notes are marcato if they are not slurred. The half-notes are full length but played with a sharp tongue stroke. Notice that there are few dynamic nuances within each level of volume. Therefore we must use an articulation that is brisk and forceful in *forte* and pointed in *piano*. There are some well-placed accents that are played quite vigorously. The accents that are imitative, such as at the beginning and before 9, are in the piano and must be very assertive.

In one of the short rest periods during a practice session, it would be interesting to count the number of times, in the horn part, that Hindemith used the signaling intervals of the perfect fourth, perfect fifth, and the octave. These intervals are to be expected in music that has strong tonal centers, but their use in horn literature, deliberately or otherwise, gives an outdoor character to the music when they are fast and loud, and a plaintive quality when they are slow and soft. We might look at each of the intervals and let them help us in our search for an appropriate spirit and style.

That Hindemith chose a rising octave for the top of the movement at 14 is certainly no accident. This is such an important moment that we must have perfect confidence in the way we have chosen to produce this octave. Remembering our principle of making the horn shorter on upward slurs, we can finger the lower note of the octave 1 on the F horn and the upper note 1 on the B-flat horn. Since, for most horn players, playing the lower note on the F horn will be slightly unusual, feeling perfectly comfortable with this fingering will require extra practice. The slur itself works well; playing the lower note *fortissimo* on the F horn must be made secure. Although Hindemith has not written a crescendo on the lower note, the air must expand toward the upper note. After arriving at the top note after a beautiful octave slur, what a pity it would be to stop the airflow before tonguing the first note in the third measure of 14.

At 16 both players have to resist an urge to gain volume before the slight crescendo before 17. At 17 the pianist should play the notes in the right hand as softly as possible so that the left hand can project the melodic line no more loudly than *pianissimo*. Hindemith has written several dynamic nuances between 17 and 18 but they should apply only to the left hand. There is a wonderful rhythmic pattern in the left hand beginning six measures before 20. Again, the right hand should not compete. Horn players should take careful notice of what the composer has written in the piano part for the last four measures. This unusual rhythmic scheme has occurred several times previously, and it must not be distorted by a rallentando as we approach the last measure. It is the fermata, not the rhythmic pattern, that ends the movement. The technique in the second movement is not difficult, but since we play rather steadily our short-term endurance must be adequate.

Between the second and third movements there can be a pause that is slightly longer than normal. During this pause all of the water is removed and we can begin to think about the tempo for the third movement. There, the 8/8 is a subdivision of 4/4 and not the 8/8 that is 3 + 2 + 3. There is a lot of activity in this movement, so we must find a tempo that sounds slow in spite of the 32nd-notes. Eighth-note equals 56 is worth considering. This movement need not be as steadily paced as the other movements, so if we gain a small amount of speed as the music progresses it will feel quite natural. The horn part at 21 should sound as different in volume from the beginning as *mezzo forte* will allow. If we start to gain some speed three measures before 22, the long note will be more manageable and the drama of the situation will be heightened. No horn player would ever break the slur to breathe before the two-octave downward leap. The breath is before the F-natural two measures before 22. The 32nd-notes at 22 are very leisurely. The ending is plain, with only a suggestion of a crescendo and diminuendo. This is the only movement that does not end with a fermata.

After a normal between-movement pause the horn player takes a few steps down-stage and recites the poetry. Just as everything else in the sonata, the poetry is studied, practiced, and rehearsed. Younger players in a music school can locate a voice teacher, a stage director, or perhaps an actor who can help with the vocal production of the poetry. We can make good use of our tape recorder to let us hear how we really sound when we speak. This can be a shock. The poetry can add a richly dramatic element to the sonata if it done seriously and well. When done poorly, everyone is embarrassed. We should prepare the poetry in exactly the same way as we prepare the music. We examine the poetry to discover its style and character.

We do the technical work necessary to produce the words, "the cornucopia's gift calls forth in us a pallid yearning." It is not easy to enunciate clearly. Then we can shape the flow of the words to give them life and meaning. After the horn player has finished speaking, the pianist can turn toward the audience while still seated, recite, and almost immediately begin the music for the opening of the fourth movement. Listeners always appreciate having the text printed in the program. The poetry is memorized, of course.

For the last movement the composer has given us a metronome setting of 60. This applies to one measure of 9/16 or one half measure of 6/8. The five-measure cue written into the horn part is helpful, but we must know the music so thoroughly that we can take a relaxed breath on the latter half of the measure at 26. The last movement looks fast but is moderate in tempo. The notes look easy, but can become difficult if our endurance is low. The articulation appears to be short, but the tempo demands a legato tongue stroke.

There is no relief for the embouchure after we have begun the last movement. We can pace ourselves by playing all of the softer dynamics very gently. This approach is also beneficial to the music, because the *fortissimo* is reserved for the last nine measures. It is tempting to play 30 more loudly than *forte* and, in doing so, expend too much embouchure energy.

Hindemith has written no pedal indications in the piano parts of either of these sonatas. Pianists are accustomed to making their own pedaling decisions based, one hopes, on an understanding of the musical consequences. Of particular concern are the repeated chords that begin two measures before 32. Pianists are very reluctant to play these chords without pedal, but they should be persuaded to consider that the descending bass line of these chords can be heard more clearly without the connecting effect of the pedal. The texture becomes bright and transparent. The non-pedal approach prepares the ear for the last two measures, which are unusually high on the keyboard. If the lower chord that begins the last two measures is not allowed to sustain through these measures, we have a completely open sound that is high and brilliant. When played this way the fermata should not last so long that the piano fades away. None of the piano writing in the last movement is commonplace; the ending could be extraordinary.

Musically, this sonata can be placed almost anywhere on a program. Physically, it is probably not wise to play it as the last work on a long recital. Even with superb physical endurance we should not have to save strength throughout the recital to meet the demands of the last work. This is not fair to the other works on the program, and the player should not have the psychological burden of wondering if the strength will be sufficient to survive to the end of the recital. Recitals drain our endurance more than rehearsals. We can gauge our endurance level by playing completely through the program in rehearsal. If we have programmed this sonata as the last work, and if our rehearsals notify us that the endurance is questionable, then, of course, we must find another place for this sonata.

## Sonata for Horn and Piano, by Bernhard Heiden

American composers have produced several fine sonatas for horn and piano. These works, with some exceptions, are in the usual three-movement pattern of fast-slow-fast, and are cast in the composers' own versions of a rather conservative tonal language. There seems to be a tendency among these sonatas to treat the piano as an accompanying instrument whenever the horn is playing, rather than having a full interplay of thematic and rhythmic gestures.

Bernhard Heiden has given us a beautifully constructed sonata, which dates from 1939. It remains among the most frequently played of the twentieth-century sonatas for horn and piano. The year of its composition is interesting because it is the same as the Hindemith Sonata. It becomes more interesting when we discover that Bernhard Heiden was a pupil of Hindemith in Berlin. Since 1946, when he began a long tenure as professor of composition at Indiana University, Heiden has written several other works for horn, including an excellent Quintet for Horn and Strings and a Concerto for Horn and Orchestra.

Aside from the similarities of the date of composition and the tonal language, the sonatas of Hindemith and Heiden are quite different. The Heiden sonata is a gentle work with a few bold and energetic moments. Whereas Hindemith wrote a piano part of complex vigor, Heiden chose to give the piano a voice that rarely converses with the horn when both instruments are playing. This approach gives us an open texture and few balance problems if both players understand their roles. A tempo of half-note equals 58–66 gives the first movement life and motion while maintaining its amiable quality. This movement will suffer greatly if there is a metronomic stiffness to the lines. The opening fourteen measures have many moving notes which can be shaped with slight rhythmic nuances to create an elastic melodic flow. These measures can be sung in the practice room to free them from the restraints of the bar lines. Of particular interest is the long arching line beginning at five measures before 3 and ending at 4. Both players must use the rising pitches, crescendo, and forward motion to fulfill the arch. It is inevitable that some speed will be gained between 3 and 5. The pianist can easily recapture the tempo three measures before 5 to restore a feeling of calm. The composer has wisely written Tempo I at 8, since between 6 and 8 the piano part is quite active and moving ahead seems natural. During the last few measures before 8 we can relax into the Tempo I. The composer chose a peaceful recapitulation at 8. We recall that Beethoven did the opposite in his Sonata Op. 17. Beginning at 12 the movement ends with a rhythmic enlargement of the main theme. Although not marked più mosso, this can be played as rapidly as half-note equals 76–80 so that the movement ends with a flourish.

In our study of this movement we should identify the passages with a spirited motion and those requiring a more placid approach. To play through the entire movement with but one tempo to fit all occasions is to deny the music its contrasts and variety. The composer has given us only the word *moderato* and, like Brahms, leaves the rest to our instincts, judgment, and experience in bringing understanding and human warmth to the music.

The second movement provides an opportunity to learn about the minuet as a musical form. There are very few minuets being written these days, so we must look backward to develop an understanding of the spirit of the music in Heiden's minuet. The article on the minuet in *The New Grove Dictionary of Music and Musicians* is a good place to start. During our study of the minuet we will find how it changed from one period to another and how each composer was able to shape the content, if not always the form, to fit his particular musical individuality. For his minuet, Bernhard Heiden chose E-flat minor, although he does not identify it as such by a key signature. He also does not give us a metronome marking, but we can take the E-flat minor as an indication that this is not a frivolous minuet. A tempo of quarter-note equals 80 seems to give a settled and stately pace to the music. Notice how the melodic line does not quite fit into a normal 3/4 metric pattern. This indicates that we must play the line with less that the customary weight on the downbeats. Notice also how skillfully Heiden smoothes out the metric disarray by the insertion of an occasional 2/4 measure or two. All is calm and genteel until the Più vivo (vivace) bursts on the scene. Dotted half-note equals

112 gives a boisterous quality if we play with aggressive accents, a large *forte*, and short, hard tongue strokes. The Più vivo ends as abruptly as it began; we should not predict the final measure with a rallentando. The return to the Tempo I restores the mood of the beginning of the movement and all is well again until the Poco più mosso, which moves ahead only slightly. Before the end of the movement we hear a faint reminiscence of the first thematic material, and the music fades away into tranquillity.

This is a movement of artful refinement, and it is a twentieth-century renewal of a dance form in the composer's personal mold. Just as Bach and Haydn animated the dance with their own personal musical identities, so has Bernhard Heiden. Just as the minuet did not spring suddenly to life in the Haydn symphonies, let us hope that this noble dance form will not expire with the Heiden sonata. The latter part of this movement is more physically demanding than it might appear, since there is very little rest from the Tempo I to the end. A well-developed and maintained embouchure is needed for this movement.

The Rondo is lighthearted with never a dull moment. The 3/8 2/4 sections are especially good-humored with their slightly unbalanced sensation. Again, a rhythmic compound flows through the bar lines that must not degenerate into its smaller units. In the practice room we can sing this rhythm, not always with pitches, until it swings most naturally. Notice how the 3/8 2/4 sounds equally valid in an aggressive setting in the horn part at numbers 4 and 10 or in a legato setting in the piano at 7. For the coda at 12 a tempo of dotted quarter-note equals 138–144 should not strain a sturdy single tongue and will end the sonata with excitement.

## Sonata for Horn and Piano, by Halsey Stevens

Completed in 1953 and published in 1955 by the Robert King Music Company, the Halsey Stevens Sonata for Horn and Piano is highly representative of music written at mid-century by those American composers who were not persuaded to follow in the theoretical footsteps of Arnold Schoenberg. In this sonata we find firmly established tonal centers and well-defined cadence points that give direction and shape to small phrases and large sections. Within the tonal framework are interesting harmonic digressions, not defined by a labeled tonality, that keep the music fresh and free of harmonic doctrine. A good example of this occurs between mm. 20 and 32 in the first movement. With only a glance at the piano part we are convinced that B-flat major, once established, is happily abandoned to memory. Further investigation shows that clearly defined harmony returns for a moment when new material is introduced and at critical points in the form. At m. 34 the elusive second theme is framed momentarily in F major, as is the beginning of the development at m. 66. The recapitulation is anchored in tonality but is a half-step higher than the beginning of the movement. The end of the movement is safe and serene in B-flat major.

Even such a cursory examination of the harmonic underpinnings is sure to numb the minds of most young horn players. Such matters are too often reminiscent of music theory classes when they are learned as a set of labels, strictures, and formulas and not as techniques for gathering information about the music we hear, play, and profess to love. It is possible for a horn player to produce, physically, all of the notes in this or most any other sonata, with little or no interest in anything beyond the notes in the horn part. This has been done, sadly, many times. To be able to see and hear more than notes and rhythms is a first step in our journey from technique to artistry. With a strong embouchure we can produce the notes, but without an informed mind we cannot understand the notes that we produce. If a work is written in a tonal idiom, the harmonic components contain vital information about style, structure and even tempo.

In our discussion of the Bernhard Heiden Sonata we observed that Heiden used the piano most often as an accompanying instrument while both instruments are playing. In the Halsey Stevens Sonata we see that the piano has several functions. It gives rhythmic punctuation as in the first measure, it provides interesting counterpoint and imitations, it acts as accompaniment in mm. 34–35, and it is a soloist with interesting parts to play from mm. 24–29 and from mm. 58–65. There are no long rests in the horn part; the piano is never silent during the first movement. Because there is so much sharing of rhythms and melodic lines between the two instruments, it is vital that the horn player spend enough time studying the piano part so that embarrassing divergences of style do not unwittingly persist or, just as distressing, an insistence on conformity or consistency does not prevail when contrariness is in order. This sonata has been edited very thoroughly by the composer. His intentions and convictions have been set before us to observe, understand, and perform. Our artistic responsibility demands that we do observe, understand, and perform to the best of our ability. At this point it is hoped that we understand something of the harmonic idiom and the composer's attitude toward the piano part.

Halsey Stevens has been careful, either through dynamic levels or textures, to give the horn a clear path for projection. Since there is little chance that the horn could overpower the piano, balancing the two instruments is mainly in the hands and feet of the pianist if we are concerned only about volume. Balance, however, is not only a matter of relative volume. It should include style, spirit, and character, most especially when there are imitations between the instruments. If a sharply articulated rhythmic figure in the horn is imitated in the piano, not only must the volume balance, but the character and spirit of the articulation must be imitative unless the composer has advised to the contrary. At any volume, a fine pianist, by skillful pedaling and other means, can create smooth melodic lines with an endless variety of subtle nuances and polished details. Horn players often do not hear this or are content with just connecting the notes. At rehearsals we can learn much by listening to our colleagues and by discussing all of the elements of balance. This discussion is most profitable if both partners are informed through study but still curious and willing to search for a better balance. Before the first rehearsal with the pianist, the horn player, through studying the piano score, must locate all imitations in both parts, evaluate all of the counterpoint in the interest of achieving clarity, and arrive at firm but not inflexible convictions as to style beyond the notes. This sonata has so much dual responsibility that it makes no sense for the horn player to give the piano part to the pianist to practice before learning the music the pianist will play.

Before leaving the first movement we should observe its jaunty and cheerful spirit as well as the wide contour of the cantabile lines. Measures 34–58 and 64–87 are examples of the need to play confidently and smoothly over a wide range. Even though the pianist plays one chord before the horn begins, it is our responsibility to start the movement with a slightly audible intake of air as an upbeat in tempo to the first chord. This must be practiced when we are alone, when we are with the pianist in rehearsal, and mentioned again off-stage just before entering the stage. Since notes near the bottom of the staff and below the staff can be readily absorbed by the piano, we should make sure that mm. 34–41 are heard clearly. There are several high As, all of which must be fingered 1 + 2. They occur as top notes of their lines and thus are vulnerable to the flatness of pitch and dullness of quality of an open fingering. Open is safer; 1 + 2 sounds better. For the artist there is no choice.

Halsey Stevens measures the length of the first movement at four minutes, five seconds. Béla Bartók, in his later works, also supplied the length for each movement as well as for the entire composition. Halsey Stevens, in addition to his work as professor of composition at the University of Southern California and his prolific output as a composer, wrote a scholarly book on Béla Bartók entitled *The Life and Music of Béla Bartók*. The first edition of the book was published in 1953, the year that this horn sonata was completed. We should be concerned if our timing strays noticeably from that of Halsey Stevens. We should also be concerned if we fail to take the next step and begin a study of the music of Béla Bartók. Halsey Stevens's book, the Music for String Instruments, Percussion, and Celesta, and the six string quartets of Bartók await those horn players who have the industry and courage to explore the unfamiliar. The easy way is to listen to a recording of the Bartók Concerto for Orchestra. The better way is to start with the Halsey Stevens book and the fifth string quartet of one of the giants of twentieth-century music.

Halsey Stevens has written a dark and introspective second movement. It is in complete contrast to the outer movements, both of which have lively rhythms and constant activity. Much of the music of the second movement has an almost stationary quality, and we should not quarrel with this but should recognize it as essential to the composer's intent. We often look for ways to move music forward, but in this movement we must be careful to maintain its somber feeling by not accumulating speed. There are a few notes above the staff, but most of the horn part is in the middle and low register. We normally develop our low register through the use of rather loud long tones and attacks. This approach teaches the embouchure the correct amount of corner firmness and an effective jaw position. In this movement all of the low notes are soft, thus requiring us to do extra low-register practice on soft attacks and soft long tones. The composer achieves much of the dark character of the movement by dwelling on the notes around middle C, which in an earlier chapter were characterized as troublesome and awkward. It is hoped that the player working on this sonata will have a good command of this register, but no harm is done by continuing to practice passing through these notes.

Stevens is fond of such directions as *poco forte, meno forte, più forte, non forte, non troppo forte, ritenuto ma fermo, sotto voce, lontano, una corda, tre corde, sonoro, ms, sp, lusingando,* and *ossia*. Very early in our study of a new work we can list all of the unfamiliar terms, define them, and enter them into our dictionary. Without precise definitions, we may distort the music.

We can plan all of our dynamics so that nothing will compete with the high point reached in mm. 35 and 36. There is no place to breathe between m. 35 and after the half-note in m. 39. All of the good work done earlier in developing air capacity will make this long phrase possible. The composer has marked a few breathing places throughout this movement and they are certainly helpful, but he gives us no alternative at this crucial moment. Other than for these few measures, sensible breathing places are always to be found.

There is a recurring four eighth-note figure in the middle of the slow movement. We are tempted to shape this figure or move it forward. This is an example of enhancing the music by doing the opposite of the habitual. Notice that in each case the composer has indicated a crescendo and diminuendo. If we can shape these notes with volume only, we keep them interesting without allowing them to move in tempo beyond a solemn, measured pace. The return of the four eighth-note figure in the piano part during the last three measures has neither a dynamic nor a rhythmic shape. For the horn player the intonation is tricky in these last three measures because of the open intervals, the fifth partial notes, and the *pianissimo*. There is good reason to believe that our notes could be flat. At every practice session and rehearsal with the pianist we must make sure that we hear and adjust if necessary. The last fermata is very long. It is much nicer not to breathe before this note and, of course, we must follow the composer's advice about when to start the last movement. This is not a good time to take care of the water in the horn.

Composers have often chosen 6/8 as the time signature for the last movement of works for horn. It does seem to be the perfect metric arrangement to convey a short, bouncy articulation that contrasts well with interjections of legato playing. As usual, Mozart showed us the way. Hindemith, in his Sonata for Alto Horn and Piano, showed us a different way. Halsey Stevens has written non legato in the piano part but, as evidence of his regard for the sound musical instincts of horn players, has given us no advice as to length of articulation. Surely this movement, with the exception of the lyrical phrases, is to be played with a short, light tongue stroke, and accented only as indicated. There is a constant use of repeated pitches, which is another reason for short playing. We see at the beginning how the composer wishes us to make clear distinctions among *mf, poco f*, and *f. Non troppo f* in m. 72 is more a warning than an actual level. Notice that Stevens uses the dot for staccato when the range or volume is low. Duplets within 6/8 or 9/8 must not slow down the pace or become accented in our zeal to be exact.

This movement is so well edited that it remains for us to understand and use all of the composer's directions. The music is written in comfortable breathing portions, high notes are approached sensibly, and the rests are well placed. We might wish to indulge ourselves with a grand allargando three measures from the end. The last note in the piano should be stunning.

It is gratifying that we have reached a point in our musical maturity where we can use, in a completely non-pejorative way, such words as *tonal* and *conservative* in describing some of the music of the twentieth century. This has not always been the case. *Serial, aleatoric, atonal, traditional, orthodox, progressive, advanced*, or *radical* are words that give but a narrow view of the music they attempt to categorize. Whether music is excellent or not, enduring or not, does not depend totally upon its theoretical techniques, or its conformity to the temporarily prevailing fad. Being old-fashioned or revolutionary has little to do with the quality of the music. Bach and Brahms were considered old-fashioned in their own time; Beethoven and Schoenberg were thought to be writing the music of the future. Great music survives everything written about it. Music that is less than great finds its own place no matter what has been written about it.

## Sonata for Horn and Piano, by Quincy Porter

In 1944 the National Association of Schools of Music undertook a study of the music its members used for the training of wind players. To no one's surprise it was determined that the music available to brass players was inadequate in quantity and much of it questionable in quality. Spurred by these conclusions, the Association in 1946 commissioned Vittorio Giannini, Howard Hanson, Quincy Porter, Robert Sanders, and Leo Sowerby to write either a concerto or a sonata for one of the brass instruments. In response to his commission, Quincy Porter wrote a sonata for horn and piano that deserves the interest of advanced players. This is not a sonata of great technical difficulty, although Porter does seem reluctant to allow the horn to remain silent, but of long flowing lines that defy the constraint of bar lines. As we have noticed in several other works, there is enough use of perfect fourths and perfect fifths to signify that the horn's outdoor heritage is recognized and acknowledged.

For the first movement Quincy Porter designed a piano part that is full of activity but consists mainly of two-part writing. Add to this the single line of the horn, and a wonderfully open texture of three contrapuntal voices is created. In general, the range of the right hand is well above that of the horn so that all lines can be heard clearly. The left hand is also active in its role of suggesting harmonies by outlining arpeggios. This three-part texture can be seen very clearly from the beginning of the movement to rehearsal letter E and from G to I. The composer has used long slur marks to indicate phrase length. Few of these marks coincide with the natural metric flow of 6/8, thus suggesting strongly that we play the lines quite independently of their metric compartments. Further evidence of this can be seen in the occasional use of beams that go through bar lines. Composers are not likely to use the term *molto espressivo* unless they mean it. All of this gives both players great freedom of rhythmic and dynamic nuances, but also the responsibility of achieving good ensemble without resorting to the prohibitions of a steady beat. Both players must insist that the melodic lines, not the placement of their notes within the meter, should govern decisions of shape and character. The flow of melodic lines independent of meter is shown very clearly in the imitations between the horn and piano at A, where the horn plays the line one octave lower and two beats later than the piano. Both of these lines should have their own freedoms. Achieving these freedoms while maintaining good ensemble should be the major concern in rehearsals. Horn players must have studied the piano part sufficiently to realize that for much of the sonata the piano does not accompany but has a voice equal to the horn's. If we play rigidly in tempo we destroy the music. If we allow our voice to dominate we miss the point of the three-part writing. If we sacrifice individual lines for simply playing together we have agreement without purpose.

We have seen how the sonatas by Hindemith, Heiden, and Stevens have readily identified tonal centers. Quincy Porter is much more elusive harmonically, perhaps as a result of his study of composition with Ernest Bloch. Although there are no key signatures in this work, the first movement makes some allusions to D major. Not until the final chord does D major emerge clearly enough to give a feeling of finality. There is very little to suggest any other tonality because the harmony and the rhythmic activity rarely come to rest. Porter's interest in the music of sixteenth century composers, and particularly that of Orlando di Lasso, might explain his long flowing melodic lines that move most often in small intervals. Horn players and pianists with an interest in learning more about the music of Quincy Porter might study his third string quartet, which also seeks rhythmic diversity by the alteration of metric character.

For the advanced player this sonata offers few technical or physical problems in any of the three movements other than those possibly caused by a lack of long-term endurance. The first two movements have a few well-placed rests and only an occasional note above the staff. In the third movement, however, the horn plays almost constantly. This sonata should be played rather early in a recital, and we should consider the physical demands of the other works on the program.

In the second movement the composer takes a further step in freeing the music from the constraints of meter by removing the bar lines. He does continue the imitation between the two instruments, and there are phrases reminiscent of those in the first movement. When two or more people play music without bar lines, the natural tendency is to play the note values very strictly so that the ensemble is perfect. This approach can cancel the freedom that the composer hoped to obtain by not confining the phrases in measures. The pianist can see the horn part in the piano score at all times. Fortunately, the publisher, The Robert King Music Company, has printed some of the piano part in the horn part. With knowledge of the other's part, and with a desire to play the music and not just the note values, both players can be elastic enough to fit the two parts together.

In the second phrase is a slur from $a^1$ to $a^2$. If it were marked *mezzo forte* or louder we would be confident of playing both notes 1 + 2 on the B-flat horn. Since the composer has written *piano* for the octave slur, the air flow does not help us very much. We can follow the principle of making the instrument shorter on upward slurs by fingering $a^1$ 1 + 2 on the F horn and $a^2$ 1 + 2 on the B-flat horn. By engaging the thumb we have shortened the instrument significantly. The fingering we must not use is open on the B-flat horn for the $a^2$, no matter what fingering we use for the lower note. The open tenth partial is noticeably low in pitch, and with the small air flow required for the piano volume we must raise the pitch with our embouchure. This is, indeed, risky business in the high register. Our success with this slur depends on having embouchure strength sufficient to produce a high A and the confidence that the fingering choice is reliable. Confidence is gained by having heard ourselves play the slur successfully many, many times in the practice room and at rehearsals. Horn players are naturally reluctant to change fingerings from their normal patterns. Good, but new, fingerings are too often abandoned after one or two unsuccessful attempts. We should always work at new fingerings by giving them a lot of air and a slower tempo until they are established. By gradually removing the air from *mezzo forte* to *piano* we can achieve a smooth, reliable slur. This process might take days rather than minutes. The note marked con sordino at the end of the movement can be played with the normal stopped horn fingering, but without any harshness of tone quality. There should be no doubt that the dramatic top of the movement arrives at N. Is it not interesting that the crucial interval is a perfect fourth?

Allegro molto, if taken literally for the last movement, could be misleading because, except for a few sixteenth-notes, the music is more lively than swift. The composer's choice of quarter-note equals 132 seems just right, but we must guard against moving the tempo ahead as our practice makes the notes easier to play. Much of the joviality and lyrical quality is lost by a tempo that is faster than the music. We seldom lose speed by practicing fast music. This is also true, unfortunately, when we practice slow music. Periodic checking with the metronome, not practicing with the metronome, will give us accurate information on tempo.

The third movement opens with many fourths and fifths, confirming once again the horn's hunting heritage. The piano part, as in the first movement, uses a two-part texture that allows the horn to be heard clearly without forcing the louder dynamics. This open texture can be seen most clearly at Q. Between R and S, Porter chose to write meter changes to fit the phrase length of the horn part but not the piano part. This dichotomy can produce an attractive rhythmic interplay if the pianist will stress slightly the first notes of the slurred groups while the horn plays its longer lines as smoothly as possible. For the horn, the changes in pitch define the rhythm. In the piano part, the stress on the first notes is necessary because the right hand has a continuous flow of eighth-notes. Between 4 and 5 and between 7 and 9, the piano and horn work together in the unequal measures. This teamwork approach is not as successful in music of varied meters, in which emphasizing the uneven bar lines is essential. For the short fanfare figure in the last six measures we can simplify the fingering of the triplets by using 2 + 3 on all of the D-sharps. By doing so we have only to raise our third finger for the

F-sharps. This probably will not work the first time it is attempted because all of us are accustomed to changing fingers on every note. After some practice it should feel comfortable and reliable. 2 + 3 on D-sharp produces a good quality and feels secure in the embouchure because it extends the ninth partial, which, on a good horn, is very stable.

As with each of these sonatas, it is hoped that this brief discussion and subsequent study of the Porter sonata will spark interest in a fine composer whose music would otherwise be unknown to horn players.

## Sonata No. 3 for Horn and Piano, by Alec Wilder

Alec Wilder wrote a large number of works for wind instruments. Many of these were written for friends who were among the finest performers on their instruments. This sonata was written for John Barrows, who edited the work and whose recording of the sonata is considered to be the model.

Alec Wilder is best known for his contributions to the field of popular music. He composed many songs in the style that was prevalent in the 1930s and 1940s, and several of these have become standards. His songs always contain unusual but commercially acceptable shifts of harmony, and this characteristic is noticeable throughout his chamber music. The music of Alec Wilder is not composed jazz (which is itself a contradiction), nor does it use the formal ingredients of the popular song or the harmonic framework of Blues. Each movement of this sonata is entirely free of historical, formal, or theoretical restraints, and therein lies the humor, the subtleties, the surprises, and the easy-going warmth of the music. It is music that will suffer from an excess of sentiment. It is vocal music played on the horn and the piano. Even the third movement, which is subtitled "with a solid beat and a jazz feeling," becomes completely singable when we use the most basic jazz vocalization of "doo-bee-doo."

With all of his freedom, Alec Wilder knew how to unite a movement through the use of recurring but altered motives. In the first movement he chose a six-note figure that is simple and easily recognized in all of its variations. We play it for the first time in the fourth measure.

Example 4-1

Since this motive is used ten times during the movement, we must use our imagination to bring something fresh and interesting to each occasion. The first time we play the motive it can be made to sound rather coy and reluctant by holding back the tempo as we move through the notes, and then resuming the tempo immediately in the fifth measure. At m. 16 we could do the opposite and move the notes ahead in tempo and volume. In mm. 75–79, Wilder asks that the motive be played very slowly. Through speed, shape, and volume we can find ways to keep all of the statements of the motive fresh and alive. These choices cannot be made without having a complete knowledge of the piano part and all of its rhythmic and harmonic implications. Measure 45, for example, could be played slowly and simply because of the stationary quality of the piano part. The metronome setting of dotted eighth-note equals 88 produces fast-sounding eighth-notes, so most of our tempo variations will be slower. It would be nice to find one occurrence that begs to be played quite rapidly. The worst thing we can do with the motive is to be consistent and predictable.

Those of us fortunate enough to have known Alec Wilder remember his dislike of all things boring, mawkish, or pompous. Since this is very personal music, we must avoid any trace of these qualities. Whenever the horn has repeated pitches on sixteenth-notes, they should be quite short. Beginning at m. 27 is a three-part canon that begins with a long note. The pianist must accent the first note sufficiently to direct the listener's ear to the entering voices. The end of the movement happens quickly and simply. Although marked poco meno mosso, we must not play so slowly that the sixteenth-note figure loses its musical identity. The music does not require a bloated ending.

In the second movement the composer uses again the recurring motive idea. This time it is varied and enlarged in most of its reappearances, and we have a considerable amount of advice from the editor in determining volume and shape. Since the music is slow and the first note of the motive is long, we are well advised to move the volume forward until the notes begin to move. The first six entrances are marked with accents. We should always consider the character of the music and the prevailing dynamic level in regulating the style and amount of accent that is appropriate. The accents in *piano* or *mezzo piano* should be heard as a solid attack rather than as an explosion. The accent in m. 37 should be colorful and exciting. There is some wonderful counterpoint between m. 50 and m. 58. The first notes of the imitations must be heard clearly.

For this sonata the straight mute should be on a flattened stand. Covering the stand with a dark cloth is helpful to absorb any sound made while handling the mute. The mute can be placed with the larger end toward the player to facilitate the grasp and the insertion. There is enough time to insert and withdraw the mute before m. 17 and after m. 27. At m. 41 we should hang the mute from our wrist because there is not enough time to reach for it before m. 63. Playing with a hanging mute is uncomfortable for some players. We could practice etudes occasionally with the mute hanging from our wrist just to become accustomed to it. We must also practice the insertion and withdrawal of the mute until the procedure is silent and quick. Twisting the mute is not necessary or advisable. We all have a tendency to overplay our mutes in soft dynamics and not to play loudly enough in *forte* or *fortissimo*. A good mute will take these extremes, but we must make the effort. At *fortissimo*, it takes a lot of energy to generate a large amount of muted volume. At *pianissimo* we are concerned with being heard and being safe. In this movement, however, we do not have either *pianissimo* or *fortissimo*, but since there is no problem of balance with the piano we can keep our soft muted playing at a very low volume. The glissando and the bend should be long and slow. Measure 63 to the end should be noticeably softer than the other muted passages.

In the third movement the composer alternates the jazz feeling, written as triplet figures, with the square feeling of the sixteenth-notes. We should not attempt to swing the sixteenth-notes. The triplet figures can be relaxed and played with a soft legato tongue. The tempo of quarter-note equals 100 is slow enough to indicate that there is little rhythmic drive or tension in the horn part. Some musicians refer to this feeling as "laid back." Except for the sixteenth-note runs that are marked with a diminuendo, we must move the air forward on all of these groups so that the ends of the groups are as clear as the beginnings. The solid beat that Wilder mentions in the title is maintained by the pianist, who is active on nearly every beat in the movement. We must be willing to play the movement at the tempo indicated and not permit it to rush ahead. The essence of the feeling of jazz is the unfailing beat against the flexibility of the melodic line. In the horn part this is heard in the loose feeling of the triplets as compared with the exact placing of every sixteenth-note. We might wish to start the meno mosso in m. 75 rather than in m. 76. Wherever we start to play more slowly it must not be slower than quarter-note equals 84.

The fourth movement is a waltz, which contrasts the exuberance of its outer sections with the restrained warmth of the poco meno mosso from m. 37 to m. 84. The change in tempo should allow the ebullience of the first tempo to be replaced by quiet nostalgia. For this section Wilder chose an accompaniment figure for the piano that is an almost constant reminder of the first section. Played at a slower tempo, it becomes ironical, since the notes are somewhat the same but their meaning is different. Wilder accomplishes this with only the perfect fifth and slow-moving harmony. Notice that the a tempo at m. 55 and m. 75 restores the prevailing meno mosso tempo. The Tempo I at m. 84 brings the music back to its original tempo.

This is not a sonata of great technical difficulty or theatrical grandeur. It is music of sophistication and subtlety for which we need a variety of tongue strokes, a willingness to be free with the tempo, some familiarity with the part of the musical world from which this music came, and both the desire and the ability to be carefree in attitude and performance.

In addition to the sonatas that have been discussed, other excellent works in this form have been written by Samuel Adler, Leslie Bassett, Edith Borroff, Robert Sanders, and Gunther Schuller. Of particular interest is the recent (1990) *Sonata da Chiesa for Horn and Piano* by Don Gillespie. Among its movements is a balanced mixture of energy and lyricism. As the title suggests, it looks back somewhat to the eighteenth century in its four-movement form and highly contrapuntal texture. As we have seen in other twentieth-century works for horn, this sonata also recalls the horn's outdoor tradition through its prominent use of the perfect intervals. The horn part is well supplied with short rests and, as the composer suggests in his preface notes, the fourth movement is the least taxing, since it is the last of a fifteen-minute work. Don Gillespie, an excellent pianist, wrote this sonata for his son Kane.

# CHAPTER 5
# CONCERTOS WITH PIANO

### The Mozart horn concertos

Most horn players are content to refer to these concertos as

Concerto No. 1 in D, K. 412
Concerto No. 2 in E-flat, K. 417
Concerto No. 3 in E-flat, K. 447
Concerto No. 4 in E-flat, K. 495.

Recent scholarship is doing much to sort out the order of composition of these works and to relieve our anxiety over why K. 412 has but two movements. The excellent article by Brian Ernest Thompson in *The Horn Call Annual* of 1989 answers some of our questions while we await further discoveries. For the next several pages, the Mozart horn concertos are identified as above.

Any discussion of the Mozart horn concertos is bound to include a horn player named Ignaz Leutgeb (or, sometimes, Leitgeb). Mozart must have found something very agreeable and entertaining in the man, who was the target of his good-natured jokes. For Ignaz Leutgeb, Mozart wrote four concertos and the Quintet for Horn and Strings, K. 407, which would seem to confirm the composer's high regard for the horn player's ability if not for his erudition. It is not likely that Leutgeb was consulted on technical or musical matters in the writing of these works, since Mozart, from his orchestral writing, understood thoroughly the instrument now referred to as the natural horn. He had no good reason to seek musical advice from Leutgeb. Thus, these concertos give us a clear picture of Mozart's view of the horn as a solo instrument with orchestral accompaniment, and of his handling of the concerto as a form to accommodate the instrument. In contrast, when Brahms wrote his violin concerto there was extensive technical and musical consultation between the composer and Joseph Joachim, who was one of the most highly respected violinists of his time.

The study of the Mozart horn concertos must reach far beyond these four works. Even a superficial study of the horn parts in the Mozart symphonies and operas reveals that he treated the orchestral horns as providers of harmony, volume, and rhythm with few melodic responsibilities. Mozart did not swerve from this well-established classical approach. Even in the last symphonies, the horns were given their traditional duties of tonic and dominant and were often paired with the oboes. With few exceptions Mozart's orchestral horn parts are written for a horn whose length corresponds to the key of the movement within the symphony, or to the aria within the opera. The horn player in the classical orchestra does not have to play many solos or notes not found in the harmonic series. It is in the chamber music, particularly in the Quintets K. 407 and K. 452, and in the concertos that Mozart reaches beyond the orchestral technique to place the horn on a more equal status with other instruments.

For brass quintet players, a study of the string quartet literature is recommended as one path toward a greater understanding of individual composers, stylistic periods, and for general musical growth beyond the limits imposed by brass literature. Along with our technical study of the solo parts of the Mozart horn concertos, a most natural companion study is that of the piano concertos of the classical period and especially those of Mozart. There are musicians who are thoroughly convinced that the genius of Mozart is most clearly evident in his operas and in his concertos for piano and orchestra.

Because Mozart wrote his piano concertos for his own use, they create a personal image of him as a composer, a pianist, and an orchestrator. They also testify to his ability to compose music of the highest quality in prodigious bursts of energy. Orchestral musicians know that Mozart composed his last three symphonies in about six weeks during the summer of 1788. Perhaps less well-known is that between 1784 and 1786, Mozart wrote twelve piano concertos, six of them composed in 1784. Our study of Mozart and the concerto could begin with any of these concertos. There is no shortage of scores or recordings of them. For horn players who are temporarily uncomfortable with studying from a full orchestral score, the accompaniments of these concertos have been arranged for a second piano. In 1785 Mozart wrote his first piano concerto in a minor key, K. 466. Its study is especially valuable for horn players, since it is a distant spiritual cousin of the Horn Concerto K. 447.

One cannot help but envy the young (perhaps fifteen years old) horn student about to embark on a study of these magnificent works. How much better to be introduced to Mozart through his greatest concertos than through the restricted use of the horn in the symphonies or through a deplorable band arrangement of *Eine Kleine Nachtmusik*! Is it not also better to look at Mozart through his music than to see the man through the vision of starry-eyed biographers, advisable to find the similarities as well as the differences between the great piano concertos and the wind concertos, and necessary to study the cadenzas of the Mozart piano concertos in preparation for the cadenzas in the horn concertos?

Nearly all of the concertos from the classical period require a cadenza in one or more movements. There are editions with cadenzas written by the editor; other editions have cadenzas written by unidentified editors; and still others mark the beginning of the cadenza by a fermata but offer no cadenza. That any horn player improvises cadenzas these days is extremely doubtful, and perhaps horn players never really did. We are left with the choice of playing someone else's cadenza or writing one for our own use. If we write our own, we should have a secure knowledge of the distinctive characteristics of the composer and the historical period.

Mozart wrote cadenzas for several of his piano concertos, and this would be a good place to begin our study. Modern editions of the Mozart piano concertos contain cadenzas written by other composers, including Muzio Clementi and Johann Nepomuk Hummel, whose names, if not much of their music, are well known to pianists, if not to horn players. More recent pianist-composers have also written cadenzas for the Mozart piano concertos.

After studying and listening to some of these cadenzas, it will be apparent that the writing of cadenzas follows no formula. We can, however, develop a sense of proportion by comparing the length of these cadenzas with the length of the various other sections of the movement to which they are attached. The internal structure can be studied by observing

1. the beginning and end of cadenzas
2. the frequency of fermatas or full-stop cadences
3. the time ratio between technical and more lyrical sections
4. the statements of main themes
5. the use of transition material
6. the use of completely new material.

Some thought should be given to whether we are bound to use only those notes that were available to Mozart and other composers writing for what is now called the *hand horn technique*. A listing of all of the notes used by Mozart in his horn concertos will reveal the extent to which he used notes outside the harmonic series. It is also evident that he used these "chromatic" notes most often in the lyrical sections. If we are concerned more with musical style than with a rigid adhesion to theory, we can construct a cadenza by following a scheme whose harmonic implications are more free in the lyrical sections and more restricted in the technical sections. If we find it necessary to use notes that Mozart did not use, we will be forgiven by all but the most intolerant of musical accountants. However, we must know the harmonic boundaries of Mozart well enough that our choices of notes do not constitute an invasion of alien harmonic territory. The harmony associated with the notes, rather than the notes themselves, should govern our choices.

Although the first movements of only the third and fourth horn concertos of Mozart require cadenzas, the majority of classical concertos follow the tradition of reserving a place for the cadenza after the recapitulation has run its course. After the cadenza there is a short coda, during which the soloist may or may not play.

In a typical classical concerto, the accompaniment has an interlude between the end of the recapitulation and the beginning of the cadenza. The interlude introduces the cadenza by its arrival at a fermata on the tonic chord. This fermata could never be mistaken to be the last chord of the movement because it has the fifth, not the root, of the chord as its lowest note. By this simple means the tonality is firmly established, but there is no sense of finality. The accompanist, pianist, or conductor makes this moment more dramatic by slowing down the tempo several beats before the fermata. Cadenzas in the second or third movements do not always have such a grand approach.

The observations that follow are not a blueprint for the writing of classical period cadenzas, but they are meant to be of help to those who are writing a cadenza for the first time. If we have had the normal training in traditional harmony, a rudimentary knowledge of notation, and have studied cadenzas by using the previously listed seven items pertinent to cadenzas, we should be equipped to make a start.

The first decision we must make concerns the use of bar lines. While it is true that bar lines have the effect of providing metric control, it is also true that cadenzas, not having the ensemble restraints imposed by an accompaniment, are played quite freely, whether there are bar lines or not. Bar lines serve to organize music into a logical and satisfying rhythmic flow and are, therefore, very helpful in the construction of phrases. Bar lines can be used during the writing of the cadenza and removed later if there is good reason to do so.

The first theme of the movement is often used to begin the cadenza. This works well if we have decided to use a three-part structure of fast-slow-fast for our cadenza. It also works well if the first theme has some rhythmic motion and energy. It does not work as well if this theme has been heard during the last part of the recapitulation or in the transition to the cadenza. For the third Mozart concerto the first theme is a good choice because it has some motion and has not been heard since the beginning of the recapitulation.

Example 5-1

By comparison, we can see that the first theme of the first movement of the fourth concerto is rather stationary:

Example 5-2

In working with the actual themes from the movement, we should present them, at least once, in the same character and spirit as portrayed by the composer. As an extreme example, one would not begin our cadenza for the third concerto by doubling or halving the note values and casting them in a minor key far removed from E-flat major. After establishing the thematic material, or part of it, we can then begin to extend it, vary it by ornamentation, make sequential patterns, and start to move toward the place where the music comes to rest on a long note, often written as a fermata. The underlying harmony at this point should suggest a noticeable departure from E-flat major. If we can manage to arrive at a concert pitch A-natural for this first fermata, we have created an interesting shift in tonality, but in doing so have reached the leading tone of B-flat major, which, as everyone knows, is the dominant of E-flat major and the tonality that is often used for second themes. Pianists can play chords and string players can use double stops to define harmony, but we have only the melodic line with which to work.

This first fermata should not be so near the beginning of the cadenza that it feels as if the music has hardly begun before it stops. In a cadenza that contains four fermatas or other definite cadence points, we should choose four pitches, and they are best distributed throughout the registers. A fermata in a cadenza serves two purposes: it brings a section to an interesting close and it creates an expectation for what is to come. Not to follow a fermata with new material makes the fermata meaningless.

After the first fermata, it is effective to rise to a higher level of technical difficulty and speed of execution. The history of the cadenza suggests that technical display was the first and main reason for its existence. Vocal cadenzas, from which our concerto cadenzas evolved, were placed near the end of arias and often had no thematic connection with the aria. When composers such as Mozart and Clementi wrote and played their own piano concertos, they began to link the cadenza thematically to the movement, if sometimes only briefly. Since we have begun our cadenza with a strong reference to one of the main themes of the movement, we are now free to find an interesting rhythmic fragment or melodic motive to act as a catalyst for this more technical section of the cadenza. Very often these figures can be found in the accompaniment, in the introduction, or in one of the transition sections. This, from measure 97, offers some possibilities:

Example 5-3

Combining this figure with a contrasting one might be interesting:

Example 5-4

If we have two motives from which to draw, we can write a rather extended passage of some technical brilliance. This part of the cadenza should gain energy and momentum to the next fermata, which is most dramatic when it is long and in either of the outer registers. It must not suggest E-flat major.

So far we have had a section with some motion with strong thematic identification, followed by technically brilliant passages based on motives from the accompaniment. We are now ready for a more relaxed lyrical feeling. The first movement has several possibilities, including

Example 5-5

or
Example 5-6

This part of the cadenza can be the most chromatic by following Mozart's habit of staying rather close to E-flat and related tonalities when technique is involved, and moving well away from the center when lyricism prevails. The close of the lyrical component of the cadenza could be very quiet in contrast to the end of the technical passages. To close the cadenza there is a need to reestablish E-flat major through a series of technical events involving scales and arpeggios that lead to a trill on concert F or B-flat. We should also begin to establish a feeling of meter and tempo before the final cadence. The most satisfying way to end a classical-period cadenza is to have the trill occupy one complete measure in the tempo of that which follows. This is not a time to be clever and deceptive but an opportunity to conclude the cadenza in an orderly and natural way. Cadenzas from the nineteenth and twentieth centuries can come to their conclusion without a strong feeling of close, but classical cadenzas seem to require a well-defined final cadence.

Again, these suggestions are only general guidelines for a first attempt at writing a cadenza. Until one has written several cadenzas, it seems prudent to outline a plan of events before writing any notes. After gaining some experience in this endeavor we will be able to plan the cadenza according to the music, rather than the reverse of fitting the music to fulfill the plan. We must have ears that are capable of imagining pitches, rhythm, and harmonic implications. Our mind's ear should be developed well enough to allow us to sit at our desks and write the music as we hear it. As in any other musical project, we gather information through study, practice by experimenting, and seek the counsel of experts. Until we have taken these steps we are correct in assuming that we cannot write a cadenza. "Consuming" another musician's cadenza is always easier than producing our own; easier is not always better. If Ignaz Leutgeb could improvise a cadenza, should it not be possible for us, after years of expensive training and study, to write our own?

Cadenzas in the first movement of classical concertos can also be quite short. Vocal cadenzas were often little more than a flourish—the length of one breath.

Occasionally there is a place for a cadenza in the slow movement of a concerto. These cadenzas should not disrupt the lyrical nature of the music, nor should they, since they often occur quite late in the movement, be so long or so active as to interfere with the natural flow toward the end. Cadenzas in the last movements should also be short and in the general spirit of the movement.

Joseph Joachim (1837–1907) was one of the great nineteenth century violinists. In addition to his career as orchestral player and soloist, he was a composer, teacher, and leader of the Joachim Quartet. His playing was known and admired by composers from Mendelssohn to Brahms. His most lasting legacy to us is his cadenzas for the violin concertos of Mozart, Beethoven, and Brahms. While playing the orchestral accompaniment to the Brahms Violin Concerto, first horn players often do not really listen to the cadenza that Joachim wrote because of concern with the *pianissimo* entrance just as the cadenza concludes. Yet this cadenza preserves the idyllic serenity, the noble grandeur, and the powerful gravity of the concerto and is an excellent example of how a cadenza begins as a continuation of the preceding tutti and ends by leading very gently into a calm final statement of the first theme. Because of his understanding of this concerto and of the concerto as a form, and because of his practiced skill as a composer and violinist, Joachim succeeded in capturing the reality of this magnificent work.

Joachim lived in the same era as Brahms and came to know the composer and his works thoroughly. We cannot know Mozart as a man, and we can only look back at his era, but we can know his music by studying the great works he produced. Our performances of the horn concertos cannot fail to be elevated by our arriving at an understanding of the composer and his other concertos.

This understanding, or maturity, if you will, seems to develop by stages. During their high school years, young players are often introduced to the third concerto because it has no high notes or because its technical demands are less than those of the second and fourth concertos. The third concerto is found to be very pleasant and a readily playable piece of music but not nearly as exciting as either of the concertos by Richard Strauss or Reinhold Glière. This attitude prevails until the college years, when the second or fourth concerto is studied and a wise and vigilant teacher insists that the technique is impeccable and matters of style are investigated. The fourth concerto takes on new meaning when it is discovered that part of it is often required for professional auditions or competitions. The third stage occurs after a professional career has begun and the player is contracted to play or record one or all of the Mozart horn concertos. At this time, intensive study of the music is undertaken, or should be; recordings by other artists are consulted, and musical decisions are made. The mature artist then is in a position to make musical decisions bolstered by scholarship but not compromised by technical apprehensions. Tempo is a good place to begin our search for musical understanding and maturity.

Composers learn, often to their sorrow, that without the right tempo music can be distorted beyond recognition. Mozart, in his letters, makes so many references to tempo that we can be assured that he was often disturbed by the differences between his conception of speed and that of many performers. Since Mozart lived before the invention of the metronome, other means, such as the human pulse, were used to convey a sense of tempo. We know now that the heart can beat at a wide range of speeds, but the most common is between 72 and 80 beats per minute. Another even more imprecise way of measuring tempo was the speed of walking. This is not to suggest that musicians of Mozart's time regularly consulted their heart beats or their footsteps to determine musical speed, but rather to indicate that 72–80 beats per minute was an ingrained part of their musical consciousness. Horn players who have served time in concert bands come to rely on Sousa marches to determine, to a fair degree of accuracy, a speed of quarter-note equals 120. Past musical experiences can also help or hinder us in our feelings about speed. If, for example, we have always heard the first movement of the Beethoven Fifth Symphony played within a range of half-note equals 100–112 we will be unhappy with a speed of 126 and will consider it to be a "wrong" tempo. The "right" tempo is identified as the speed at which a composition has been most often played or recorded. Whether the tempo conforms to the composer's tempo or is appropriate musically is another matter.

We can begin to narrow the range of speed for the movements of the four horn concertos by looking at the words Mozart chose to indicate tempo and character:

| Concerto No. 1 | Movement I | Allegro |
| | Movement II | Allegro |
| Concerto No. 2 | Movement I | Allegro maestoso |
| | Movement II | Andante |
| | Movement III | Allegro |

| Concerto No. 3 | Movement I | Allegro |
| | Movement II | Larghetto |
| | Movement III | Allegro |
| Concerto No. 4 | Movement I | Allegro moderato |
| | Movement II | Andante |
| | Movement III | Allegro vivace |

If we take these words as Mozart's own we find that he used allegro eight times in the eleven movements, andante twice, and larghetto once. There is no allegro assai, allegro molto, presto, adagio, largo, or lento, all of which Mozart used in his piano concertos and other works. Allegro moderato is used as a precaution against excessive speed and allegro vivace is meant to be lively in spirit but not necessarily faster than allegro. Allegro maestoso is also used to indicate spirit and character. There is no compelling evidence to suggest that movements marked only allegro must vary greatly in speed from those marked allegro moderato, allegro maestoso, or allegro vivace. Larghetto and andante are among the most problematic of all tempo indications. Folk wisdom tells us that andante moves at a walking speed, but that gives us a too-broad range of choices. Larghetto, as the ending implies, is a diminutive of largo and is used correctly as a tempo less slow than largo.

If we take quarter-note equals 72–80 as a middle ground of speed and andante as a middle point between largo and presto, we can establish a basis for larghetto on the slower side of andante and allegro on the faster side. We must never be influenced by where the manufacturers of metronomes place their boundaries of the various words for speed. We know, for example, that moderato cannot be confined between 108 and 120, as it appears on some metronomes.

The second movement of the fourth concerto is marked andante. If we set our metronome at quarter-note equals 69 and sing, not play, the first phrase, we have a very agreeable tempo.

Example 5-7

By testing the tempo in the middle section of the movement (beginning at m. 41), we find that it works well for this material also. All of us have heard this movement played with a disturbing più mosso in the middle section. We should find a general tempo that serves the music throughout the movement. When we play the first four measures on the horn at this tempo, we may be temporarily uneasy with the speed of the sixteenth-notes. We must make sure that we do not reduce the time available for these sixteenth-notes by moving late after the tied note. It is helpful to think of the sixteenth-notes as ornamental passing tones. Practicing the phrase without the sixteenth-notes is also helpful:

Example 5-8

By doing so we discover that the phrase could prosper without the sixteenth-notes and that their true function is ornamental. Another consideration is the relative speed of the triplets and sixteenth-notes. We can think of the triplets as being played as slowly as the tempo will allow and the sixteenth-notes as quickly as the tempo will allow. One hastens to add the stipulations that all notes must be heard clearly, the note values must not be distorted, and there is never a feeling of rushing or of tension. By singing the phrase before playing it we have an opportunity of arriving at a tempo and style through our experiences and instincts. By first playing the phrase we are more likely to be influenced by physical and technical limitations to the detriment of the music. We develop our technique to serve the music. We must never alter the music to accommodate our inadequacies.

Since Mozart also used andante for the tempo indication of the second movement of the second concerto, it would be interesting to sing through several phrases to see whether a metronome setting of eighth-note equals 72 might be appropriate for this movement. Because slow music depends on harmonic motion as well as melodic and rhythmic motion, we must be able to imagine the harmony of the accompaniment as we sing the melodic line. Eighth-note equals 72 seems to be a tempo that pleases many horn players and it also seems to fit both musically and physically until we reach mm. 38–45. Musically there is no acceptable place to breathe during these measures, and we cannot justify speeding up the tempo to accommodate a lack of capacity. This phrase lasts approximately seventeen seconds. By setting our metronome at 60 and holding a long tone for seventeen beats we can strengthen our capacity and develop a feeling of pacing our air supply. It is best, at first, to practice holding these long tones at *mezzo forte* rather than at *piano* and then gradually reduce the volume to *piano*. Players with a well-developed capacity will find little difficulty with these measures; others will have to work to achieve a good air supply. In the second movement of the fourth concerto there is another of these long phrases between mm. 34 and 41.

The slow movement of the third concerto is marked larghetto, not andante. If we believe that these words are, indeed, Mozart's own and that he did not choose these words frivolously, it follows that this movement should have a pulse slower than the 69 of the Andante movements of the second and fourth concertos. Using our procedure of singing before playing, we find that quarter-note equals 60 produces a tempo that fits the color and serious quality of the music while also permitting a flow of motion through the eighth-notes. It is sometimes played as quickly as quarter-note equals 76. One hopes that this faster tempo was chosen after wide study and long deliberation.

All of the final movements of these concertos have a time signature of 6/8. All are marked allegro except in the fourth concerto, where it is allegro vivace. Even though they all recall their hunting ancestry, there is no reason to play them at the same tempo, or, since all are rondos, to play all of the material in these movements at the same tempo. The thematic material of the last movements of the third and fourth concertos have repeated pitches as their main source of rhythmic energy, while the first and second concertos rely more upon arpeggiated figures. In acknowledging the subjectivity of the means used to arrive at the conclusion, it seems reasonable to play the final movements of the first and second concertos somewhat slower than the final movements of the third and fourth concertos. Is it not interesting that Mozart wrote the same sixteenth-note figure in the celli and basses of the orchestra in the fourth measure of the third movement of both the second and fourth concertos? This figure should not influence, unduly, our decisions on tempi. If we believe that the nature of the music should guide us toward an appropriate tempo we might consider the following for the rondo movements:

Concerto No. 1: dotted quarter equals 76
Concerto No. 2: dotted quarter equals 96
Concerto No. 3: dotted quarter equals 116
Concerto No. 4: dotted quarter equals 120–126.

The first movements of these concertos have many similarities.

1.  All are in 4/4.
2.  All begin with an introduction in the accompaniment only.
3.  All are lyrical movements with a few technical passages.
4.  All have a modified sonata-allegro form.
5.  All are more chromatic in their second (development) section than in their outer (exposition and recapitulation) sections.
6.  All are more lyrical in their second sections.
7.  With the exception of the first concerto, there are no references to the main themes in the sections usually labeled development.
8.  There are stronger and more numerous cadence points in the outer sections.
9.  All flow very well at speeds between quarter-note equals 100 and 116.

All of this suggests that Mozart wrote these first movements from an orderly and pre-conceived plan that drew upon his experience with sonata-allegro form. His use of new material in what would be the development section is far from unique. We can speculate that his close adherence to tonic and dominant in the outer sections prompted him to seek contrast in the middle sections by the use of new and more chromatic material. Whatever the motivation, these middle sections serve to confirm that the sonata-allegro form can be very flexible; they attest to Mozart's ability to use the form in his own way. Never at a loss for an irresistible combination of melodic lines and harmonic elegance, Mozart used these sections as small arias for the horn to sing. They all have very simple accompaniments that outline an eloquent harmonic background without becoming competitive.

For the lyrical playing in these first movements we must have a tongue stroke that is perfectly balanced between attack and air flow. It must be reliable in all registers, speeds, and dynamic levels. This type of tongue stroke is particularly necessary for the first notes after silences. It can be practiced in the warm-up as outlined in Part I, Example 1-1. This is especially advisable for orchestral players who are often required to use a heavier attack. For the technical playing we can develop a tongue stroke that is short but not blunt, pointed but not accented. One way to acquire this stroke is to practice the following at quarter-note equals 112:

Example 5-9

For the half-notes a completely legato stroke should be used. As the notes become quicker, we shorten the ends of the notes but do not change the style of the beginning of the notes. For some players this is a natural stroke; others must work to maintain the integrity of the beginnings of the notes while shortening the length of the notes as they become faster. The tape recorder is necessary for this exercise since we can easily mistake the effort for the result. While we hope that playing these first movements faster than quarter-note equals 112 will never be necessary, we should practice this stroke at every metronome setting between 96 and 126. Each note value in the exercise can be repeated as many times as necessary. This stroke is most successful when the tongue moves the shortest possible distance, and the response is most reliable when the corners are firm. It can be practiced at all dynamic levels but should be practiced most often at a volume consistent with its use in these concertos. It can be practiced on any pitch found in the Mozart horn concertos.

It is generally understood that the highest volume level in a Mozart concerto will be less than that of a concerto by Richard Strauss or Reinhold Glière, but the lowest level will be much the same. Because the horn is the soloist and, therefore, must be heard as a solo voice and not as a blending inner voice, we need to find that point in our volume scale below which we cease to have the projection necessary to be heard above the accompaniment. This lowest volume will be higher when we play with an orchestra than when we play with a piano. There is also the quality of sound to consider. Below a certain volume level the horn sound loses its ringing quality and its ability to separate from the tones around it. This is one of its virtues as an ensemble instrument, but, within reason, the role of the soloist is not to blend but to be the leading voice. Horn players with dark tone qualities must be especially sensitive to when their softer dynamic levels become dull rather than rich and vibrant. Bright players must know when their higher dynamic levels become strident. Judging these matters in a small, dead practice room without the accompaniment is difficult. Words such as *strident, vibrant, rich, bright, dark*, and *dull* give only a faint description of the sound. We must not be so absorbed in our own part that we forget that the accompaniment, whether it is piano or orchestra, must have its own resonance. To soften the accompaniment to the point that it has no vitality will destroy the spirit of the music. The total sound of volume and quality must be in balance.

Pianists, singers, and violinists must also make adjustments in their technical, musical, and volume patterns to conform to a classical style. Their adjustments are much like our own in attacks, releases, and restraints of tempo and volume. Having touched upon attacks, tempo, and volume, we can turn our attention to releases. In the movements with time signatures of 3/4 or 4/4, nearly every phrase ends with a quarter-note. Even in the second movement of the second concerto, which is in 3/8, the last notes of phrases are often quarter-notes. These final notes must be full value and end with a tapered release. We can refer again to Example 1-1 and our releases of long notes. Where the harmony does not change immediately after our release, we can afford ourselves the luxury of a slightly longer final note and an even more elegant release. We also must develop a quickly tapered release for occasions when we must breathe and reenter. We should plan to arrive at these final notes of phrases with enough volume to complete the phrase and be able to taper the volume down to silence. In long phrases our good breathing and body support techniques will be valuable.

The ancestry of the piano accompaniments of the Mozart horn concertos can be traced back to Henri Adrien Louis Kling (1842–1918) otherwise identified as Henry Kling, H. von Kling, or simply H. Kling. He is known today for his training method entitled *Horn-Schule*, from which etudes and exercises have been extracted by various editors. These etudes are written in the style of Kopprasch, with much more emphasis on patterns, sequences, and repetitions.

Kling followed the accompaniment scheme of Mozart in which the first violins (right hand) have the melody and the three lower voices (left hand) have the harmony and rhythm. Kling often chose to use either repeated chords for the harmony or the arpeggiated figures known as Alberti bass. These devices were standard classic fare used by Haydn, Mozart, and Beethoven in all of their piano writing and can be seen throughout Kling's piano reductions of the orchestral scores of the Mozart horn concertos. Experienced and sensitive pianists realize that repeated chords on the piano sound quite different from repeated bow strokes in the second violins and violas, especially when the chords are thickened by the use of the damper pedal. Alberti bass, named for Domenico Alberti (c. 1710–1740), when played on the harpsichord can give an open-textured harmonic background and rhythmic energy. Played on the modern piano it can sound heavy, competitive, and distracting. When the horn is playing, the pianist must play these accompaniment patterns with great restraint. We should remember that these piano arrangements of orchestral scores were intended more as study aids than for recital purposes.

Henri Kling, who was a horn player, teacher, composer, and organist, provided dynamics, slurs, dots, and such words as *espressivo, grazioso, dolce*, etc. These notes give us Kling's opinions on these matters. When Leutgeb played these concertos, we can imagine that he was given not much more than Mozart's notes and rests with the expectation that he would provide everything else he thought necessary. This became the Leutgeb "edition," never published, as far as we know, but perhaps this was the beginning of a tradition, for good or evil, which led to the Kling edition. The Kling phrasing and articulations seem right to us mainly because we hear them, or something similar, most often. It is comforting to see that some of our greatest contemporary artists have ventured into the troubled waters of editing, thus giving us the benefit of their scholarship, musicianship, and experience. Eventually we all make our own editions of these concertos for our own performances just as Leutgeb did. One hopes that our scholarship, musicianship, and experiences are sufficient for the task.

Throughout these four concertos is the traditional sixteenth-note articulation of two notes slurred and two notes tongued. This articulation pattern seems to fit the Mozart concertos, since the slurred notes soften the effect of the tongue. The slur must not be constant or automatic. If we feel that a tongued passage could be described as grazioso, we could consider using the two-slurred, two-tongued grouping. We can tongue each note if we feel that a more energetic character is needed. If we choose to slur the first two notes of the groups, we must blow completely through the second note so that it will project enough to be heard as a note equal in volume to the tongued notes. It is the only note in the pattern that does not begin with a tongue. Peter Damm has written more about Mozart editions and articulation in a fine article in *The Horn Call* of November, 1978.

## Concerto No. 1 in D, K. 412

We should not be greatly concerned that we now have three Mozart horn concertos in E-flat and only one in D. By Mozart's time, the middle lengths of horns—F, E, E-flat, and D—were well established as being appropriate for solo playing. We should be concerned with the intonation considerations connected with playing in D major. For the first concerto, these notes, written here for convenience as horn in F, need special attention:

Example 5-10

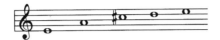

Horn players know that e¹ is the fifth partial on the F horn and is noticeably flat when left uncorrected. Normally, when playing with the piano we tune the F side of the double horn by using the sixth partial (g¹) as our tuning note. If g¹ is in tune with the piano, and if we have done nothing with our embouchures or our right hand to alter the pitch, we can assume that our main slide and our F slides are in good positions for most of the F horn notes. Our e¹, however, is still low in pitch. This note is very important in the tonality of D major, since it is the fifth scale degree. A large majority of the phrases in this concerto contain this note. Many times throughout the concerto this flat note is followed by a¹, which tends to be sharp when played with its normal fingering of 1 + 2 on the B-flat horn. When we consider all of this information we see the benefit of tuning the F side of the double horn slightly higher than usual. Checking e¹ and a¹ with the piano is a good idea to see how much embouchure adjustment is necessary to play these notes exactly in tune. We can raise the e¹ with the F slide without affecting the B-flat side of the horn. If we try to lower the a¹ by pulling out the main slide, we also lower the e¹ on the F horn. We can, however, lower the a¹ and d² on the B-flat horn by extending slightly the first valve slide on the B-flat horn. We must not also pull out the second valve slide because it must be in a good position to produce e². (All of these references to pitch are for horn in F.) The 2 + 3 combination also needs attention for playing in D major. When the main slide and the first and second slides are in position, we should check the 2 + 3 on the B-flat horn to see whether the C-sharp and G-sharp are high enough. The third valve slide on either side of the double horn is often extended a routine quarter of an inch. If, in checking our 2 + 3 with the piano, we find that it is low, we should feel free to push the third B-flat slide all of the way in, if necessary, to bring our 2 + 3 up to pitch. Again, do not move the second slide, since we use the second valve by itself so often. To review our procedures for setting the slides for playing in D major:

1. Check the sixth partial notes (g¹ and c²) as usual to see whether the general pitch of the horn is reasonable. Do not alter the pitch by adjusting the embouchure, right hand, or air stream. *Mezzo forte* on a horn at room temperature should produce a reliable pitch.
2. Test the e¹ with the piano. If it is low in pitch push in the F tuning slide. It may be necessary to push in the F slide as much as a quarter inch or more. Our goal is to raise the F horn enough that the e¹ can be played with a minimum of embouchure adjustment, but not so much that all other notes on the F horn are unacceptably high. There are very few notes on any horn that do not need some pitch adjustment. A horn that is well in tune is a horn that is played well in tune. Slide placement can keep these adjustments to a comfortable minimum.

3. Check the 1 + 2 combinations on the B-flat horn. If they are high we can lower them by extending the first slide, but not the second.
4. Tune the 2 + 3 combinations with the piano. If they are low we can raise them by pushing in the third valve slide but not the second.

These manipulations do not guarantee perfect intonation, of course. Only our ears can do that. Our purpose here is to allow us to make all of the physical adjustments of pitch as small as possible. The less we do with our embouchure the greater our accuracy will be. The less we do with our right hand the more even our tone quality will be. We must always remember that the pianist cannot make any pitch adjustment to accommodate our instrument. Intonation is always much easier when we play with another instrument that can conform to our pitch deviations. The trombone, after all, is one long tuning slide. Intonation training for young players should begin as soon as the embouchure has gained enough strength and flexibility to be able to move the pitch on middle-register notes. Working with the tuner is just fine. Sustaining intervals with the private teacher is very good experience in listening and adjusting. The college years are rather late in the training to begin a serious and orderly study of intonation. After four or more precollege years of not being concerned with intonation, the ears have become accustomed to accepting whatever the embouchure produces. The sounding of an A or B-flat at the beginning of an orchestra or band rehearsal does very little for the horn player's intonation skills. Watching the electronic tuner, matching unison pitches with the piano, playing intervals with teachers or colleagues are all ways of working on intonation. During performances we must never allow our attention to be diverted from intonation. A performance with otherwise perfect technique and musicianship is ruined by faulty intonation.

There is a difficult lip trill at m. 51, or rehearsal letter C, in some editions of the Mozart first horn concerto. A fingering of 2 + 3 on the F horn gives the best intonation for this trill. 2 + 3 makes the horn quite long. For these long trills, our trilling motions should be somewhat larger and more aggressive than for trills on open notes. Fingered 2 + 3, the lower note of the trill is an extension of the seventh partial. Most lip trills on the F horn have the eighth or a higher partial as the lower note. We know from our study of the harmonic series that there is more than a whole step from the seventh to the eighth partial. The longer trill created by the 2 + 3 fingering and the longer distance between the seventh and eighth partials conspire to make this fingering more difficult physically than trills that have the eighth partial as the lower note. We can perfect this lip trill by practicing all of the seventh to eighth partial trills that start on the open seventh partial. After several days of practicing the open trill, we can begin to add the second finger, then the first finger, and 1 + 2, and finally 2 + 3. Notice how wide the whole step sounds when it is played open. Notice how the intonation improves with every addition of valve tubing. Notice how each addition of tubing makes the notes feel less well-centered. If we extend the exercise to include 1 + 3 and 1 + 2 + 3, notice how the notes become even more insecure. By using 2 + 3 on this trill we have chosen to use the fingering that gives the best result rather than a fingering that is easier instantly. Easier is better only if the result is better. The work done to perfect the more difficult lip trills will surely help the "easier" lip trills.

Most musicians agree that Mozart sounds natural, simple, and spontaneous. One of the reasons his music seems uncomplicated is his use of long melodic lines. If we look at the first eight measures of the horn part of the first concerto, we find that there is, indeed, a melody that lasts for eight measures.

Example 5-11

The quarter-rest in the fourth measure does not interrupt the flow of melody but does offer a convenient breathing place. We can test this by playing through the quarter-rest. There is a general upward direction to the line, and the most energetic moment occurs at the end of the phrase. This is not a phrase that arches toward the middle only to relax toward the end. The activity and the pitches rise as the phrase unfolds. Those who wish to pursue further the subject of phrase contours might compare this phrase with the first eight measures of the second movement of the Beethoven Second Symphony, where there is a perfectly symmetrical melodic arch of four rising measures and four descending measures.

Example 5-12

Notice also how Beethoven used one moving measure and one stationary measure to build his arch. Mozart's line has its apex at the end of the phrase; Beethoven's arch has its apex in the middle of the phrase. There is no better, worse, right, or wrong in this comparison, but rather two master composers at work, each in his own way. This view of Mozart's phrase tells us that we must keep the volume and the energy moving toward the final note and not treat the quarter-rest as signifying a phrase ending that must be relaxed.

All of the sixteenth-note passages in the first movement should be played with a feeling of gentleness rather than excitement. This is more readily accomplished at a metronome setting nearer 100 than 112. We must not react to all the sixteenth-notes by playing aggressively. At m. 135, which is eleven measures from the end of the movement, we can begin to predict the end of the movement by using a more marcato tongue stroke and making a crescendo toward the final cadence.

Ludwig Ritter von Köchel (1800–1877) was the first to catalog the more than 600 works of Mozart. His catalog, which dates from 1862, listed both movements of the first concerto as K. 412. This catalog also lists a rondo in D major as K. 514. The K. 514 rondo is the one that has been joined with the separate movement of K. 412 to form the Concerto No. 1 as we now know it. One of the reasons that these two movements seem to combine so well is that both are gentle in nature. In the first movement all of the technical passages are confined to a narrow pitch range, and in the Rondo the sixteenth-notes are of the ornamental or passing-note variety. This seems to indicate that a somewhat restrained tempo and style would be appropriate.

In the Rondo we should avoid the typical 6/8 subdivision of a strong pulse on the first and fourth eighth-notes so that the music can flow from the first beat of the measure. Notice how the rondo theme has an upward direction, and how it does not come to rest at the fourth measure. Here again is the long line that is orderly, but that begs to be free from the constraints of the bar lines and the pulsations within them.

The only contrasting material in the movement begins at m. 59, where the music is lyrical and the mode is minor. This is also where Mozart chose to be the most chromatic. In the accompaniment there is an elegant modulation between m. 63 and m. 67 during which every note must be allowed to sound clearly. Throughout the rondo the left hand has repeated chords and arpeggiated figures that must not become thick or energetic.

This rondo movement is often played faster than dotted-quarter equals 76. At this tempo the music has a chance to be amiable, but never forceful. It is not music for virtuoso display. There are no high notes, no low notes, no passages to astound the audience with brilliant technique, and no cadenza.

### Concerto No. 2 in E-flat, K. 417

With this concerto Mozart establishes a larger framework for both the accompaniment and the soloist. Here we can see a wider range of pitches and a more extensive use of technical passages, although nearly all of the sixteenth-notes move in scale step patterns. The tempo for the first movement should reflect this expanded approach and should be close to quarter-note equals 116. When we practice with only the horn part on the music stand, the tempo of 116 can be misleading because our first entrance starts with a whole note followed by a dotted half-note. These notes seem very long and stationary without the underlying rhythm of the accompaniment. There must be complete understanding and agreement about tempo between the soloist and the accompanist. Pianists seem more likely than conductors to gain speed during the twenty-four measure introduction. At our first entrance, the pianist should provide only a soft background of E-flat major and not insist on a trenchant rhythm of sixteenth-notes in the arpeggiated figures. In the third measure of the solo part, the horn player must release the tied note exactly on time so that the sixteenth-notes will not have to be rushed to arrive at the downbeat in the fourth measure. It is a very uncomfortable feeling to have to make up for lost time on the sixteenth-notes; it is also unacceptable musically. In mm. 38–40 we can linger on the first of the sixteenth-notes and in this way define the rising line. The second theme, in the expected key of B-flat major, must be played very smoothly in contrast to the short sixteenth-notes we have just played. In m. 62 we have another lip trill whose lower note is an extension of the seventh partial. This trill, fingered 1 + 2, does not feel as wide as the trill one half step lower in the first concerto. At this tempo the *nachschlag* after the trill fits very nicely and does not sound hurried when it is played as two sixteenth-notes after the fourth beat. In some editions there is an unfortunate articulation in m. 81, or two measures before rehearsal letter F. If we slur the sixteenth-notes as printed, we lose much of the energy needed to drive toward the final cadence. It is better to articulate this measure:

Example 5-13

At m. 91 or letter G we arrive at some of the most glorious measures in all of the Mozart horn concertos. B-flat minor and the diminished seventh interval are both indications of darkness and mystery. We should play very smoothly and with only the slightest dynamic nuances between letters G and H. Notice that the harmony moves very slowly until two measures before H. These eight measures between G and H set the stage for the wonderful events between H and I. Looking at just the horn part we see three statements of the same phrase, with each statement starting a whole step higher than its predecessor. The exotic interval of the diminished seventh has been replaced by the even more enticing interval known as a tritone. Notice that, as in the beginning of the movement, this melody starts with a whole-note followed by a dotted half-note. Notice, also, that the energy and the activity happen at the end of the phrase. The tritone also occurs at the end of the phrase.

Example 5-14

We can use all of this information about the structure of phrases to help us decide how best to shape this remarkable set of sequences. We must consider the measures between H and I to be one connected rising line. The first statement at H should be *piano*, the second statement should be *mezzo piano*, the third *mezzo forte*. Within each statement we elevate the volume in preparation for the next statement by making an appropriate crescendo during the tritone. The third statement, which begins *mezzo forte*, then continues the line by raising the volume to *forte* at letter I. There is one more extraordinary feature of these sequences. The first one starts in D-flat major. The sequences then lead the music to G major at I. G is a tritone away from D-flat. Mozart, as always, makes all of this sound natural and inevitable. Understanding phrase structure and harmony can make the difference between playing the notes and playing the music.

The music between rehearsal letter G and six measures after letter I would ordinarily be labeled as the development section. The recapitulation is orderly and presents little new material. As at the beginning of the movement, the accompanist has the responsibility of delivering the right tempo for our entrance at letter K.

The second movement is very simple in design, with melodic lines that are constantly passed from the accompanist to the soloist and back again. In this way the flow of melody never stops and the harmonic cadences are not melodic resting places. A good example of this can be seen in mm. 27–28, where the accompaniment settles into F major while the soloist continues in full stride. Since most of the solo line is in the rich vocal area of the upper middle register, there should be no great balance problems. The accompanist must be willing to become soloist when taking over the melodic responsibilities. This requires agreement between the two players on matters of style and phrasing, since they often play the same phrase. One wonders whether horn players listen while the pianist is playing. This movement never rises to a great volume of sound or to any dramatic elevation; its main appeal lies in the simple elegance of an unbroken melodic line.

The Rondo of this concerto is not a movement of technical exhibition demanding a fast tempo. At dotted quarter equals 96, its rollicking outdoor quality is fulfilled and its more gentle phrases do not seem hurried. This tempo will also allow us to use a single tongue on the sixteenth-note figure that Mozart uses during transitions. These figures are repeated pitches, and because most of them are rather low we must have a strong tongue stroke on the second sixteenth-note. When double tongued these notes are likely to be indistinct and more nearly 32nd-notes than sixteenths. In spite of their insignificant appearance, these notes are important because they are used to connect the sections of the rondo form. At m. 112, or one measure after letter I, the music suddenly becomes serene, with slow-moving harmony and the simple motion in the horn line. We can enhance the calm feeling by a slight meno mosso and by not hurrying the last two eighth-notes in these measures. The accompaniment, when it takes over the melody, must be equally tranquil. At letter K we suddenly break the quiet with our sixteenth-note repeated-pitch figure, which Mozart uses once again as a transition device. When these same notes appear five measures before the end of the movement they must be *forte* and firm as though to remind us that they have been important throughout the Rondo.

## Concerto No. 3 in E-flat, K. 447

The third horn concerto seems to be ideal for introducing a young player to the classical horn solo literature. It has lip trills, a few technical moments, well-defined forms, attractive melodic lines, and a cadenza. It has no high notes, low notes, and no endurance or special technical problems. It is available in several editions and has been recorded many times. It sounds quite pleasing with a piano accompaniment, and listeners feel at ease with it. Having played it in the early high school years, many horn players are reluctant to return to it during their college training because they have played it before, and feel that it is not very challenging. Unfortunately, it is also regarded as the concerto that is played by those without a high register. When played for competitions, auditions, or recitals, there is always the question of whether it was chosen to avoid the demands of other concertos. Whatever one's feelings about this concerto, the music itself remains direct, uncomplicated, thoroughly Mozartian, and completely idiomatic for the instrument of the classical era and our own.

In the first movement at m. 29, the horn begins to play the same music that the strings have played during the first four measures of the concerto. This theme, as played by the first violins, is legato and without any noticeable articulation. At m. 51 we play the same music that the first violins have played beginning in m. 9. There is more sharing of themes between the first violins and the horn at m. 32 and m. 36. In general, the phrasing and articulation should be consistent between the horn and the accompaniment. Judging from the phrasing in the strings, Mozart apparently wished these melodic elements to be very smooth and simple. The repeated notes in the accompaniment, whether played in the strings or on the piano, should not contradict the lyrical feeling of the melodic lines. Throughout the first movement, the more aggressive moments are in the accompaniment, not in the solo part. We have nothing but lyrical playing until we approach the strong cadence in m. 69. After the first four measures, most of the introduction in the accompaniment is rather vigorous, with wide leaps and downward sixteenth-note scale passages. We should not let this influence our approach to the solo lines because, once we enter at m. 28, the horn part is relaxed and graceful. All of the work done to perfect a legato tongue articulation will be helpful in this movement. For the lip trill in m. 68 we can use the 1 + 2 fingering on the F horn. This trill must not become lost in the volume created by the accompaniment. Since the 1 + 2 fingering results in a rather long tube length, we must have a vigorous trilling motion and a strong air stream with a crescendo. We could practice this trill at *fortissimo* for several days before returning it to *forte*.

Between m. 69 and m. 84 the transition in the accompaniment from the exposition to the development consists mainly of the wide leaps and downward scale passages heard earlier. By the time we enter at m. 85, the music has become calm again, and the accompaniment is very simple. At m. 92 we see more evidence of Mozart's use of the accompaniment to provide energy while the solo line is slow moving and undisturbed by the activity. The recapitulation re-states the music of the exposition with the expected shifts in harmony necessary to fulfill the form. At m. 161 the articulation of the triplets should be short and light, but not marcato. There should be no crescendo until m. 165. Notice how Mozart, once again, uses the wide-leap motive to bring the music to the cadenza.

This is the first of the four Mozart horn concertos that requires a cadenza. In writing our cadenza we should be reminded that although Mozart wrote a very lyrical horn part, there is considerable rhythmic energy in the accompaniment during the interludes. The wide leaps and the sixteenth-note figures in mm. 14–19 and at mm. 97–113 could be used as a basis for the more technical passages of the cadenza. Because the music following the cadenza is quite active, it seems appropriate that the cadenza should conclude in the same way. We might consider ending the cadenza not with the usual trill, but with a sixteenth-note scale pattern ending on E-flat. Starting the cadenza for this movement with the melodic line that opens the concerto has become traditional. There is no great harm in doing so, since this theme has not been heard since the beginning of the recapitulation. We can also draw upon the music heard in mm. 57 and 58 for our more lyrical sections.

The second movement is warm, rich, and serious. The term *larghetto* seems to indicate a tempo slower than andante. Younger players might be temporarily impatient with a metronome setting of quarter-note equals 60, but we should consider that this tempo offers the possibility of some forward motion while still maintaining a tempo slower than quarter-note equals 72. This slower tempo might present a slight breathing problem for players who have not developed a large air capacity. Notice that the music does not stop between the first measure and m. 9. The best place to breathe is before the fourth beat in the third measure. Following our principle of not adjusting the music to accommodate our deficiencies, we must work to expand our capacity rather than resort to speeding up the music. Mozart did not provide a dynamic level for the first eight measures of the horn part but the nature of the music suggests that a rich *mezzo forte* would fit the music. Nearly every edition has *piano* or *mezzo piano*. We must be careful that our choice of a volume level less than *mezzo forte* does not suggest a tone quality that is pale or fragile, but does result in a quality that is full without being forceful. When the first eight measures are played *piano*, the *forte* entrance at m. 9 seems to be more of an intrusion than a continuation of the theme. We can follow the same reasoning for our entrance at m. 17 and m. 21, each of which is followed by *forte* in the accompaniment. At m. 24 the sixteenth-notes can start *piano* and, at m. 25, we can be forgiven if we begin a crescendo in preparation for the *forte* at m. 27. In some editions the wonderful dissonance created by the E-flat in the left hand has been bowdlerized by changing the E-flat to D-natural. E-flat it surely must remain.

There is a feeling of coda beginning after the third beat in m. 66. To announce the coda properly, the accompaniment should not hurry past the third beat. From m. 66 to the end all is placid. The last three measures must not be slow, slower, and still slower, but rather the second beat in the final measure can be late and the last note can be lengthened.

In contrast to the serious nature of the second movement, the third movement is full of energy, and the articulation of the repeated pitches should be quite short. The volume level of the first eight measures should be strong enough to suggest jocularity. The fermata in m. 22 need not be very long because the movement has just begun. In some editions the hunting calls in mm. 55 to 56 have been slurred in various ways. We evoke more of the heritage of the hunt by tonguing every note quite vigorously.

At m. 98 there is a sly reference to the theme of the second movement. We should maintain the tempo but should also play these notes with a completely legato tongue stroke. In m. 105 we must be careful to play the last three sixteenth-notes in the measure as real sixteenths and not as a triplet. These notes are tongued, of course.

It has become traditional to choose one of the returns of the rondo theme to be played more softly than expected. If we follow the tradition, m. 155 could be the place to do so. In m. 184 the sixteenth-notes must be single tongued quite forcefully, and we should not lose volume on the descending arpeggios in mm. 186 to 188. The fermata in m. 196 should be surprisingly long. In the last three measures, the horn part should not become lost in the orchestral or piano accompaniment. There is no need to slow the tempo at the end.

## Concerto No. 4 in E-flat, K. 495

The first movement of this concerto starts quite vigorously with thematic material that is never played by the horn unless we include some of it in our cadenza. The second concerto begins in the same way. The first and third concertos start with the main theme in the accompaniment. We are on shaky ground if we try to see a pattern emerge from Mozart's having started the two more gentle concertos with an announcement of the main theme, and the two more energetic concertos with material that never finds its way into the solo part. What is evident, however, is that in the horn concertos Mozart reveals the general nature of the first movement in the first few measures. Near the end of the introduction, Mozart has written a lyrical line for the solo horn that is doubled at the octave with the orchestral oboe. The pairing of horn and oboe was not unusual in classical orchestration. Looking ahead one hundred years, we seen that the horn and oboe were a favorite combination of Johannes Brahms.

The first theme, at m. 43, begins with long note values, as did the corresponding measures in the second concerto. Since there is little opportunity to adjust the tempo during these measures, we must rely upon the accompanist to deliver a tempo that is very close to quarter-note equals 116. As is the case throughout these concertos, the repeated chord type of piano accompaniment figures must be played with much restraint and little volume. Since nearly every phrase ends on a quarter-note, we should practice our elegantly tapered releases. At this tempo they must be done rather quickly, and particularly so in the measures in which the harmony changes on the beat after our release. Notice how Mozart, once again, shapes the first twelve measures by starting with long note values and gradually increasing the activity as the music proceeds. Measures 47 and 51 have exactly the same notes, but because m. 51 is four measures further into the long line, it must be played with more energy than m. 47. When we include the accompaniment in our study and analysis we find that in spite of the rests in the horn part, the motion of the music never stops during these twelve measures. The forward direction of volume and motion should be subtle enough that there is no feeling of crescendo or accelerando, but real enough that the shape of the line is always evident. Recognizing that insipid correctness is just as evil as rampant rubato is part of musical maturity; our good judgment in these matters can be enhanced by a constant study of the era and the composer. If we play the Mozart fourth concerto in much the same way at ages 18 and 38, we have grown older but have not grown musically.

In mm. 65 to 70 the sixteenth-notes have more sparkle when each note is tongued—single tongue, of course—rather than two notes slurred and two notes tongued. In most editions there is a crescendo printed one or two measures before the strong cadence in m. 87. This seems much too late to establish the feeling that we have arrived at the end of the exposition and are ready for the transition to the development. Upon consulting the accompaniment we find that there is a Rossini type of rising figure beginning in m. 79, which seems to beg to go ahead in intensity and motion. We cannot discover this by looking only at the horn part.

The music between mm. 97 and 132 occupies the place normally reserved for the development section. Following his usual pattern of the horn concertos, Mozart makes no reference to the main themes of the movement. It is completely lyrical in nature but not as chromatic as the corresponding section in the second concerto. In mm. 114 and 115 there is an upward leap of one octave and a perfect fifth. We really must not break this interval with a breath but must have the courage and the ability to connect these notes with a legato tongue. The lip trills in mm. 117 and 118 are very fast and free. In m. 131 the low notes should sound strong and healthy, and should not lag behind in tempo. The B-flat horn gives a quick and reliable response to the tongue but, for some players, the F horn produces a better tone quality. Each of us should decide on the fingering by listening to how these notes sound, not by how they feel.

There are no surprises in the recapitulation. Notice that our Rossini rising figure starts again in m. 177, and this time the solo part contributes to the forward motion toward the cadence in m. 189.

The cadenza can start vigorously. If we decide to do so we should play immediately after the release of the fermata in the accompaniment. We might consider beginning the cadenza with the motive that is heard in the bass line of the accompaniment in mm. 189 and 190. There is so much interesting music in the interludes and transitions that we need not include very much of the solo part in the cadenza, but it should include more technical display than the cadenza in the third concerto. We should avoid the figure that the accompaniment plays immediately after the cadenza. Mozart balances the coda with the introduction by using the same oboe and horn melody that was heard earlier.

The second movement of this concerto has several phrases that demand a plentiful air supply. The first of these is from m. 5 to m. 10. We must arrive at m. 10 with a strong sound in preparation for the crescendo in m. 10 and the consequent *forte* in the accompaniment in m. 11. The first phrases of this movement are marked *piano* in most editions. Here we need a volume that allows the horn to sing with its true soloistic voice and not one that is so soft that it blends rather than projects. Part of our preparation for playing the Mozart concertos should be an investigation of the relationships among volume, tone quality, and register. All of us should know when we have reached a softness that is suitable for an inside harmony part but insufficient for solo playing. Similarly, we must temper our loud playing to the historical period, the accompaniment, and the register. Rarely in the classical concertos should we ask the listener to search for the solo line.

Beginning at m. 50 our attention must be directed toward the shape of the phrases. For the first eight measures the music consists of a rising set of sequences, during which we can follow the upward line with increasing volume. At m. 59 we start an unbroken line that ends at m. 78. During these measures all of our breaths must be taken very quickly to keep the line intact. Mozart has provided eighth-rests at the proper places for breathing. At m. 67 we must take a breath that is sufficient to last until m. 73. Mozart could have written a rest for breathing in m. 68, but he did not, so we must not compose a breathing place and thereby break the line. The coda begins in m. 78 and from that point the music should remain calm. The four sixteenth-notes in m. 87 add a nice touch of ornamentation before the final cadence. They must not be played slowly just because we are so near the end of the movement. The long pedal point on B-flat, beginning in m. 78 and lasting until nearly the final measure, provides an expectation of the end of the movement. We can control the last two measures by thinking a slightly slower subdivision of eighth-notes while playing the quarter-notes.

The Rondo, marked allegro vivace, seems to be most playful at dotted quarter-note equals 120–126. In the orchestral accompaniment Mozart slurred the tenth and fourteenth measures, which correspond to our second and sixth measures. This could be taken to mean that the horn player should do the same. When we slur these measures we lose much of the bounce and liveliness of the theme. We are left with making a choice between musical conviction and consistency. Measures 42–45 are slurred in the first violins just after we have played the same phrase. On the horn it seems perfectly natural to tongue all of the notes in the hunting call tradition. Once again we have to decide between conviction and consistency. Being consistent is often very convenient, since we have only to repeat a previous pattern. Lack of consistency is not always a virtue either unless it can be defended by solid information. We can feel rather confident that Leutgeb was not constrained by either conviction or consistency. After much thought, study, analysis, and consultation with experts on authenticity, we still must decide by singing and playing the passage both tongued and slurred before choosing the way that best serves the music. There is no right way to play these passages. Conviction backed by scholarship is the only way to decide.

The interlude in C minor at m. 84 can be played with a legato tongue stroke and with a feeling of unhurried calm. Measure 100 marks the beginning of a 21-measure long arch of melody and volume that contains many imitations between the horn and the accompaniment. The imitation of the dotted half-notes between mm. 110 and 120 should begin with a slight accent to point out the dissonances in the accompaniment and the responses by the horn. This is a remarkable succession of events in which the details of the imitation and the dynamic and melodic contour must be made very clear. The dynamic arch has its highest point in m. 118, and then recedes to the statement of the rondo theme in m. 121. The fermata in m. 178 invites a brief cadenza, which could be a slightly ornamented downward arpeggio. We can follow Mozart's orchestral dynamics and play the coda, beginning in m. 198, quite softly until the last three measures.

There are those who dismiss the Mozart horn concertos as being somewhat entertaining but not of much importance except to horn players. It must be remembered that in Mozart's time and, sadly, until the time of Dennis Brain, the playing of horn concertos with an orchestra was considered by the public to be an almost freakish novelty. In these few pages we have seen how Mozart wrote music of charm and wit for an instrument of limitation and hazard. For the young horn player, these concertos offer a first step toward the truly great music of Mozart.

# The Richard Strauss concertos

## Horn Concerto No. 1, Op. 11

It is probably safe to assume that Richard Strauss is the only celebrated composer who wrote two excellent horn concertos nearly sixty years apart. Both concertos remain among the most popular for the instrument, and no horn player's training and experience can be considered complete without them.

During 1882–1883 (his eighteenth and nineteenth years), Strauss was occupied with several large works:

| | |
|---|---|
| Concerto for Violin and Orchestra | 1881–1882 |
| Serenade for Thirteen Wind Instruments | 1882 |
| Sonata for Cello and Piano | 1882–1883 |
| Concerto No. 1 for Horn and Orchestra | 1882–1884 |
| Suite for Wind Instruments | 1883–1884 |
| Symphony in F minor | 1883–1884 |

With the exception of the Serenade for Thirteen Wind Instruments, all are full-scale works and represent the threshold over which Strauss was to step into his maturity. Given that his father was the leading horn player of his time, it seems natural that Richard Strauss would have a love for the instrument, one that is manifest in all of the orchestral works and that lasted throughout his life. His other great love was the human voice, also family-connected, since his wife Pauline was a soprano. Between his sixth and nineteenth years he wrote at least forty-seven songs, and his poignantly nostalgic *Four Last Songs* were the last compositions that he completed. The total output of over 200 songs would flow from his pen almost without interruption.

The years between 1942 and 1948 parallel, somewhat, the years from 1881–1884:

| | |
|---|---|
| Concerto No. 2 for Horn and Orchestra | 1942 |
| Sonatina No. 1 for Wind Instruments | 1943 |
| *Metamorphosen* for 23 Solo Strings | 1945 |
| Concerto for Oboe and Orchestra | 1946 |
| Duet-Concertino for Clarinet, Bassoon, Strings and Harp | 1947 |
| *Four Last Songs* | 1948 |

Again, there are two works for wind ensemble, a horn concerto, plus solo works for oboe, clarinet, and bassoon. Surely these works must be studied by every horn player aspiring to play the second concerto. Horn and voice were almost as one with Strauss. Is it only a pleasant coincidence that Op. 10, which contains eight songs, was followed by Op. 11, the first horn concerto, and the *Weinheber Songs* of 1942 were followed by the second horn concerto?

The Horn Concerto No. 1 is often played by talented students during their high school years, and from that experience a pattern is set for future performances. The same is true for the Mozart concertos. During the college years young players should be willing to take a fresh and penetrating look at works studied earlier. This restudy is especially important for the Mozart and Strauss concertos because they are works that we will play during all our performing years.

This new look at the Strauss first concerto can begin with the first measure. Notice that the fermata on the third beat suspends all feeling of meter. Accompanists, whether pianists or conductors, must often be urged to hold the fermata long enough to create a feeling of majestic energy and expectation. A fermata whose length is ordinary and predictable is not a real fermata. We should not breathe until after the fermata is released. The first dotted eighth and sixteenth-note figure is played in tempo and with great energy:

Example 5-15

The dotted half-note can be held slightly longer than notated and its release has a quick taper. It is nice to start the next dotted figure a little late, slower, and softer, and then create a forward-moving line to the two half-notes. These half-notes must be exactly in tempo, and the accompaniment must respond with identical half-notes in the sixth measure.

Horn players understand that the first notes we play in a work are often made more difficult simply because they are first. Therefore, we plan our physical actions completely and precisely for these opening measures. In our practice we repeat these measures enough times that they become, in the best sense, automatic. In our rehearsals with the accompaniment, we rehearse the placing of the breath and the first entrance enough times that there are no surprises at the concert. Before every practice session and rehearsal we should check quarter-note equals 112 again, since even though the accompanist is heard before we play, there is no tempo until we play. This is a true 4/4 with stable first and third beats and more active second and fourth beats, and is pointed out most clearly in the opening fanfare. This is important when we see how often the lyrical phrases in the first movement begin on fourth beats and how the triplet figures are almost always on two and four. Following our custom of singing in the practice room, we could choose one of the lyrical passages, turn on the metronome at 112, sing along with the metronome for a few beats, turn off the metronome, and continue singing for several measures. In this way the tempo grows out of the music and becomes a natural expression. Very often, in the heat of battle, we play too fast (rarely too slowly) and live to regret it. By having a musical grip on the tempo we can avoid this hazard.

For the F octave slur at our next entrance, several fingerings are possible:

Example 5-16

A. B-flat horn open to B-flat horn open
B. F horn 1 to B-flat horn open
C. F horn 1 to B-flat 1
D. B-flat 2 + 3 to B-flat open.

We can probably rule out A since that fingering puts all of the responsibility on the embouchure to place the upper F. B follows our plan of making the horn shorter on upward slurs. C does the same, but the embouchure is not very accustomed to playing the upper F with the first finger. D is a good choice because it really does shorten the instrument, does not change from F to B-flat, and the upper F is played on one of the most stable notes on the B-flat horn. Any of these fingerings should be in tune unless our slide settings are eccentric. The 2 + 3 on the lower F produces a surprisingly good tone quality on most horns. There may be some adventurers who would choose to play the upper F 2 + 3 on the B-flat horn. We wish them every success. This octave slur occurs at such a critical point in the concerto that we must select a fingering in which we have the most steadfast faith. By testing each of the fingerings many times we can discover one that sounds and feels just right. This process of discovery need not be hurried. Without meaning to influence the choice, 2 + 3 on the B-flat horn to open on the B-flat horn deserves a fair trial.

It is hoped that the accompaniment has not accelerated during the tutti before our entrance on the F octave. In any case we should breathe on the second beat of the measure of our entrance. Breathing on the third beat does seem more natural, but by breathing on the second beat we can take a longer, slower, fuller, more relaxed breath before this crucial entrance. We must practice taking this earlier breath so that it feels secure. The pianist should be happy to play several measures preceding our entrance so that we may practice this slightly unusual timing of the breath.

Anyone who plays this concerto must have a reliable high B-flat. Strauss has given us every opportunity for success by leading up to it with a crescendo and by placing an accent on the top note. In the practice room we approach the B-flat by exaggerating the crescendo and the accent. When this becomes secure we can then begin to play the phrase at the proper volume. The high B-flat is not a soft note in the performance. When this phrase is not solid in the performance, it is often because we have not done on stage exactly what we did in the practice room.

Our entrance after the next tutti can be dramatically *fortissimo* and energetic if we take full advantage of the accents. The sixteenth-notes in the upward scale must be single tongued to preserve the *fortissimo* and the marcato. It is interesting to see how quickly Strauss brings the music back to a gentle lyrical feeling after this outburst. There probably should be a *mezzo forte* after the tied low B-flat rather than a continuation of *fortissimo*. Until we begin the triplets we should play very calmly, but with many small dynamic nuances. The rising triplet figures should enter quietly and must be very short, since they arise from the bottom of the staff. The end of the movement is very grand and never hurried.

The music throughout this concerto seems to flow in an uninterrupted stream, not only because the movements are joined but also because of the thematic material the eighteen year-old Strauss chose for the tutti sections and the transitions between the movements. The dotted rhythms, the rising triplets, references to melodic lines that appear later in the solo part, and references to themes heard earlier all serve to knit the concerto into a logical series of events. There are no jolts or surprises, but rather order and control, as illustrated by his use of the dotted figure and the rising triplets to move so naturally into the second movement.

A-flat minor, with its seven flats, must have raised a few conservative eyebrows in 1882. It does sound perfectly natural at the beginning of the second movement because Strauss has led the music from E-flat major to A-flat major (nothing startling there) and simply lowered the third of A-flat major to become A-flat minor. The transition is so smooth that some players must be reminded that the 3/8 of the second movement starts with the change from major to minor. The rising triplets then become the main accompaniment figure for the second movement. The wonderful economy and simplicity of means looks back to Mendelssohn and not yet ahead to the Strauss of the abruptly shifting harmonies of *Salome* and *Elektra*.

The opening theme of the second movement sounds stationary until we play it with the accompaniment. We must not choose a tempo without considering the effect of the motion provided by the triplets in the accompaniment. The triplets must not be played mechanically but should have a slight forward motion. With this activity in the accompaniment, eighth-note equals 69 feels right. At this speed the horn line can float unhurriedly with only small dynamic nuances. There is ample time for breathing. The ascent to the high B-flat should result in a *forte* that is rich but does not contradict the generally placid quality of the music thus far.

Notice how, at the double bar, the A-flat of A-flat minor becomes the G-sharp of E-major. By the simple device of what was once called modulation by common tone, Strauss moves the music from the darkness of A-flat minor to the brilliance of E major. Here is the first harmonic surprise of the concerto, and we must make the most of it through the *fortissimo* and the accents. At the double bar our goal is to make the music sound as different as we can from the first time that we played it near the beginning of the first movement. Here we have E major, not E-flat major; *fortissimo*, not *piano*; accents, not legato. Contrary to what is printed in the piano part at the double bar, the pedal must not be held through the second beats. In the orchestral accompaniment those second beats are scored for high woodwinds, which sound transparent. If the pianist holds the pedal through as indicated, we have a roar and a rumble instead of brilliance. The fermata that ends the movement need not be very long. We must remain motionless during the fermata and not attend to any water in the horn until after the accompaniment has resumed. Once again Strauss uses the dotted figure as transitional material; this time it leads us into the third movement.

In the Rondo we have to consider the lyrical elements of the music when establishing the tempo. Dotted quarter-note equals 132 allows the legato phrases to sound unhurried and the staccato main theme to project clearly. We play the theme twice for a total of thirty-two measures, while we have more than 100 measures of lyrical playing. The coda, not the whole movement, is the virtuoso part of this concerto.

As one might expect, the theme is sixteen measures in length. In eight of these measures we evade the second beat with a tied note. We must give ourselves a strong mental second beat in these measures, since there is no physical action on the second beats. If the tied note is too long we must then hurry through the remaining notes to be on time for the next downbeat, thereby destroying the natural flow of 6/8. The theme has a bold and jolly feeling and the high B-flat has a confident accent. The notes after the highest note remain *forte*.

All of the lyrical playing that we do after the Rondo theme should be unhurried, and shaped dynamically, with the rise and fall of the lines. The pianist should use a minimum of pedal to create a very open texture, particularly in the *pianissimo* phrases. With all of the activity in the right hand there is a tendency to accumulate both volume and speed. All of the rising arpeggios marked *mezzo forte* should be played boldly enough to create a fine contrast to the more subdued lyrical playing.

At the 4/4 there is a problem with the metronome marking. Here Strauss has interjected a reminiscence of the beginning of the first movement. We are advised to play these four measures at the same speed as the Rondo, which is 132. The first movement is 112. Since echoes and reminiscences are usually played more slowly than their first statements, we could consider a tempo of quarter-note equals 96–104 for these four measures. If we play these four measures at 132 we do not have a feeling of recollection of the first movement, or the temporary disengagement from the steadiness of the 6/8 motion. The fermata at the end of these four measures should be long and full of anticipation for the return of the energy of the 6/8.

If we have, indeed, played the Rondo at dotted quarter-note equals 132 we must move the coda to at least 144 to create a noticeable poco più mosso. At this speed we need an evenness of volume between the tongued notes and the slurred notes. Listening to a playback of the whole coda is helpful to make sure that all of the notes project at this tempo. There is little competition for volume with the piano part, since it is light and open. Slowing the tempo during the last three measures has become traditional. If we can achieve a sense of forward motion it might be appropriate to maintain the speed to the very end. One suspects that the tradition of slowing down was born out of apprehension over the two-octave leap in the third measure from the end.

## Horn Concerto No. 2

Just as the first horn concerto lets us see the composer as a superbly gifted youth of eighteen in 1882, the second horn concerto allows us a view of the seventy-eight-year-old composer in 1942. The old man of the twentieth century was not so different from the young man of the nineteenth century. Highly chromatic, but always tonal, formally balanced even when formally free, essentially lyrical, lavishly nostalgic in the *Four Last Songs*, boisterous and witty in the Rondo of the second horn concerto, he continued to write his own nineteenth-century music completely unswayed by the musical tides around him. With excellent craftsmanship and enormous energy, he drew from only his own musical treasury until the very end.

A glance at the first two movements of this concerto reveals that nearly everything is slurred, confirming, once again, that Strauss heard the horn as a human vocal expression. Tempo and style begin to be formed from this conviction. Late twentieth-century horn technique will produce all of the notes very rapidly. The players, then, must look past the speed of the notes to find the music and should, as in the first concerto, use their own voices to capture the predominately lyrical quality of the first movement. Harmonic motion is another factor in trying to establish tempo and style. Notice that for the first twenty-six measures the harmony, except for a few digressions, is slow-moving. At rehearsal number 2 it begins to stray noticeably from E-flat major and to move more quickly toward the peak two measures before number 4. The composer has given us few directions for volume other than *forte* and *piano*, but that does not release us from our allegiance to espressivo. We must search for a *forte* that is large without brightness, a *piano* that will project with clarity, and an F horn tone quality that recalls Strauss's long and fond association with the Vienna Philharmonic. Given all of the above, the music seems to defy any attempt to confine it to a number on the metronome, but, if sorely pressed to do so, quarter-note equals 104 would be a good place to start; surely no one would ever practice the first movement with the metronome beating the music into mindless precision.

The first page of the horn part is a wonder to behold, with its long slurs and unending lyricism. There are only two measures of rest, and most of the music is rather high. Our short-term endurance (long-term endurance defined as that required to play the whole concerto) must be adequate to play with a large voice from the top to the bottom of this magnificent page of music.

The first two measures must be played boldly, but beginning with the third measure we can relax as the line descends and the diminuendo takes effect. The fifth measure brings us back to E-flat major after the chromaticism of the triplets, and we should establish the tonality by broadening slightly the first beat and then resuming motion to the *forte* in m. 6. These first six measures are crucial because they are first, but also because they introduce five of the motives that Strauss uses throughout the movement. Never again does the opening two-measure motive appear in the horn part, but Strauss does use it throughout the movement in the accompaniment to mark the beginning of sections. We should practice the first six measures, and the next four measures, separately. It is perfectly reasonable to practice these measures quite mechanically until the notes are secure. After the notes are solid we can add their musical values. These first ten measures are easily memorized. Memory permits us to observe our fingers to make sure that they are arched, relaxed, and always in contact with the valve keys. In the seventh measure, the sixteenth-notes can start slower and begin to move ahead, creating a line of motion that culminates in the tenth measure. The tape recorder can be of help in listening for clarity, and in allowing us to judge whether the musical freedoms are appropriate and effective. Above all, we must not hurry anything, since the real pace of the movement is not established until the thirteenth measure. Speed without clarity destroys the music.

From two measures before rehearsal number 1 to the bottom of the first page of the horn part extends an almost unbroken lyrical expression. There are no "correct" places to breathe but we should keep in mind these guidelines: (1) breathe after longer notes; (2) breathe often enough to maintain the *forte* until the next breathing place; (3) breathe quickly enough that the line seems unbroken. This is not music that has definite phrase beginnings and endings so we must concentrate on achieving a constant flow of lyrical energy. At six measures before number 4, each downward arpeggio can be more bold than its predecessor so that we have, in effect, *più forte* two measures before number 4. We move forward into number 5 and should not hold back for the cadence; though our part finishes, the music continues unhesitatingly in the accompaniment.

We have to know the music so thoroughly between number 6 and our entrance at 7 that we can take a long, confident, relaxed breath on the third beat one measure before 7. The music in the accompaniment gives no invitation; we simply have to know when this measure arrives. Knowing the music is so much better than counting measures because if we mistrust or question our counting, we are lost and the music is damaged. We cannot hesitate or be in doubt about breathing. The *etwas gemächlich* is in exactly the right place to introduce the thematic material at number 8. The *mezzo forte* three measures before number 9 is also well placed. The poco meno after 9 slows down the music even more. Notice how the motive, which begins with the ornament, is heard first in the accompaniment and is *forte* against our *pianissimo*. We should urge the accompanist to follow this good advice. From number 8 to 11 the music sounds leisurely in spite of all the fast notes. At 11 the tempo primo must be exactly tempo primo, since the motive that begins the movement is in the bass of the accompaniment. Our solo part is important counterpoint to this motive. If we reestablish quarter-note equals 104 at number 11, the slurred notes will sound very clear. Too often in our zeal to play the sixteenth-notes with great speed and volume we miss the counterpoint. In the practice room, numbers 11 to 12 must be memorized both physically and musically. After these measures are learned thoroughly we must be willing to repeat the process of starting slowly and building up the speed. This passage can leave our fingers if we neglect practicing it after it is learned.

For our entrance at 13 we, again, must know the music that precedes our entrance so that we can take a strong, confident breath on the third beat of the measure before 13. At number 14 the accompaniment should be outspoken on the triplets in the left hand to echo our triplets.

The *ruhiger* one measure before number 18 gives us the opportunity to slow down by placing the second eighth-note quite late and by continuing to play more slowly through the next eighth-notes. It is very effective to bring the music to a complete halt before beginning the sixteenth-notes at the end of the measure. All of the music between 18 and 19 is slow and peaceful in spite of all of the sixteenth-notes.

At number 20 the Boosey and Hawkes piano edition does not give the accompaniment a dynamic level after the diminuendo. In consideration of the *piano* in the horn part, *pianissimo* seems wise. In following Strauss's tempo primo, we will play at quarter-note equals 104, cantabile, and without a trace of rhythmic tension. The music should not move forward but should feel suspended over the slow-moving harmony. At 21 the urge to create a line of crescendo as the melodic line moves upward is common. It is much more eloquent to reserve the crescendo for the downward part of the arch as written. Once again the composer is right. Coming at the end of this long and difficult movement, the slur up to the written G in the measure before 22 can be hazardous. If we stay on the F horn through the D we can shorten the instrument by going to the B-flat horn on the G and remain there for the next slur downward. Once again, shortening the instrument on upward slurs is helpful.

After we finish our part at 22 we stand perfectly still until the accompanist has played several measures of the second movement. To move about or to begin to remove the water during this sublime epilogue indicates that we do not consider the music to be important unless *we* are playing. All on-stage water removal is done silently and with as little motion as possible.

The second movement is an aria in form and content. This movement is not especially slow if we consider the composer's choice of andante con moto and 6/8 rather than 3/4. Eighth-note equals 88 seems to be slow enough for the gentle quality of the music while permitting a feeling of motion. Notice the rhythmic motive in the left hand of the accompaniment at the beginning of the movement. The three sixteenth-notes provide motion within the measures. This motive appears in twenty-six of the first thirty-one measures of the slow movement and is reminiscent of the triplet figures that Strauss used throughout the slow movement of the first concerto. The Più mosso section can move ahead to about eighth-note equals 112. In the short middle section the accompanist should accept the fact that the music meanders, has no discernible melodic shape, and serves only to separate the two statements of the main thematic material. It is important to hear the imitation of the triplets between the two hands.

At the return of the first theme at number 27, the triplet figure from the Più mosso section is resumed in the accompaniment. This gives even more motion within each measure, but the tempo should not exceed eighth-note equals 88. The end of the movement remains very calm, and the fermata in the last measure is long.

The slur marks at 24 and 27 are not very helpful in deciding where to breathe, since they seem to have no connection to the phrase structure. If our capacity is sufficient it is nice to breathe before the last eighth-note in the fourth measure of 24. If need be we can take a quick breath after the dotted eighth-note in the second measure of 24. The *mezzo forte* at 24 should be rich and vibrant for its own sake and because the return at 27 is *piano*. In the middle section the two notes marked sforzando are *piano* and rather gentle.

Virtuoso horn players are always pleased to see a movement marked allegro molto. In the Rondo there are several reasons for a swift tempo. A glance through the movement reveals that, for the most part, the harmonic background stays quite close to the home base of E-flat major while the horn is playing. The harmony becomes slightly more complex at 35, which is marked *ruhiger*, and is the most complex at 36, where the horn does not play. This seems to be evidence that harmonic motion, at least in this movement, is no deterrent to speed.

Notice, also, how each segment of the rondo theme starts either on beat 2 or 5, and never on 1 or 4 of the 6/8. This device indicates that well-defined main beats in 6/8 are not the principal source of rhythmic energy. This also suggests that if we must practice this movement with the metronome, it should be set to give only the first beats in each measure. We could consider a tempo in the range of dotted quarter-note equals 132–138. At this tempo the tongue has three notes to play on each beat. If we have developed our single tongue to play four notes on each beat at 138, the speed of the last movement should not be unreasonable as far as the tongue is concerned. This tempo allows a feeling of playing through each segment of the rondo theme without pointing out beats 1 and 4 in each measure. At number 29 we have to add a little volume in the second octave of the arpeggios as they go below the staff, but otherwise resist any urge to gain volume before the crescendo five measures before 30.

If we have maintained a speed of 138, slowing the tempo down to 96 at 35 is effective. Both the soloist and the accompanist should accent slightly the tied notes before the slurred sixteenth-notes. This points out the first notes of the imitations. Number 38 should be spectacularly *fortissimo*. Choose a fingering for the low written E that gives a good *fortissimo*, produces a good quality of tone, speaks rapidly, and is in tune. Third finger on the B-flat horn should do all of this, and we might as well stay on the B-flat horn for the rest of the arpeggio. At the sixth measure after 39 we must resist any urge to compose a crescendo so that the *forte* at the return of the rondo theme comes as a surprise. Notice the articulation below the long slur. It is seldom played but adds an interesting touch. From this point to 44 there is much repetition of previous material. At 49 it has become traditional to relax the tempo. This is fine, but we should note that Strauss was always capable of writing *meno mosso* or *ruhiger* when he wanted the music to slow down.

One of the important moments for the soloist occurs at six measures before 48 with the written high Ds. The problem, if any, seems to be with the second high D and not the first. If we do not use at least as much tongue energy on the second D as the first we are quite likely to play a lower or an indistinct pitch on the second note. We must breathe on the second half of the measure before the entrance. To breathe on the eighth-rest before the entrance is simply too late. This is applicable throughout the movement; breathe a half measure before each entrance whenever possible. The movement ends in tempo.

This is not a movement that benefits from the time-honored, but deplorable, practice of "taking it a little slower so that all of the notes will sound." Of course all of the notes must sound, but they must be in the right tempo. We must never vandalize the music to conceal an inadequate technique.

It is hoped that these observations will help young horn players to form a basis for making decisions concerning tempo, articulation, volume, style, and breathing.


## Horn Concerto Op. 91, by Reinhold Glière

To most orchestral players, Reinhold Glière means the ballet *The Red Poppy* and an occasional performance of his Symphony No. 3 (Ilya Murometz). Horn players have a special fondness for his short pieces for horn and piano, which include an Intermezzo, Nocturne, and Romance. His horn concerto is also a favorite among advanced high school and college players. It is a big concerto of at least twenty-five minutes and is full of long, romantic, melodic lines. Its technical moments have the virtue of sounding both dazzling and difficult. This concerto requires an embouchure that has good short-term endurance for playing nonstop from the beginning of the first movement to m. 39, and from m. 63 to m. 103. It also requires a long-term endurance that will be refreshed and ready to proceed after a reasonable amount of rest.

Glière wrote this concerto in 1950 and dedicated it to Valery Polekh, who edited it and recorded it in 1954. Polekh also wrote a stunning cadenza for the first movement. The piano reduction and the Polekh cadenza are published by International Music Corporation. Horn players have begun to write their own cadenzas for this concerto. Here is an opportunity to write a long, romantic, free cadenza in keeping with the spirit of the concerto. In spite of having been written in 1950, this is a thoroughly late-nineteenth-century work in the tradition of Borodin and Glazunov.

The first measure of the horn part will present a problem for any horn player who lacks a responsive low register. There is no alternative; we simply have to produce a low A as the first note. We also have to play smoothly through two octaves that contain the troublesome "break" register notes. Those who have practiced Kopprasch and similar etudes one octave lower and those who have practiced slurring through the harmonic series will be ready for this unusual passage. The first several measures are difficult also because they are the first notes we play after having arrived on stage. Part of our preparation for this concerto must be directed toward gaining confidence that we can, without question, play the opening measures flawlessly. Constant repetition once the notes are mastered will relieve any doubts. The first six measures are played quite slowly and freely. We can pause slightly after the first eighth-note in the second measure and again after the first note in the third measure. For the syncopation in mm. 26 to 30 we should stress the first note of each group, not the second. In this way the profile of the crescendo will be heard as a rising melodic line. While not syncopated, mm. 30 and 32 should have a slight emphasis on the first of the two eighth-notes as the line rises. The editor has given us a breath after the first eighth-note in m. 35. Here the music can sound quite grand if we use the breathing time to delay the reentry and broaden the next several notes before proceeding to the cadence in m. 39. Horn players who have been unduly restrained by the metronome or the baton are always reluctant to alter the regularity of beats. Cellists are taught to play the music, not the beats.

At m. 63 Glière has written tranquillo. There will be nothing tranquil about the music if we continue a speed of quarter-note equals 120, which the editor has suggested for the beginning of the movement. If we relax the tempo to quarter-note equals 88 we have a tranquil feeling, a noticeable contrast to the first section, and the opportunity to start moving ahead with the tempo in m. 85. At m. 93 we have regained our speed of quarter-note equals 120. At this point the horn part is counterpoint to the melody in the accompaniment. The tempo should remain steady until the molto ritardando in m. 101.

The animato at m. 140 should be more lively than fast. If we follow the editor's articulation and play all of the staccato notes very short, we achieve both clarity and lightness. Measures 140 to 154 should be practiced in the same way as we practice technical etudes. We should memorize these measures as soon as possible so that we do not have to rely upon the printed page. For horn players, the sight of an E-sharp, C-double-sharp, or F-double-sharp can be distressing. Following the procedure for memorizing, as outlined in the chapter on etudes, we can learn the notes both physically and mentally. This passage is not difficult to play when the notes are learned thoroughly. It is not easy to play as long as we have to look at the notes. Once learned, it is a passage that must be played through many times. A quick breath after the first note in m. 152 is very helpful for the ascent to the high A-sharp.

The cadenza by Valery Polekh is written with bar lines, but we should not feel that our freedom of expression is limited by their presence. There is a slight lack of agreement between the accompaniment and the solo part in the measure before the cadenza begins. When playing the Polekh cadenza we should change the quarter-rest to a half-rest and place a fermata on the half-rest. If we should play the short Glière cadenza, the notation is correct as printed.

The cadenza has been edited very thoroughly. Notice that the fermatas are widely spaced and infrequent. This suggests that the music should have a dynamic and rhythmic flow toward these stopping points. The first phrase is a good example of using rising height, speed, and volume to move toward a dramatic pause. There are four fermatas in the cadenza. We can vary the length of the fermatas and the speed with which we reenter after each fermata. Since the cadenza has just begun, the first fermata can be rather short and the reentry almost immediate. The second fermata, since it occurs on an exceptionally low note, could be very long and the reentry delayed. The third fermata, in spite of the *forte*, is not very dramatic and does not seem to require much length or a late reentry. The last fermata can also be quite short so that we do not lose the effect of the Es covering three octaves.

At the top of page 3 we should break slightly before the stopped notes and then connect the stopped notes to the two slurred notes with a legato tongue. By doing so we observe the dash on the stopped notes and have given our embouchure a moment to feel the next stopped note. These four measures must not be hurried so that the technique is clear and the notes are accurate. Although Polekh has not given us a volume level for the end of the cadenza, we should continue his crescendo to arrive at *forte* on the low E and finish the cadenza with a crescendo on the trill. The quarter-notes preceding the trill should be played at quarter-note equals 120 so that the accompanist can enter without a gesture from the soloist. The music then proceeds at 120 after the trill.

The tranquillo at m. 200 is played at the same tempo as the tranquillo at m. 63. Notice, however, that the volume is now *mezzo forte*, not *piano*, and the accompaniment is more elaborate. If we have not exceeded our speed of quarter-note equals 88 the triplets from m. 227 to m. 230 will sound very relaxed. Notice that the first movement ends not with our last note but with the più mosso in m. 239. From mm. 200 to 239 we must remain in the tranquillo tempo. During the più mosso we should stand very still and not take care of the water before the music has finished. Since we have just played a long movement, we can take enough time to ensure that the instrument is completely dry before starting the Andante. With the exception of the animato between mm. 140 and 156, the horn part in the first movement is mainly lyrical. Glière has given the more energetic music to the accompaniment.

We can develop a greater feeling for the second movement by singing it many times before playing it on the horn. It is music that begs to be free of any impediments of embouchure, fingers, tongue, or air capacity. Therefore we must arrive at our musical convictions by musical means and not be influenced by technical or physical expediency. This is beautiful music played on the horn, not music written to conform to the horn's idiosyncrasy.

Glière wrote a very simple accompaniment for the horn entrance at m. 10. The harmony is slow moving and the rhythm is calm and regular. The horn melody moves generally upward in narrow intervals. This suggests that the melody should be played very simply, not hurried, and that we should follow the direction of the line with our dynamic nuances. At m. 23 there is more activity in the solo part, but the general feeling of calm prevails. The interlude in the accompaniment between mm. 31 and 39 continues to be serene and does not rise in volume.

At m. 40 the poco agitato can be played at quarter-note equals 72. At m. 48 the speed can increase to 84. There is a very quick diminuendo at the end of m. 50, which is more effective if we slow the tempo on the third beat. We can resume the tempo in m. 51 before the accelerando in m. 55. At the più mosso in m. 58 a tempo of quarter-note equals 96 will complete an escalation of tempo and activity that began in m. 40. We must have each of these tempi under complete control so that the forward motion is continuous and logical. Each new tempo can be practiced separately until all are natural and reliable.

In the small cadenza from m. 72 to m. 78 the first grouping of notes leads to the C in m. 73. The second grouping leads to the G in m. 74 and the third to the F in m. 76. Notice how each of these notes appears one beat later than its predecessor. We can fulfill the feeling of ad libitum by moving forward toward each of these notes and pausing slightly before moving ahead to the next. All of this cadenza is *forte* with no diminuendo in m. 77.

The tempo from m. 78 to m. 90 is quarter-note equals 64, which is exactly the speed of the opening of the movement. This return of the first theme is often played too rapidly because of the volume and the motion in the accompaniment figures. There is only a slight change of tempo for the animando at m. 90. All of the music from m. 78 to m. 102 is slow and majestic, not hurried and tense. Notice that the a tempo in m. 102 restores a speed of 64, not the animando tempo.

The tranquillo at m. 121 can be as slow as quarter-note equals 52. We can establish this new feeling by being rather late with our entrance in m. 121. We all must search for a good fingering for the last note of the movement, since stopped notes can feel quite different on various models of horns. After testing every combination of fingers on both the F and B-flat horns, we can surely find a reliable fingering. On some instruments open on the B-flat horn feels solid and is in tune. A small crescendo on the last three eighth-notes is helpful.

The second movement is written in a format of A (beginning to m. 40), B (m. 40 to m. 78), A (m. 78 to m. 121), coda (m. 121 to the end). We also find that each section has its own quality: A (simplicity), B (agitation), A (grandeur), coda (serenity). The horn part is written in the most agreeable part of the range, and the accompaniment interludes are frequent and of such length that there is no good reason for fatigue. Therefore, our greatest concern in the practice room is not for the notes. Each section of the movement must be practiced for control over its place in a very orderly framework. Each tempo must fit with what has gone before and with that which is to follow. Each dynamic level must correspond to its place in the scheme. Each nuance must be in agreement with its surroundings. We can best serve the music by practicing each section separately to establish control over its special quality. Only after each section is understood and mastered should we begin to play through the movement. Each section is separated by an interlude in the accompaniment. This relieves us of the burden of making the transitions between sections.

Some players might insist on playing this movement as they "feel" it and not wish to be inconvenienced by a consideration of form and content. This movement offers an opportunity to combine "feeling" with an understanding of the composer's intent. Our feeling of music is conditioned by past experiences. No one could be expected to "feel" Palestrina without some understanding of his historical period, style, and sixteenth-century counterpoint. Similarly, no one could be expected to play the Blues without a knowledge of its harmonic and formal structure. The romantic period and its general style are much more familiar to us, since we can hardly avoid hearing and playing nineteenth-century music. To this general understanding from experience, we can enlarge our knowledge of each composer and each work by detailed analysis. A thorough examination of the music does not stifle instinct or cancel the benefits of experience. Understanding and instinct, if each is of a high order, can combine to produce superb feeling.

At the beginning of the third movement Glière allows the music to continue, but briefly, the gentle quality of the end of the second movement before introducing the main theme at m. 19. We do not play the theme until m. 53, but we must be prepared to play music that is fast and light. Our entrance at m. 53 can be troublesome unless we know the piano part thoroughly. The accents in the right hand can guide us in preparing for the entrance. At quarter-note equals 144 we should breathe one measure before our entrance. We must know where the accents begin and how many measures to count before we take this important breath.

In the theme all staccato notes are very short. The dotted eighth-notes should be separated from the following sixteenth-notes and the second notes of the slurs can be short. This theme is found throughout the movement and it is always short and spirited. At m. 107 we can begin to predict the more lyrical material of m. 121 by not shortening the second notes of slurs. The latter half of m. 120 can be broadened slightly to introduce the new theme. There are good breathing places at the middle of m. 130 and at m. 135. We need a good supply of air for the slurs to the high A. From m. 185 to m. 229 there is always a tendency to gain speed. We should guard against any accelerando because Glière moved the speed ahead with the introduction of triplets in m. 223. If we have not gained speed before arriving at the triplets, we can play as the composer suggests and make only a poco (small) allargando one measure before the a tempo in m. 229.

The metronome marking at m. 326 should be corrected to read half-note equals 72. For the più mosso at m. 342 we will need a tempo that will allow the sixteenth-notes at m. 350 to sound strong and clearly projected. In m. 356 and m. 357, a strong accent on the first note of each group of sixteenth-notes will outline the arpeggio and stabilize the rhythm. The pianist should be urged to play very softly from m. 342 until the crescendo begins in m. 352 so that the horn's lower notes can be heard. There is no ritardando until the last three measures.

This concerto is very effective with its piano accompaniment. Despite its length, it does not pose serious endurance problems for players with strong embouchures. There are long piano interludes and no long, high, sustained passages. For student recitals it is often the last work on the program. For less formal occasions the second movement is a very effective separate piece.

Horn players who wish to learn more about Reinhold Glière might study his Concerto for Coloratura Soprano and Orchestra.

## Concerto for Horn and Strings, by Gordon Jacob

The technical perfection and impeccable musical taste of Dennis Brain served to inspire such composers as Paul Hindemith, Benjamin Britten, Francis Poulenc, and Gordon Jacob to create works for the horn. His solo playing opened the door for his successors, who continue to play and record much of the same literature that Dennis Brain brought to life in the late 1940s and 1950s. Composers responded to his consummate artistry by writing music of technical brilliance and musical excellence. Benjamin Britten's Serenade for Tenor, Horn and Strings, written in 1943, proclaimed that the horn no longer need be confined to the rear of the orchestra but can frolic and sing, shout and echo, evoke tears of joy and mourning, and reach back into human history with its ancient signals. Never again would missed attacks, unreliable techniques, or inadequate musicianship be accepted as the price we pay to hear the horn's glorious voice.

The Gordon Jacob concerto demands a solid, conventional technique and a single tongue that can produce four sixteenth-notes at quarter-note equals 132. This speed is reasonable for a well-developed single tongue. The first and third movements are more technical than lyrical. The second movement sings a persistently melancholy song with only one note above the staff. The piano reduction of the string orchestra accompaniment is well-written and not difficult.

The opening theme of the first movement contains a typical brass articulation pattern of an eighth-note and two sixteenth-notes. When this pattern is on repeated pitches, all three of the notes will probably sound with clarity and evenness of volume. When the second of the two sixteenth-notes changes pitch by a perfect fourth or a wider interval we must use a more aggressive tongue stroke on the second sixteenth-note. This is an articulation that can feel as though the notes are projected evenly, but can sound otherwise. After listening to a tape playback we can determine whether all of the notes are articulated clearly and evenly.

The composer advises that rehearsal letter C should proceed at the same tempo. *L'istesso tempo* is a term that composers use to remind us that the speed of the pulse remains the same when the general feeling of the music is changed. It is interesting that letter M contains the same thematic material as E but is marked meno mosso. At G the music begins a long build-up of energy and volume, which culminates in the high C at H. This is one of the difficult moments in the concerto because there is no place to breathe after the tied-over eighth-note four measures before H. Here our air capacity will be sorely tested. We can, however, conserve some air by decreasing the volume four measures before H and then making a crescendo two measures before H. Releasing the tied note four measures before H will help us take our largest breath. Notice that the accented notes three measures after H continue at *fortissimo*. The accents in the horn and the pianist's left hand should match in style and intensity. There should be a minimum of pedal from H to J in the hope that the imitation between the horn and the left hand can be heard clearly.

From rehearsal letter K to L, neither the solo nor the accompaniment rises in volume above *piano*. All of the repeated chords in the piano must remain short and soft and not be allowed to accumulate volume from the use of the pedal. If we follow the composer's directions, letter M will be slower than E.

Gordon Jacob has written a fine, brilliant cadenza containing some of the themes from the movement and some new material. The accompaniment stops abruptly and the horn begins the cadenza without delay. It is a restless cadenza; the tempo and style constantly change. It does not come to rest until just before we start the Più vivo section. Since this is the only moment of repose, we should pause slightly before resuming. It is very effective if letter O is played faster than Tempo I and the last four measures push aggressively to the end.

The composer's choice of adagio molto for the second movement seems to indicate a very slow tempo, but the metronome marking of quarter-note equals 60 and the motion within the phrases should prevent the music from becoming lifeless. We can take full advantage of the molto espressive to invent both dynamic and rhythmic nuances. We see how necessary it is to do so when we discover that each of the first eight measures of the solo part begins with a dotted quarter-note. Six of these eight notes are $e^2$.

The music seems to move ahead slightly at letter C. The highest note and the most dramatic moment occur in the fourth measure of E. We should sustain this measure at *mezzo forte* and then begin a diminuendo to *pianissimo* at F. From G to the end of the movement the music continues its inscrutable calm.

After the melancholy of the second movement, the last movement bursts forth with exhilarating energy. All of the sixteenth-notes must be single tongued. A slow double tongue does not give the spirited marcato necessary for the repeated pitches. We can be forgiven if we add a crescendo in the descending line two measures before B. At C the tempo must not lag as the music becomes more lyrical. All of the technical passages from the beginning to letter G should be practiced at a *forte* volume to achieve clarity. We can then begin to relax back to *mezzo forte*. Listening to a tape playback of these passages will help us locate those notes that do not speak clearly.

At letter G the music becomes playful with a light accompaniment, some displaced accents, and syncopation. Letter H is missing but it should occur twenty-two measures before J. At K the volume does not rise above *piano* and all of the notes in both parts must be very short until L.

At letter N the melodic line is taken from the second movement, but the harmony is extremely chromatic and the volume is *fortissimo*. The tempo should be slow enough that the rapidly changing harmonies are not blurred. The horn's entrance in the seventh measure of N can be preceded by a slight ritardando. The two measures marked con sordino may be played stopped, but very softly and slowly to give the impression of an echo.

The coda at letter O should be as fast as our single tongue can produce all of the notes clearly and precisely. There is no ritardando at the end of the movement.

# CHAPTER 6

# CHAMBER MUSIC

Most musicians agree that the string quartets of Beethoven are among the most sublime and enduring of all musical creations. Although often technically demanding, they do not depend upon technical display, but rather require that each player has a complete command of every musical element. One cannot imagine a fine performance of Op. 131, for example, that is not built upon an understanding of its historical, theoretical, and formal ingredients.

During our younger years we learn how to play our instruments. During our middle and later years, if we study and are receptive, we learn how to play the music. Performance of chamber music, since it depends entirely upon the musical judgment of skilled and informed players, offers a fine combination of responsibilities, opportunities, and satisfactions that solo playing and orchestral membership cannot match.

A lot of wind and brass chamber music is played these days. Nearly every college music faculty of any size has trios, quartets, or quintets. Many symphony orchestras have several chamber music groups operating along with the regular season. Sadly, chamber music has not begun to flourish in the pre-college years, but it is being studied seriously by students at our leading schools of music.

Horn players are doubly blessed, since we have a voice in both the traditional wind and brass quintets. More diverse groups whose instrumentations vary widely, but often include horn, are becoming more active. A chamber music group consisting of piano, soprano, oboe, and horn can, with skill and imagination, play interesting and valid concerts by choosing music for various combinations from within the group. These diverse ensembles can also have an important role in enriching the literature by encouraging and commissioning new works for a specific and unusual combination of instruments and singers. All of this activity is a part of the growing desire of wind and brass players to shape the direction of their musical and professional careers and to lead a varied musical life beyond the confines of the orchestral section or the teaching studio.

Chamber music requires that all participants assume responsibility for the preparation and performance of the music. The musicians themselves must make decisions regarding tempi, phrasing, balance, style, articulation, dynamics, choice of music, dress, scheduling, library, travel arrangements, finances, and goals. In its highest form, chamber music is an effort among equals in which each must make an equal effort.

Orchestral playing demands a thorough knowledge of one's own part and a general knowledge of all other parts. Chamber music demands a thorough knowledge of one's own part and of all other parts. Obviously, much time must be devoted to studying scores to achieve this knowledge. It is also obvious that the ears of chamber music players must be capable of hearing all of the other parts in score study, rehearsals, and performance. Developing this ability to hear completely through the ensemble is a difficult, elusive, and time-consuming pursuit, but one that can be learned through patience and effort.

In studying a chamber music score, it is best to begin with one's own part by looking at its rhythmic elements. One must be able to feel, verbalize, and hear every rhythmic figure in the horn part. The time devoted to rhythms will naturally be less in studying a Samuel Scheidt transcription than an original work written today. After the horn part is searched thoroughly for rhythmic events, each of the other parts should be examined similarly. Horn players will find that the other parts are often more complex rhythmically. The emphasis must be on feeling and hearing with the mind's ear. If a work is notated properly, there should be no unsolved mysteries.

Avoid using the metronome when hearing mentally. At best it is a distraction and at worst it develops a dependency. One of the great joys of chamber music comes from the inner control that each player has over all of the musical elements. To allow an outside force such as a conductor or a metronome to take over any of these elements destroys the spirit of chamber music completely.

New notation presents new challenges and demands new thinking, but if the composer has written with logic and skill, players must respond with determination and enthusiasm. When each part has been analyzed and understood for its rhythmic content, we can begin to concentrate on the melodic elements.

Hearing pitches is essential to any musical activity. In music schools much emphasis is placed on training ears through sight-singing and dictation. All too often any skills thereby attained are lost through subsequent neglect. Except for those with "perfect" pitch, hearing pitches is a skill that needs constant nurturing through practice. Unfortunately, most brass players look upon ear training as a bothersome course to be passed rather than a course through which life-long skills are obtained. A fine horn player can produce on the instrument all the pitches of the horn part. There remain all the other pitches in all the other parts to be accounted for. Few brass players are proficient enough at the piano for it to be of much help. We are left with only our own ears to convert ink into sound while studying.

This is a complex procedure and one that is best developed by adding voices one at a time. Start by looking at the most predictably tonal duets that you can find. Try to hear each part separately and then try to hear the two parts together. Trios follow duets and are followed by four or more parts. This activity is also good for horn players' eyes, since when we play we seldom deal with more than one line. When we can hear the pitches in four or five wind or brass parts complete with their different clefs and transpositions, we have taken a large step toward hearing through our eyes. It is easy to become discouraged in the early stages of this process. Small steps should produce steady results if one does not add the third voice until two voices can be heard reliably. Adding a fourth voice is more difficult than adding a third voice, since two different clefs are commonly used for four-part writing. Bach chorales, in addition to being fascinating music, are an excellent choice for four-part study. Some movements of the Haydn string quartets might be the next logical step, since three clefs are usually involved. Haydn string quartets are so far removed from the usual training diet of horn players that a broadening of horizon is almost inevitable. This is also good preliminary exercise for studying a wind quintet score, which might contain flute and oboe in concert pitch, clarinet in B-flat, A, or possibly E-flat, horn in F and possibly other keys, and bassoon in tenor or bass clef. We have all heard musicians say, and often without shame, that they cannot "read a score." Of course they cannot until the proper eye and ear training has made it possible.

After the elements of pitch and rhythm are understood we should return to our own part in the score to determine its place in the dynamic design. In a general way the dynamic marks indicate importance. It is possible, however, that even if all the parts have the same dynamic marks they are not intended to be equally prominent. In a wind quintet, a horn player's *fortissimo* must be calculated after a careful consideration of other factors. Are all of the parts *fortissimo*? Are they in their most brilliant registers? Is our part the highest, lowest, or an inner voice? Is our part important thematically? Is the general style of the music such that a large orchestral *fortissimo* is appropriate? Composers must hear the density, color, and volume of what they write just as players must evaluate these elements in study, rehearsal, and performance. Many composers are reluctant to use the word *solo* in chamber music. In older music, solo lines and accompaniment figures are rather easily identified as such and a sensitive player will adjust accordingly. In more recent music, the textures often do not so readily separate into solo and accompaniment. Each dynamic situation should be analyzed first with the eyes and then with the ears. Hearing colors and volumes is quite different and far more elusive than hearing rhythms and pitches.

Composers must invent and store an enormous inventory of sounds, colors, combinations, and balances. Orchestral conductors, from study and experience, must have an aural vision of the music before daring to tread the path to the podium. Listening to another conductor's recording gives only an indication of another conductor's opinions. Orchestral players rely upon their own experience, tradition, and to some extent the conductor to achieve a reasonable dynamic balance. Chamber music demands that each player be responsible for knowing and producing the appropriate volume and color.

*Pianissimo* is one of the more troublesome of all dynamic levels for horn players. We too often will add volume "to make sure it speaks," thereby distorting the composer's intentions. Taken literally, *pianissimo* means an absolute superlative degree of softness. This definition is often ignored or not understood, and instead a safe degree of softness is substituted. An absolute superlative degree of softness should arise from a position of artistic excellence and not from physical infirmity. There may be a dimension of softness unexplored by wind and brass groups. Is it possible that in striving for the sensational *fortissimo* we have neglected the sublime *pianissimo*?

*Piano* can have several levels of intensity, depending on the context. To have a fixed level of *piano* and to insist that it works for all occasions would seem to show a lack of sensitivity and understanding. A *piano* volume without much life or projection might be perfect for a note in the middle of a soft woodwind chord, but completely wrong for a gentle melodic line in a brass group. Musicians know that *piano* means soft. How soft can be calculated by score study and confirmed by rehearsal and performance. The span between *piano* and *mezzo piano* in a well-developed horn player can be quite wide and at times overlapping. To insist that a passage marked *piano espressivo* never touch the sacred ground of *pianissimo* or the richer soil of *mezzo piano* sets severe limits upon the freedom implied in espressivo.

*Mezzo piano* is also impossible to categorize out of context. Its span is greater on the trombone than on the bassoon, for example. Generally, its span is greater in middle registers than in outer registers. It probably has less character of its own than any other level and is troublesome for composers because it nearly always encroaches on its neighboring dynamics. *Mezzo piano* does not exist on its own but depends entirely on relevancy and purpose.

For horn players, *mezzo forte* can be described as rich and full without the edge, brightness, or tension of *forte* or *fortissimo*. It can be an all-purpose level, and this can lead to using it excessively. Obviously, orchestral horn players must be sensitive to the difference in *mezzo forte* in a chord with the full brass section and the same chord with the woodwinds and horns in pairs. Horn parts are most often in the middle of the texture—third voice down from the top of the brass quintet, second voice up from the bottom of a wind quintet, and right in the middle of an orchestral wind and brass section. This traditional scoring demands that we be very flexible in our dynamics generally and in *mezzo forte* particularly. It also points out the need to study the voicing of other instruments to determine our own volume. How low are the flutes? Are the trumpets in unison? Trombones in our octave? Clarinets high or low? Bright top to the scoring with piccolo, flutes, clarinets, oboes, trumpets in high register? Is there overlapping among trombones and horns or is each section in its own territory? In chamber music, the same questions are valid. Where are we in the scoring and what is our function? Answers to these questions are necessary in determining *mezzo forte* or any other level.

That every horn player develop the best possible *forte* and *fortissimo* is imperative. Every horn player also must understand the difference between *forte* and *fortissimo* as most composers have used these terms. In the wrong hands mere volume can be a weapon. It can force other players to match it and thereby destroy the composer's intent, or it can be left on its own to persist, heedless of civility.

For *forte*, a good model is the level that fine horn players use for the glorious solo in the introduction of the fourth movement of the Brahms First Symphony. It is a typically outdoor expression and one that must travel and project. Brahms wrote it for a long instrument (C horn), thus indicating that it must be powerful but rich, intense but not bright. Another good model is the first page of the Second Horn Concerto of Richard Strauss, where the emphasis is on fullness and richness, not on stridency and clamor.

A true *fortissimo*—absolute superlative degree of loudness—occurs more often in orchestral literature than in chamber music, and more often in brass quintets than in wind quintets. Both the string quartet and the brass quintet can produce a uniformity of quality, volume, and blend, since like instruments are involved. With such a rich variety of sounds, the wind quintet need not, and perhaps should not, place the same emphasis on the choir concepts of balance, blend, and uniformity. Much of the literature for wind quintet has been written from this choir-blend approach, however, and this has given the wind quintet its familiar and unique sound. Each instrument is customarily assigned its place in the "choir," beginning with the flute at the top, and proceeding down in order through oboe, clarinet, horn, and bassoon. This traditional scoring forces the horn to play a subordinate role in the volume and, except for an occasional solo, the horn seldom releases its full volume. In the wind quintet's striving for blend, all instruments sacrifice some of their individuality. This is as it should be for most of the works written before 1960. For example, one cannot imagine the wonderful wind parts in the Mozart Quintet K. 452 played in any other way. In more recent works, composers have broken free of the procedure and have placed a greater importance on allowing each instrument to speak with its own true voice without the distortion of blend. For some works, players should not sit in a tight U-shape in exactly the center of the stage. The group can choose to stand or sit anywhere they agree will best serve the music. These freedoms do not absolve the players from the responsibility of an intelligent appraisal of dynamic relationships. A controlled, brilliant, and appropriate *fortissimo* is a most welcome addition to the sound spectrum of the wind quintet.

*Fortissimo* in brass chamber music is governed by each player's ability to control the technical elements of accuracy, pitch, and quality. These are obviously the same elements that must be controlled in any dynamic level. The horn player in a brass quintet more often feels a kinship with the lower trio of tuba, horn, and trombone than with the higher trio of two trumpets and horn. Since our range most closely parallels that of the trombone and our quality relates well to the tuba, it seems a natural alliance. This lower trio works well at all levels from *piano* to *forte*. At *fortissimo*, however, the trombone seems brighter and more penetrating than either the horn or tuba. This is due to the direction of the bells, the shape of the tubing, and the shape of the mouthpiece. Trombonists can produce an astonishing if not stunning amount of volume and seem willing to do so on any occasion. Horn players must be prepared physically and convinced musically that *fortissimo*, according to definition, is to be sought, used, and admired in brass chamber music. It should not be tempered by timidity. If the pitch suffers in *fortissimo*, fix the pitch, not the volume. If accuracy is not reliable, fix the accuracy, but do not reduce the volume. If the quality is not appropriate, practice to achieve the "right" quality but do not sacrifice the volume. We all have known players who try to play more loudly than they can. This should not deter any of us from developing the very best *fortissimo*; it can and must be superlative.

The last and most important element for consideration is the music itself. Musicianship, in its broadest terms, has two main components: the instinctive and the learned. This can be illustrated by recalling the life and work of Mozart. Few would disagree that Mozart had superb musical instincts, yet he felt indebted to his father, to Joseph Haydn, and to Johann Christian Bach for what he learned from them. His travels as a child brought him into contact with some of the leading performers and composers of his time, thereby enriching his musical treasury. His mind's ear was developed to the extent that entire movements could flow directly from his ear to the page. We have all read accounts of his ability to work out compositions mentally while playing billiards, or of his writing canons for relaxation. Apparently his musical mind and ears were constantly being exercised and extended. Those of us with lesser gifts must do no less.

We live in an age of wide availability of good music instruction. Mozart did not live in such an age. We also enjoy easy access to scores, recordings, and information about music. Mozart did not. We live in an age of unsurpassed technical accomplishment in performance. Mozart must have heard some terrible performances of his works compared to present standards. These riches around us make our learning easier and more convenient but they do not exempt us from the hard work of continuing to build upon our natural gifts. We all know of orchestral players whose musical horizons never expand beyond their own parts, and of academic musicians who show up for work only to regale their students with stories of the good old days.

Chamber music demands a constantly developing musical comprehension, and the best way for us to accomplish this is to study music beyond the limits of wind music.

For the horn player in the wind quintet or brass quintet, it seems most natural and advantageous to learn as much as possible about the literature for string quartet. Fortunately there is no shortage of fine recordings of all of the great works for string quartet, and the music is readily available in study scores or collected editions.

A good place to start is with the quartets of Haydn. The easy way is to listen to recordings. A better way is to listen to recordings while looking at the scores. The best way is to study the score thoroughly and only then listen with the score. Haydn, like so many composers, wrote string quartets throughout his productive life. A study of Haydn's quartets can serve as a study of the growth and development of Haydn as a composer and the string quartet as a form. Haydn leads naturally to Mozart and Beethoven. It is in the string quartets and piano sonatas, not the symphonies, that we can see the real evolution of Beethoven. If one has studied the earlier quartets with diligence and enthusiasm, the complex late quartets of Beethoven will not seem impenetrable. A great reward awaits the horn player who is ready to experience the Beethoven Quartet Op. 131 for the first time.

The chronological pursuit continues through the nineteenth and twentieth centuries to Shostakovich, Bartók, and beyond. Always study, then listen. Eyes and ears are strengthened. Musical minds are expanded. As with the Beethoven Quartet Op. 131, another great reward awaits the horn player who is prepared to gather the riches of the eighth and twelfth quartets of Shostakovich or the fifth and sixth quartets of Bartók.

Horn players often speak of singing on their instruments and yet few have studied the great nineteenth- and twentieth-century song literature. Horn players, for whom Brahms means four symphonies, four concertos, two serenades, two overtures, and the Trio Op. 40, should consult a catalog of Brahms's works to see listed the vast amount of music he created for the human voice. In studying vocal literature the same procedures apply—always try to hear as much as possible through score study before listening. One could start with Schubert and then proceed through the nineteenth and twentieth centuries, not neglecting the French composers. Nearly all composers who wrote orchestral works also wrote extensively for the voice, Hugo Wolf a notable exception.

The string instrument that most closely parallels the horn in range and color is the cello. Although it does not have a solo literature as extensive as that of the violin, for example, horn players can learn much about lyric playing, rhythmic nuance, shadings of color, and freedom of line from listening to cellists.

Just as sight-singing and dictation classes should lead to the greatest possible development of our ears, our music history and literature classes should open the way to a life-long curiosity about the full range of musical activity and accomplishment. There is no possibility of overly developed ears and no possibility that acquired knowledge about any area of music can inhibit one's performing ability. Having fully developed musical instincts is the goal. Mozart is the model.

Duet playing is another way to develop the kind of ears necessary for chamber music. In duets, discrepancies of all kinds are readily apparent if one can hear beyond one's own part. We should work with a partner, not necessarily another horn player, playing all of the intervals for intonation, all common rhythmic figures for precision, and matching attacks, releases, colors, and dynamics. Duet playing is the best mechanical groundwork for chamber music. It is also good preparation for orchestral playing, because nearly all of the classical period orchestral music containing horns is written for a pair of horns, and some of the nineteenth-century orchestral composers treated a section of four horns as two pairs. Trios and quartets are also good training for other kinds of chamber music, since all participants must hear thoroughly while playing.

Four good horn players, after some diligent rehearsal, will play with generally the same tone quality, style, dynamics, good intonation, spirit, and conviction. When one of these same four horn players is seated in a wind quintet, a whole new set of concerns becomes apparent.

## Wind quintet

The orchestral horn player has to make conscious and deliberate adjustments in volume, articulation, and release in order to play the traditional music written for wind quintet. The beginning notes must be practiced at all volume levels and in all registers to remove any bluntness or accents. We must practice this type of attack well in advance of the first rehearsal to become comfortable with it physically and psychologically.

Playing duets with a clarinetist can be revealing. Clarinet players can start and end notes with no discernible attack or release. Their softest notes can be barely audible and their loudest notes have brilliance and projection. The tone quality changes dramatically from soft to loud and from low to high. Because they play a highly mechanized instrument, they can move with an astounding rapidity. Clarinetists, like other woodwind players, generally have an attitude toward phrase shape that is much less metronomically bound than brass players. This can be temporarily uncomfortable for horn players in the timing of breaths and entrances. The clarinet and the horn sound combine well when the volume is neither very soft nor very loud and when the distance between the parts is not very great.

Playing duets with oboists confirms that the qualities of the two instruments are so different that they will never blend in the customary way. It is better to find ways to use the wonderful differences in quality between these two instruments rather than to distort one or the other, or both, in an attempt to "blend." In a wind quintet this blend can result in "bland" when the unique tone quality of each instrument is sacrificed to the whole. Since there are no pairs of like instruments in a wind quintet, there cannot be the same "choir blend" that is possible in a Mozart wind serenade. With such a variety of colors available to the wind quintet, all of the players must develop ears capable of hearing much more than pitches and rhythms. Wind quintets can sound flavorless, particularly in older music, if there is not constant attention directed toward how the group really sounds. Fortunately, most twentieth century composers have made a fine effort to exploit the exotic possibilities of these instruments rather than follow the usual orchestral approach.

Playing duets with the bassoon will show the dynamic boundaries of the two instruments. Bassoonists are naturally more accustomed to playing with the clarinet than with the horn, but since we share a similar range and somewhat similar tone quality we can balance well except at the higher dynamic levels.

Composers who take an orchestral approach to scoring for the wind quintet have not often used the horn as a bass voice. A well-developed low register on the horn provides volume and a rich texture to the group. This means reliable attacks at all volume levels, impeccable intonation, firm rather than bright quality, and agility. The ideal low register makes no concession to lack of height.

The flute, like the clarinet, is highly mechanized, and, depending on the register, can offer a range of colors from dark to bright. The flute staccato has more ring than the oboe or bassoon, and its highest octave can usually dominate the wind quintet. Traditionally, the flute is placed as the highest voice in the wind quintet but, like the horn, can provide a rich inner voice at softer dynamics. The horn player must always be sensitive to the register assigned to the flute when all five instruments are playing, since the flute projects considerably less well in the staff than above it. Attentive ears and a knowledge of the score are essential to adjusting the volume.

Horn players must become accustomed to playing wind quintet rehearsals and concerts that have only a few loud moments. A good preparation for this is to practice Kopprasch, Mueller, or similar etudes for about two hours with a short intermission and only occasionally playing louder than a *piano* level. This is roughly equivalent to a full-length wind quintet concert.

This type of playing, if done exclusively for any length of time, can result in a smaller air capacity, smaller volume of sound, and a psychological acceptance of these limitations. Wind quintet players must establish and maintain a superb endurance, since, as compared with orchestral playing, there is very little rest. Unless the horn player foresees a life sentence of playing only wind quintets, it seems prudent to keep a balance in daily practice among all types of playing. One's skills in wind quintet can then be regarded as an important extension beyond skills in orchestra, solo, and brass quintet. Loud, long tones in all registers will help preserve the more soloistic elements of horn playing. Loud, long tones in the lower octave are particularly helpful because they allow the upper lip to vibrate with less mouthpiece pressure than in other registers. Whether or not one plays in a wind quintet, long tones are essential to the embouchure and to the air supply.

Wind quintet playing can have a refining effect on horn players, particularly in the areas of style, balance, attacks, dynamics, and rhythmic nuances. Woodwind players tend to use dynamic and rhythmic nuances more freely than brass players. This probably is due to their having a richer fund of solo literature. Brass players prize power and precision; woodwind players prize line and elegance. These two attitudes can merge in a wind quintet if horn players are willing to expand their musicianship to include these freedoms.

Unlike the string quartet, brass quintet, or symphony orchestra, the wind quintet has five separately distinct sounds. This creates a new set of calculations for all players and most especially for the horn player. The first flute and first oboe sit side by side in the orchestra and rightfully pride themselves in matching, blending, and creating a uniformity of style, color, balance, and articulation without losing their individual musical identities. Exactly the same can be said of the first clarinet and first bassoon in an orchestra. The horn player's natural partner is another horn, not a clarinet, flute, or bassoon, and most certainly not an oboe. Horn players who are serious about playing in a wind quintet should spend a lot of time listening to and playing with each of the other instruments. Horn players also must develop a willingness to trade the glamour of the leading voice for the nobility of playing an inner voice superbly. This can be a difficult adjustment for an orchestral player for whom "projection" is very important.

For most of the traditional literature of the wind quintet, the horn player is seated at the back of the group facing the audience. This arrangement gives us good eye contact with each of the other players. It also permits us to make good use of the stage area behind the bell for the refinement and enrichment of the horn sound. Ideally there should be at least fifteen feet of space between the bell and the backdrop. Wood is the best surface for reflecting the tone of the horn. Curtains at the rear and sides of the stage muffle the volume of the group, dull the tone quality, and distort the balances. Curtains cause less blending and more separation of tone qualities, causing the horn player to feel that every note is too loud and every attack and release is blunt. On some stages this acoustical difficulty can be partially remedied by seating the group further downstage. Any major adjustment in seating must be tried in rehearsal and evaluated by a trusted colleague listening in the house. There is seldom much to be gained by moving the group any great distance upstage. Most stages have an area toward the front and center that feels good, looks right, and sounds best. Large stages and halls normally used for bands and orchestras present the most problems for wind quintets. In a hall seating three thousand, the wind quintet will always look and sound small.

Seating and balance problems become more acute when the piano is added to the wind quartet or quintet. The Mozart Quintet for Piano and Winds, K. 452 and the Beethoven Quintet Op. 16 are among the finest and most often played works for oboe, clarinet, horn, bassoon, and piano. In these works there is no good place for the horn to sit. If we sit stage right our bell is toward the audience. If we sit stage left our bell is close to the piano lid. If we sit facing the audience we lose contact with the pianist and the wind group appears unbalanced, since there are two players stage right and one stage left. One solution is to move the piano several feet upstage and to move the wind players slightly downstage. This arrangement allows the horn player to sit stage left but gives some room for the horn sound to develop.

In any work for winds and piano, the richness of the lower half of the keyboard absorbs some of the horn and bassoon sounds. A skillful and sensitive pianist can make the necessary adjustments when the texture is light or when the piano part serves as an accompaniment. When the piano part is prominent, weighty, and forceful, the lower wind voices can suffer from lack of projection. Horn players should have developed sufficient volume and an appropriate tone quality to meet these occasions without sounding bright and orchestral. With a fine pianist playing a fine piano, the sound is so magnificent that it seems shameful to ask the pianist to restrict the volume in an important passage because the lower notes of the horn and bassoon are not projecting. It is the horn player's responsibility to meet the volume requirements in an artistically responsible manner.

Some horn players view the wind quintet as a chamber music group in which every player, other than the horn player, has interesting parts, can play with a full range of volume, and has abundant opportunity for expressive and technical display. In the more traditional works for wind quintet, the horn does seem to be safely tucked away on an inside part with only an occasional leading voice. Violists might feel the same about the string quartets of Haydn and Mozart. Cellists might feel much the same about eighteenth-century literature for piano trio. Other horn players find great satisfaction in wind quintet playing because it demands ears that can solve intonation, balance, and color problems. Being so often in the middle of the scoring we must listen for intonation and balance with the instruments above us and below us. We have no natural tone color ally in the wind quintet, so we must know the scoring well enough to react to the brighter flute, or the darker clarinet or bassoon. Attacks in the extreme dynamics are a constant challenge for the horn player in a wind quintet. In *pianissimo* there is always the dread of an attack that speaks late, inaccurately, or not at all. In *fortissimo*, brass player attacks sound accented to woodwind ears, so we must be able to temper the force of the attack without losing volume. Compared with brass players, woodwind players have a less militaristic attitude toward rhythmic precision, and seem willing to shape the rhythm and motion to serve the music. Woodwind players like to play their solo lines rather freely, thus requiring that horn players be flexible with accompaniment figures. In addition to their ability to play very rapidly, woodwind players are often very leisurely in slow movements and do not see why there should not be extra time for breathing, phrase endings, cadences, and reentries. They can play very quick ornaments and fast trills; horn players have speed limits.

These are some of the concerns that a horn player brings to the wind quintet. They illustrate that in addition to having a beautiful voice, the horn can integrate with almost any other instrument. In the orchestra this has always been one of its virtues; in wind chamber music, it is a necessity. All of the work done to perfect a variety of attacks will pay musical dividends; all of the embouchure strength needed to play softly will be called upon; all of the time spent in ear training will be valuable for score study and intonation; all of the technical etudes we practice will give us a chance to match the speed of the flute and the clarinet.

Several works for woodwind quintet, or quartet, stand apart from the rest of the literature. The quintets for piano and winds by Mozart, K. 452, and Beethoven, Op. 16, are among the finest music written for any chamber music group. From the twentieth century, Carl Nielsen and Samuel Barber have composed works that are played frequently and are extremely valuable as training pieces for young players.

In his Wind Quintet Op. 43, written in 1922, Nielsen wrote a horn part that is not confined to providing an inner supporting voice. There are solo lines within the ensemble, duos and trios that feature the horn, and even a variation for horn alone. At every moment the horn player must know how each part fits into the texture. Score study is the first step, followed by listening with prepared ears during rehearsals and concerts. As a result of score study, horn players might wish to develop a system of marks for their part that reflects the changing nature of Nielsen's scoring as it moves from inner voice to solo prominence, from rhythmic activity to color blending, from listening to and watching the bassoon in a duet setting to providing volume and color in a *fortissimo* chord. In this work every player has a part that is remarkable for its variety, completely suitable for the instrument and for the ensemble, and unhampered by dependence upon earlier techniques.

Samuel Barber's *Summer Music*, Op. 31, was written in 1955 and published in 1957. Its score makes a fascinating study, showing Barber's refusal to cast these five instruments in their usual roles and positions. The low register of the flute appears as a harmonic voice below that of the oboe, clarinet, and horn. The high register of the bassoon is occasionally the highest voice of the sonority. The clarinet and the flute have most of the virtuoso writing; the horn and the oboe are the most lyrical; and the bassoon is, at various times, a traditional bass voice, an Alberti-like bass, a pedal, a participant in melodic counterpoint and rhythmic imitation, an occasional soloist, an infrequent virtuoso, but always a bassoon. Each player must know all of the other parts well enough to contribute informed opinions during rehearsals and to play appropriately at all times. Much of *Summer Music* is rhapsodic and freely moving. Other moments, such as rehearsal numbers 5 to 13 and 26 to 30, must be played quite strictly. Even in these passages there must be no beating of time or pounding of feet. The horn part has everything that is contained in any of the other parts, except for the velocity of some of the writing for the flute and clarinet. By not following a traditional vertical (flute down to bassoon) approach to scoring, Barber avoided the wind quintet sound sometimes referred to as bland. Instead he created changing patterns of texture, color, speed, and sonority. The score is a delight to see; the music ranges, as Barber indicated, from the indolent to the exultant. Such magic happens only if all players have worked at the music, not just at their own parts.

Other fine works have been written for the standard instrumentation of the wind quintet by Elliott Carter, Alvin Etler, Irving Fine, Jean Françaix, Paul Hindemith, Darius Milhaud, Vincent Persichetti, Walter Piston, Mel Powell, Arnold Schoenberg, Gunther Schuller, and Alec Wilder.

## Brass quintet

Many horn players find the brass quintet to be the ideal performing medium. The literature for brass chamber music has had huge growth since about 1960, mainly because brass quintet players have created their own libraries of arrangements and original works. String quartets can draw upon works by virtually all of the leading composers from Joseph Haydn to the present. Wind quintets have a few works from the classic period and some fine compositions from the twentieth century. Brass quintets, until recently, have had to build their programs around arrangements of Renaissance and baroque pieces and original twentieth-century compositions. The classic and romantic eras were seldom represented. More recently, popular American forms such as jazz, rags, marches, and rock appear on brass quintet programs and such diverse composers as Debussy, Mendelssohn, Shostakovich, and J. C. Bach also are heard in arrangements. Twentieth-century composers, with a few notable exceptions, have not made a substantial contribution to the brass chamber music literature. One hopes that this will not be true of the twenty-first century.

Because the literature is so diverse, brass chamber music players must be able to play in a wide range of styles and periods. This requirement goes well beyond producing the notes efficiently. Each musical era has its own idiosyncrasies of style, notation, tempo, and ornamentation. Since we live in an age of "authentic" recordings and books on performing practice by theorists and musicologists, it is now possible to make use of these resources to guide us in our musical decisions. Orchestral players, for better or worse, have nearly all of their decisions made for them by the conductor, and string quartets have a vast number of recordings of their literature available for consultation and guidance. String quartets also have a rich traditional heritage passed along from generation to generation, since many of our leading string quartets are now active in training and sponsoring their successors.

Brass players confronted with an edition of a Scheidt canzona, a Weelkes madrigal, or a Joplin rag will have to draw upon their own scholarship and research to produce a good result. This study of styles should be considered an important part of the preparation for brass chamber music performances, and can help fill in some areas not covered in the traditional education and training of brass players.

Since so much of the brass quintet literature consists of adaptations of music from the late Renaissance and baroque periods, and since most brass players have a limited performing experience with the original music of these periods, it seems wise to broaden our knowledge by looking at the music, reading about it, listening to responsible performances and recordings, and consulting authorities. Most music schools have collected historical editions of older music for us to examine. Musicology continues to produce a steady stream of information on music of all periods in books and periodicals. Record companies have been willing to invest some resources in baroque music but have not seen fit to explore the Renaissance to any great extent.

College music history courses can be very helpful if they evoke a continuing appetite to pursue the music itself. One is reminded of the college English major who, upon graduation, remarked that it certainly would be nice never to have to read another book. The knowledge and skills acquired in theory courses are too often allowed to wither and fade through neglect. Ear training for the horn player should not stop with the final theory examination. The pursuit of knowledge about music of all periods should not end with the final history examination.

We are now at an interesting point in the evolution of brass chamber music literature. The popular commercial quintets must feed mainly upon audience appeal, since their existence depends on selling tickets and recordings. This obviously influences their choice of literature. They rarely play original works because they have decided that audiences do not like serious music. The result has been the temporary stagnation in the development of important chamber music for brass.

The literature now being played by commercial brass quintets can be compared to the literature of concert bands of the late nineteenth and early twentieth centuries. American concert band programs then consisted of music that had great audience appeal, often performed by players of rather shallow virtuosity. Transcriptions of lighter orchestral works alternated with marches and musically trivial display pieces for soloists. Quite often these marches and solo pieces were written by the band director or by the soloist. The great traveling bands were extinguished economically by the Great Depression and musically by an artistic vision that did not extend beyond selling tickets and paying salaries.

Much the same can be said of the great swing bands of the 1930s and 1940s. They were nearly always led by a virtuoso player. Their literature consisted of arrangements of currently popular tunes, with only an occasional original work. All musical decisions were based on commercial considerations. These bands died out in the late 1940s for the same artistic and economic reasons that killed the traveling concert bands.

The concert band now exists professionally as a historical curiosity and educationally as a place for college students to play. It has been almost entirely replaced by the academically based and nurtured wind ensemble. With, theoretically, no musical decisions dictated to it by commercial restraints, the wind ensemble has been free to evolve toward its own stature. Since about 1950, composers have produced for the wind ensemble a large fund of serious works, some of which may prove to be valuable and enduring and quite able to withstand the next economic distress. The swing band has evolved into the academically based "big band" and exists mainly to train players and arrangers for careers in commercial music.

There are very few brass quintets whose members have no other source of income. There are hundreds of brass quintets whose members are employed either by a symphony orchestra or an academic institution. The technical and musical accomplishments of brass players, and of orchestral players and academically based performers in general, have never been higher. This would seem to be a propitious time, under the economic shelter of the academy, for brass chamber music to shed its unfortunate image as pop-commercial entertainment and begin to make the next fifty years a true golden age of brass.

The brass quintet is a popular vehicle for demonstrating instruments to young children. Indeed, many quintets play nothing but concerts for young audiences. The commanding tone of the trumpet, the elegant shape and sound of the horn, the fascinating slide of the trombone, and the majestic bulk and deep voice of the tuba all appeal to the eyes and ears of young people. Programs designed mainly to hold the attention of very young listeners consist of many short, fast pieces, some simple information about each instrument, the ubiquitous hose-horn, funny hats, clown shoes—all lasting between thirty and forty-five minutes. Whether such exhibitions have done much to create future audiences and to prepare young people for real music, brass or otherwise, remains to be seen. This style, in its choice of music and in its presentation, has created an expectation that a brass quintet exists to entertain.

Each brass quintet, and especially those in academic residencies, should develop its own musical mission. Whether that mission attempts to mimic vaudeville or seeks to bring brass chamber music to its deserved eminence are the two distinct choices. There is little middle ground.

The latter part of the twentieth century has seen a refreshing reluctance by composers and performers to limit themselves to the traditional groups of string quartet, piano trio, wind quintet, brass quintet, etc. Composers, writing for friends and colleagues, have created interesting and challenging music for combinations once thought to be eccentric and incompatible. These newer combinations often require new thinking and new techniques from the players, while also requiring the traditional dedication to study, thorough rehearsal, and a keen commitment to excellence.

The tuba choir, trombone choir, trumpet ensemble, clarinet choir, saxophone quartet, etc. are examples of like-instrument groupings for which arrangements and a few original works are being written. Larger than the usual chamber music groups, and often conducted, these choirs exist mainly in academic settings. They provide an unusual musical training and experience.

Unfortunately, the term *academic* has been distorted by some to imply an attitude of formalism, conventionality, and conservatism. The original meaning of *academy* refers to a place where there is constant questioning of assumptions, where learned individuals gather for the advancement of the arts, sciences, and literature. We all look forward to the day, perhaps in another thirty years, when brass chamber music has evolved from its present reliance upon arrangements to a time when composers are writing brass quintets of the same quantity and quality as their string quartets. This will not happen as long as the brass quintet is perceived as intellectually trivial and musically meretricious. The market place has produced the musical equivalent of comic books. The academy is the place to produce the musical equivalent of Shakespeare.

There is no standard seating arrangement for the brass quintet. Some quintets never sit, but choose to stand and walk about during the performance. Others play most or all of their concerts from memory and are thereby freed from the music stand and a fixed location. Compositions and arrangements are being written with flexibility of staging as an important ingredient. The whole auditorium and the areas off stage become part of the performing arena. This searching for new ways of presentation is another indication that each brass quintet, lacking an inherited literature, is creating its own version of chamber music. This bodes well for the future if intelligent, educated, industrious, and dedicated brass players with taste are willing to lift the brass quintet out of its pop commercial arrangement doldrums to an exciting new era of musical greatness.

Whatever the future holds for the brass quintet, their horn players will continue to need embouchure strength, volume, every tonguing skill, a complete range, a good memory, an enlightened historical grasp of styles, industry, and a devotion to excellence.

As we have seen, embouchure strength is built, carefully but relentlessly, during the training years. Brass quintet players need both short- and long-term endurance because we must play shorter works, or movements where there is little or no rest, and long evening concerts of up to two hours. Practicing the more difficult etudes by playing through them nonstop is one way to develop short-term endurance, but we should not attempt this kind of practicing until our general strength has been secured by following the principle of work and rest. When a high level of strength is obtained we can play with a low level of mouthpiece pressure, which, in turn, allows us to play for longer and longer periods without rest. A healthy, well-conditioned embouchure reacts very well to short periods of rest between movements, between works, and at intermissions. We all need those breaks in the music to refresh the vitality of the embouchure, but in some works the composers have not provided them. Therefore, we need a strategy to develop short-term endurance. Long-term endurance begins with good warm-up and practice habits. It continues to be developed by the quintet's rehearsal techniques. Rehearsals in which there is much conversation and little playing do not give an accurate sense of long-term endurance requirements, nor do they add to our fund of strength. Just as we practice and rehearse the notes, the ensemble, and the musical values of the performance, we should practice and rehearse the physical demands of the whole concert. This is most often done during the last few rehearsals before the concert. Very often the last piece on a concert is at least as taxing, physically, as any other. Our play-through rehearsals can show us how much strength we need at various times during the program and what we can expect to have left for the last work. Not many brass quintets play two hundred concerts a year. Those who do can use the physical work-out of the concerts to stay in shape. Those in quintets playing on a less regular schedule need to balance and integrate their practice and rehearsal strategies to build strength for the performances. Our daily routine keeps us on a plateau of endurance. Rehearsals add the particular kinds of strengths needed for the event.

Embouchure strength plays a role in the order that works appear on a concert and in the selection or rejection of certain works. Programming is most often discussed and agreed upon by the whole group. Sometimes a work will make extraordinary demands on one or more players. Care should be taken to ensure that the order of the program works for the good of the music.

Very often in brass quintet literature, the horn must match volume with the trombone. The burden is on the trombone to match the *pianissimo* of the horn, but a greater burden is on the horn player to match the *fortissimo* of the trombonist. The middle dynamics are more easily matched. We should all spend enough time with our trombone colleague to arrive at an agreement on volume levels and how they are affected by register. Since the ranges of the two instruments are comparable, it is safe to say that we can never match the *fortissimo* or the tone quality that the trombone produces in the low register, nor, perhaps would we want to match it. In the middle register, the tone qualities of the two instruments become more compatible, but horn players are still hard-pressed to play as loudly as most trombonists. In the top octave the instruments have a greater similarity of tone quality and the horn is able to compete well for volume. These comparisons are very general, of course. We can come to understand the trombone tone quality and volume capability by consultation, by listening to each other, and by playing duets. The ideal brass quintet trombone player, from a horn player's perspective, is one who has a bass trombonist's richness of sound, a superb high register, and the facility made possible by valves. Trombonists might wish to work with a horn player who never plays very softly, has a bright tone quality, and has a staggering *fortissimo* in all registers.

In traditional scoring for brass quintet, notes are rarely doubled at the unison, so we are on our own in contrapuntal lines and in chords to provide a proper balance with each of the other instruments. When the whole group is playing we are seldom very low or very high, but are most often in our least-projecting middle register. A well-balanced *forte* brass quintet chord can be glorious, but only if there is enough horn volume to complete the sonority.

Horn players usually begin to develop their fast tonguing skills considerably later than trumpet players. We lack the equivalent of the J. B. Arban Method or the virtuoso cornet solos that emphasize multiple tonguing. Most of our etudes, solo literature, chamber music, and orchestral parts can be played with the single tongue. A benchmark speed of four notes single tongued at metronome marking 138–144 will continue to be our goal, but there is the occasional need for double and triple tonguing. One cannot imagine a trumpet player going twenty-four hours without multiple tonguing, but horn players have to make a special effort to maintain these skills. Once learned, multiple tonguing can be kept in shape by reserving a place for it in our daily routine. We should practice the basic unit, as described in the discussion of tonguing, and check frequently for speed and efficiency. As with other physical skills, tonguing is most difficult at the extremes of volume and register. Fast single tonguing above the treble staff at a low volume requires an embouchure that has the strength to speak when given little air. Fast multiple tonguing above the staff at a low volume requires an embouchure that has the strength to speak when we use the "ku" stroke. It is interesting to practice a series of multiple tongued groups starting at *mezzo forte* and fading to *pianissimo*. Notice how the need for firm corners and body support grows as the volume decreases. Most of our multiple tonguing in the brass quintet literature will be of short duration, at a higher dynamic level, and in the middle register. Nevertheless, for the sake of a complete technique, we cannot neglect or postpone working on any manner of tonguing.

Dynamic balances are often set from the trumpets downward through the quintet because the trumpets usually have the leading voice when the whole group is playing. Again, it is the extremes that can cause concern. On a *fortissimo* final chord, the horn sound must bridge the gap between the brightness of the trumpets and the darker qualities of the tuba and trombone. These chords can become rich, full, and blended when the horn supplies a strong middle voice. This kind of balance can be difficult to hear from inside the group. A good rehearsal technique is to start with the horn and the first trumpet playing their chord members. When all are agreed that these two players are well-balanced, add the second trumpet, followed by the trombone and finally the tuba. Whenever possible, the quintet should check balances in the hall where the performances occur. In a small rehearsal room the balances might seem just fine. In a larger auditorium the horn and the tuba lose more projection than the trumpets and trombone. Trumpet players and trombonists must be consistent in how much they angle their bells toward the audience. When their bells are toward the audience, the horn player hears and reacts to less volume than when the bells are angled across the stage. College faculty quintets who play regularly in their own campus hall soon learn its idiosyncrasies and can make the necessary adjustments. Quintets who travel a lot are able to react quickly to almost any peculiarity of a hall. Within reason, every brass player likes a live hall, which allows releases to ring a little longer and blends the voices together into a richer sound. Dead halls seem to shorten the releases, separate the voices, and affect the projection of the tuba and horn (the conical instruments) more than the trumpets and trombone (the cylindrical instruments). In a dead hall, the question is always whether there is enough horn in the loud moments. Since this cannot always be ascertained from the stage, we should find another brass player to listen from the hall and evaluate the hall in terms of horn volume. Typically, the quintet might play a short afternoon rehearsal in the performance hall and become convinced that the hall is pleasantly live. That evening the same hall, filled with people, will lose some of its life. A live hall can do a lot for a brass quintet. Unfortunately, the finest hall cannot improve intonation.

While there has been significant growth in brass players' technique during the latter part of the twentieth century, the creation of serious works for the brass quintet has not kept pace. Fine original works, however, have been written by Samuel Adler, Ingolf Dahl, Peter Maxwell Davies, Eric Ewazen, Arthur Frackenpohl, John Harbison, Sydney Hodkinson, Karel Husa, Byron McCulloh, Vincent Persichetti, Mel Powell, Anthony Plog, André Previn, Christopher Rouse, Gunther Schuller, John Stevens, and Alec Wilder.

Arrangements abound. Some are serious efforts to bring music from the Renaissance and baroque into the brass chamber music literature. Ralph Sauer has arranged *The Art of Fugue*, by J. S. Bach, in its entirety, for brass quintet, and I have compiled a series of twelve suites, called *Centone*, of music ranging from Dufay to Mendelssohn. It remains for brass players themselves to build on the work of the composers listed above and to interest other composers in writing brass chamber music. The level of performance by young brass players continues to advance, and training in the art of chamber music performance is available at many fine schools. Brass players can choose to feed upon the work of others or to take responsibility for the future.

## Chamber music rehearsals

Developing the ability to rehearse efficiently and effectively is both an individual responsibility and a musical necessity. Most chamber ensembles claim to be more or less democratic. Democracy depends upon equality in order to function. This equality is best maintained by the willingness of all players to participate fully in all discussions and decisions, musical and otherwise. Reluctance or failure to participate in this way eventually weakens the group by depriving it of the experience and the intellectual resources of one or more of its members. A quintet, ideally, consists of people with strong musical convictions. This strength of conviction is less than helpful if it is manifestly stubborn, defensive, arrogant, or self-serving. It is most prized when it is generous enough to cherish discussion, large enough to accept counsel, and wise enough to welcome strength in others. In an ideal quintet, each player is convinced that each of the other players has a total commitment to excellence. Obviously, this conviction is not established overnight but grows out of a constant exhibition of the highest personal, professional, and artistic standards.

Our ideal quintet must find ways to resolve differences of opinion. Some matters are settled easily through discussion that leads to consensus. Other questions can be decided by each member stating a preference. A quintet produces a majority if all members participate. Sometimes a decision is best delayed until more rehearsal, more individual practice, or more information can lead to a solution. Occasionally the group will agree that a certain member has greater expertise in an area (baroque ornamentation, for example) and will gratefully accept guidance. All of this suggests that flexibility in procedure is important, and that the opinions of all members must be sought and respected. Opinions should be offered frankly, not frivolously, and in a tone of voice that is free of tension or threat. Some people simply talk too much in rehearsals. Others are reluctant to contribute. A good chamber music citizen finds ways to elicit participation and knows when to bring the discussion to a conclusion. There are really no rules beyond those that apply to civilized behavior. Respect for each member and the recognition of the value of independent thinking are two of those rules.

Very fortunate, indeed, are training quintets that can spend four years working with fine coaches during the college years. The first several months of the freshman year can be the most difficult because, in addition to the usual college adjustments, a newly organized group must begin to develop a new set of attitudes toward playing and toward colleagues.

During the early months of a quintet's existence, a young group will most likely confront problems related to diversity of personalities, backgrounds, and temperaments. This might be, for some players, their first experience with settling differences within an organized, cooperative venture. The full resources of the ensemble, including the coach, should be brought into action.

If a conflict is between two members, the first step might be for the differing parties to attempt conciliation through private conversation. If this fails, one or more additional quintet members might be brought into the discussion. If there is some progress, but no settlement, then perhaps the full quintet plus the coach can work toward a solution. In all of these efforts, the rules of civil conduct must apply; no tempers, no shouting, no name-calling or slander, no interrupting, no sulking. Even to try to understand an opposing view is one step toward maturity. Each party must have thought completely through the reasons for the differences and have command of the language sufficient to make a calm, orderly, and concise case. These conversations must be confined to the issues at hand and not allowed to veer into irrelevancies. To define a problem to the satisfaction of both parties is a necessary first step. To discover which parts of the discussion hold promise for agreement is the next step. To defer those parts of the conflict which are likely to remain at least temporarily unsolved will divide the negotiations into manageable segments. To demonstrate at all times that the welfare of the ensemble is paramount will elevate the discussion above the personal and the trivial. A quick and easy solution is to disband the group or to replace one or more members, but this should be a last resort. To prevail over difficulties can strengthen the quintet's resolve to deal with future trials in a calm, orderly, mature, and intelligent way. The quintet gains composure; the individuals gain experience and skill in working with colleagues.

During the high school years, our quintet's horn player probably played in the school band and in regional youth orchestras. Little individual effort was required beyond being on time and playing the assigned part. The music was chosen by the conductor, parts were provided and distributed by the librarian, rehearsal space and times were arranged by the staff, and all musical matters were dictated by the conductor. No discussion, no negotiation. Be on time and play the part. Now, suddenly, college chamber music requires that most of the operation of the quintet has to come from within the group.

It is helpful early in the first semester to convene a business meeting of the players and coach to set up a working agenda and goals. The agenda must include rehearsal times and coaching times. Rehearsals must be regular and often. Coaching times should be regular and often enough to provide stimulus. At this meeting the coach should outline the short-term (one semester) goals and the long-range (four year) goals. From the beginning, all agree that this is a serious musical endeavor and not something to do because it is "fun." Groups can stagnate without enough rehearsal times, or with irregular rehearsal times. Short-term goals should include the scheduling of performances. These earlier performances need not be full-length evening concerts or confined to school premises. Finding, booking, and managing off-campus playing opportunities can be both short- and long-term goals, and provide valuable experience for the group, since they involve both music and business. Long-term goals should include pointing toward national competitions in the third and fourth years. Long-term planning is necessary to chart a logical exploration of the literature. Another long-term project should deal with the development of literature from within the group. Many brass quintets have at least one member who feels a responsibility to produce literature, not just consume it, and is equipped with the industry and the skills necessary to do so. Often it is the horn player.

College daily schedules tend to be based on sixty-minute segments. This timing is good bookkeeping but it does not work well for chamber music rehearsals. Even if everyone arrives at the rehearsal room on time, many minutes are consumed by unpacking, warming up, finding the music, a mute, and a missing stand, oiling valves, and discussing musical or other matters. The quintet might consider having one-hour rehearsals during the day to conform with the regular school schedule, and having evening rehearsals of at least ninety minutes.

Rehearsal and performance need leadership but of a kind that inspires confidence rather than commands obedience. This leadership role most naturally, most often, and traditionally falls upon the first violin in the string quartet, the flute in the wind quintet, and the first trumpet in the brass quintet, but only because each of these instruments is likely to have the highest voice. Horn players also have to lead when starting movements, releasing fermatas or final chords, changing meter or tempo, indicating ritardando or accelerando, and signaling entrances. Brass players, particularly horn and tuba players, are often uncomfortable and reluctant when called upon to lead by body movement. Horn players, especially those who play with the bell on the leg, can ease this discomfort by practicing the appropriate motions while standing and then gradually converting these motions to a sitting position.

Leadership constantly shifts from one member to another according to the requirements of the music. If a work begins with a five-voice chord, and if there is good reason for the horn player to "lead" the preparation and entrance, so be it. All chamber music depends upon the players' willingness and ability to do this. This leadership is accomplished mainly by subtle body movements, and it offers the possibility of freeing the music from the custody of the "beat." Body motions can be very useful in rehearsals, since, unlike string players, wind players cannot speak while playing. Freedom of movement can also have a beneficial effect upon the rhythmic nuances of phrases.

One body motion never used is foot-tapping. Foot-tapping often is the result of the urging of a well-meaning junior high school band director to "keep time" with the feet, or of the continued use of the metronome while practicing. Although consulting a metronome occasionally for tempo is helpful, its continued use can only inhibit the freedom and spontaneity essential to chamber music. The metronome has no place in the chamber music rehearsal except for checking tempi. Brass quintets have great problems changing tempo as a result of metronome "addiction." This seems to be less true of wind quintets and no problem at all for string quartets. Thoughtless insistence on a "steady beat" is just fine for rock and country and western. It is deadly for serious chamber music.

Since wind and brass chamber music players have probably served time in a conducted musical organization, it is natural that the usual orchestral or band rehearsal sequence of (1) playing through, (2) working out, (3) playing through again, will be transferred to chamber music rehearsals. As a rehearsal prototype this works fairly well for chamber music, but the time given to each phase must be enlarged and apportioned differently.

Professional orchestras must rely more on the playing-through phases for reasons of time and also, since most of the players have played most of the literature many, many times, the playing-through can serve to refresh and stabilize the performance. Rarely played or completely new works require relatively more time for working out details. Orchestral musicians evaluate conductors according to the clarity of "beating time" and the proficiency of rehearsal technique. "Conductor X has a clear beat and knows how to rehearse," is high praise, indeed. Knowing how to rehearse includes apportioning time intelligently among works, and between working out and playing through.

Without suggesting that details are not as important in conducted organizations, a trio, quartet, or quintet must devote a much larger share of rehearsal time to working out smaller musical segments. For younger quintets to start each rehearsal with a Bach chorale is advisable for the same reasons that Pablo Casals started each day at the piano playing from *The Well-Tempered Clavier* or from the unaccompanied cello suites. Bach chorales—four parts with the bass doubled at the octave—have a cleansing and calming effect on the ensemble. These chorales can provide a spiritual and musical link with the Master. Brass players' literature does not provide many links to Palestrina, Schütz, any of the Bach family, Haydn, Mozart, Beethoven, Schubert, or Chopin, to name but a few masters. Because there is no great difficulty in reading or producing the notes of a chorale, players can concentrate on intonation, balance, dynamics, and rhythmic ensemble. Every training group should produce for its own use a collection of chorales, mainly by J. S. Bach. A few minutes spent on chorales will focus the group on fundamental concerns and will allow the quintet really to listen to itself. Perhaps one or more members might be moved to research the history of the chorale and thereby begin to understand its psychological importance to church-goers of earlier times. Chorales, because they contain fermatas, are excellent material for the practice of starting, holding, releasing, and restarting. At each rehearsal, a different player could be responsible for leading the chorales.

Quintet rehearsals need not follow an unyielding pattern, nor should they be improvisatory. One especially productive way of rehearsing is for the group to decide to stop and repair immediately any blemish of ensemble, every intonation misdemeanor, each dynamic imbalance, and all rhythmic eccentricities. This raises the level of concentration on one's own part while requiring that each player listen analytically to all other parts. Hearing completely through the ensemble while playing is the essence of chamber music. This approach to rehearsing also raises the level of effort to achieve performance excellence, particularly in technical matters. Late responses, intonation lapses, careless rhythms, vague dynamics, all can result from a lax attitude in rehearsals. Left unchallenged and uncorrected, these defects are not likely to disappear miraculously at the concert. Wind and brass players, sadly, are often content in rehearsals to tolerate and dismiss flaws that would be unacceptable at a performance. One hears "It just spoke late," as an exoneration of careless attacks, or "Sorry, I didn't notice the *pianissimo*."

This type of rehearsing is intense, but efficient and rewarding if all players have the strength to continue to exhibit civility and good nature. After a quintet has worked together for several years there can develop an almost tribal bond and collegial spirit, growing out of respect for each other and the sharing of good times and bad. This kind of rehearsing is also time-consuming, not "fun" in the playground sense, and requires several different kinds of strengths from all players. Each has to be strong enough to follow as well as lead, strong enough not to retaliate defensively when defects are mentioned, strong enough not to fight a major battle over a tiny and temporary difference of opinion, and wise enough to recognize that, at times, each of us can be wrong, sharp, flat, late, early, too soft, too loud, uninformed, narrow, and insensitive.

These rehearsals lay bare and scrub clean the skeleton of the music. At this point, it is tempting to be satisfied with that which approaches mechanical precision, especially when it has been gained at great cost in time and effort. Such punctilious orthodoxy can easily be worshipped for its own sake, rather than recognized as only a necessary step in a larger process. Elevating this skeleton of precision into music is the next step, and one that requires the playing through of longer sections. Freedom without loss of precision now becomes the main concern. Now all of the collective wisdom and experience of every player must be available so that the theoretical, historical, and stylistic implications of the music can be discussed, understood, and agreed upon. A complete knowledge of the score is indispensable. This includes an understanding of the stylistic traits of the various historical periods, so that Gabrieli and Mendelssohn each retain their historical propriety, for example, and a transcription of an English madrigal does not suggest Stephen Foster.

It is not unusual for pianists, for example, in preparing a work by Robert Schumann, to study and review many other works, not just works for piano by Schumann, to develop an increased understanding of the composer, the music, and the period. Brass chamber music with all of its transcriptions, plus its twentieth-century works, spans at least four hundred years and includes styles ranging from the magnificence of the late Renaissance to the insignificance of the latest commercial pandering. That a quintet will evolve its own distinct "style," which is then applied to all works regardless of suitability, is always a danger. Since symphony orchestras play mainly nineteenth-century works and since quintet players have often had some orchestral experience, it is understandable that romantic tendencies are apt to infect the music of other periods. The diversity of styles in brass chamber music literature offers an alluring opportunity for individuals to grow musically and intellectually, and for the group to play with authority and integrity. Study and learn, read and grow, listen and mature.

One of the more troublesome areas in quintet playing is the tailoring of accompaniment figures to fit the solo line. Very often, in both original works and arrangements, rhythmically intricate accompaniment patterns are invented that can become obstinate after a few measures. Accompaniment figures, by their nature, usually have three or four voices against the solo line and can easily create a dynamic and musical imbalance. A fine piano accompanist provides a rhythmic, dynamic, and harmonic background, vital in itself but seldom competitive or restrictive. The pianist accomplishes this through listening, experience, instinct, and a realization of what the musical situation calls for. For wind players, the study of the songs of Franz Schubert should be interesting and helpful. Many of Schubert's songs have accompaniments with rhythmically persistent patterns; *Auf dem Strom* is no exception. Accompanists pride themselves, and rightly so, on their ability to vary the speed, texture, and volume of repetitious figures to follow the freedom of the solo voice.

In rehearsals, accompanying members should often not play but rather listen to the solo line played alone. Without the restriction of the accompaniment, the solo line can move with appropriate dynamic and rhythmic freedom; the accompanying players can hear clearly what must be done to accommodate those freedoms and thus supply a background that supports and enriches. Again, it is wise to consult the string quartet literature, beginning with Haydn. Notice, through score study, how often the composer has written three accompanying voices and one solo (first violin) line. Notice, through listening, how skillfully the accompanying players move with, rather than restrain, the leading voice. String players have a huge advantage because they train on the quartets of Haydn, Mozart, Beethoven. There is nothing remotely comparable in wind and brass literature.

In other, longer play-through rehearsals it is easy to develop a complacent attitude toward established, and often orchestral, habits of musicianship. Since most of the early training literature for horn players (Kopprasch being the perfect example) consists of short pieces with sequences and other repetitions of patterns, we learn to be "exact" and "perfect" by playing each repetition of material precisely the same. This is just fine for mechanical training, but from the beginning a wise teacher shows that music goes beyond mere reproduction. Being consistent with repetitions is not necessarily an automatic musical virtue.

When we play works in a forthright sonata-allegro form, is it really necessary to play every reference to the thematic material with exactly same articulation or dynamic shape? Does this not disregard the intention, purpose, and function of the development section and, quite possibly, the recapitulation? I do not argue for a prohibition of consistency but rather for a questioning of its rigid use. The same applies to the returns of rondo material in works of the classical period. The second movement of the Mozart First Horn Concerto is an obvious example; chamber music literature presents many examples. These deviations from the typical must be evaluated in relation to their impact upon the whole movement and not on their momentary charm. Playing nonstop through a movement is a good way to judge the appropriateness of these departures.

Playing through an entire movement or work helps to provide a complete picture of the dynamic scheme. Often there is a true dynamic summit in a movement. This point could well be marked *fortissimo*, but other passages could also be marked similarly. If, by playing through a movement, the group can decide that mm. 232–241 are the dynamic top, that decision can influence how the volume and energy are handled on both slopes of the summit. Brass players particularly are likely to be impatient with pacing the ascent, the stay at the top, and the descent. Rhythmic motion can be of great help in dynamic shaping, but, of course, this is impossible if the group is content with a metronome approach to musicianship.

On rare occasions, non-espressivo can be intensely expressive. It is most effective at *pianissimo* or *fortissimo* and must not be used too frequently or last too long. The total absence of variation in dynamics, rhythm, color, speed, articulation, or even body movement can be used if the best interest of the music is served thereby.

Playing through can give an indication of the physical and emotional pacing required in a work of difficulty and length. Playing through an entire concert lasting from one and one-half to two hours is also necessary to achieve a sense of how all events, musical and other, are linked. Intermissions and time spent offstage between works should be "rehearsed," timed, and evaluated. The order of works on a program can be confirmed as logical or altered as necessary after one or more runs-through.

## Intonation

Rhythmic precision, accuracy, good tone quality, and every other manifestation of musicianship mean very little in a rehearsal or performance marred by bad intonation. Chamber music intonation means that a tone is "in tune" with at least one other tone. When we are alone in the practice room, the other tone is represented by the visual display of the electronic tuner. We use the tuner to show the general pitch of our instrument (A440 is a good place to begin) and to show where each note is in relation to other notes. We can use this information to adjust pitches when we play with the tuner, but only our ears can supply this pitch information when we play with others. The role of the tuner, then, is to provide information and to give us experience in adjusting pitches. The tuner also shows us in which direction we should adjust; without the tuner our ears have to tell us. The tuner is especially helpful with linear intonation of slow, moving lines. It is of no help in vertical intonation, since we are apt to have variables in the other parts. Armed with information and experience, we can arrive at the rehearsal with some knowledge of our own intonation tendencies. After playing for months or years with our colleagues, we should have some comprehension of their intonation also.

One should not feel that using a tuner is an indication of having bad ears. Rather it should be seen as a very helpful device, and, like the metronome, one that supplies unbiased information. Of course, it is not enough to see on the tuner's display that a note is sharp or flat; we must hear it.

Vertically there is always the necessity of aligning all of the chord members. In tonal music it is logical to find the perfect intervals (unisons, fourths, fifths, and octaves) and align them in that order. The intonation of the perfect intervals is not a matter of opinion. They are either in tune or not in tune, and the ear can hear the beats that indicate discrepancies. When the perfect intervals are in good order, the major-minor intervals can be added from lower to higher, one at a time. Thirds are fairly easy to tune when they are close to the root of the chord. Thirds are even easier to tune if they can be related to a tonic scale degree. A good exercise for this is to practice a major scale with only whole steps very slowly with a tuner, thus: C-D-E; F-G-A; G-A-B; and then another C. This exercise implants an aural picture of the quality of major thirds as they relate to a tonic. Similar exercises can be devised for minor thirds. That we must not just look, but look and listen, cannot be too heavily emphasized. Third problems are compounded by inversions, which tend to obscure the tonic-third relationship. Thirds that are widely separated between bassoon and flute or between tuba and trumpet, for example, are further complicated by difference in timbre. A myth exists among brass players that lowering the third of a chord will automatically solve intonation problems. Lowering the third when it is too high seems more reasonable.

It is best to fix a problem chord by isolating it, aligning its perfect intervals, then its major-minor intervals, and then holding it several times to solidify it. The task is not completed until the group has approached the trouble spot from a measure or two earlier so that the players can make the necessary adjustments in context. This takes rehearsal time and unfortunately there is no guarantee that a chord fixed today will remain fixed tomorrow. Constant vigilance gradually produces consistent intonation. It is remarkable how much a quintet's sound is warmed and enriched when the intonation is correct.

In nontonal music, intonation difficulties are more severe because, generally, there are fewer perfect intervals on which to anchor the tuning. The same procedure applies as in tonal music: find the perfect intervals, if any, and then proceed through the major-minor intervals before adding tritones, seconds, and sevenths. These nontonal harmonies begin to sound logical and even brilliant when tuned properly.

Problems arise when the upper voice in a melodic line does not sound in tune with a more stationary harmonic background. It helps to hear the melodic voice played by itself to verify its integrity. When it is agreed that this line is correct, it can be played against one harmonic voice, then against two, and then three or more. By adding harmonic voices one at a time, the offending intervals can be heard clearly, identified, and repaired.

Working on intonation at rehearsals tests each player's ability to hear, to adjust, and to maintain a calm and cooperative attitude. This ensemble attitude does not develop through the normal process of learning to play our instrument. Instrumental training is mostly a sequestered and personal pursuit in which we have private lessons, we practice in solitude, we play solos, we have our own instrument, mouthpiece, mutes, and are often praised unduly by teachers. It is not surprising, therefore, that college music majors view themselves and their endeavors quite differently from, for example, English literature majors, who are constantly studying the works of others and are not concerned exclusively with themselves. This ego-centrism of performing musicians, the need to excel and the desire to exhibit excellence, the need to be right, the best, and to be recognized and admired, are all parts of the psychological profile of the solo performer. The solo virtuoso tends to glow more brightly than the music. The ensemble musician needs all of the above in reasonable and balanced amounts, plus a conviction that the player is the servant of the music. This conviction need not dim the brilliance of execution, or make unnecessary the striving for great accomplishments, but rather allows the musician to rise above self-interest to a higher artistic realm. If this convic-tion is firm enough, the ensemble musician can regard bad intonation, even if pointed out by a colleague, as a temporary frailty to which all of us are subject. Our frailties do not serve music; our strengths serve music. A belligerent reaction to a colleague's observation about intonation serves no purpose other than to delay the resolution of the problem that prompted the observation. A cooperative attitude toward suggestions about intonation or any other ensemble matter indicates benevolent strength.

Inevitably, every chamber group must read through new works, which could range from simple transcriptions of older music to original compositions of great difficulty. Transcrip-tions are usually notated in a traditional manner and offer few difficulties. Composers of the late twentieth century often notate in a very personal style that requires players to under-stand and react to new symbols and directions. Some players are either amused or scornful at the prospect of having to study the list of symbol explanations often included with the score and parts.

New notation is here to stay. It has freed the composer to explore a much wider field of expression while requiring performers to learn about new notational techniques. Most new chamber works should not be read in the conventional way, but should be read by the group only after each member has studied the music sufficiently to comprehend the information supplied by the notation. We cannot read and understand a book written in French without understanding the French language. A casual reading of a new composition (new to the group) before the notation is understood can lead to a totally false and embarrassing evaluation of the music. This is an injustice to the composer and can deprive the group of the possibility of adding a rich and exciting new work to its repertory.

## Specific works

### Quintet for Violin, Two Violas, Cello and Horn, K. 407, by W. A. Mozart

Mozart wrote six quintets for strings. All are scored for two violins, two violas, and cello. According to *The New Grove Dictionary of Music and Musicians*, Luigi Boccherini (1743–1805) wrote an astounding total of 125 quintets for strings; 113 are scored for two violins, viola, and two celli; the remaining twelve are scored for two violins, two violas, and cello. Perhaps it is from a combination of these patterns that Mozart chose to include two violas rather than two violins for his quintet for horn and strings. For his quintet for clarinet and strings K. 581, he chose the conventional string quartet. The inclusion of the second viola in the horn quintet is pertinent more for the type of music Mozart wrote in the quintet rather than for its link to the six string quintets.

The horn quintet and, to some extent, the clarinet quintet, are solo works with string accompaniment. Written for Ignaz Leutgeb, the horn quintet contains more rapid technical playing than any of the concertos. It is not necessarily more difficult to play, since most of the notes are in the middle register. Harmonically it does not stray very far from E-flat major and B-flat major. It lacks the beautifully modulatory middle sections of the concertos. It is happy, uncomplicated music. Horn players are more fond of it than are string players.

The violin in the quintet often has dialogue with the horn, and is nearly always the top voice of the accompaniment. The cello provides the customary bass line and is heard only rarely in any other capacity. While the horn is playing, the two violas are used mainly as inside harmony voices in accompaniment figures. Examples of these figures can be seen in the first movement in mm. 18–29, 34–56, and 72 to the end. The other two movements contain similar passages. From their experiences in playing string quartets, violists develop a sense of dynamic balance based more upon four equal string voices rather than a balance that grows out of accompanying a dialogue between the horn and the violin. Most of the accompaniment figures in the two violas are not very interesting in themselves, are repetitious, and are on the lower strings of the instrument. Great care must be taken in rehearsals to ensure that the volume and style of the three lower voices do not overwhelm the dialogue between the horn and the violin. For this discussion, the score of the Rudolf Gerber edition as published by Eulenburg was consulted. The string parts seem to be well edited with slurs, dots, and phrase marks. Some dynamic marks are missing in individual string parts. These can be discussed and corrected during rehearsals. The horn part often lacks dynamic marks at entrances, but these can also be agreed upon at rehearsals.

In the first movement, some horn players will question the slurs in mm. 34, 36, 116, 132, and 134. We could consider using the traditional pattern of two notes slurred and two notes tongued. The scales in mm. 58, 60, 62, and 63 will not suffer from being slurred. Horn players, probably including Leutgeb, have never been slaves to Mozart editors. This is as it should be, as long as our decisions are based upon scholarship, understanding, and good judgment.

It is always helpful for the violinist and the horn player to have a separate rehearsal before the general rehearsals to play and discuss phrases that they have in common and other stylistic and articulation considerations. Very often a sensitive and reasonable violinist will change the bowing and articulation after hearing a certain phrase played on the horn. We also must be willing to listen and learn from string players, who probably have played much more Mozart chamber music than we have.

For the first movement, quarter-note equals 120 is a tempo that allows for brilliance and clarity in the rapid figures. Notice that in m. 34 Mozart has taken us to a solid B-flat major cadence, where we would expect a second theme that is lyrical in nature. Instead, we have rapid downward scales and no cantabile phrases in spite of the editor's slur. The music simply shifts to the dominant and goes on its merry path to the end of the movement. The only relatively inactive moments are in mm. 5–12 and mm. 77–82. In these measures the accompaniment should be very soft and without extravagance of nuance. These moments are to be cherished in a movement full of untroubled energy. From mm. 18 to 28, and from mm. 90 to 102, the three lower string parts must not intrude upon the dialogue between the violin and the horn. The exposition repeat should be made.

In the first eighteen measures of the second movement, the strings can play with their accustomed string-quartet equality of voices. There is enough imitation of figures to allow all voices to be prominent upon occasion. When the horn enters in m. 19, the accompanying balances must be restored. A glorious dissonance is found on the third eighth-note in m. 26. It occurs very naturally as a result of the imitations of the dotted eighth-note figure. On the third eighth-note the horn and the second viola have E-natural while the first viola has F-natural one half-step higher. This dissonance is resolved immediately but it is great while it lasts. We should neither emphasize it nor shy away from it. Apparently, this dissonance so offended some editors that it was bowdlerized by changing the rhythm to make it less offensive to their own ears. Another of these unexpected dissonances occurs in m. 46, where the A-flat in the first viola is sounded with the G-natural in the cello. All becomes friendly again when the cello moves up to imitate the first viola in m. 47. Here the first violist and cellist should emphasize their A-flat to point out how the momentary dissonance is resolved by imitating the figure that caused the dissonance. In m. 56, the horn arrives at a written high C and immediately becomes a secondary voice to the imitations in the string parts. Since our part is singularly uninteresting between m. 56 and m. 59, we can reduce the volume after the high note in m. 56.

In m. 104 there are two fermatas; one is on the first eighth-note in the horn part and the other is on the third eighth-note in the string parts. The strings release their eighth-note without regard for the fermata in the horn part. The horn then holds its fermata until all metric pulse has been suspended. When the horn moves after its fermata is completed, the meter is resumed in all parts. In this way the strings' fermata is completed when the horn begins to move. This can cause confusion if all of the players have not studied the score before the first rehearsal. Passing the score around the group at the rehearsal should clear away any uncertainty. The end of the movement should be played very simply, with only a slight delay before the final note. A tempo of eighth-note equals 88 seems appropriate for this movement.

Starting the third movement almost immediately will help the listener to be aware of the thematic connections between the second and third movements. The second viola has a very busy part during the first eight measures. It is often played too loudly. We should not ignore the dynamics as written: eight measures *piano* while the horn is playing, and eight measures *forte* while the strings play without the horn. The horn's volume during all of the technical passages should be strong enough to ensure a rapid response to the tongue and a crisp staccato. It must sound more joyous than soft. There is always the danger that we will lose volume as the scale proceeds downward in the first two measures. This is especially so if we slur the second group of sixteenth-notes as edited. No harm is done if we follow the traditional two-slurred, two-tongued articulation for the theme. We should feel a slight crescendo on the second group of sixteenth-notes. Here is a passage where effort can be mistaken for result. Listening to a taped play-back is wise to make sure that our efforts are resulting in clarity and projection of every note.

Quarter-note equals 126 will give the third movement a jovial feeling and should present no problem for horn players with a well-developed tongue. We can experiment with various articulation patterns for mm. 25 to 32. Slurring most of the notes takes away the sparkle. The familiar style of two notes slurred, two notes tongued seems to fit the music here also. The accompaniment during these technical passages must remain very steady and very soft. Playing from m. 37 to m. 48 in one breath is effective. The ornaments in m. 49 are exact imitations of the violinist's ornaments in m. 47.

There is a double bar in the middle of m. 73, after which the horn enters to begin the

next section. It always seems to be musically courteous to let the strings finish their last note
in tempo and then pause slightly before resuming in the latter half of m. 73. We do observe
the repeat in m. 81 after taking enough time for a full breath. It is better not to take the repeat
in m. 105, since it contains a repeat of m. 73 to m. 81. At the fermata in m. 126 we can play a
short cadenza consisting of a slightly ornamented downward B-flat major (actual pitch) arpeggio. From m. 143 to m. 167, tonguing the notes will add to the lightness and clarity. The
imitations among the strings and horn begun in m. 157 should be *forte* and each should gain
some vitality. In other editions the volume is reduced to *piano* in m. 178. That the Eulenburg-
Gerber edition permits the music to finish with energy and dash is reassuring.

## Trio for Piano, Violin and Horn, Op. 40, by Johannes Brahms

From the following list we can see that Brahms was concerned between 1860 and 1866
with large works for solo piano and with chamber music. In addition to these works, he composed many songs with piano and several short choral works during this period.

| | | |
|---|---|---|
| String Sextet | Op. 18 | 1860 |
| Variations and Fugue on a Theme by Handel, for piano | Op. 24 | 1861 |
| Piano Quartet | Op 25 | 1862 |
| Piano Quartet | Op. 26 | 1862 |
| Variations on a Theme by Paganini, for piano | Op. 35 | 1863 |
| Piano Quintet | Op. 34a | 1864 |
| String Sextet | Op. 36 | 1864 |
| Cello Sonata | Op. 38 | 1865 |
| Horn Trio | Op. 40 | 1865 |
| *A German Requiem* | Op. 45 | 1857–1866 |

Of these ten works, seven are chamber music for strings, five are for piano and strings, two are
for solo piano, one is for solo voices, chorus, and orchestra, and one includes the horn. We see
that Brahms, from rather early in his career, often wrote works for similar instrumentation
quite close together, with string sextets in 1860 and 1864, piano quartets in 1861 and 1862,
piano variations in 1861 and 1863, as well as the two orchestral overtures in 1881, orchestral
serenades in 1858 and 1859, and two sonatas for piano and clarinet in 1894. Sadly, for horn
players, of the twenty-four chamber works he wrote during his life there is only one that
includes the horn. There are more than 220 songs for solo voice and piano, and nearly 150
songs for two or more voices. By comparison, the orchestral music of Brahms is only a small
part of his total work; all of it remains in the standard repertory.

The title of this trio is interesting because it mentions the piano first and the horn last.
Until the Sonata for Violin and Pianoforte, Op. 108, written in 1887, Brahms and his publisher (Simrock) always listed the piano first in any chamber music that included the piano.
Today, Op. 40 is known simply as the horn trio. The International Music Company reprint
of this work retains the title of Trio for Piano, Violin and Horn.

The early 1860s saw a great flourish of chamber music from Brahms. It was also the
period of the American Civil War and the most productive years for Walt Whitman and
Emily Dickinson. By this time the valve horn was well-established but had not made the nat-

ural horn obsolete, since many players continued to play it in addition to the valve horn. Most horn players would have had their early instruction, if any, on the natural horn and only later turned to the valve horn. The valve mechanism and the general workmanship of the early valve instruments must have caused many problems until late in the nineteenth century. By then the orchestral horn parts of Strauss and others had become so complex that a true chromatic horn was needed. In 1865 the sound of the natural horn, or waldhorn as it was known in Germany and Austria, still lingered in Brahms's ear, as did the less than pleasing sound of some of the valve horn playing that he must have heard. As a child, Brahms had studied each of the instruments in the trio, and from this experience his preference for the waldhorn remained. Brahms played the piano part in several of the early performances of the trio and always asked for a waldhorn player. In recent years there has been a revival of interest in playing the natural horn. Many of our finest artists are playing it without abandoning the modern instrument. One suspects that the natural horn has never been played as well as it is being played today.

Brahms's predilection for the natural horn can be seen as a part of his conviction that music is a historical continuity. By his twentieth year he had begun to develop a life-long interest in early music. Before the age of Xerox he copied by hand works of Palestrina, Frescobaldi, Giovanni Gabrieli, Hassler, Schütz, Michael Praetorious, J. S. Bach, and other less well known composers. His library, which is preserved in the Archives of the Gesellschaft der Musikfreunde in Vienna, contains these hand-written pages, as well as the books, music, and autograph scores that he collected. The influence of the late Renaissance and early baroque composers can be seen most clearly in his choral writing. He also was an editor for the preparation of modern editions of works by Couperin, Carl Philipp Emanuel Bach, Wilhelm Friedemann Bach, Mozart, Schubert, Schumann, and Chopin. This was during the time that Liszt and Wagner were writing the "music of the future." To label Brahms as simply a backward-looking conservative composer is not helpful. Labels cannot convey a sense of the composer's strong musical individuality, his close ties to the musical scholarship of his time, his early classical musical training, his professional activities as pianist and conductor, or any meaningful evaluation of his music from our twentieth-century perspective. His music endures regardless of anything written about it during his lifetime.

Brahms was born shortly after Mendelssohn's revival of J. S. Bach's *St. Matthew Passion*. He died in 1897 during the decade in which the first wave of twentieth-century American composers were born. Paul Hindemith, although not strictly an American composer, was born in 1895. Walter Piston (1894), Roger Sessions (1896), Howard Hanson (1896), and George Gershwin (1898) each in his own way represented the new American music. Brahms's life span also encompassed the development and general acceptance of the valve horn. It is heart-warming, but mistaken, for horn players to believe that our instrument was Brahms's favorite. We must take our place somewhere behind the piano, the human voice, and string chamber music. There is no Brahms horn sonata, horn concerto, or quintet with strings. Brahms came upon the clarinet very late in his life thanks to the artistry of Richard Mühlfeld. The Trio Op. 114 (1891), the Quintet with Strings, Op. 115 (also 1891), and the two sonatas with piano were all written for Mühlfeld and are further evidence of Brahms's habit of writing more than one work for the same forces during a short period. We can speculate, with idleness, upon the riches lost to the horn community because Brahms's favorite wind player was a clarinetist, not a horn player; rejoice that we have a trio by Brahms; enrich our lives by studying the rest of his chamber music, his songs and his piano music; understand more fully his horn trio after becoming acquainted with the composer through studying his music. We will never again think of Brahms as a composer who wrote only middle-register solos for the first and third orchestral horns.

We can all profit from a detailed study of the last piano compositions of Brahms. Opuses 117, 118, and 119 contain shorter works that combine elegance with logic, intensity with resignation. This is not music for the self-important virtuoso or for the listener seeking diversion. When played with elegance, logic, intensity, resignation, and understanding, these works take the informed listener beyond the performer and the piano, and into the world of the music itself. This journey should be our goal when playing the trio or any of the orchestral music of Brahms.

From the beginning of the first movement of the horn trio, we are met with considerations of articulation and note length. Horn players are familiar with Brahms's use of dots under slurs, since this notational device occurs rather frequently in the orchestral music. Violinists occasionally ignore this marking or are puzzled by it. For horn players the dots mean that the notes are articulated with the tongue. The slurs mean that the notes are connected. We can best accomplish this by adding a slight taper between the eighth-notes and before the quarter-notes. The tongue stroke must be smooth and not accented. Some violinists find this articulation unfamiliar and awkward. At the first rehearsal we can speak of the virtues of consistency between the violin and the horn and might offer to demonstrate this articulation. Violinists, after some experimenting, can work wonders with stopping the bow very slightly between the eighth-notes and before the quarter-notes. This will sound very similar to our momentary tapering of the air stream between the notes. The pianist never plays this phrase during the movement, but can offer a listener's evaluation of progress. Taking enough time at rehearsals to agree on this articulation is worthwhile.

That the horn trio begins with an upward perfect fifth is no accident. Violinists are often concerned about making the shift to the second note so that the interval of the fifth is played rather tentatively. In this case, the *piano dolce* should not result in a small, lifeless sound from the violin. Neither the horn player nor the violinist should emphasize the first of the two eighth-notes. To do so would not allow the eighth-notes to be heard as upbeats that provide motion across the bar line.

Throughout the trio, each player must be aware of his or her instrument's role. These roles are constantly changing but can usually be identified as leading voice, equal voice, secondary voice, and accompaniment. The violin is the leading voice for the first eight measures but becomes, suddenly, part of the accompaniment in the ninth measure. In mm. 17–20 all three instruments are of equal importance. Much of our study and rehearsal of the trio should be devoted to arriving at an understanding and consensus on these matters.

Another interesting comparison of articulations occurs at rehearsal letter A. There the piano begins with two half-notes, which are imitated by the violin in the third measure and by the horn in the ninth measure. The piano cannot, of course, enter softly and add vibrato and crescendo after the key is struck for the half-notes. One often hears a violinist altering the volume and color of the sound after a note has begun. In the third measure of letter A, the violinist should imitate the pianist's articulation as closely as possible, and not swell on the half-notes. Notice that from the horn's entrance in the ninth measure of A, the violin and the horn are of equal importance. From the seventeenth measure of A to B the right hand of the pianist, the horn, and the violin are all of equal importance. All three players must adjust their volume (not necessarily downward) to achieve this type of balance. At letter B the pianist's left hand, the violin, and the horn are, again, of equal importance. The piano's half-step figures and the violin's motive will become important factors in the coda.

At the Poco più animato section, the character of the music must change noticeably. Several things are different. The harmony is much less rooted in E-flat major; it is in 9/8, not 2/4; the thematic material is long and flowing; the tempo is slightly faster and there is a feeling of restlessness. It is not sufficient simply to play more rapidly. The rather staid vertical quality of the first section must now be replaced by a freedom of line and nuance. In the ninth measure of the Poco più animato the pianist should bring out the half-step figures in the left hand, and three measures before letter C the left hand should supply a strong lower voice. Notice that there is no diminuendo before C.

At C we have, again, equal roles among the violin, the horn, and the dotted quarter-notes in the pianist's left hand. During rehearsals all three players must listen and strive for a balance that will allow this remarkable counterpoint to be heard clearly. It is often the pianist's right hand that is heard too prominently. At five measures before D the piano part is marked *dolce*. The violinist can anticipate the more relaxed feeling by playing the octaves very gently. At letter D there is a beautiful descending line in the pianist's left hand that must not be obscured by the right hand. For the transition back to Tempo I, the pianist has the main responsibility for shaping the ritardando. Ideally, the speed of the rising perfect fifth in the violin and later in the horn should be identical. This is possible since Brahms has written duplets in the piano part to continue the feeling of ritardando.

At letter E, the horn has a secondary voice and must not compete with the violin. At the ninth measure of E is another example of the equal importance of the violin, the horn, and the pianist's left hand. This left-hand figure also becomes prominent in the coda. The approach to the Poco più animato is handled in the same way as before. Brahms, predicting our tendency to slow down as the music fades, admonishes us with senza ritardando before the 9/8.

This Poco più animato section is much shorter than its predecessor after B. The same restless quality is present but this time the piano has the role of accompanist. The constant eighth-notes in the right hand can distract from the melodic lines in the horn and piano if the pianist allows the volume to become overpowering. The return to the 2/4 is exactly the same as before.

At the Tempo I after letter G, all instruments are *pianissimo* in preparation for the long crescendo and accelerando to follow. There must be no change of volume until the slight crescendo eight measures before H. Here the piano must lead the crescendo with the half-step figures between the hands. The animato must not be anticipated but, once begun, it must go forward immediately. Notice that the horn arrives at *forte* before the violin and the piano. At the double bar before I, Brahms has written optional rests under the notes in the first three measures, just as he did at H. In both instances he provided a moment's rest for the horn player before the ascent to the high B-flat. Horn players with well-developed embouchures need not observe the rests.

At letter I Brahms has written *p* in the piano part but not in the other parts. This is puzzling, since in the third measure of I he writes *sempre diminuendo e ritard, poco a poco*. We then have no other dynamic mark until eighteen measures later, where there is *pianissimo*. It seems appropriate that the left hand of the pianist should remain strong enough to lead the diminuendo until the twelfth measure of I, where the piano part abruptly changes its configuration. At this twelfth measure after I the horn has become the leading voice in preparation for the end of the movement. If all three players are *piano* at this point, the descent from the *forte* will seem well-paced and the diminuendo can still proceed to the *pianissimo* in the last three measures.

This is the only time that Brahms abandoned his beloved sonata form in the first movement of any of his twenty-four chamber music compositions. Out of his own wisdom he chose to alternate 2/4 and 9/8 sections which can be shown as ABABA. The sections are proportioned superbly; the outer A sections are the longest. Each of the inner BAB sections is shorter than its predecessor. All that really matters is the control Brahms maintained over his material.

Before arriving at a tempo for the Scherzo we should study the whole movement to find the real character of the music. If we are searching for an ancestral kin, it would more likely be the Scherzo from the Beethoven Fifth Symphony than the Scherzo from Mendelssohn's *Midsummer Night's Dream*. This Brahms scherzo is solid and serious, not transparent and light. It is not relentlessly energetic; there are moments of grace and tenderness. The trio of this scherzo does not provide contrast by becoming witty and frolicsome; it becomes melancholy. There is no dazzle of virtuosity in this movement; it speaks of substance rather than frivolity. All of this seems to lead us to a tempo that is fast enough to be powerfully energetic at times and gracefully reflective at others. We have all heard performances of this scherzo that were so fast that the music between letters C and E was a technical and musical jumble. Obviously, in seeking an appropriate tempo we must consider much more than the pianist's first twelve measures. The horn's melody at B, the effect of the periodic insertion of duplets into an otherwise triple meter, and the melody and its accompaniment at C are all pertinent to establishing a musically rational tempo. Dotted half-note equals 100 gives us a starting tempo that feels steadfast but is not so rapid that a relaxation of energy during the lyrical moments will sound fabricated. We must be in control of the tempo so that letters A and E are exactly the same speed in spite of all of the music in between. We should not confuse speed with energy. This is a movement that can easily accumulate speed as it progresses if we are less than vigilant. It is also a movement in which nearly all of it can sound either *fortissimo* or *mezzo forte*, rather than *forte* or *piano*. We must not confuse volume with energy.

The first twelve measures are played extremely short, *piano*, not *mezzo piano*, unaccented, with slightly more left hand than right, and without crescendo. Pianists are reluctant to do all of this. We should not ignore the staccato mark on the second note in the second measure of A. The pianist has the responsibility of ensuring the stability of the tempo after the duplets at A. At twenty measures before B, the violin and horn have to play very softly accompanying the piano. At fifteen measures before B, notice how Brahms uses a duple device known as hemiola to help the music relax slightly. At thirteen measures before B the horn accompanies only and must stay in the background. At dotted half-note equals 100 the horn line at B can sound broad, lyrical, and unhurried.

Five measures after the double bar before C, Brahms begins a twenty-measure transition into the more lyrical music at C. Notice how once again Brahms uses duplets to slow the forward motion of the music. On paper, it seems quite drastic to suggest that C should be played at dotted half-note equals 84 after having started the music at 100. It is enlightening to listen to the metronome set at 84 for several beats and then play C at this speed. Suddenly the horn and the violin can play a calm dolce and the pianist can play the eighth-notes lightly and without tension. It is important that the pianist observe the quarter-rests as they occur after C. Releasing the accumulation of sound helps to keep the texture open and light. The violinist's eighth-notes seven measures before D will sound controlled and relaxed at 84. Brahms has given us twenty measures of transition before C to move gradually to the slower tempo. His duplets give us the means to do so. At the double bar after D, we have fourteen measures to ease the tempo back to 100 at E. Twenty-five measures after E the *piano* dynamic stays in effect until eight before F. Starting the crescendo much sooner is always tempting. The horn part is a secondary voice from E until thirteen after F. The chords and the cadence six measures before the double bar after G must be strictly in time and the violinst's entrance after the double bar should not be delayed.

The pianist has eight measures to change the tempo between the two double bars. Notice that Brahms wrote molto meno allegro, not adagio or lento for the trio. This seems to indicate that we should preserve the pulse of one beat per measure. At dotted half-note equals 40–44 we can still feel the music in one beat per measure and there remains a hint of allegro in the speed of the quarter-notes. Notice how, at the beginning of the trio, the harmony in the piano does not change for eight measures. Notice, also, that there are no full cadences in this trio of seventy-six measures. The eighth-note movement is constant until the sixty-seventh measure. During the last nine measures of the trio, the violinist and the horn player remain motionless until the pianist has played several measures of the da capo. There is plenty of time to turn back the pages to the beginning of the movement. The pianist should ask the page turner not to turn back the pages until sometime after A. The pianist will be happy to play these few measures from memory. All of the da capo is played exactly as before. The pianist's chords in the fourth measure before the *fine* should be played rather late, and the last sustained chord is also delayed, but not lengthened. These measures were not held back before going on to the trio.

Composers have written the word *mesto* to indicate intense grief. Beethoven used the term in the second movement of his Piano Sonata Op. 10, No. 3. There, the meter is 6/8 and the interval of the half-step is prominent in the melodic line. Béla Bartók used *mesto* for the first, second, and fourth movement of his sixth string quartet. The meter is 6/8 in these movements and the half-step is prominent. Brahms used *adagio mesto* as an indication of tempo and sadness in the third movement of his horn trio. The meter is 6/8 and the interval of the half-step is very important in the beginning and throughout the movement. Brahms surely knew the Op. 10, No. 3 of Beethoven; Bartók must have known both the Beethoven Sonata and the Brahms Horn Trio.

In arriving at a tempo for the third movement, we have to find that point where slowness causes us to hear individual stationary notes and not their motion within the phrase. Slow music can become vertical rather than horizontal. For this third movement, the stationary feeling begins at approximately eighth-note equals 52. If we believe that 56–58 is an appropriate general tempo for this movement, we are free to move slightly in either direction as the music suggests. Because of the arpeggio effect that Brahms used in the first four measures of the piano part, the tempo will seem slightly slower than 56–58. These chords must be arpeggiated so that the melodic notes are sounded together in both hands. In addition to using the *una corda* pedal, the pianist can darken these measures even more by having more weight on the left hand than the right. This seems backward to most pianists but it is worth investigating. In spite of the diminuendo in the fourth measure, there should be no ritardando and no break in the line before the violin and horn enter in m. 5. This has always been a troublesome entrance for horn players. It can be less hazardous if the players agree that the downbeat in m. 5 is not delayed and the volume is a healthy *piano*, as written, and not *pianissimo*. If there is a natural feeling of rhythm from the sixth eighth-note in m. 4 to the first eighth-note in m. 5, we can breathe confidently on the sixth beat and release the tongue precisely on the first beat.

This breath must be full and relaxed, since there is no good place to breathe during the next five measures. Good eye contact and slight body motions on the preparatory beat are also helpful. We can perfect the mechanics of this entrance by setting the metronome at 56–58 and practicing the timing of the air intake and tongue release. Our confidence will be improved by having a method that works.

Beginning eight measures before rehearsal letter A, the violinist should play the next five measures on the A and D strings. Violinists are often reluctant to play high on the A string when the E string is so comfortable and available for the higher notes. There is, however, a real feeling of anguish connected with playing high on the A string that is not matched on the E string.

At letter A, the three instruments are of equal importance until the ninth measure. At letter B, the stringendo does not begin until the second half of the measure. Notice that the stringendo remains in effect during the diminuendo in the fifth measure. In the eighth measure after B the stringendo is canceled by the poco a poco leading to the in tempo at the twelfth measure. For Brahms this is a complex set of directions, but if we play exactly as he directed us, all will be well. The low A-flat in mm. 9–11 after B becomes sublimely dissonant when the harmony changes in the latter half of these measures. Our volume should be sufficient to make the dissonance very clear. Brahms asks the violinist to play *quasi niente* in the twelfth measure of B. Although these two measures are often played without vibrato, nothing in the word *niente* prohibits vibrato. Notice that the piano is now *pianissimo*, compared with *piano* at the beginning, and the violin is *ppp* with a diminuendo.

At letter C there is momentary relief from the darkness of E-flat minor and a harbinger of the last movement's thematic material. We can forecast the spirit, if not the liveliness, of the next movement by playing C slightly faster. This leads us into the poco accelerando in the ninth measure of C. After holding back the tempo and volume for so long, the *forte passionato* should appear as a sudden outpouring of grief continuing even as the octaves become lower and lower. We simply must continue the *fortissimo* as the notes descend to the low F. To maintain the volume we can take a quick breath after the first eighth-note in the second measure of letter D. This is the first time that Brahms used *fortissimo* in the trio; he used it once more at the end of the fourth movement. Brahms did not use passionato or *fortissimo* routinely or frequently. Beginning seven measures before D, the pianist must observe the rests in the right hand by not holding the chords or allowing the pedal to sustain the harmony through the rests. When the rests are observed, the bass line is clear. This is especially necessary at D as the left hand begins its descent to the low C-flat one measure before Tempo I. Whatever speed has been accumulating during the poco accelerando and passionato must not dissipate until the poco ritardando one measure before Tempo I. The C-natural in this measure must be very strong and very late to accomplish the poco ritardando in only one measure. In the third measure of the Tempo I, the left hand of the pianist becomes prominent as it begins another descent, which settles on the E-flat to D half-step figure that began the movement. The sforzando four measures from the end should not be startling but should be heard as a final expression of a painful melancholy.

The horn part in the Finale is full of the typical hunting signal at the rising fourth and fifth. Most of these signals are *forte* and, except for those at letter E, all are slurred. Just as in the Scherzo, we must not overplay either the *forte* or the *piano* dynamic levels. Horn players, of course, are rarely guilty of this. The first phrase between the violin and the piano is often played too loudly, thus destroying the gradual rise in volume toward the *forte* eight measures after letter A. Ten measures after B the ensemble must not exceed *piano*. Playing the first ending and the repeat shows respect for Brahms and our understanding of the structure of the movement. The return to the first measure is exactly in time as if it were written out rather than repeated.

Our big moment is at F, where Brahms wrote twenty-four measures of lyrical playing based upon the hunting signals. Notice that the piano is most often soft during these measures when our part is *forte*. The eighth-note of the signal must not hurry across the bar line. By arriving at the eighth-note early enough, we can play it strongly and at least full value. It is not just an upbeat, but a vital member of the signal. One measure before letter I, we are all tempted to play the high C very loudly. This could be described as playing the note at the expense of the music. The real *fortissimo* is eleven measures before the end of the movement. This is music that can suffer from an embarrassing accumulation of uncontrolled speed. Dotted eighth-note equals 126 seems to be the speed limit. As in the Scherzo, it is tempting to confuse speed with energy.

A detailed study of the piano part reveals that the pianist supplies most of the energy of the finale. Some of this energy is generated by a marcato accompaniment whenever the main thematic material is presented. Notice how the texture is changed when the volume is altered. This can be seen clearly by comparing the first eight measures with what follows at A. When the violin plays at the beginning, there is no octave-doubling in the left hand of the piano part and only a few notes in the right hand, thus creating an open and light texture most appropriate for the *p* dynamic level. At letter A a much richer fabric is created by enlarging the piano part in both hands and by adding the horn. Here we are not less important than the violin, and as a new voice our presence must be felt from our first note.

Brahms obtains another type of energy by using the rhythmic device of the hemiola. A hint of this can be seen in the accents in mm. 3 and 4, and mm. 3 and 4 after A. At C and D all six eighth-notes are beamed together, telling the pianist to abandon the conventional 6/8 rhythmic practice of dividing the measure into two groups of three eighth-notes. It now has become three groups of two notes. This shifting of the rhythmic pulse is quite subtle at C but more pronounced at D, where both hands and eventually the violin participate in this shifting of pulse.

For a few horn players the rhythm at six measures before C and six measures before H can be troublesome. We dare not wait until the first rehearsal to perfect this rhythm. We can see that the pianist will give very strong accents on the main beats in these measures. We have no choice but to trust the pianist to do so. In the privacy of our practice room we can set the metronome at dotted quarter-note equals 126 and play the rhythm against its beats. No tongue stroke should coincide with any of the beats. It is always helpful to take away the ties and tongue all of the six notes in these measures. When the notes are secure we can begin to restore the tie in the sixth measure, then in the fifth measure, and continue adding measures until we can play the proper rhythm from the first measure. Listen to the piano to establish this rhythm two measures before playing it. If we are late in beginning this pattern, catching up is almost impossible. In the seventh measure before C and H we can release the long note early enough to be set for beginning this rhythm. These passages must be played very boldly by all three players. All of the notes must be equal in volume. It is very disconcerting for the pianist and the violinist to have to teach the horn player how to play this rhythm correctly during any of the rehearsals. Violinists and pianists rarely have trouble with it. A somewhat similar rhythm appears at m. 135 in the first movement of the Brahms Second Symphony.

The horn is only heard by itself for two measures at A in the third movement. With this exception, Brahms always supplies a cushion of piano sound for us. As in the orchestral works, he gives the horn player the basic information of dynamic levels, and some indication of style. It remains for us to study the score to determine how our part fits into the general categories of leading voice, equal voice, secondary voice, and accompaniment. Perhaps we can assume that the violinist has played the Brahms sonatas or other chamber music works with piano, and is therefore accustomed to the richness of the piano writing. Surely the pianist is not playing Brahms for the first time. For the horn player, this could well be the first venture into chamber music with piano and violin. If so we must rely more on our study of the music than on our past experience.

In this work the horn must always be heard clearly and with its own distinctive voice. This does not mean that *forte* and *fortissimo* passages are played with an orchestral extravagance or the *pianissimo* passages with a tone so small that it becomes dull and lifeless. The horn sound must retain its individuality whether it is the leading voice or the accompanying voice. The piano does not sound unlike a piano when it has an accompanying role. To be so subservient in volume as to lose our musical identity does not serve the music. To "blend" so well as to become inconspicuous defeats the logic of Brahms's choices of instruments for this trio. A viola would probably blend better with the violin, but then we would no longer have a horn trio.

## Trio for Violin, Horn and Piano, Op. 44, by Lennox Berkeley

Although commissioned by Colin Horsley and dedicated to Shiela Robertson, this trio is another work written for and introduced by Dennis Brain. It was written in 1952, and was performed for the first time in 1953 while Brain was at the height of his career as soloist, chamber music player, and orchestral musician. This trio has very little in common with the Brahms Trio Op. 40; to point out their differences does no disservice to either work.

Whereas the Brahms Trio has a feeling of melancholy for three of its four movements, the Berkeley Trio is more optimistic throughout its three movements. Brahms's piano writing is often dark, rich, and favors the lower portion of the keyboard. Berkeley has written a transparent piano part that is most often contrapuntal. In only a few instances are conventional accompaniment figures used. Berkeley writes long passages for piano and violin, or piano and horn, or one instrument by itself. In the Brahms Trio, all three of the instruments play together much of the time.

These differences are apparent from the first measure of the first movement. The horn begins with a bold statement of rising fourths against a contrasting contrapuntal line in the piano. The accents in the horn are strong and the *forte* is intense. This is completely different from the first several measures of the Brahms Trio. Berkeley asks the players and the listener to be accountable for two main thematic lines played simultaneously; Brahms introduces his theme with the most simple of accompaniments. Lennox Berkeley's long study, from 1927 to 1932, with Nadia Boulanger could be responsible for his natural flow of counterpoint.

In the fifth measure of rehearsal number 4, a dynamic mark of *piano* is missing in the piano part. It is very rewarding to relax the tempo slightly in the fourth measure of 4. From 5 to 7 Berkeley has written a series of events that move forward in intensity and height. We can enhance the activity by allowing the speed to move along to the high B at 7. The violin entrance at 7 should be accented rather heavily.

The recapitulation at 10 is more powerful when it is not preceded by a ritardando. Notice that the composer has distributed the thematic and contrapuntal responsibilities differently from the way he began the movement, but again we hear these two strands together. From the fifth to the eighth measures of 10 we must tongue the sixteenth-notes very sharply, since they are followed by the same pitch. At 11 the downward scale must have no diminuendo. At 13 we have no choice but to enter with a bold confidence on the high A-flat. Here, again, we need short and strongly accented sixteenth-notes. This is the dramatic and dynamic peak of the movement. The descent to the final measures begins in the fifth measure of 13. The triplets five measures after 14 are light, not marcato, and only slightly accented.

The second movement is more gentle than sad and more resigned than dramatic. This is music that requires great patience from the players because of the slow tempo. Several very soft entrances below the staff demand our best legato attack. The horn part is full of fourths and fifths that recall, once again, an ancient battle or hunt. These figures are played very gently and never hurried. It is appropriate that these remembrances occur only in the horn part and most often as a distant background to the violin. Examples are at six measures before 16, nine measures after 16, and ten measures after 17. Not by chance is the first interval in the horn part a rising perfect fifth. The notes in the second movement are not difficult. The style is not puzzling if we are content to play with restraint.

Curiously, throughout the trio the metronome markings have been omitted in the violin and horn parts. The piano score has all of these markings except for the beginning of the third movement. Eighth-note equals 116 seems appropriate. Since this movement is written as a theme with ten variations, we expect to find a variety of styles and tempi and a few references to the theme. The most distinctive feature of the theme is the interval of the minor seventh. It is easily recognized and is heard prominently in eight of the ten variations.

After the rather easy-going theme, the first variation is very lively, with accents, fast notes, and an almost Stravinsky-like neo-classical feeling. We must not be shy with the accents, bland with the staccato notes, or moderate with the *fortissimo*. A slight pause is necessary before starting the second variation.

The volume does not rise above *mezzo piano* during the second variation. It must have a feeling of smoothness and hushed calm. The sixteenth-notes in the piano should not create excitement or intensity.

The third variation is for horn and piano. It appears to have much in common with the third movement of the Brahms Horn Trio, with its slow-moving 6/8 meter, its use of half-steps, and its thick darkness. The pianist should try to bring out the half-steps in the outer voices during the first six measures. The horn part is taken from the two measures before 18 in the statement of the theme. It revolves around the half-step from B-flat to B-natural. In this variation we should remain content with the slow pace of the music, and the pianist should not move the tempo ahead at 24. The last five measures are in exactly the same tempo as the beginning of the variation. The third measure from the end is played with regular stopped horn fingerings. Because of the glissando, the last two measures are played with the second valve on the F horn with the hand closed enough to bring the pitch down to B-flat. We can open the hand to its usual position for the B-natural and slowly close it again for the glissando to the B-flat. By studying the piano part of this variation we can see the ingenious way the composer handled the half-steps in both hands of the pianist and in the horn part. Here, again, it is not by chance that the horn part centers around the infamous seventh partial.

The fourth variation is for violin and piano. Though not very fast, its jaunty feeling seems perfect after the solemnity of Variation III. We should not move until the violinist has played several measures of Variation IV. Only then should we attend to the water in silence and with propriety.

Because the horn begins Variation V, we must have the tempo firmly in mind before playing the first note. Tempos are easily remembered when they can be associated with a melodic line or a conspicuous rhythm. This rhythm is mechanically precise and must be especially so during the last five measures. For orchestral musicians to slow the tempo upon seeing *pesante* has become habitual. Lennox Berkeley has used the eighth-note rhythm throughout the variation as a steady rhythmic ostinato. We should use the literal meaning of *pesante*, which is heavy, not slower, and increase the volume and lengthen the notes. The last note is massive.

The music in Variation VI flows very freely at dotted half-note equals 46. It loses much of its graceful charm when each quarter-note is felt. The horn part is made entirely from perfect fifths. We must observe the fermata over the bar line at the end of Variation VI so that the austerity of Variation VII is felt immediately.

In Variation VII the theme is in the left hand of the pianist; the horn part is a counter melody. The balance is difficult to achieve if the harmony in the right hand is too loud. The violinist can check the balance from a distance to ensure that the two strands of melody are heard very clearly. From the beginning to the end of this variation, the left hand must be heard clearly as a melodic voice.

Variation VIII is a brief intermezzo in which the interval of the seventh is featured. Most of the dialogue is between the piano and the violin. The horn player must be ready to set the tempo in Variation IX, since there is no pause after Variation VIII. The music in Variation IX has a perpetual motion feeling as it goes forward relentlessly. The *fortissimo* five measures before the end of the variation is brilliant. There is no ritardando before the beginning of Variation X. The pianist starts Variation X in exactly the same tempo as was used for the statement of the theme at the beginning of the movement. This variation is a gentle reminiscence of the theme and is dolce and cantabile throughout. The ending will not seem abrupt if the last few notes are slower than the rest of the variation. The reentry after the second fermata is not difficult if the pianist gives a strong gesture on the fifth eighth-note in the penultimate measure.

Horn players who wish to do more than play the notes will want to study this trio to discover more than these paragraphs have revealed. It would be interesting to learn how Lennox Berkeley arranged the order of the variations to achieve both unity and contrast. This quest could lead to studying the Brahms Variations on a Theme by Haydn or the Elgar *Enigma Variations* for the same purpose.

### Serenade for Tenor Solo, Horn and Strings, Op. 31, by Benjamin Britten

To discuss the Serenade under the heading of chamber music seems appropriate even though it is conducted in performance. It is most often performed with a small string group rather than with the string section of a symphony orchestra. The strings act as accompanist throughout the work, and there are no extended tutti passages demanding a large sonorous string section. The violins and violas are often quite high in register while the celli and basses are low, thus giving the middle ground to the tenor and horn. Examples of this can be seen at rehearsal number 7 in the Nocturne and throughout the Sonnet. The strings have only an occasional *forte* or *fortissimo* but many times are asked to play *forte piano*, accents, sforzando, marcato, divisi, and soli. Every note in the Hymn is pizzicato. Only in the Dirge, and at 7 in the Nocturne do the string parts engage in melodic counterpoint with the tenor or the horn. The string parts are edited meticulously with all of the information necessary for producing an accompaniment that is inconspicuous in the Pastoral, brilliant in the beginning of the Nocturne, dark and threatening in the Elegy, grotesque in the Dirge, simple in the Hymn, and transpicuous in the Sonnet.

On the title page of the full score, printed by Boosey and Hawkes in 1944, this work is called Serenade for Tenor Solo, Horn and Strings. Horn players refer to it as the Britten Serenade, not the Horn Serenade. Horn players and other musicians are fond of reducing names and titles to their most bare necessities—horn trio, Till, short call, Tchaik. The word *solo* in the title should not trouble horn players, since it establishes that the tenor is the protagonist. The horn has a variety of roles. It is, at times, soloist, equal partner with the tenor, or obbligato (which means necessary), but is never completely in the background. Except for the Prologue and the Epilogue the strings play almost constantly but always in support of the tenor or horn.

In studying the score, the conductor must be concerned with matters of volume, style, balance, color, pacing and shape of the movements, and dramatic effects. The "beating" of time—another unfortunate term, which is, however, descriptive of many conductors—should be the least of the conductor's concerns. That conductors will be able to understand, remember, and follow the composer's wishes for tempo is assumed.

We, likewise, must study the score to determine how our part fits into the scheme. We are also concerned with volume, style, balance, color, and dramatic effects. We will need soft high attacks, rapid single tongue, bold accents, a reliable high C, a pedal F, soft low notes, and a dynamic range from a soothing *pianissimo* to a searing *fortissimo*.

Providing the audience with a copy of the text to follow during a vocal performance has become almost acceptable. This practice has been described as a courtesy to the listeners but could also be described as an admission that the singer lacks the ability to project the words. Attending a vocal recital during which the audience is looking at the text rather than at the stage is disturbing. The listener's attention is diverted from the total performance toward the attempt to follow the text. It has even been suggested that the stage manager, on occasion, has not provided enough house light for the listeners to read their texts. Is the expectation unreasonable that American singers will sing English words clearly enough that English-speaking people can understand them? Does providing the audience with texts exonerate the singer from the burden of the words? Is it enough to sing only pitches and rhythms?

During the performance of the Serenade, the horn player stands on stage right (the conductor's left) and the tenor on stage left. Much of the effect is lost if the horn player sits among the strings. Ideally, both the tenor and the horn player perform the Serenade from memory. A performance of the Serenade in which the tenor sings from memory while the horn player cowers behind a music stand ratifies the belief that tenors have sufficient musical industry and intelligence to memorize, and horn players do not. It has been suggested that since orchestral horn players always have their music to look at, they are, thereby, excused from memorizing anything. Any horn player with the technical skills and musical sophistication necessary to play this magnificent work will not be content until the music is memorized. A tiny number of celebrated soloists from the recent past apparently could not memorize. Their weakness must not be seen as justification for our lack of industry in preparation, or courage in performance.

The Serenade, written for Dennis Brain and Peter Pears, is yet another work born out of a composer's admiration for the musicianship of specific artists. It suggests to horn players that we should search out gifted composers and interest them in writing for us. This effort can begin during the college years, when horn players and composers are studying under the same roof, and is often a mutually beneficial association. For horn players, this could be a first step toward removing the fear and loathing of today's music from those unacquainted with its notation and aesthetics. Composers need to accumulate an enormous warehouse of sounds and techniques to draw upon. They need to know how the horn really sounds in all its registers and volumes. On the practical side, composers must know what works against their intentions. Musicians are fond of saying that a piece of music or a technique "works." There is no doubt that everything works in the Britten Serenade. The horn sings, it is technically brilliant, the complete three and one-half octave range is covered intelligently, the horn's unique history is evident in the Prologue and the Epilogue, and the muted and stopped horn are used in a musically appropriate setting.

Some thought should be given to when we should start to play the Prologue. We arrive on stage and there is applause. The audience then needs a few moments to settle into a receptive calm. Our actions on stage must do nothing to interrupt the transition from applause to receptivity. Tuning on stage is always disconcerting and playing a few warm-up notes is even worse. The horn must be completely dry before we enter the stage so that the spell is not broken by noisy water removal. Our posture and demeanor must be in keeping with the serenity of the beginning of the Prologue. When there is total silence and everyone in the audience has stopped rattling the pages of the text, we can count approximately ten seconds before raising the horn to begin the Serenade.

The Prologue is written with bar lines but no time signatures. The *sempre ad libitum* gives us the opportunity to shape the phrases but not the license to distort the relative lengths of note values. A quarter-note remains approximately twice the length of an eighth-note, etc. In performance, the longest note values can be more felt than counted. In the practice room we can begin by playing exact note values to establish a feeling for the lengths of notes. In doing so we must not try to force the notes into conventional patterns of 3/4, 4/4, or 5/4. Britten was perfectly capable of writing the Prologue with changing meters. He chose not to do so. There are fourteen measures of varying lengths in the Prologue; twelve of them start with an eighth-note followed by a longer value. This indicates that the eighth-notes are never felt as upbeats to the longer value, but that the weight of these figures falls upon the shorter note, not the longer. This becomes quite evident in the ninth measure, where Britten has written accents over the eighth-notes, but it applies as well to every measure that begins with an eighth-note. The feeling of short-long is not syncopation with its usual stress on the longer value. Only when this relationship of note values is natural and reliable can we begin to apply the freedoms indicated by the composer. We should not listen to any of the fine recordings of the Serenade merely to mimic the soloist's playing of these rhythms. We must become very sure of our understanding of the rhythmic subtleties and nuances before being influenced by even the finest of recordings. We all can learn from the playing of great artists, but listening to their recordings is not a substitute for understanding what the composer wrote.

For the Prologue, Britten used the extremes of soft and loud, but not the middle levels of *mezzo piano* and *mezzo forte*. *Più forte* means more loudly than the preceding, but in this case the preceding refers to the first measure, which is *piano*. We are more accustomed to fitting *più forte* between *forte* and *fortissimo*, but here Britten has used *più* in its literal sense. Notice how mm. 1, 6, and 11 contain the same music and nearly the same notation. Through the use of *a tempo*, those measures are all the same speed. We should make a distinction between Britten's use of the comma for breathing and his use of the quarter-rests for longer silences. All the increases of volume and all the freedom of accelerando and animando must lead to the *fortissimo* in m. 11. This is the ultimate outdoor signal. It should strain the volume of the F side of the horn.

Obviously, our embouchure must be completely warmed up before starting the Prologue, since we have delicate playing, fairly wide leaps, a sudden *pianissimo*, and a shouting *fortissimo* to play just after having entered the stage. Nearly all of this is in a seldom-used register of the F horn. The notes feel very slippery and close together. For several weeks before the performance we can devote a good share of our practice time to this unfamiliar part of the instrument for the sake of accuracy and our confidence. Since the composer calls for the Prologue to be played on the natural harmonics, we have no choice but to use the F horn, although one suspects that more than one horn player has used the B-flat horn for the first measure.

We should not try to "tune" the seventh, eleventh, or thirteenth partials. They are "in tune" with the harmonic series but sound strange to equal temperament ears. The odd partials give the Prologue a feeling of the remote past and are not to be confused with modern natural horn playing, whose practitioners make a valiant attempt to "correct" the pitch of these partials. If program notes are given to the listeners, include a brief mention of the acoustical considerations of the Prologue and the Epilogue so that no one is distracted by what might seem to be very bad intonation. Most horn players play the high A as a fourteenth partial.

With the Prologue and the Pastoral we begin to see the economy of means with which Britten achieves variety in the Serenade. The Prologue has its short-long two-note rhythmic grouping, which is continued into the accompaniment of the Pastoral. The horn part of the Pastoral is made almost exclusively from downward arpeggios. For the Pastoral we need confidence in our high soft entrances and our legato attacks. With the exception of the entrance eight measures after 2, the harmony in the accompaniment prepares our ears for the first notes. There is always enough time to hear and feel the note on which we enter. We can practice these entrances by setting the metronome at 54 and timing our breath over two beats. None of these phrases requires a large intake of air, but we need a slow breath and time enough at the top of the breath to hear and feel the note before releasing the tongue. The highest entrance is the softest, of course. Our method of breathing should not change for this entrance. Although Britten has written *ppp sempre* at 3, this low A-flat (D-flat concert pitch) must be heard clearly enough to form a tritone with the Gs in the accompaniment.

In the Nocturne we have, once again, the short-long rhythmic coupling of note values. Except for the soft trills that accompany the cadenzas, this distinctive rhythm is always present in the strings. The horn part, most appropriately, is a series of bugle calls. Britten has given us specific note values, articulation lengths, and dynamics for each call. Through his use of the word *simile* we understand that each call has an accelerando and ritardando. We must take care that the two eighth-notes after the triplets are not so slow that the 3 to 2 ratio of triplet to duplet is destroyed by the ritardando. One often hears these calls played as if each of the eighth-notes had been written as a quarter-note. Before adding the accelerando and ritardando we must be sure that we can play the calls strictly in time. The second call is not different in any way from the first. The third and fourth calls are *più* (more) *forte* (loud), but not louder than *forte*. The top of the fifth call is a generous *forte*. Notice that beginning with the fifth call we enter after a quarter-rest. All of the other calls have begun after longer rests. The sixth call is marked *mezzo forte*, not *più forte*. The last note before 5 is very long; the fermata does not begin until after the last note in the strings.

The muted calls in the cadenza at 6 are *come sopra*, which means as above, or as before. The pacing of the calls is the same as before, but the volume in the fourth call after 8 rises to *fortissimo*, not *forte*, as before. Our straight mute must be able to produce a blazing *fortissimo*. This can be an extraordinarily thrilling sound. Since we rarely play tongued muted notes this loudly, we have to practice for accuracy, volume, and confidence. This is not the place to be timid in performance.

For the third set of calls Britten adds vivace to *come sopra*. Now everything is faster but shaped the same as before. The tenor often takes more time with the last "dying, dying." The conductor must observe a long fermata before continuing at 9. If we use the mute, as Britten suggests, for the last two measures, its insertion must coincide precisely with the string entrance. Some horn players prefer to stop the horn. The third valve on the F horn produces a reliable pitch for the stopped note.

Some horn players may have played the Nocturne without having read the text. The image drawn by the line of poetry that precedes each of the three sets of calls is very clear: (1) "And the wild cataract leaps in glory"; (2) "The horns of Elfland faintly blowing"; (3) "Our echoes roll from soul to soul And grow forever and forever." It is also possible that some horn players have attempted to play this work without looking at the music written for the tenor. In the vocal part of the cadenzas Britten continues his use of the short-long rhythmic grouping. This is particularly fitting for words such as *bugle, echoes, answer, flying,* and *dying.*

We have seen how Beethoven in his Piano Sonata Op. 10, No. 3, and Brahms in the third movement of the Horn Trio have used the interval of the descending half-step to express grief. The entire horn part of the Elegy is composed with half-steps; only three of them are upward. As we might expect, Britten uses the short-long rhythmic grouping again. This time it is extremely slow. Compare this version of the rhythm with that used in the Nocturne. The Elegy is really a horn solo, since there are only eight measures for the tenor to sing. We must resist, mightily, any suggestion by the tenor or the conductor to speed up the tempo to "keep it moving," or to make the phrases more comfortable to play or sing. Slow music is slow music. To "move" it destroys its essence.

The form of the Elegy is a simple ABA. The B section is a short accompanied recitativo by the tenor and is somewhat free. The horn plays only during the A sections. When the horn plays, the music plods slowly and laboriously. This is not pretty music, but music about hideous death. Each section of the Elegy begins G-sharp and G-natural, and those two notes end the piece. This is economy, logic, unity, and superb technique.

The Serenade cannot be performed by any horn player who lacks a high C or the confidence to attack it softly. We can practice these entrances by a series of five attacks:

Example 6-1

When, after several weeks, we have achieved a high rate of accuracy, we can begin to add the G before the high C, and gradually add more notes until the complete phrase is played in the proper volume. This exercise must not be done on fatigued lips, and we should pause several seconds before each attempt. We time our breathing precisely with the metronome and enter exactly one eighth-note after the next beat. We then have an orderly and proven method of playing this difficult part of the Elegy. The more times we hear ourselves play this passage successfully, the more reason we have to expect success at the concert. Hope is fine; confidence born of hard work and thoughtful repetition is better.

At 12 the strings and the horn start more softly than at the beginning, but the music is otherwise the same. To begin the Dirge the tenor repeats the pitches of the last two measures of the Elegy. There should be only a slight pause before the tenor sings.

Another composer might have separated the Elegy and Dirge, but Britten placed these two songs of death together. In the Dirge he reversed the order by having the horn play only in the middle of the song rather than at the beginning and the end as in the Elegy. He abandons the use of the short-long rhythm in favor of a group of five notes that is heard in nearly every measure of the Dirge. The first thirty measures are essentially a long crescendo and a gathering of energy in preparation for the horn entrance at 17. All of the strings and the horn player must be rigidly precise in playing the five-note figures. Too often these notes are played as sixteenth-note triplets

Example 6-2

rather than five thirty-second notes on the latter half of the second beat. At quarter-note equals 60 the difference is significant. If we wait for the latter half of the second beat we will probably play the rhythm correctly. Notice the thoroughness of the editing in the first measure of 17 where we have *molto forte*, dashes, dots, a wedge shape and an accent, plus *largamente*. Each of these is meant to be played to the fullest intensity. The glissando in the third measure of 17 must contain as many intervening notes as possible. This can be accomplished by using the first finger on the F horn for the glissando and starting down immediately upon arriving at the fourth beat. The same fingering can be used for the glissando in the fourth measure of 17. In the fifth measure we should change to 2 + 3 on the F horn for the glissando. The diminuendo one measure before 18 remains in effect until 19; *sempre più piano* means always more softly.

The Hymn is the technical showpiece for both the tenor and the horn player. For this piece there is no substitute for a fast single tongue. We strengthen our tonguing speed by setting the metronome at 88 and practicing six tongued notes per beat. Repeated pitches in the middle register are best, and we can vary the volume from *piano* to *forte*. We should play as many groups of six notes as our air capacity will allow. Repeated pitches are followed by chromatic scales one octave up and one octave down. Chromatic scales are followed by major and minor scales of one octave and a sixth, up and down. This expanding process could take several weeks or more, but it will result in the velocity and response needed for the Hymn. Brass players may convince themselves that they have a slow tongue, but most slow tongues are simply tongues that have not been developed by months and years of effort.

The reentry in the third measure of 21 is difficult because it is in the middle of the measure. It is helpful to think a very strong first beat in the second measure of 21 and to play a strong accent on the first note of the fifth measure of 21. The dots under the notes at 25 are a reminder that all tongued notes in the Hymn are staccato. Three measures before 26 we dare not slow the tempo, and we hope that the conductor will not linger unduly over the quarter-note triplets one measure before 26. The juxtaposition of 2/4 and 6/8 is in itself an invitation to become laggard with the duplets. After the Hymn we should leave the stage before the Sonnet begins.

Offstage horn, trumpet, and perhaps viola, can have a magical quality. Much depends on finding the right place to play and the correct direction of the bell. Within reason, the farther we are from the stage the better the sound will be if we are interested in creating a feeling of distance or echo. Sometimes we can leave the backstage entirely and play from an adjoining corridor. Generally we should avoid playing close to the stage because the audience can locate the sound rather readily and much of the effect is lost. If given a choice, we should play from the center of the backstage area rather than from one side. We can also play from the front vestibule of the hall or from a basement area. Since every hall is different, a thorough survey of the premises could reveal an unusual, but ideal, location for offstage playing. Having another horn player play from various positions while we listen from the hall is wise so that we can decide which place best serves the music. For the Epilogue, the horn should sound very distant but with some reverberation, if possible.

The beginning of the Epilogue should not intrude upon the end of the Sonnet, but should start soon enough that the F (concert pitch) will impinge slightly upon the memory of the F-sharp in the last string chord of the Sonnet. On stage, the conductor's hands must stay up until the horn has started to play so that the joy of expectation is not interrupted by applause. The tenor and the string players remain motionless until after the Epilogue is finished. We play the Epilogue in the same way that we played the Prologue, except that the last three measures can be slower and the last note longer. We must not forget that the Sonnet is also about death and its last line is "And seal the hushed casket of my Soul."

# CHAPTER 7

# TEACHING THE HORN

Our discussion of teaching the horn will be confined mainly to the private lesson in an academic setting, where nearly all of our fine young players are now trained. In this context the music student is given the most personal and direct kind of teaching while simultaneously receiving instruction in a variety of other ways, including classroom lectures, independent studies, large ensemble rehearsals, and chamber music coaching. The private lesson remains the chief means of transmitting information about playing any instrument. It is rare to find a successful horn player whose background does not include significant study in an academic institution.

Nearly every leading horn player teaches. In our larger cities these teachers are often members of the local symphony orchestra and have part-time employment in the music departments of nearby colleges. In smaller cities, college music teachers often play in their community's orchestra and chamber music groups while maintaining a full academic appointment. This would seem to be the perfect arrangement whereby fine players become teachers and pass along their expertise.

It does not follow automatically that successful orchestral horn players are fine teachers, however. The typical undergraduate educational experience does not provide the broad musical and intellectual background that has become necessary for college teaching, nor does membership in a professional orchestra's horn section always lead to a rich pattern of musical growth. It was once believed that several year's experience in a symphony orchestra was prerequisite to college teaching, or, after long service in an orchestra, a "college teaching job" would be a fine way to finish one's musical life. Few college positions in applied music today do not demand a high level of performing ability and an educational record that signifies intellectual breadth and vigor. This combination of strengths is needed to obtain a professorship, to advance in the academic world, and to prosper in the private studio.

The teacher functions in the studio by looking, listening, evaluating, and explaining. Intonation, rhythm, and style must be heard and evaluated constantly. Teachers must also listen with ears that can evaluate progress since last week, last month, and last year. Writing and filing a monthly or quarterly report on student improvement is helpful. This record can help us separate the occasional unsatisfactory lesson from the larger picture of progress. Some elements of horn playing change more rapidly than others. Air capacity can show almost immediate improvement when good breathing techniques are begun. Capacity will decrease slowly if breathing exercises are abandoned. Tonguing speed will improve quickly for a few weeks and then begin to improve at a slower rate. Endurance can have both long-term trends and day-by-day fluctuations. When practice hours are well spaced and consistent, endurance usually has a slow and steady improvement. A hard rehearsal and concert, lack of sleep, a fever, or a series of days with too much or too little playing will cause a decline in endurance. For young embouchures, the high register is especially sensitive to what and how much one played yesterday and how carefully one warmed up today. The low register, once learned, seems to stay in place rather well. Horn students seem to have their own individual timetables of progress. Some exhibit a slow, steady increase in ability; others improve by moving from one plateau to the next after periods of little progress; still others show quick improvement in some areas and little in others. For each student, all of this information is needed for the teacher to make proper assignments of literature and special exercises, for adjusting embouchures and changing equipment, and for evaluating the efficiency of practice habits. It allows the teacher to be more flexible in providing both short-term and long-term solutions to problems. No two players and no two embouchures are identical; having a large fund of information about each student could prevent long-term damage developing from a short-term solution.

Teachers' ears and eyes have to be alert for trends that signal difficulties for the future. Excessive pressure will not go away if not brought under control by the methods described in the section on long tones. Pulling up the lower jaw when ascending to the high register is often related to pressure, and any work done to relieve pressure should include watching the lower jaw in a mirror to ensure that it does not move upward. We should watch for any noticeable change in the angle at which the lips meet the mouthpiece. The teacher must maintain a clear memory of each student's embouchure and be ready to evaluate any change in its appearance. Those who play with the bell resting on the right leg must maintain the same distance from lips to leg while sitting on chairs of different heights or chairs whose seats have a pronounced backward slope. The teacher must remember the student's sitting and standing posture and be willing to adjust it if necessary. An observant teacher will notice when the jaw moves in connection with the tongue stroke. This can be corrected by an enriched diet of tonguing at moderate speed on repeated pitches and small intervals while looking at a mirror. Often the player is not aware of the jaw movement. It can cause inaccuracies, late responses, and slow tonguing speed. Fingers must be watched to prevent flatness, or lack of contact with the keys. The left arm can become tense if the shoulders are too high at the top of the breath, or if the stretch from the thumb to the little finger is too great. For an average size hand the stretch should be approximately that of a sixth on the piano keyboard. A stretch that is too long will cause trouble in holding the instrument comfortably. All of these items can be observed at each lesson. If the teacher has a good memory of the student's history, the evaluations and options for solutions can be made from reliable information. Looking, listening, and evaluating are the prelude to explaining.

We should follow no formula to determine when to talk, when to play, and when to listen during lessons. The student is in the studio to play and the teacher is there to analyze, illustrate, and comment. The time allotted to playing and speaking during lessons can change drastically from one student to the next and from lesson to lesson with the same student. The amount of playing done by the teacher during lessons is also not subject to a formula. It is, however, absolutely necessary that the young player hear fine horn playing during the early part of the training. For a beginner to hear only the sounds of other beginners cannot be helpful in forming a concept of tone quality. For the more advanced player, the teacher can demonstrate how the finished product should sound, but imitation of the teacher's playing is only the starting point. Well-chosen words must explain how, why, and when. Very often explanations must be made from a historical, stylistic, theoretical, or aesthetic perspective. The teacher has to decide at what stage of development the student will benefit more from a longer and more detailed analysis or from a shorter and immediately practical description of cause and effect. Small answers to large questions run the risk of becoming much less than half-truths. A freshman in the first semester of college theory and history will, perhaps, benefit less than a senior from a detailed discussion of why the horn parts in the orchestral works of Brahms and Dvořák are so different from each other.

Most speaking in the studio is related to correcting mistakes and making suggestions for improvement. Teachers tend to develop and rely on their own jargon and labels for the larger issues of horn playing. These terms, even if they are rather home-spun, can be useful if both parties agree on their precise meaning and application. "Air stream" is often used to describe the movement of air from the lungs, past the lips, and into the horn. If the teacher and student agree that "air stream" is shorthand for the means by which our lips are made to vibrate, all is well as long as both parties agree that "air stream" by itself is meaningless. "Air column" is another favorite label that needs a precise definition before it can become pertinent to horn playing. Is it the same as air stream, and does it function with or apart from air stream? Why column? We hear of fast air, slow air, warm air, hot air, abbreviated air, more air, compressed air, and free air. All of these can become useful at the moment that they are defined fully and applied to a specific task. They are not useful when they divert attention away from good breathing techniques. At the very least they confirm that the horn is, indeed, played with air.

Teachers must have strong convictions and control over the language that is used to convey their convictions. All teachers can profit from an examination of their specific terminology and general teaching vocabulary to test its authenticity and precision. Convictions are excellent when they are grounded on scholarship and proven by experience. They become less so when they are used by teachers to create students who are replicas of themselves. As students become more advanced they will begin to exhibit musical convictions of their own. If we have taught them well, they will have the technique to play from the depths of their convictions. If we and our academic colleagues have opened their minds to the world of musical scholarship that lies beyond playing the horn, they will be able to support and defend their convictions. For horn players, musical literacy is even more important now that technique can free us from always treading in the narrow footsteps of tradition.

A good teacher is an interesting person, at least while teaching. This does not mean that teachers are entertainers. It does mean that word choices are elevated but not obscure, and explanations are clear without being commonplace. Our teaching vocabulary need not be limited to the restricted language of brass playing if we continue to read and to learn. We must be willing to build on the skills that our theory teachers tried so hard to drill into us, and be prepared to expand our knowledge of the whole of music literature. Through our increasing knowledge we come to realize that teaching does not stop at 5:30 on Friday afternoon. We continue to teach through our research, and by writing and publishing, coaching chamber music groups, conducting, performing and promoting new music and old, even by composing and arranging. All of this activity demands that we have the intellectual energy and musical sagacity to perform well in each of these areas. If we are content with teaching as we were taught, with feeding upon the labor of others who provide us with music and information, and are satisfied with playing and teaching the same music year after year, our students are likely to follow our example. This is not teaching as it is understood in most disciplines. In their undergraduate years our students are especially sensitive to the models they see around them. These are the years that set up lifelong patterns of attitudes, industry, and behavior.

Just as our musical life outside the studio is one of energy and productivity, our actions within the studio must be efficient and orderly. The teacher controls how the lesson time is divided between playing and speaking, how it is divided among etudes, orchestral literature, and solo material, and how much time can be spent on discussing concerns or events beyond the usual scope of the studio. As teachers we need to keep a long-term balance among all of these compartments so that each receives its proper attention over several lessons. During the weeks prior to a solo recital our emphasis is, naturally, upon that event. Before an audition with required repertoire we can focus on those works. If the school orchestra is rehearsing a Mahler symphony, we can spend time with those parts. All of this must be blended into a larger pattern of physical development and musical growth. Make brief notes on each student between lessons or at the end of the teaching day. These notes can then be reviewed before the next lesson to help us make the best possible use of time. An absent-minded professor is a dangerous personage in the private studio. Classroom teachers usually have their material planned for a semester or a year and follow it, one hopes, on a clear path from one class meeting to the next. The private teacher's path has many diversions, but we should establish some general guidelines for each semester's work.

The first semester of the freshman year should concentrate on the calisthenic and technical elements of playing. Most teachers have developed their own series of exercises for the warm-up and for the basic technical procedures. Through speaking about these elemental ideas, a fund of shared information and a set of working principles can be established. One of the earlier lessons can be devoted to breathing exercises and the preparation of the body and mind before playing the first note of the day. At this lesson the private teacher becomes a lecturer. Students may wish to take notes and can be encouraged to do so. Young teachers will want to spend some time in preparing this lecture and may wish to review and revise it for several years. Every word that we say in the studio carries the potential for benefit or harm. The ability to speak clearly, to present ideas in a structured sequence, and to provide accurate information are all the product of a disciplined and industrious mind. Beware of "in other words." If we have chosen our words wisely, other words should not be necessary. Beware of playing illustrations that show *fortissimo* or fast single tonguing, for example, but do not reveal the steps necessary to achieve volume or speed of tongue. Do not hurry the presentation. It is better to be thorough than fast. Do not be sidetracked by questions. There will be plenty of time for discussion during the next four years. Hearing one's own voice on a taped playback can be shocking, but hearing is a necessary, if painful, part of our preparation for speaking. Our preparation notes and tapes can be preserved for future reference.

If we have decided that lessons, generally, are to be divided between technique and musicianship, or more specifically, among etudes or exercises, orchestral parts, and solo literature, we are not bound to include all of these items in every lesson, especially during the early part of the freshman year. After the preparatory lecture, the next several lessons could well be devoted primarily to introducing the actual procedures involved in breathing exercises, attacks, long tones, releases, tonguing, and slurring. Again, the presentation of this material should be orderly and unhurried. During these lessons, questions are answered and discussion is encouraged. Students vary widely in their ability to frame pertinent questions. Eighteen-year-old students are often more interested in talking about themselves than asking questions about technical or musical matters. Their questions beg for quick, easy answers. "How do you lip trill?" cannot be answered adequately without reference to the methods used to develop the lip trill. Some teachers who work primarily with young children have to be ready with shallow answers to deep questions, but to the college freshman who desires to devote a lifetime to horn playing we owe a complete explanation.

After we are satisfied that the list of breathing, warm-up, attacks, long tones, releases, tonguing, and slurring has been explored in a preliminary way, we can start to work on orchestral literature. At first glance it might seem decisive, but unreasoned, to study the orchestral literature alphabetically by composer, with as few exceptions as possible. Granted, Bach comes before Beethoven in several ways, but the Beethoven horn parts offer an opportunity to work on the orchestral discipline of style and rhythmic precision. Complete first horn parts of Beethoven and other major composers are now available. Excerpt books usually do not include more than a few of the prominent solos and tutti passages. Buying the complete parts is a lifelong investment, and studying the complete parts is a necessary component of the training of horn players who want to play in a symphony orchestra.

Every Beethoven symphony, with the exception of the first, has passages that horn players have come to regard as solos. All of these solos must be learned thoroughly and committed to memory during the undergraduate years so that the student will accumulate a rather complete inventory of standard orchestral solos ranging alphabetically from Bach to Wagner. Much of the time spent on orchestral literature will be devoted to these solos, many of which have become required material for professional orchestral auditions. The training of aspiring orchestral horn players does not stop when the most frequently encountered solos are learned, but must be extended to include tutti passages. Trusting that dedicated teachers and serious students will join together to explore all of the important solos from the orchestral literature, we can turn our attention to some of the more challenging tutti passages in the Beethoven symphonies.

In most Beethoven orchestral works there are only two horns. They function as part of the middle voices of the woodwind section. Our choices of volume and styles of attack should reflect our knowledge of how we fit into the orchestration. It is best to start with the Second Symphony. The introduction in the first movement, when taken measure by measure, presents several features of the classical style of orchestral playing, including our understanding of dynamics, tongue strokes, note length, D horn transposition and its intonation hazards, and mental subdivisions of rhythms. The notes themselves are quite simple to produce, but the discipline of style and the precision of note values are very important. We can expect that a freshman entering college as a performance major can read horn in D, has a secure knowledge of rhythmic notation, and has played or heard the Beethoven Second Symphony. It should be made clear that the student will be asked to sing the major themes from all of the movements and will have listened to a recording several times while watching the score, not just the horn part. Any institution that grants degrees in horn playing will surely have recordings and study scores of the Beethoven symphonies. Any horn student who wants to become a member of a professional symphony orchestra surely will welcome the opportunity to study the music— not just the horn solos—that will be played throughout a long and distinguished career. The teacher can bracket the passages that will need special attention. Playing every long, held note in every movement is not necessary, but every rhythm must be perfect and every dynamic must be at the proper level. Orchestral playing allows no latitude in those areas.

The complete introduction in the first movement of the Second Symphony is studied as an exercise in classical-period orchestral playing. The first note that we play is a 32nd-note before a fermata. Before the conductor has made any motion to begin the symphony we should start a mental subdivision of 32nd-notes so that our first note will be confident and well placed rhythmically. Not only must the 32nd-note be played at exactly the right moment, but the articulated and rhythmic space before the next note must be correct. In school orchestras these first two notes are rehearsed many times, or should be, to achieve ensemble precision. Professional orchestras remember from year to year; school orchestras playing this work for the first time must remember from one rehearsal to the next. We should use the few seconds before the symphony begins to review the placing of the first two notes. There should be no decrease in volume on the fermata until the conductor gives a motion to indicate that the fermata is about to be concluded. In the studio, the teacher can act the role of the conductor by giving small beats and other motions against which the student can play. In m. 8 Beethoven has written dots on repeated pitches under a curved line. We use a legato tongue stroke to begin each note but decrease the volume slightly before the next tongue stroke. Five notes in m. 8 are shaped as just described while making a crescendo to the sforzando in m. 9. The crescendo is not completed until we reach the end of m. 11. Beginning with our entrance in m. 13 we have a series of notes marked sforzando. We find, upon consulting the score, that our sforzando notes are in *piano*, not *forte*. The doubly dotted eighth-notes one measure before A will be precise if we match them to a mental subdivision of 32nd-notes. The articulation of the group of six notes four measures after A should match that of the woodwinds earlier in the measure. The crescendo in the measure before the double bar should result in a small *forte* and must not detract from the downward scale in the first violins.

This detailed description of the introduction is meant to show the needs for teachers to have the orchestral score close at hand during lessons on orchestral literature and for precision in the realization of all editing marks. Professional players know from experience how to deal with these common symbols, but students should learn as much as possible about them in the private studio. In school orchestras not very much time may be devoted to such matters.

After the notes in the first horn part in the introduction have become secure, the teacher or another student can add the second horn part. Notice that the two parts contain only octaves, fifths, and unisons. This is not unusual in an orchestral work of the classical period. Great care must be taken to ensure that these perfect intervals are, indeed, perfectly in tune.

It is not possible to comment in such detail here on all of the other tutti passages that deserve attention, but I hope that all horn teachers will spend enough time with the scores of the Beethoven symphonies and all other orchestral works in the standard repertory to become familiar with the musical setting in which these passages occur. While there is no substitute for actually playing these works in an orchestra, our students can gain much from our informed counsel in the private studio and the class lesson.

In the Allegro con brio following the introduction, four measures before B and three measures before G can be troublesome because of the speed at which the leaps must be played. From eleven measures after K to the end of the movement, the rhythmic precision and intonation must be perfect. Beginning in the ninth measure of the second movement, we have another example of repeated pitches with dots under a curved line. These are played exactly as those in the first movement introduction. Horn players feel that seven measures before C and seven measures after G are horn solos; whenever we think of the Beethoven Second Symphony we are reminded of these measures because they are high and soft. It is helpful to practice these two passages quite loudly for several days and then begin to reduce the volume gradually until a piano level is reached. This process could consume nine days if we practice these two passages *forte*, *mezzo forte*, and *mezzo piano* each for three days before beginning to practice at *piano*. If we always practice these measures at *piano* and are not successful because of the lack of volume, we are teaching ourselves that we cannot play these passages. By teaching our embouchures how to play these notes with a substantial flow of air, we gain confidence before beginning to reduce the air to an acceptable level. All of this depends, of course, on whether our embouchure is developed enough to produce high B. If we have a high B in our lips, our practicing in this manner will allow us to hear ourselves play these difficult measures perfectly many, many times. Upon such repetition a justified expectation of success is founded. Following the principle of making the horn shorter on upward slurs we should try a fingering of 1 + 2 on the note before the highest note in both passages.

In Symphony No. 3, the Presto at the end of the fourth movement is difficult; the second and third horn parts are considerably more difficult than the first horn part. Even if the conductor follows the printed tempo of quarter-note equals 116, the speed of the sixteenth-notes should not cause difficulty for a player with a well-developed single tongue. Double tonguing is not appropriate because of the moderate speed and the repeated pitches. Most of the second horn part is near the bottom of the staff or below the staff. *Fortissimo* in this register is not easy for many horn players. Developing volume in this register begins with long tones at *fortissimo*, followed by legato tonguing, which is followed by staccato tonguing all on repeated pitches. This process could take months. Here is a perfect opportunity for students to write a short exercise that includes tonguing at *fortissimo* in this register, sforzando attacks, and arpeggios. The B-flat horn can be used for the entire Presto, since it yields more volume and a quicker response than the F horn.

The Fourth Symphony is noted, among horn players at least, for the high soft entrance in the second movement. The low C (for horn in B-flat basso) that begins the first movement is often overlooked. For the second horn it can be difficult because it is *pianissimo*, long, low, and the first note in the symphony. The note must not be accented or late in responding. It must be exactly in tune with the right volume to support three octaves of B-flat above it. This note is the pride and joy of the great second horn players throughout the world. Sustaining the note is less of a problem than attacking the note softly. We can use several strategies in practicing the attack. We can slur scale-wise down to the low written C from a more comfortable higher note and, after arriving on the low C, we can begin to use a legato tongue stroke on the low note. This exercise should begin at *mezzo forte* and the repeated tongue strokes should be played with a diminuendo to *pianissimo*. For this exercise the starting note can be lowered gradually after several days or weeks until the low written C becomes the starting note. Next, we can attack a more comfortable higher note and slur without any intervening notes down to the low C and begin our legato tongued notes. Again, the starting notes can be lowered gradually. When this is producing results we can begin to attack the low C at *mezzo forte* and, on the same breath, repeat the note several times with a diminuendo to *piano*. Finally we are ready to practice the *pianissimo* attack. These attacks must always be done by removing the mouthpiece from the lips between each attack. All of these methods of practicing start with something that we can do rather easily and consistently. From this position of strength we move gradually into the area of difficulty. To try, time and time again, to attack the low C at *pianissimo* with little or no success results in practicing our failure. By relating the low C to a note that responds more readily we can move gradually toward our goal of attacking the low note successfully.

Symphony No. 5, like Symphony No. 3, has in the last movement a coda marked presto. There the difficulty is not in the volume, the notes, or the register, but in the notation. Our eyes and minds are not accustomed to whole-note equals 112. The notes are quite easy to produce, but we seem to rebel at seeing quarter notes go by so swiftly. The rests can also be puzzling at this speed. When practicing the coda with the metronome, we should take special notice of measures in which the rhythmic patterns change. The most annoying measures are those in which we enter after a quarter rest. Our eyes have to move more rapidly than usual and we have time to think only the first beats in the measures. Singing the complete coda until the notation seems very natural is helpful. We should also practice starting twenty-six measures before the Presto. The metronome will be of no help here because of the *sempre più allegro*, but we can try to predict what the conductor will attempt to do in moving the tempo from half-note equals 84 to whole-note equals 112. In the studio the teacher can beat through the accelerando.

The Sixth Symphony has no concealed difficulties. Eight measures before A in the third movement, we must remember that the notes without sforzando are *fortissimo* and that there is no diminuendo before we complete the passage four measures after A. When the passage is repeated in the last eight measures of the movement, the tempo is presto, not allegro. This has been known to escape the attention of conductors. We should practice both of these passages very loudly so that we can gain the confidence necessary to play very aggressively at the concert. This is no time to play it safe by holding back on volume. Horn players can only hope that we are never asked to play with a crescendo during the last five measures of the fifth movement.

The Seventh Symphony is the most demanding, physically, of the nine symphonies of Beethoven. It requires both short-term and long-term endurance, and great volume in the high register. No great harm is done if the teacher decides to postpone work on this symphony until the high register is strong and the endurance is resilient. At B in the first movement we have to give ourselves a strong mental second beat in each of the first eight measures because the second beat is so often evaded by the tied notes. We practice this passage many times by adding the fermata in the measure before B. We must also practice without the fermata, since conductors in rehearsals like to start at B rather than one measure before B. One wonders why Beethoven did not include the horns in the repeat of this material at H. To play perfectly from M to the end of the first movement requires superb short-term endurance. We can increase our endurance by starting to practice ten measures from the end of the movement and, after a few days, adding four measures. When this is going well we can continue to add measures until we are starting at M. Of course we must not practice this passage on fatigued lips, but it must be practiced at *fortissimo* and in tempo. The dotted 6/8 rhythm that runs throughout the movement can degenerate easily into 4/8 if we play the sixteenth-note too soon or if we accent the third and sixth beats. As a last resort we can always pronounce "Amsterdam," "Rotterdam," or "Albany," but never "Aberdeen" or "Liverpool" in an attempt to "feel" the rhythm.

There are a few surprises between the beginning of the last movement and thirteen measures after A. Our eyes must be ready for the repeat and our embouchures and breathing have to be ready for A. It is much better to breathe one measure before A rather than just before the higher note at A. Notice that we are no longer important thematically in the third measure after A. We play continuously from four measures before Q to the end of the movement. Every note is loud and much of it is high. We can begin by practicing the last fourteen measures and then gradually add measures until we are starting at four measures before Q, not forgetting to add volume for the *fff*. This symphony always seems long (long can be good) when we play it. Its feeling of length could come from the form of the scherzo which has two trios rather than one. This unusual structure means that we hear the scherzo material three times rather than two. This is a symphony without a slow movement despite the way it is often conducted and recorded.

The Beethoven Symphony No. 8 is often thought to be one of the more gentle symphonies, in the style of the fourth and sixth rather than in the more dramatic and energetic style of the third, fifth, seventh, and ninth symphonies. The horn parts of the first and fourth movements of the eighth symphony do not conform to this generalization. Nearly everything that we play in the first movement is *f*, *ff*, or *fff*, and sforzando abounds. During the few times that the horns are asked to play softly we are part of the woodwind choir and have an inside supporting role. A glance at the first eight measures illustrates very clearly how the classical orchestra horns are required to supply volume to the inner voices when the dynamic level is *forte*, and to become a blending voice when the dynamic level is *piano*. Our entrance in the sixth measure must not be an intrusion on the soft woodwind quartet of two clarinets and two bassoons. The texture is warmed and enriched, not changed abruptly, when we enter the established sonority. For this first movement we need three well-defined levels of sound for *f*, *ff*, and *fff*. The *forte* in the first four measures is at a volume that fills out the middle voices of the orchestration but does not compete for attention with the thematic line in the upper strings. The first sforzando appears four measures before A. Since the prevailing level is *forte*, we can use a vigorous tongue stroke on the sforzando and on the following sixteenth-notes. This sixteenth-note is often not played loudly enough and the energy of the dotted eighth and sixteenth-note is lost. The first *ff* is at four measures before B. This volume level must be unmistakably louder than the previous *f*. The first *fff* occurs at the recapitulation at D. Beethoven did not use this marking frivolously or lavishly, and it is no accident that he chose to introduce this heightened level of volume at the restatement of the first theme. This can be a glorious moment if every orchestra member understands Beethoven's use of this unusual volume level and is willing to expend the effort necessary to achieve a dramatic result.

In the teaching studio the emphasis is upon rhythmic precision and a clear definition of dynamics. Each level and its concomitant tone quality can be discussed and demonstrated by the teacher. Some students are reluctant to add the top layer of volume that distinguishes *fff* from *ff*. A skillful demonstration by the teacher can be very enlightening and persuasive. In the practice room the student should not be reluctant to try for this intense level of volume. It may sound very harsh at first but a well-developed embouchure can, with practice, be encouraged to accept a large amount of air. Students are also reluctant to practice elements that do not sound acceptable until they are mastered. (Someone may be listening outside the door!) Teachers can mitigate some of the anxiety by reminding the student of the future benefits of practicing to achieve control over all volume levels.

In the first movement of the Eighth Symphony, Beethoven chose to use sforzando rather than accents as a symbol for emphasis. A sforzando can be imagined to be a flash of bright color at the beginning of a note, after which the volume returns to the prevailing level. This is different from *fp*, which assures that the volume will revert to *piano* immediately after the attack. Composers are not always clear in their use of *sf* and *fp*. A conscientious orchestral horn player will look to the score for help in making decisions concerning the meaning of these two common terms. Very often common musical sense will provide the answer after the score has been consulted. Surely it is not possible that orchestral horn players would play the Beethoven Eighth Symphony without ever having seen the score. Surely no college teacher of horn would be without a copy of the score in the studio for quick reference.

From their appearance one would not suspect that the horn parts in the second movement of this symphony had been written by Beethoven. They may not look like Beethoven but they do look exactly like the music should sound. All of the tongued sixteenth-notes are very short and very soft. They are at least as short as those played by the oboes and bassoons. It is always helpful to ask an oboe player to demonstrate the shortest notes the oboe can play. We also must not become hypnotized by the sameness of the part or allow the *pianissimo* to drift into "mezzo something." Throughout the movement we keep in mind that our part hardly moves and does not have any thematic importance. Supplying a nonobtrusive inner voice is a valid part of orchestral horn playing.

For horn players, the duet in the trio of the minuet is the high point of the symphony. In every measure of the trio the celli have triplets. We must maintain a strong duple feeling against the triplets, especially in the measures that have a dotted quarter- and eighth-note. We distinguish clearly between the dots under the curved line and the dots without the curved line. The first clarinet contributes at least as much to the trio as do the horns. If we are secure in our part we can listen to the clarinet and try to match styles and note lengths. One hopes that the clarinet player will do the same.

In the fourth movement Beethoven again uses the metric notation of a whole-note to the measure. This time the speed is 84. Our first entrance could be laggard if we are merely counting bars and are not alert to how swiftly the music is moving. We have to wait until m. 438 before the horns are heard as a leading voice. For the rest of the movement we have a typical classical role of supplying harmony, long-held notes, and volume to the loud measures.

As stated above, not every long note in orchestral parts need be played in the studio. The long note at the beginning of the Ninth Symphony, however, must be practiced and played in the studio. The conductor, understandably, wants the symphony to start as softly as possible, and horn players want to start softly but with confidence and accuracy. We can practice starting this note while listening to the metronome, and in the studio the teacher can supply a beat for the student. We do not get a breath before the fourteenth measure. This means that we must take a large breath and produce a small amount of volume. This seems to be a contradiction but it is so, and it must be practiced. Pencil in the measure numbers up to 14 so that there is no uncertainty. In the studio the teacher can give the beats for the long notes and provide counsel on the crescendo and intonation. At rehearsals and performances the second horn must rely upon the first horn, not the conductor, for the timing of the attack and the consistency of the intonation. The first horn, through a slightly audible breath and a discreet body motion, can be of great help to the second horn in producing a perfectly timed and articulated attack. After several years of playing together, first and second horns can develop a confidence in their partner's reliability. For a first horn player there are few greater comforts in this world than having an excellent second horn player. In school orchestras the wind players are not usually assigned a permanent chair, with the result that the bond of mutual reliance is not easily forged. In the studio, the teacher can use the beginning of the Ninth Symphony, and other similar passages, to exemplify the need for establishing this feeling between first and second players. When we are free, finally, of the long note, we join the rest of the orchestra in a statement of the first theme in m. 16. The opening long note and the statement of the theme goes on the teacher's list of passages to be played perfectly many consecutive times in the practice room and in the studio. Missed notes are always damaging but are particularly so in unison passages in *fortissimo*.

In the Scherzo, the basic rhythm is similar to that of the first movement in the Seventh Symphony. There it is written in 3/4, not 6/8. This rhythm feels quite comfortable when it is played softly. When it is played loudly and repeated for many measures it can become sluggish and fall behind. In the practice room this tendency can be remedied by leaving out the eighth-note in every other measure, thus establishing the true location of the first and third beats in each measure. If the eighth-note is late, the third beat will also be late. Practicing as described and thinking an early eighth-note will stabilize the rhythm.

The Adagio within the third movement contains some of the most inspired writing for the horn in all orchestral literature. We all identify these sixteen measures as "the fourth horn solo" in the Beethoven Ninth Symphony. In reality, this is not a horn solo. The horn line is but one of four and eventually five contrapuntal lines that are woven together into a quintet of flute, two clarinets, bassoon, and horn. In this context the passage could be called more reasonably the first clarinet solo from the Ninth Symphony were it not that the clarinet has countless moments of prominence throughout the symphony. The only time that the horn is truly solo is three measures before the 12/8 when no one else is playing. Still, this is remarkable writing for the horn and all the more so because Beethoven did not give it to the first horn to play. Horn teachers have been known to assemble one flute, two clarinets, one bassoon, and one horn player in the studio to play through these sixteen measures without the string pizzicato accompaniment. We can then hear that this is a vocal quintet in which the melodic responsibilities shift from one instrument to another. During these sixteen measures, the horn part has a range of three octaves and one half-step. It is, at various times, a bass voice supporting the quintet, an equal contrapuntal partner, and, finally, a soloist. All of this is totally out of character for a classical orchestral horn part. All horn players should study, with reverence, these sixteen measures to discover their greatness and to place the horn line in its proper perspective.

By following the alphabet, the next prominent composer of orchestral works is Johannes Brahms. We have seen that a knowledge of the score is essential for understanding the horn parts of the Beethoven symphonies. Score study is even more important in the orchestral works of Brahms. By the middle of the nineteenth century composers had made the horn section a fully participating member of both the woodwind and brass sections. With the advent of the valve horn composers were no longer confined to writing only notes that were available, by one means or another, on the valveless horn. Brahms, and other composers, still notated their horn parts for a specific length of horn. These lengths were closely related to the harmonic structure of the various movements of symphonies or other large works. Most of the first and second horn parts were written in the key of the movement; the first and second horn parts of the first symphony are written as horn in C, since the symphony and its first movement are in C minor. The third and fourth horn parts of the first movement are written as horn in E-flat; E-flat makes the difference between C major and C minor. In the fourth movement of the first symphony the first pair of horns is written in C, but the third and fourth horns are written as horn in E because the movement, except for its introduction, is in C major; E-natural makes the difference between C minor and C major. The horn parts in the inner movements of the symphonies reflect the tonality of the movement. The second movement of the Brahms Second Symphony, for example, is in B major and the first and second horn parts are in H (B-natural). This strange transposition continues to plague student horn players, who remain firmly aground in F. Brahms wrote comparatively little for the trumpets, but their parts are usually written in the tonic key of the movement.

Brahms filled his horn parts with interesting lines of secondary importance. A good example of this occurs in the first measure of the first symphony where the third and fourth horns enter to play a descending scale line. Too often horn players, in manifestation of their respect for Brahms, will play this line at a volume that competes with the upward curve of the great melodic arch that Brahms wrote for the violins and the celli. This horn line looks enticing but the primary melodic line is elsewhere. Throughout the symphonies and other orchestral works, our *forte* level is most often one that fits into a woodwind sonority. In the first symphony we have to wait until N in the fourth movement before we have a true brass section *fortissimo* with trumpets, horns, and trombones. We can also be guided by Brahms's well-known preference for the longer lengths of horns. Horn parts in D, C, H, and low B-flat are more common than F and G. There is no symphony in A major, where the more strident *forte* and *fortissimo* of the Beethoven Seventh Symphony would perhaps be appropriate. One of the most over-played passages in the first movement of the first symphony is at L where the accompanying figure of repeated pitches is marked *forte*. We probably will not overpower the first violins or the celli, but our part is not of equal importance. Thirteen measures before P the horn parts are marked *fortissimo*. When these measures are over-played the dialogue between the strings and the upper woodwinds is not clear. The most important notes in the first four measures of these brass chords are in the fourth horn, who has the seventh of the chords in the bass. One hopes that trumpet players will not insist that their repeated Cs constitute an important melodic line.

Our intention is not to comment upon every instance where dynamic balances might become faulty. This is the job of the conductor in rehearsals. The teacher, however, can make good use of the score during lessons to show the student the importance of relating volume to the orchestration. When the student sees the scoring six measures after A in the second movement, it becomes clear instantly that our crescendo and subsequent *forte* must not compete for attention with the upper strings or overwhelm the bassoons. Similarly, the orchestration at E is completely different from the orchestration in the tenth measure of E, but first horn players, if unaware of this, will continue to play in the same volume and style. The orchestration at E looks and sounds rich and thick; at the tenth measure it looks and sounds thin. We should not be annoyed that Brahms wrote "Violin Solo" at E. *Solo* indicates that only one of the first violins should play the melodic line.

The first horn part in the first ten measures of the third movement is another example of Brahms's ability to write interesting inner voices. A glance at the score confirms that we are the tenor voice in a quartet of clarinets, horn, and bassoon and, as such, we must not encroach upon the dynamic territory of the clarinet whose part is marked *piano*. While looking at the score we can see an even more interesting line that Brahms wrote for the pizzicato celli during these same measures. No conductor would permit the cello line to compete with the clarinet, but some seem to be content when the horn imposes. The third and fourth horn are written in the dreaded horn in H in this movement. Their first entrance at the thirteenth measure of D is quite bold and should never hint that it is written in an unfamiliar transposition.

The introduction to the fourth movement contains one of the most famous of all horn solos. Our responsibility to Brahms and the listeners begins before we have played the first note of the solo. Since we are seated near the back of the orchestra, we sometimes forget that the audience can see us if risers are used. If the hall is pitched rather steeply, most of the audience can watch our movements even if we are on a flat stage. Many listeners who attend orchestral concerts regularly know very well when the horn solo is about to begin, and their eyes will turn toward the first horn several measures before the entrance. Much of the magic is lost if we are blowing out the water, emptying slides, twirling the horn in search of water, turning the page, or are in any pose other than that of majestic calm. As it happens, there is a page turn just before the solo, and we do have to play the solo on a completely dry horn, but surely we can play these few measures from memory and not turn the page. There is time between the third and fourth movements to take care of the water if the conductor does not start the fourth movement immediately, or the assistant horn can play part of the introduction so that the first horn is ready for the solo.

It is best to be able to play this solo without having to adjust the pitch of any of the notes with our embouchure. The high G and the D are often sharp when they are fingered 1 + 2 on the B-flat horn. Since no note in the solo requires us to use the first valve on the B-flat horn by itself, we can pull the first B-flat slide out far enough to bring down the pitch on the D and high G. The low G is often played first finger on the F horn, and is flat. Most horn players play with the first slide on the F horn pulled out approximately one quarter inch. Since we play no note other than the low G with the first valve, we can push in the first valve slide on the F horn far enough to correct the pitch. All of this must be done with a tuner, because even the finest of ears can grow accustomed to hearing these notes in their old familiar places. By not having to adjust these notes with the embouchure, our accuracy will be more certain and the tone quality will be even.

As with the Beethoven symphonies, the teacher can mark the tutti passages in all of the movements that will need the student's attention. The coda of the fourth movement, which begins at the più allegro, will surely be one of these passages. The triplets with the missing members can easily go astray, and we have to reserve our largest volume for the *fortissimo* that persists to the end of the movement. It is the hope of every horn player to be allowed to play the coda as Brahms wrote it. There really is no largamente when the trombones enter in the seventeenth measure of the coda, even though there is a tradition that calls for one. Brahms lived twenty more years after the first printing of the score of the first symphony. That would seem to be sufficient time for him to correct the score for later printings if some indication of a slower tempo had been omitted. A brief history of corrections, additions, and deletions is contained in the Editor's Preface of the Dover Publications 1974 edition of the scores of the Brahms symphonies. No reference is made of Brahms's addition of a slower tempo when the trombones enter. This seems to be yet another unfortunate tradition that has been allowed to persevere.

One could choose from a wide variety of adjectives in attempting to describe the second symphony of Johannes Brahms. It has been called sunny, mellow, optimistic, brooding, happy, resigned. Such generalities are helpful if we are willing to search the score for evidence of their appropriateness. Horn players are interested, naturally, in how a composer treats the other members of the brass family. In the second symphony we see a remarkable increase in the use of the three trombones. They are usually in the low and middle register, slow moving, soft, and positioned closely together. For this symphony Brahms added the tuba, which, with the three trombones, makes a quartet of tenor and bass voices. Brahms wasted no time in introducing this quartet; its first appearance is thirteen measures before A in the first movement. The tuba appears also in its traditional role of reinforcing the bass line. Brahms wrote very little for the trumpets until the last nine measures of the fourth movement. The brass writing is mainly for richness, not volume, and could be characterized as mellow. Brahms, as always, was prudent in his choices of moments to break the mellow mold of the trombones. The entrance of the first trombone on the high D fifteen measures after P in the last movement, and the sustained D major chord in the fifth measure from the end of the symphony are both thrilling moments in their own right, and made all the more so by an understanding of their relation to the way Brahms used the trombones in the rest of the symphony. The neglect of the trumpets until the final nine measures is a masterstroke.

This insight into the brass scoring probably will not help our accuracy or our tone quality to any noticeable extent, but it does offer clues about how our tone quality and volume are affected by the orchestration. Each teacher will have to decide how much lesson time can be devoted to looking at the score. As the students move through the undergraduate years, their theory and history classes are supposed to add the skills and knowledge necessary for productive score study. Freshmen are slightly curious about scores but remain fearful because the pages look so complex to those accustomed to seeing only one or two staves of music. As private teachers we can reinforce our requests for louder or softer with specific illustrations from the score. Conductors of student orchestras can also help by speaking occasionally about matters of orchestration. Fortunate, indeed, is the student horn player whose conductors can arouse curiosity about how the composer achieved a certain orchestral sound. As the student moves through the undergraduate years, we can increase our references to the scores.

The first several measures of the Brahms Symphony No. 3 give us an excellent opportunity to observe the composer's wind scoring and his use of the F-A-flat-F motive. We can see which of the four horns has the most important voice in the first two measures, why Brahms did not use the trombones until the third measure, and which of the three trombones should be prominent in the third, fourth, and fifth measures. All of this information has a bearing on how we play our parts. The teacher can also show how G starts as a horn solo, becomes a duet with the oboe in the fifth measure, and changes to a horn duet in the ninth measure. It is also interesting to see how the scoring changes with each reappearance of the opening chords.

In the first twenty-three measures of the second movement, Brahms uses rather simple means to achieve magical results. Starting with the basic woodwind quartet of two clarinets and two bassoons, he adds two horns and two low flutes after the quartet has begun. The ends of the phrases are echoed by the divided lower strings. All of this overlaps so that the phrases seem to be in constant flow. Brahms does this not once but five times. After seeing the orchestration, horn players will understand that our entrances must not disturb the quiet sonority of the woodwind quartet but should darken and thicken the texture. The opening of this movement can be ruined by horn players who believe that their every note is important for its prominence. In these measures our importance lies in our ability to add a soft, dark enrichment to the woodwind quartet. Our aim is to conceal the fact that we enter and exit five times. We have not done so if our entrances are too loud or have even a hint of accent, or if our exits are blunt. One cannot help but admire Brahms's limited use of the trombone section in this movement. We hope that trombone players have consulted the score at E in their desire to fit their parts into the dialogue between the flute and the clarinet.

Another well-known horn solo occurs at B and at F in the third movement. Here we see how the orchestration at B differs from that at F. Because the horn is surrounded by sound at B we must play on the large side of *mezzo piano*. At F the scoring is very simple and open, leaving us free to play softly with a hint of nostalgic reminiscence. Since the notes at B and F are almost identical, horn players too often assume that the music is identical. A wise conductor does not destroy the music in the pursuit of consistency. The same can be said of horn players. The private teacher can make sure that both the arithmetic and the character of the dotted sixteenth- and 32nd-notes are correct. Taking a breath has become traditional after the first eighth-note eight measures after B and eight measures after F. We can hope that young players now in training will develop their air capacity sufficiently to make this interruption of the phrase unnecessary.

In the fourth movement, the rhythm at F and at thirteen before N can be troublesome. There the teacher can ask the student to conduct the beats (two beats per measure) and to sing the rhythm while beating the time. A typical freshman reply is "I can't conduct." The teacher has now been provided an opportunity to explain the difference between conducting and "beating" time. Eleven measures before the end of the movement the third horn has a gentle reminder of the F-A-flat motive from the first movement. Conductors enjoy holding the last chord much longer in concerts than in rehearsals. Be prepared.

In the Fourth Symphony, Brahms divides the important horn parts almost equally between the two pairs of horns. As usual, each pair has its own transposition. The music for all of the horns contains many accidentals, which make the transpositions more difficult at first reading. The parts might be easier to read had they been written for the familiar horn in F, but orchestral players do not "read" their parts, they learn them. We can respect Brahms for his steadfast convictions concerning horn notation, while we master his orchestral parts. In the first movement there are some interesting rhythmic patterns in the horn parts at nine measures after B and ten measures before D. In both cases the players must keep the triple and the duple feeling well defined. This is especially important ten measures before D, where the sforzando notes must be heard distinctly in both pairs of horns. The teacher can use the score to show how the sforzando notes occur at slightly different times between the pairs of horns. Young horn players are often cautious when confronted with a sforzando. It is hoped that after seeing how Brahms distributed the sforzando throughout the orchestra, caution will be replaced by courage. A tempo that is too fast will not permit the interplay between the duple and triple to be heard clearly. The first movement is full of this juxtaposition.

The teacher can draw the student's attention to the string scoring nine measures after E in the second movement. An alert student, upon hearing a recording or performance of this symphony, may well marvel at the opulence of the string writing at this point. As far as the harmony is concerned, Brahms could have written the usual four parts with the bass doubled. Instead he created eight parts by dividing the second violins, violas, celli, and occasionally the basses. We should notice how dense the scoring is and how Brahms does not hesitate to write thirds much lower than a lesser composer might dare. Young horn players usually have little interest in anything connected with string playing, but perhaps after hearing these measures and seeing how the sound was created, our brightest players will be moved to listen to the strings with more inquisitive ears. They might also be interested to observe how few conductors insist upon *poco forte* nine measures after E.

Horn players should take full advantage of the many opportunities to play *forte*, *fortissimo*, accents, and sforzando during the third movement of the fourth symphony. Our loud moments should be played with a brawny energy in keeping with the robust quality of the movement. At long last the trumpets have something to play at K. We join them in their brief moment of eminence.

The last movement of the Brahms Fourth Symphony is one of the miracles of the musical world. Every musician, regardless of instrument or vocal range, should know this movement and how it is constructed. This information is usually available in courses labeled History of the Symphony, or Symphonic Literature, but orchestral players owe it to Brahms and themselves to investigate on their own the wonders of this movement. Horn teachers can help by asking the student to speak for five minutes at the next lesson on the form of the movement. For young students this will cause much momentary consternation, but it is one small step toward understanding Brahms and his greatest orchestral achievement. After the student has spoken, the teacher, with the score on the music stand, can continue the discussion for the rest of the lesson, if possible. Both parties should enter into this project with the clear purpose of learning about music by looking at the notes. Classroom lectures are fine, listening to recordings is excellent, reading about music is enlightening, but there is no substitute for discovering the greatness of great music by seeing it on the page. The teacher's attitude should be one of encouragement and support, with the hope that this enterprise will lead toward a lifetime of learning about the vast literature of music beyond the orchestra and its horn parts.

After the symphonies, concertos, serenades, and other orchestral works of Brahms are studied, we can turn to Dvořák. In the last three symphonies of Dvořák it becomes clear that his horn parts are more chromatic and more challenging technically than those of Brahms. In the second movement of his cello concerto, Dvořák wrote a lyrical and dramatic horn trio, which must be practiced for balance and intonation before the first orchestral rehearsal. The horn section of a fine professional orchestra can rely upon its experience to ensure a fine performance every time this work is rehearsed or performed. In school orchestras, the members of the horn section may not have played together very long and may not have played the Dvořák cello concerto. The teacher can use this as an opportunity to coach the horn section before orchestral rehearsals begin. The composer, conductor, the horn section, the rest of the orchestra, the soloist, and the audience will profit from our early preparation of this part of the concerto. In a well-managed school orchestra, the programs are announced for the year and personnel lists are posted well in advance of the first rehearsal. The teacher can encourage the first horn player to organize a sectional rehearsal before the players bring the trio into the teacher's studio for coaching.

Managing sectional rehearsals is good practice in leadership, musical and otherwise, for student horn players. It requires communication skill to persuade other student players to participate and a demeanor that will elicit positive reactions to suggestions. Young horn players often feel that parts other than the principal part are not very important. Sectional rehearsals can help players realize that every part must be played as perfectly as possible. The trio in the Dvořák cello concerto can be embarrassing for everyone if intonation, accuracy, balance, dynamics, style, and ensemble have to be rehearsed in front of the whole orchestra. Such rehearsal within a rehearsal is not an efficient way to spend the orchestra's time. Conductors vary in their ability to give sound advice to horn players on matters other than ensemble and style. At the first orchestral rehearsal it is much better to present the conductor with a trio that needs few suggestions for improvement.

Each teacher will have to make decisions concerning how much lesson and practice time can be devoted to the study of orchestral parts. College teachers also have to consider the career goals of each student, and how important having a comprehensive knowledge of the orchestral literature will be in achieving those goals. Not every freshman who has a fierce desire to play in a fine professional orchestra will feel the same way as a senior. Teachers who have fulfilled their musical and educational responsibilities to the student will have opened the door to pursuits beyond the orchestra. Balancing the emphasis among etudes, orchestral literature, chamber music, and solo playing should be done after consideration of the student's ambitions and current ability. Work on the opening of *Ein Heldenleben* makes no sense if the prerequisite work on pertinent etudes and exercises has not been done. The balance can shift during the four undergraduate years, but a general policy of becoming acquainted with the horn parts of the standard orchestral literature can guide the teacher's decisions. Obviously, becoming familiar with the twenty most often played orchestral excerpts does not prepare a student for a lifetime of musical achievement.

Some thought should be given to fitting the orchestral studies into the four undergraduate years. Under ideal conditions a horn performance major will have gone through the composers alphabetically in three years, leaving the senior year for review and audition preparation. Some students are ready for the Mahler symphonies earlier than other students. No harm is done by coming back to Mahler after the alphabet is completed. Other students will not have studied the Beethoven Seventh Symphony in the expected order because of its unusual physical demands. These and other works can be taken out of sequence if the teacher feels that the student needs more time for embouchure development. The senior year can be used for a thorough review of all important passages and for working on the required lists of works for professional and other auditions.

It is hoped that teachers and students can use this discussion of the orchestral horn parts of Beethoven and Brahms as a guide for studying the whole of the orchestral literature. Works such as Richard Strauss's *Don Juan* or *Till Eulenspiegels Lustige Streiche* require that nearly every measure be studied and perfected; for others, such as the one and only symphony by César Franck, we need to concentrate on the solos. Memorization is important as a matter of discipline and for its effect on concentration in the practice room. Orchestral parts, unlike etudes, are meant to be played in public; studio class meetings can be used for performance of orchestral parts. It is the teacher's responsibility to place each composer in the proper historical context, to locate each work in the composer's output, and to relate each solo or tutti passage to its orchestral framework. Listening to recordings and studying scores are considered to be part of practicing but are performed in addition to regular practice hours. Even if horn students spend two hours per day in listening and studying, they still will fall very short of the total hours that pianists and string players spend practicing. It is a happy coincidence that most of the more difficult orchestral literature lies toward the end of the alphabet. The student often reaches such composers as Strauss, Tchaikovsky, Wagner, and Stravinsky in the junior year, when etudes and exercises have produced a strong embouchure and technical skills have improved.

Solo literature provides an opportunity for personal expression and musical growth. Whereas orchestral playing does not permit very much freedom from convention, solo playing is governed by musical intelligence and stylistic integrity. Each teacher can establish a list of solo works that are the most appropriate for college-age study and performance. Most of the works discussed in the chapter on playing with the piano would probably be included on such a list. Teachers have a three-fold responsibility when teaching the solo literature. One is to give the student experience with a broad range of styles from the Baroque to the present. Another is to acquaint the student with the special characteristics, if any, of music from such countries as England, Austria, France, Italy, Russia, Germany, and the United States. The third responsibility is to arouse an interest in the creation and promotion of new and unknown music. Teachers can lead the way by being actively engaged in enriching the solo literature through commissioning and playing new music. Teachers can also assign students to write music for their own recitals or to be responsible in other ways for the creation of new solo music for horn.

Nearly every freshman entering college has played at least one of the Mozart horn concertos. Nonetheless, beginning the freshman year with one of the Mozart concertos is not unreasonable. The third concerto, with its emphasis on lyrical playing rather than technical display, is a perfect choice because the teacher can insist that preparation begins with notes but does not end until every element of performance is mastered. During the freshman year, teachers and students should not be hindered by deadlines on the preparation of solo works. Within reason, teachers should take whatever time is necessary to perfect the first solo work, since this will set the pattern for the future. Much of what is learned by studying the Mozart Concerto No. 3 will be applied to other classical works.

There is not much in the solo horn literature to suggest that a chronological order of study is of particular value. A Mozart concerto could well be followed by one of the Hindemith sonatas with the hope that the same care and understanding will be applied to both works. Either of the Hindemith sonatas provides the student with valuable experience in working with a pianist as an equal partner. The horn teacher must be prepared to offer advice to both players on rhythm, articulation, balance, style, and tempo. The teacher must obviously have ears that can detect and correct wrong notes in either part. The horn teacher can urge that the horn student receive coaching from the pianist's teacher also and can devise stratagems to get the horn students into the studio of many teachers. Just as our horn students can benefit from time spent in a piano teacher's studio, we are responsible for the musical, if not the technical, enlightenment of student pianists who come to our studio.

Occasionally a student will be less than enthusiastic about starting a new solo work. Quite often young players form attitudes based upon their previously inadequate technique or immature musical understanding. Almost every student retains the memory of an unfortunate experience with the public performance of a work that was too difficult or insufficiently prepared. To avoid another negative event, teachers must develop a keen sense of how each student will react to technical and musical challenges and should always make clear their purpose in assigning a particular work. Not every solo work that is practiced will be performed in the semester or the year that it is assigned. Some works—Richard Strauss's Concerto No. 2, Schumann's Adagio and Allegro, Glière's Concerto—can be worked on during the sophomore year and performed in the senior year. Other works, or movements of works, can be chosen just for their technical features. Generally, however, the solo literature should enrich the student's grasp of various styles and historical periods. Thus, some of the more lighthearted French solos could follow the Hindemith Sonata, which, in time, could be followed by a truly romantic work such as the Rheinberger Sonata. Whenever possible the teacher can use solo or chamber music literature as a way of enlarging the student's knowledge of similar works or forms. A study of one of the Hindemith horn sonatas could be expanded to an investigation of Hindemith's sonatas for other wind instruments and piano, which could lead toward an interest in the Hindemith sonatas for viola and *Ludus Tonalis*.

In the chapter on etudes we established a sequence of Kopprasch, Maxime-Alphonse, Barboteu, and Reynolds, augmented by Hill, Schuller, and Decker. In the orchestral studies we followed the alphabet. The solo literature for horn does not lend itself to such an orderly approach. Even though the solo literature is not large, as compared with that for the violin, for example, it is impossible during the college years to become acquainted with more than a sampling of its main categories. Each teacher can divide the literature by period, by degrees of difficulty, or by style, and within each division can decide upon works that best suit the student's needs and abilities. Teachers must keep a balance among periods and styles so that Mozart is not neglected or the twentieth century ignored.

After they leave school, horn players will have to teach themselves new solo works. By insisting upon stylistic integrity, and by requiring that horn players venture beyond the horn literature, teachers can help their students to develop a comprehensive musicianship. When we teach the etudes, we teach a disciplined technique. When we teach the orchestral works, we pass along tradition. When we teach the solo and chamber music literature, we teach music.

A fine studio teacher continues to learn. Just as fine players must set aside time for practice in order to progress, studio teachers should organize their professional and academic lives to include reading and research. A day without reading can be compared to a day without practice. We practice because it is an indispensable part of being an academic musician. Teachers of any subject grow as teachers by their constant absorption of experiences at their work place, be it classroom or private studio, and by their independent ventures in the laboratory or library. We have all heard teachers proclaim that they "learn so much from their students." One suspects that even more can be learned when teachers keep an account of what they profess to learn from their students, and use this information to become more effective teachers.

Academic performing musicians have the heavy time burdens of teaching, playing, practicing, and research. There is no point in ranking these duties in order of their importance, since each is essential. To prosper as a performer in an academic setting, we must practice. It should be equally apparent that to prosper as a teacher in an academic setting, we must contribute to the sum of knowledge and to the treasury of literature in our own field.

An outstanding private teacher understands when patience is a virtue and when it is no longer producing results. Few would argue that the first semester of the first college year can be a trying time for some students. The transition from high school to college is pleasant for some, but difficult and intimidating for others. Similarly, the transition to a new private teacher can be temporarily disturbing, and especially so for those who have had the same teacher for a number of years. A college freshman who, as a high school senior, was an outstanding player, is suddenly surrounded by more advanced and experienced players. College teachers must be able to evaluate their incoming freshman class rather quickly and accurately to determine which students are secure in their playing and have settled into college life, and which need more time to react to the new environment.

Patience, by both the teacher and student, is needed when major changes are made. Quite often an entering freshman has been playing the same instrument and the same mouthpiece for several years. The mouthpiece, particularly, was chosen to fit the embouchure and body strength of a young player, or simply because it came with the instrument. A gifted fourteen year-old who has worked diligently is no longer the same player, physically, at eighteen years of age, yet is playing on the same equipment. Most often the first change that a college-age horn student must make is to go to a larger mouthpiece. Larger mouthpieces allow for a free air flow, a larger volume of sound, a richer tone quality, and a better low register. Air flow, volume, tone quality, and low register seem to improve almost immediately, but a price is paid in endurance and high register. Young players and teachers who work with beginning students tend to judge a mouthpiece by how well it produces high notes on an undeveloped embouchure. Patience is required of both teacher and student during the weeks and months that it takes to rebuild the strength needed to play a larger mouthpiece.

During the first several weeks the teacher can determine which changes should be made immediately, and which can be introduced more gradually. Breathing technique can be altered quite early, if need be; right-hand position and bell on the leg or off can be discussed later. Posture, as it affects breathing and body support, can be adjusted early; playing while standing can be phased in slowly. Accuracy and good intonation are required from the first lesson to the last; lip trills and multiple tonguing can be postponed until a strong embouchure and a rapid single tongue are developed. In all of these areas students must be kept informed of what they are doing, why they are doing it, and how they are progressing. We cannot set a timetable for progress, but over a period of months some things will improve dramatically, others less so, and some very little, if any. The most patience is required for establishing a reliable high register and for building confidence during performances. A wise teacher is willing to allow enough time for changes and new procedures to produce the desired results. A wise teacher also has freshman-to-senior goals in place that can be flexible during the earlier semesters but become much more firm in the later semesters. Patience can follow the same general path. Patience during the first year must not sink into indulgence in the senior year. Confidence, embouchure strength, and the high register are built in the early years and are proven in the later years.

A successful private teacher combines kindness with determination. The teacher's effectiveness is not lessened by a genial countenance. Kindliness is a manifestation of benevolent strength. Determination is strength of conviction aided by perseverance and confidence. All of these—determination, strength of conviction, perseverance, and confidence—are qualities that a fine private teacher strives to instill in students; they are also qualities that must be present in the teacher.

A dedicated teacher does not look upon teaching as an advantageous way to occupy hours not spent in serving the local symphony orchestra. Membership in a professional orchestra is not, in itself, incompatible with fine teaching, but is only one of the ingredients that might contribute to successful teaching. It was once believed that one was not qualified to teach the horn or other wind instruments without having served many years in an orchestra. Now many of our most promising young horn teachers choose to bypass professional orchestral playing in order to concentrate upon preparing for the rich and more varied life of the performing musician in an academic community.

Other personal qualities of the good teacher are those that are found in the exemplary citizen. A teacher is an informed member of the community who participates in its governance. A teacher never violates confidences or speaks ill of students or colleagues. A teacher recognizes responsibility to the individual student and to the art of music. A teacher produces and gives, not consumes and takes. A teacher opens doors intellectually, artistically, and professionally. A teacher's door is not closed after the student graduates. A teacher continues to grow until the final lesson is given.

A good teacher realizes the importance of concentrating on the student for sixty minutes of the teaching hour. Toward this end, it is interesting for the teacher to record several lessons during the year. Hearing our own voices and becoming aware of how much time is spent on irrelevancies can be helpful in arriving at a balance among speaking, demonstrating, and listening to the student playing and speaking. Older teachers often have fond memories of earlier experiences, and it is natural for them to want to share them with students. Younger teachers sometimes feel the need to drop names and to dwell upon their recent accomplishments. Many teachers urge students to hear their own playing on tape as a regular part of the learning experience. Teachers can also use tape to become more efficient in their use of lesson time. In an academic setting, it is necessary to stay on schedule. Private teachers and conductors must respect the time framework in which a music school operates. To run a lesson or rehearsal overtime and thereby cause a student or another teacher to be inconvenienced is ill-mannered and, in the case of the conductor, often indicates poor preparation and rehearsal technique. We have all heard of occasions when teachers, outside the academic community, were able to devote three or more hours to a lesson. Long lessons are fine, provided the instruction is on a high level.

That a successful horn player would not have a well-developed sense of pitch is inconceivable. That a horn teacher cannot tell whether a student is producing the correct pitches is impossible to imagine. Horn players and horn teachers have the burden of identifying pitches in at least ten transpositions and two clefs. When coaching chamber music, horn teachers have to be comfortable with four clefs and transpositions within each clef. First-year college students often view their ear training classes as a useless bother. Private teachers can help to change this unfortunate attitude by requiring students to memorize pitches, and by devising practical exercises in ear training. During the earlier semesters the student can be asked to sing the first pitch that is played after each silence. In later semesters the teacher can declare that at the next lesson the student is to be prepared to sing F-sharp (or any other pitch) as it sounds in each of the transpositions. These pitches can be sung during the small breaks that occur naturally in any lesson. To sing a written F-sharp in horn in D immediately after playing a written A in horn in B-flat will surely test the ears of both teacher and student. During the week the student can use the embouchure-resting moments of the practice hour to work on such ear-training exercises. During the four undergraduate years, horn students can develop ears that are capable of hearing horizontal lines, vertical combinations in transpositions and clefs, and discrepancies in intonation. Theory classes offer ear training that is designed to give a general introduction to the subject. Too often the training of ears ceases when the last theory class has been taken. After consultation with the theory faculty, horn teachers can begin to compile a collection of ear-training exercises that progress in difficulty and are designed to meet the specific needs of horn players. The training of ears thus becomes an integrated and indispensable part of learning to play the horn. Horn students with absolute pitch are not automatically exempt from expanding the usefulness of their ears.

In the chapter on practicing, we established links leading from the practice room through the private lesson, class lessons, and rehearsals to the performance. A more elusive but equally important set of links can be established to connect the practical with the ideal. Imagine a series of doors behind which horn players are practicing the first horn part of the Beethoven Seventh Symphony. The teacher opens each door and asks why the student is practicing this symphony. Their replies might be as follows:

Door 1. I am practicing because I have a lesson on it tomorrow.
Door 2. I am practicing because I have a rehearsal on it next month.
Door 3. I am practicing because the concert is in two months.
Door 4. I am practicing because the symphony is a challenge.
Door 5. I am practicing because I like to play the horn.
Door 6. I am practicing because I like to play in an orchestra.
Door 7. I am practicing because it is such a neat part.
Door 8. I am practicing because I like the symphony.
Door 9. I am practicing because I like Beethoven.
Door 10. I am practicing because I love music.

Notice how each reply elevates the purpose and enlarges the significance of practicing. Notice also how we must wait until Door 7 is opened before the focus begins to shift from the personal to the music itself. The progression from the personal to the musical shows a gradual maturation of motivation from meeting tomorrow's deadline to a love of music. Preparing for tomorrow's lesson is a very practical thing to do. Loving music is the ideal.

## Auditions

In our larger communities, membership in a youth orchestra is often obtained as the result of an audition or upon the recommendation of a teacher. Auditions, like any other performance, can be devastating for the unprepared, disappointing for the unsuccessful, and reassuring for those who are chosen. Teachers should, of course, always help in the preparation of the music required for the audition. Work on the audition list must start well in advance of the event.

At an audition, all of the fundamentals of horn playing suddenly take on a greater and a more practical importance. Accuracy, rhythm, and intonation are the three most significant technical ingredients of any successful audition. Everyone within earshot becomes a music critic when accuracy is the topic. Accuracy is not moot; either playing is accurate or it is not. Accuracy is the result of having all of the physical components of horn playing under control and working together. It begins with hearing every pitch before it is played, and depends on making a mental connection between how a pitch sounds and how it feels. Accuracy is strengthened by playing thousands of timed attacks during years of warm-up sessions. It is increased by thoughtful repetition of difficult passages and is decreased by faltering concentration. Accuracy suffers from poor warm-up procedures. It plunges with fatigue and is lost when "nerves" win. Every part of the accuracy complex is related to and dependent upon every other part. We can hear every pitch but fail to make the physical connection. Teachers can guide students through this labyrinth by placing each instance of inaccuracy in its proper category of ear, air, or embouchure, and by suggesting specific methods for improvement. In these pages I have offered some solutions for problems in each of these areas. Teachers and players must never accept inaccurate playing. The day is long gone when any horn player can hope to succeed without a superlative degree of accuracy.

The second of our technical ingredients is rhythm. For this discussion we can limit the definition of rhythm to the integrity of note values. Quite apart from any considerations of style or expressive devices, the note values for auditions and orchestral playing in general must be precise. Of our three categories—accuracy, rhythm, and intonation—rhythm seems to be the least controlled by young players.

In an ideal musical world we all would learn about rhythm (the relative value of notes) before anything else. Our system of notation is based upon large units (whole-notes), which are divided by half (half-notes) and divided by half again (quarter-notes) and continue to be divided by half until very small units have been created. This would seem to be one of the most direct and easily accomplished of all arithmetic computations. Its main obstacle is that the computations have to be done while the mind and parts of the body are otherwise engaged. If we can learn to divide mentally by two for simple meter, by three for compound meter, and can maintain a mental subdivision of these divisions, we have struck an enduring blow for the early rhythmic education of performing musicians. Every performing musician who teaches understands this. Every musician who teaches beginners of any instrument has a duty to correct this most fundamental frailty before moving to the next level of instruction. Rhythm, like embouchure, becomes more and more difficult to correct as the months and years of instruction go by.

During the college years, teachers should have the student solve all rhythmic problems by simple arithmetic, not by imitation. If a rhythmic configuration is notated properly there can be no unsolvable mysteries. The quick and easy way is for the teacher to demonstrate, for example, the common rhythm of the dotted eighth- and sixteenth-notes. The best way is for the student to divide the rhythm physically and mentally into four equal parts. Just as no inaccuracy can ever be left to cure itself, no rhythmic aberration can be allowed to fester.

In placing intonation third on our list of fundamental technical ingredients, the intent was not to make it less important than accuracy or rhythm. Sadly, for some young horn players, it is far down on the roster of important concerns.

We learn much about intonation from making comparisons between what we play and what we hear from another instrument, and what we see on the tuner. We can take as long as we wish to make adjustments when working with the tuner. When playing with other instruments we generally have at least one other pitch with which to compare our own, but a limited amount of time to alter the pitch or to confirm that all is well. Chamber music groups have been known to remark, jokingly it is hoped, that all chords will eventually be in tune if they are held long enough. When playing by ourselves at auditions, and on other occasions, we do not have the benefit of tuning to pitches from another instrument; we can tune only to the note that we have just played. It is fine to lower $d^2$ on the B-flat horn or to raise $d^1$ on the F horn, but we must also know and remember how these notes sound as a linear (moving) interval as well as a vertical (stationary) interval. Therefore, our work with the tuner will be more complete if we can invent exercises that allow us to hear our corrected D in a moving intervallic relationship with the notes around it. Listening with total concentration is necessary when looking at the tuner. Memory can work for us or against us. If we have played either D incorrectly for several years, our memory tells us that the familiar is acceptable. Memory works for us when the adjustments become the familiar. As with accuracy and rhythm, intonation is best seen, heard, and corrected in the very young.

Auditions are performances that are prepared as thoroughly as any recital or concert. They are a series of gateways through which young players pass to reach the next level of recognition and accomplishment. They are a firmly established process by which players are chosen for entry into youth orchestras, music schools, training ensembles within music schools, graduate schools, professional orchestras, chamber music groups, and academic performing and teaching positions. Learning the technique of auditioning has become an important part of the education of performing musicians.

Preparation and experience hold the key to successful auditioning. Required music for orchestral auditions usually consists of a movement from a standard concerto, a list of well-known orchestral passages, and sight reading. In the interest of fairness and reliability, all players are expected to perform the same music. First impressions are most important at auditions. A missed note, a shaky tone, an incorrect rhythm, or questionable intonation within the first several measures are all that is needed for the audition committee to reject an applicant. Erasing the negative impact of a bad beginning is nearly impossible. Preparation must convince the player that all of the music is under control. Simulated auditions can be of some help in discovering whether the player is ready for the audition, but there is no substitute for experience gained from the real thing. The actual audition is not the place to discover that preparation has not been complete.

After each audition, successful or not, the player should write a complete account of the experience. These records will sort out the procedures that worked from those that should be altered for the next audition. Detailed appraisals are better than a general recollection of events. Many young players can recall only what went astray during an audition and thereby invite an expectation of failure at the next auditions. Others have some difficulty in finding areas that need improvement. Realistic evaluation of one's own playing is not simple, but, once again, experience and the teacher's guidance will be of great importance. Nearly every horn player has been advised to forget a bad experience and go toward the next occasion. Surely there is something to be learned from failure as well as from success.

Musicologists, composers, and theorists have common interests in the study of music, and have formed strong links interconnecting their activities of research and creativity. Less strong are the links to the private studio. Without the free trade of ideas and information, the private studio has seceded from the alliance of scholarship and creativity. The unity and strength of the musical commonwealth is maintained by teachers of the classroom and studio whose commitment is tenacious enough, whose love is profound enough, whose knowledge is broad enough, whose industry is tireless enough to join the glory of performance with the nobility of scholarship. What better place for this union to flourish than in the calm intellectual chambers of the academy? What better time than now?

# EPILOGUE I

# REMINDERS

1. The most critical session of practice each day is the first.
2. Practice demands analysis.
3. Just as it is necessary to recognize deficiency, it is essential to acknowledge accomplishment.
4. We are constantly evaluated by listeners whether we like it or not, whether it is fair or not, whether it is informed or not.
5. Popular psychology should not become a substitute for logic.
6. We never outgrow our need for long tones.
7. A fast single tongue is the horn player's best friend.
8. In its highest form, chamber music is an effort among equals in which each must make an equal effort.
9. We have all heard musicians say, and often without shame, that they cannot "read a score."
10. Is it possible that in striving for the sensational *fortissimo* we have neglected the sublime *pianissimo*?
11. Many brass quintets seem to have at least one member who feels a responsibility to produce literature, not just consume it, and is equipped with the industry and skills necessary to do so. Often it is the horn player.
12. The egocentrism of the performing musician, the need to excel, and the desire to exhibit excellence, the need to be right, to be the best, and to be recognized are all parts of the psychological profile of the solo performer.
13. The superb accompanist enriches the music by freeing and exhilarating the soloist.

14. To play solo works while looking at the music serves to reinforce the belief that brass players are intellectually incapable of memorizing music, and are therefore exempted from doing what singers, pianists, and string players regard as proper, expected, and routine.

15. A great reward awaits the horn player who is ready to experience the Beethoven Quartet Op. 131 for the first time.

16. We grow through searching; we stagnate when content with the obvious.

17. By doing nothing beyond the mechanical reproduction of notation we have grammar but not Emily Dickinson.

18. We must never make music the victim of our inadequacies.

19. In the catalog of musical sins, boring is on the same page as lazy.

20. No horn player has ever suffered permanent damage from applying pencil to staff paper.

21. Is it not better to look directly at Mozart through his music than to try to see the man through the vision of starry-eyed biographers?

22. With a well-developed embouchure we can produce notes, but without an informed mind we cannot understand the notes we produce.

23. Easier is better only if the result is better.

24. Small answers to large questions run the risk of becoming much less than half-truths.

25. Convictions are excellent when they are grounded on scholarship and proven by experience.

26. Great music survives everything written about it.

# EPILOGUE II

# THE ESSENTIAL HORN

Stated in the bluntest of terms, the horn is only a narrow, conical, coiled tube, which expands to a widely flaring bell, facing backward, and is often made of silver, which isn't silver at all. For this tube, composers for nearly five hundred years have written music depicting feelings ranging from carefree exultation to the most impassioned tragedy.

Which instrument is called upon to evoke the hunt? The horn, of course. Which instrument did Beethoven and Wagner choose to symbolize heroism? The horn, of course. Which instrument did Tchaikovsky, Brahms, Schumann, Mahler, and Bruckner, to name a few, turn to for special moments of tender eloquence? On which instrument did Mozart bestow four concertos and numerous chamber works? Which brass instrument has a range most nearly parallel to that of a chorus of mixed voices? Which instrument has been played by musicians sitting, standing, on horseback, outdoors, indoors, on mountain tops, in huge auditoria, in small recital halls, in recording studios, in practice rooms, at weddings and memorial services, on street corners, on parade, on the football field, on radio, on television, at Christmas and the Fourth of July, in solo recitals, in chamber music, in bands and orchestras, choirs, jazz groups, rock concerts?

Which instrument requires the physique of an athlete and the heart of a poet? Which instrument demands dedication, perseverance, industry, honesty, and an indefinable musical gift? Which instrument rewards the player and the listener with perfect joy?

The horn, the horn, the horn, of course.

# INDEX